Mediating Languages and C
Towards an Intercultural Th
Language Education

Multilingual Matters

Age in Second Language Acquisition
  BIRGIT HARLEY
Bicultural and Trilingual Education
  MICHAEL BYRAM and JOHAN LEMAN (eds)
Cultural Studies in Foreign Language Education
  MICHAEL BYRAM
Current Trends in European Second Language Acquisition Research
  HANS W. DECHERT (ed.)
Dialect and Education: Some European Perspectives
  J. CHESHIRE, V. EDWARDS, H. MUNSTERMANN, B. WELTENS (eds)
Individualizing the Assessment of Language Abilities
  John H.A.L. de JONG and D.G. STEVENSON (eds)
Introspection in Second Language Research
  C. FAERCH and G. KASPER (eds)
Key Issues in Bilingualism and Bilingual Education
  COLIN BAKER
Language Acquisition: The Age Factor
  D.M. SINGLETON
Language Distribution Issues in Bilingual Schooling
  R. JACOBSON and C. FALTIS (eds)
Language Policy Across the Curriculum
  DAVID CORSON
Marriage Across Frontiers
  A. BARBARA
The Management of Change
  P. LOMAX (ed.)
The Moving Experience: A Practical Guide to Psychological Survival
  G. MELTZER and E. GRANDJEAN
Modelling and Assessing Second Language Acquisition
  K. HYLTENSTAM and M. PIENEMANN (eds)
Oral Language Across the Curriculum
  DAVID CORSON
Raising Children Bilingually: The Pre-School Years
  LENORE ARNBERG
The Role of the First Language in Second Language Learning
  HÅKAN RINGBOM
Second Language Acquisition — Foreign Language Learning
  B. VanPATTEN and J.F. LEE (eds)
Story as Vehicle
  EDIE GARVIE
Teaching and Learning English Worldwide
  J. BRITTON, R.E. SHAFER and K. WATSON (eds)
Variation in Second Language Acquisition: Vol. I and Vol. II
  S. GASS, C. MADDEN, D. PRESTON and L. SELINKER (eds)

Please contact us for the latest book information:
Multilingual Matters,
Bank House, 8a Hill Rd,
Clevedon, Avon BS21 7HH,
England

MULTILINGUAL MATTERS 60
Series Editor: Derrick Sharp

Mediating Languages and Cultures: Towards an Intercultural Theory of Foreign Language Education

Edited by
Dieter Buttjes and Michael Byram

MULTILINGUAL MATTERS LTD
Clevedon • Philadelphia

For:
Alice, Andrea, Elke, Ian,
Marie Thérèse and Stefanie

Library of Congress Cataloging in Publication Data

Mediating Languages and Cultures: Towards an Intercultural Theory of Foreign Language Education/Edited by Dieter Buttjes and Michael Byram.
p. cm. (Multilingual Matters: 60)
Includes bibliographic references.
1. Intercultural education — Europe. 2. Languages, modern — Study and teaching — Europe.
I. Buttjes, Dieter. II. Byram, Michael. III Series: Multilingual Matters (Series): 60.
LC1099.5E85M43   1990
270.19′6′   dc20

British Library Cataloguing in Publication Data

Mediating Languages and Cultures: Towards an Intercultural Theory of Foreign Language Education (Multilingual Matters: 60)
1. Foreign languages. Learning
I. Buttjes, Dieter. II. Byram, Michael
418′.007

ISBN 1-85359-071-1
ISBN 1-85359-070-3 (pbk)

Multilingual Matters Ltd
Bank House, 8a Hill Road,   &   1900 Frost Road, Suite 101
Clevedon, Avon BS21 7HH   Bristol, PA 19007
England   USA

Copyright © 1991 Dieter Buttjes, Michael Byram and the authors of individual chapters.

All rights reserved. No part of this work may be reproduced in any form or by any means without permission in writing from the publisher.

Typeset by Action Typesetting Ltd, Gloucester
Printed and bound in Great Britain by Dotesios Printers Ltd.

Contents

Preface ix

Acknowledgements x

PART I: TOWARDS AN INTERCULTURAL THEORY OF LANGUAGE EDUCATION

1. Mediating languages and cultures: the social and intercultural dimension restored
   Dieter Buttjes 3

2. Teaching culture and language: towards an integrated model
   Michael Byram 17

PART II: TOWARDS A SOCIAL HISTORY OF LANGUAGE TEACHING IN EUROPE

3. Cultural studies and foreign language teaching after World War II: the international debate as received in the Scandinavian countries
   Karen Risager 33

4. Culture in German foreign language teaching: making use of an ambiguous past
   Dieter Buttjes 47

5. Area Studies in the German Democratic Republic: theoretical aspects of a discipline in evolution
   Dieter Kerl 63

6. 'Background Studies' in English foreign language teaching: lost opportunities in the comprehensive school debate
   Michael Byram 73

7. Interculturalising the French educational system: towards a common European perspective
   François Mariet 84

PART III: TOWARDS A RESEARCH-BASED THEORY OF INTERCULTURAL COMMUNICATION

8. Young people's perceptions of other cultures: the role of foreign language teaching
   Michael Byram, Veronica Esarte-Sarries, Susan Taylor and Patricia Allatt 103

9. Stereotypes in intercultural communication: effects of German–British pupil exchanges
   Gottfried Keller 120

10. Developing transcultural competence: case studies of advanced foreign language learners
    Meinert Meyer 136

11. Culture and 'hidden culture' in Moscow: a contrastive analysis of West German and Soviet perceptions
    Astrid Ertelt-Vieth 159

PART IV: TOWARDS A REVISION OF INTERCULTURAL TEACHING MEDIA

12. Cultural references in European textbooks: an evaluation of recent tendencies
    Karen Risager 181

13. Presenting distant cultures: the Third World in West German English language textbooks
    Angelika Kubanek 193

14. World Studies and foreign language teaching: converging approaches in textbook writing
    Hugh Starkey 209

15. Relating experience, culture and language: a German–French video project for language teaching
    Gisela Baumgratz-Gangl 228

PREFACE   vii

PART V: TOWARDS AN INTERCULTURAL TEACHER EDUCATION

16. The acquisition of cultural competence: an ethnographic framework for cultural studies curricula
    Laurence Kane 239

17. The observation diary: an ethnographic approach to teacher education
    Geneviève Zarate 248

18. From integrative studies to context theory: a project in in-service education
    Franz Kuna 261

PART VI: TOWARDS AN INTEGRATED VIEW OF LANGUAGE LEARNING

19. Intercultural pedagogy: foundations and principles
    Michele Borrelli 275

20. Intercultural learning at school: limits and possibilities
    Hagen Kordes 287

21. Language education across Europe: towards an intercultural perspective
    John Broadbent and Leonardo Oriolo 306

List of Contributors 323

Index 325

Preface

This volume owes its origin to a symposium organised by the editors in 1986 and held in Durham. The symposium was our first attempt to bring an international perspective to the question of cultural content in foreign language teaching. It was a stimulating and enjoyable occasion and it seemed important to make the papers presented more widely available. At the same time it was evident that the value of a collection of papers would be enhanced by contributions from other sources too. In the meantime there have been several indications that the Durham symposium anticipated a revival of interest among language teachers and researchers in the cultural content and political and educational purposes of foreign language teaching. It is our hope that, in bringing together contributors from several European countries and from several traditions of language teaching, the present volume will stimulate that interest further. The editors are convinced that such an interest can only increase both the social usefulness and the educational value of foreign language teaching. Learning another language would then, in our view, be a major contribution both to communication across international boundaries between societies and individuals, and to the enrichment of people's lives irrespective of their national and social origins.

We are grateful, for financial support for the original symposium, to the Deutsche Forschungsgemeinschaft (Bonn), to the Economic and Social Research Council (London) and to the Danish Ministry of Education (Copenhagen). We are grateful to Mrs Doreen Wilson, secretary to the Durham research project on foreign language teaching, who did most of the hard work of organising the symposium. Finally, we were gratified by the willingness of colleagues in various parts of Europe to contribute to this volume, thus making it a truly intercultural endeavour.

Dieter Buttjes	**Michael Byram**
(Dortmund)	(Durham)

Acknowledgements

Versions of the following chapters have appeared elsewhere:

Michael Byram, 'Teaching culture and language: towards an integrated model' in *Cultural Studies in Foreign Language Education* (Clevedon: Multilingual Matters).

Gisela Baumgratz-Gangl, 'Relating experience, culture and language: a German – French video project' as 'Das Unterrichtskonzept *Vivre l'école* als Beispiel für die Verknüpfung von Eigenerfahrung, Zugang zur fremden Wirklichkeit und Spracherweb' in *Aspekte einer Interkulturellen Didaktik* (Munich: Goethe Insitut).

Geneviève Zarate, 'The observation diary: an ethnographic approach to teacher education' as 'Le journal d'observation ou la mise en question de l'évidence immediate' in *Etudes de Linguistique Appliquée, No. 69*.

Hugh Starkey: extracts from *Orientations* by R. Aplin, A. Miller and H. Starkey (London: Hodder and Stoughton).

Part 1

Towards an Intercultural Theory of Language Education

Part I

1 Mediating Languages and Cultures: The Social and Intercultural Dimension Restored

DIETER BUTTJES

Mediating Language and Culture

We are usually not aware or conscious of the way we learn our first languages or teach them to our children. Perhaps that is why the informal and apparently 'natural' process of first language acquisition seems such an intriguing model for second and foreign language teaching, even though the ways of learning language are so different. Most of us are even less aware of the intricate and subliminal processes by which all of us are socialised into our native first cultures. Our subjectivities and identities have been shaped as members of a specific gender, social class, religion or nation long before we can be aware of these formative influences. And language plays a crucial role from early childhood on.

Acquiring language and culture

Recent studies in the language development of children are capable of enhancing our appreciation of how fundamentally language acquisition is embedded in socialisation and of what role language plays in the acquisition and transmission of sociocultural knowledge. Cross-cultural comparison of the language of children and their caregivers shows that these early language interactions are 'neither universal nor necessary for language to be acquired'. What this ethnographic approach to language development reveals is that 'every society orchestrates the ways in which children participate in social situations, and this, in turn, affects ... children's utterances' (Ochs & Schieffelin, 1984; 310).

The primary concern of caregivers in different cultures is not to provide grammatical input, but to 'ensure that their children are able to display and understand behaviours appropriate to social situations' (Ochs & Schieffelin, 1984; 276). Therefore, children in Hawaii learn to use languages for 'negotiating status', and Black American kids in South Baltimore are taught teasing and pretend play to sensitise them to the 'potential of language for ... self-assertion' and for 'some of the playful and transforming possibilities of language' (Schieffelin & Ochs, 1986: 94, 210–11). Due to this early mutual experience of language use mediating culture and of cultural initiation affecting language, adolescents are trained 'not simply to utter grammatical sentences, but to ... convey the full range of meanings .. available in the speech economy of any society and culture' (Ibid: 95).

From oracy to literacy

In contrast to these early phases of 'natural' language development, later stages of formal language education tend to dissociate rather than mediate language and culture. The first indication of a separation of experience from language can be seen in the revolutionary transition from oracy to literacy at the beginning of modern European history. This critical historical phase has had many social and cultural consequences in general, but also profound consequences on schooling and knowledge. Moving from oral to literate representations of knowledge and away from oral speech to the written text has weakened the social context of language and its material base in the social experience. Words in a written or printed form appear in isolation and removed from the extratextual context, whereas spoken discourse always refers to a given, complex, social and interpersonal situation which includes non-verbal information (Ong, 1982).

The graphic coding of speech – aggravated by its representation in printing – has accelerated the decontextualisation and reification of language as an abstract system of symbols. In effect, language became text, and text became knowledge (Buttjes, 1988: 51–52). These concepts of literacy and language have influenced European ideas about education and schooling: 'At the basis of our notion of schooling is the assumption that information is transformed through the written record into organized knowledge' (Cook-Gumperz, 1986: 14).

Ideally, it should be through language interaction in the classroom that sociolinguistic understanding is gained and shared, thereby continuing cultural mediation via language in childhood. However, critics of formal public schooling emphasise that the way language is used and knowledge presented often discourages or even excludes the everyday knowledge and commonsense arguments of many children (Cook-Gumperz, 1986: 4). Furthermore, notions of schooled literacy, especially in language teaching, tended to emphasise grammar and correctness which in itself goes back to the long process of 'fixing' a standard national language as a prerequisite for a centralised school system and for the beginnings of formal and of foreign language teaching as such (Howatt, 1984: 75; Michael, 1987: 380).

The formation of nation-states and the new language question

These centralising tendencies found in most Western nation-states could not be favourable to the mediation of culture and language. It took some time for national languages to emerge and for national school systems to evolve, but this historical struggle has often meant homogenising and thereby suppressing cultural variation. England and Germany have seen compulsory schooling for less than 150 years, and working towards a single standardised literacy for all citizens must be seen as 'a twentieth century notion' (Cook-Gumperz, 1986: 22).

By offering education and equality of opportunity for all, mass schooling has in effect attempted to socialise children into established cultural diversity and discourage subcultural deviation. In a similar way, the struggle to impose standard languages on more or less unwilling populations, as has been the case in Italy, was bound to eradicate oral dialects along with their heritage and potential of cultural expression. It is sobering to remember that Frederick the Great of Prussia found it 'a perfectly normal thing for a German prince' to speak French two centuries ago, and that 'not more than 2 to 3% of the Italian population would have understood Italian' at the time of the formation of a unified nation-state in Italy a century ago (Steinberg, 1987: 198).

That national identity should find expression in one standard language is a notion clearly connected with the emerging nation-states in Europe. Intraculturally this has meant hegemony at the expense of variety, and interculturally it has led to rivalry and conflict affecting language teaching as well (cf. Chapter 4). But the situation is changing in most European states and in other parts of the world. With joint markets and global communication, mass tourism and mass migration, the *'questione della lingua'* is returning (Steinberg, 1987). The need to mediate between languages and cultures increases with the presence in classrooms of children speaking something other than the standard national language, with television programmes from foreign countries received in many livingrooms, and with the exchange of commerce and the increasing international contact at workplaces (cf. Chapters 21 and 7). This may lead to new notions of transnational and intercultural literacy which would recognise that 'communication with others who do not share our background' and 'exposure to and contact with other modes of thinking' is becoming essential to our daily lives (Cook-Gumperz, 1986: 43).

It is in the language learning experience of immigrants that cultural mediation has been most clearly identified. Under these circumstances, acquisition of the second language seems possible only as part of a wider process of acculturation (Schumann, 1978: 47). Where acculturation does not take place because immigrants avoid contact with members of the host society, language learning cannot be successful. Therefore, 'second language learning is often second culture learning' (Brown, 1986: 33). However, simple notions of acquisition or adaptation may not do justice to the 'larger web of culturally institutionalized patterns of social relations' that ethnolinguistic minority children encounter in their vacillations between two cultures (McLaughlin & Matute-Bianchi, 1987: 271). If language learning can be seen as 'cultural transmission', serious bilingual education will have to be truly bicultural, allowing children to make use of their native cultural potential in order to develop their own (inter)cultural strategies in response to their specific experience.

Mediating across Nations and Traditions

After reviewing some aspects of mediating language and culture within one cultural setting, we now look at how language teaching transcends national cultural and traditional disciplinary divisions.

International language teaching and the discourse across cultures

There is growing concern in the international language teaching profession that the social dimension and intercultural function of language be restored. The 'big business' of English language teaching may have been less sensitive to the intercultural problems and objectives connected with its work around the world. English – as the global *lingua franca* – has become increasingly depoliticised and culturally neutralised in the process of separation from its native-speaking sources in Britain or the United States (Bowers, 1986: 402). TENOR — 'teaching English for no obvious reason' — may be the reason many students continue to learn English for instrumental rather than intergrative purposes, and many teachers of English still focus on the language for 'purposes not directly related to culture' (Ashworth, 1985: 119; Strevens, 1987: 173).

Yet even in this context more 'holistic' or 'synthetic' approaches to language teaching have been advocated recently. Such approaches would bring language and culture into 'interactive relation in successful discourse' (Smith, 1987: vii) and 'look outside language to see how it works within a broader cultural framework' (Bowers, 1986: 403). The conviction is growing that narrow linguistic notions of language that disregard the social and cultural context of language use and learning can do justice to neither the language learning process nor its objective of cross-cultural communication. The reasons for frustration in language learning and failure in cross-cultural communication are increasingly seen to be cultural rather than linguistic in nature. If successful 'discourse across cultures' is to be the testing case of language teaching, much more comprehensive ideas about language, culture and language education are required.

Language studies, ethnography and cultural studies

It is fortunate for our purposes that among the disciplines concerned with language and those concerned with culture agreement is increasing in the way they both define the object and methods of their study. It seems that linguistics more frequently includes culture and cultural studies generally integrate language. Linguists like Halliday have for long insisted that any text is 'a sociological event, a semiotic encounter through which the meanings that constitute the social system are exchanged' (Halliday, 1978: 139). And from psycholinguistic theory we learn that human language serves to expand the orientation within people's environments (Obuchowski, 1982: 59). Language therefore functions as a vessel of individual and collective social experience and as a vehicle for acquiring an operative knowledge of the world.

The ethnographic study of language development describes the socialising function of languages in terms which are very close to the ethnographic approach within cultural studies. Where linguists discover in language training 'the full range of meanings ... available in ... any society and culture' (Schieffelin & Ochs, 1986: 95), cultural studies are concerned with the generation and circulation of 'all the meanings of ... living within an industrial society' (Fiske, 1987: 254). It seems that ethnography is providing the missing link between language and culture studies (cf. Chapter 15–17). In fact, British cultural studies are pervaded by notions borrowed from linguistic and literary discourse.

The American ethnographer Geertz may have been one of the first to foresee that 'the concern with linguistic categories' was going to be 'a methodological theme in ethnography and beyond' (Geertz, 1983: 157). A more sociological approach to cultural analysis insists on including the actual 'manipulation of the material world' besides the 'discussion of values'. Even then culture is seen as 'the symbolic-expressive dimension of behaviour', subsuming not only the verbal discourse, 'but also the dramatizations of everyday life and the ritualized aspects of social arrangements' (Wuthnow *et al.*, 1984: 255). But whoever leaves his or her familiar domain of verbal and social behaviour is bound to undergo a dual process in which the two languages are increasingly separated, but the two cultures 'increasingly unified ... at the level of meaning and thought' (John-Steiner, 1985: 368). Therefore, a lot more is involved in language teaching than a mere exchange of linguistic labels; subjective experience and personal identity are at stake (cf. Chapters 10 and 20).

Traditions and objectives in intercultural language teaching

The psychological concern with language learners' cultural identities may be a rather recent discovery. But the role of culture in foreign language teaching can be traced back to more than one origin. The pragmatic motive has seen culture in language courses as preparation for international contact and communication, quite often in specific fields like trade and commerce. The educational motive for culture in language teaching was discovered later and refers to the individual's enrichment through the acquisition of a wider world-view and through an access to the non-native cultural capital. Intercultural studies should try to reunite these separate origins by using the immediate educational effect of mediating between culture and language in the foreign language classroom for the intermediate benefit of transcultural communication and interaction.

It was the modern language reform movement that transformed the European language teaching scene a century ago and that paved the way for our present concern of mediating culture and language in more than one respect. Modern languages had, after a century of struggle, found their way into British and German school curricula albeit only within the confines of élite education. In addition to their emphasis on spoken discourse, the language reformers addressed the established models available in both native and classical language teaching in order to win prestige and legitimacy in the school curriculum and among the teaching profession. Their focus on the authentic, 'connected' text was not only linguistically motivated: it was also invited by such traditional holistic notions as 'English education' or 'Roman civilisation' that could be found in other European curricula as well. In both these strands of language teaching practice texts were not treated as resources of grammar, but as sources of 'causal knowledge' (Manicas, 1987) about culture.

If culture is to permeate all levels and stages of modern language teaching today, not only texts will be affected (cf. Chapters 12–14). Figure 1.1 lists some of the roles that culture can be seen to play in a foreign language classroom if both interlingual and intercultural competence are intended. Even in the early phases the motivation for learning another language can be raised through cultural awareness, and language acquisition can be facilitated through culturally 'thick' and socially realistic textbook presentation. Intercultural competence as such may refer to either information or mediation skills, allowing for an insider's view of the foreign culture and encouraging the negotiation of meaning across cultures.

Intercultural studies must thus be a socially informed discipline. That is why social studies and cultural studies provide the foundation and the frameworks even if language discourse or literary texts are the objects of research and learning. But culture clearly differs from and transcends the traditional linguistic or literary dimensions of language teaching. 'The treatment of culture in the language programmes largely – and we suggest, quite legitimately – concentrates on non-linguistic features in the life of society' (Stern, 1983: 256).

Finally, a new intercultural rationale for language teaching is required to integrate aspects of communication and education. If classroom practice can be seen as a continuing effort at simulating a foreign environment, this learning experience may as such enhance tolerance of ambiguity and empathy with others (Beattie, 1986: 129). Presenting cultural and social alternatives may provide new orientations for the individual who is led to respect the plurality of thought and the historicity of cultural practice (cf. Chapter 19). At a time of increasing international dependency and imminent global threats, this may prove to be a rationale both necessary and appropriate for language teaching.

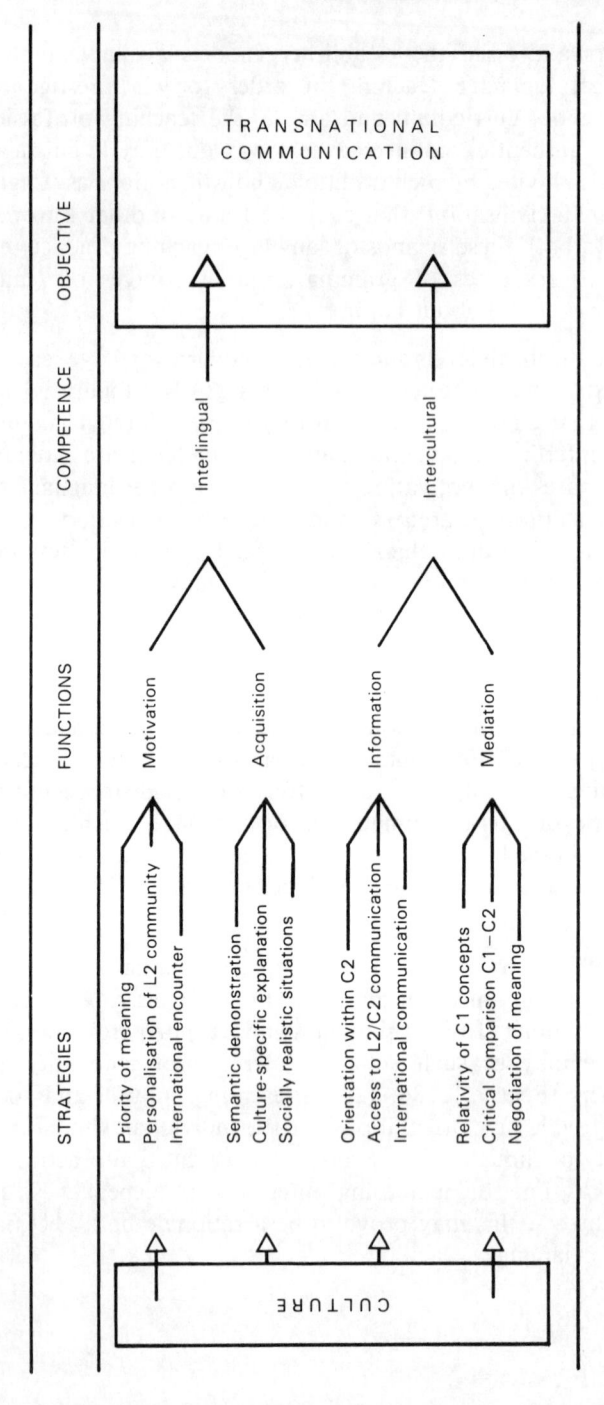

FIGURE 1.1 *Foreign language and intercultural learning*

Mediating Intercultural Research

The intercultural debate in language teaching expanded in scope and volume during the 1980s. Mediating some of the results of this reseach is in itself an attempt to 'interculturalise' specific national studies, general language teaching theory and the emerging international debate. It also means mediating the contributions from different national and educational contexts assembled in this volume.

The new cultural emphasis in language teaching

Concern with culture among United States language educators goes back beyond the 1970s, but was renewed in the 1980s (Seelye,1984; Valdes, 1986; Kramsch, 1989). Studies focusing on the mediation of language and culture in the foreign language classroom have been published in Britain (Loveday, 1982; Byram, 1989), in West Germany (cf. Chapter 4), and France (Zarate, 1986). In West Germany French Studies and German Studies have, more than others, placed cultural and intercultural studies at the core of their self-identity as academic disciplines (Höhne & Kolboom, 1982; Wierlacher, 1987).

In general language teaching theory, (inter)cultural studies may, in fact, be in the process of assuming the position and prestige that literary studies used to have. The least that can be said is that the intercultural rationale can be used for providing a framework and legitimation for literature in foreign language courses. A recent foreign language conference and a new comprehensive handbook in West Germany offer proof of the shift from literature to culture (Doyé, 1988; Bausch *et al.*, 1989). This transition, which may at some later time be considered paradigmatic in retrospect, was announced by Stern's monumental international study which draws on language and society or culture – rather than literature – for the fundamental concepts of language teaching (Stern, 1983).

Yet, international discussion about cultural studies in language teaching has been conspicuously missing. An exchange across national boundaries, cultural traditions and educational systems would have been more than appropriate in this discourse. But the beginnings were made during the second half of the 1980s with European language agencies co-operating and language departments of universities collaborating. Thus, Austria and Denmark have seen international conferences on literary and cultural studies at university level (Kuna & Tschachler, 1986; Jensen & Nielsen, 1988). Other international conferences on intercultural language teaching have included the Netherlands (Sixt, 1985), Poland (Piepho *et al.*, 1987) and in triangular co-operation Britain, France and West Germany (Goethe-Institut, 1988).

Interculturalising the intercultural debate

It is in this context of 'interculturalising' (cf. Chapter 7) both language education and the debate about it that the First Durham Symposium (see Preface) and the present volume must be seen. Foreign language theory has lacked the kind of discourse across nations and disciplines that gave momentum to the first modern language reform movement (Howatt, 1984; 169). Participants in such transnational communication cannot accept any hegemony in theory or practice, but need to expect variety in educational systems and teacher training no less than in the ways curricula are constructed and educational theories advanced.

Even in writing and reading cultural variation cannot be denied. Thus, Anglo-Saxon readers may miss linearity and relevance in German academic discourse, German readers 'may seek in vain for textual and syntactic markers of . . . academic register' in English-language contributions (Clyne, 1987: 79–80), and French readers may be confused by the lack of a clear tripartite structure so familiar to them from essay writing. Patience and persistence will be required for any intercultural reading because the contributions are bound to be different in reasoning and style. Even translations into English and English-language versions by non-native authors cannot meet all the cultural reading expectations of an international audience.

Yet, important areas of overlap and agreement have emerged after less than five years of intercultural debate. Here are some of the corresponding notions, most of them arrived at independently.

1. The comprehensive nature of intercultural learning means:
    – that learners' identities must be respected as starting-points and receiving ends in intercultural mediation (Chapters 10, 15 and 20);
    – that language teaching can be only one of several influences on the formation of intercultural competence (Chapters 8, 9 and 10);
    – that 'interculturalising' education reaches beyond language teaching (Chapters 7 and 19).
2. The interdisciplinary approach of intercultural studies assumes:
    – that ethnographic observation is useful both in constructing teaching material and in training teachers (Chapters 15, 16 and 17).

THE SOCIAL AND INTERCULTURAL DIMENSION 13

- research and learning must include a critical evaluation of established cultural values and academic disciplines (Chapters 5 and 19);
- that intellectual climates and international debates must be considered in describing educational or academic discourse within a social-historical context (Chapters 3, 4 and 6).

3. The transnational scope of intercultural language teaching envisages:
   - that mediating languages and cultures requires cross-cultural comparison and, finally, transcultural values (Chapters 11, 13 and 14);
   - that Europe may offer a common vantage point for both second and foreign intercultural language learning (Chapters 7 and 21);
   - that national and cultural loyalties may be questioned in the process of intercultural language learning (Chapters 4, 19 and 21).

Connecting the contributions in this volume

Different routes can be followed in reading this collection of papers. Many contributions focus on teaching in schools and at university (see Chapters 2, 6, 7, 12 – 14 and 16 – 18), others focus on the description of learning processes and processes of cultural mediation (Chapters 8, 10 and 20). There are empirical field studies covering areas outside school (Chapters 9, 11 and 15) and historical and systematic studies of curricula and teaching traditions (Chapters 3 – 5 and 16). And there are, finally, papers including observations on first language acquisition and second language learning (Chapters 1, 19 and 21). But if readers follow the sequence of chapters as suggested, they start with the editors' view on mediating language and culture in theory and practice (Chapters 1 and 2). These introductions intend to establish a framework for the development of an intercultural theory of language teaching.

In Chapters 3 to 7 authors from Denmark, the Federal Republic of Germany, the German Democratic Republic, the United Kingdom and France discuss the state of affairs in their countries. All of them put the educational trends portrayed into a wider social and historical context.

Samples of European research in intercultural communication and language learning are presented in Chapters 8 to 11. They are taken from observation in classrooms, in student exchange, in intercultural mini-lessons, and in the contrastive perceptions of everyday life in Moscow. The four contributions see communication as an active and comprehensive process of mediating or negotiating meaning rather than as a one-way flow of cultural information.

Practitioners and teachers who look for advice in using or producing teaching material, even before research results are available, may consult Chapters 12 to 15. They are all concerned with criticising the cultural contents of textbooks and offer alternatives in teaching culture and language. The textbook-writing experience in a related subject is presented and media other than textbooks are offered, too.

It is in teacher training that theory and practice need to be mediated. The case studies presented in Chapters 16 to 18 offer practical advice based on teaching experience in sociological, ethnographic and literary approaches to cultural studies. The courses described were tried out in West Germany, France and Austria.

The final three chapters are by Italian, West German and British authors and work towards integrating views of language learning and teaching. They emphasise that intercultural learning is not restricted to the foreign language classroom and may have effects that transcend language learning (see Chapters 19–21). From this perspective, our views of intercultural education in language teaching can be enhanced.

References

ASHWORTH, M 1985, *Beyond Methodology: Second Language Teaching and the Community.* Cambridge: Cambridge University Press.
BAUSCH, K. R. *et al.* (eds) 1989, *Handbuch Fremdsprachenunterricht.* Tübingen: Francke.
BEATTIE, N. 1986, Use or ornament? Values in the teaching and learning of modern languages. In P. TOMLINSON and M. QUINTON (eds) *Values Across the Curriculum,* pp. 109–33, London: Falmer Press.
BOWERS, R. 1986, English in the world: Aims and achievements in English Language Teaching. *TESOL Quarterly* 20, 393–409.
BROWN, H. D. 1986, Learning a Second Culture. In VALDES (ed.), pp. 33–48.
BUTTJES, D. 1988, Kontakt and Distanz: Fremdkulturelles Lernen im Englischchunterricht. In GOETHE-INSTITUT (ed.), pp. 49–58.
BYRAM, M. 1989, *Cultural Studies in Foreign Language Education.* Clevedon & Philadelphia: Multilingual Matters.
CLYNE, M. 1987, Discourse structures and discourse expectations: Implications for Anglo-German academic communication in English. In SMITH (ed.), pp. 73–83.
COOK-GUMPERZ, J. (ed.) 1986, *The Social Construction of Literacy.* Cambridge: Cambridge University Press.
DOYÉ, P. *et al.* (eds) 1988, *Die Beziehung der Fremdsprachendidaktik zu ihren Referenzwissenschaften.* Tübingen: Narr.
FISKE, J. 1987, British cultural studies and television. In R. C. ALLEN (ed.) *Channels of Discourse,* pp. 254–90. Chapel Hill & London: North Carolina Press.

GEERTZ, C. 1983, *Local Knowledge.* New York: Basic Books.
GOETHE-INSTITUT (ed.) 1988, – *Interkulturelle Kommunikation und Fremdsprachen Lernen/Culture and Language Learning/Communication inter-culturelle et apprentissage des langues* (Triangle 7). Paris: Didier Erudition.
HALLIDAY, M. A. K. 1978, *Language as Social Semiotic: The Social Interpretation of Language and Meaning.* London: Arnold.
HÖHNE, R. A. and KOLBOOM, I. (eds) 1982, *Von der Landeskunde zur Landeswissenschaft.* Rheinfelden: Schäuble.
HOWATT, A. P. R. 1984, *A History of English Language Teaching.* Oxford: Oxford University Press.
JENSEN, T. and NIELSEN, H. (eds) 1988, *Landeskunde im universitären Bereich.* Copenhagen/Munich: Fink.
JOHN-STEINER, V. 1985, The road to competence in an alien land: a Vygotskian perspective on bilingualism. In J. V. WERTSCH (ed.) *Culture, Communication and Cognition: Vygotskian Perspectives,* pp. 348–71. Cambridge: Cambridge University Press.
KRAMSCH, C. J. 1989, *New Directions in the Teaching of Language and Culture.* Washington: National Foreign Language Center at the Johns Hopkins University.
KUNA, F. and TSCHACHLER, H. (eds) 1986, *Dialog der Texte: Literatur und Landeskunde.* Tübingen: Narr.
LOVEDAY, L. 1982 *The Socio-Linguistics of Learning and Using a Nonnative Language.* Oxford: Pergamon.
MANICAS, P. T. 1987, *A History and Philosophy of the Social Sciences.* Oxford: Blackwell.
MCLAUGHLIN, B. and MATUTE-BIANCHI, M. E. 1987, The role of cultural factors in classroom second-language learning. In E. OKSAAR (ed.) *Sociocultural Perspectives of Multilingualism and Language Acquisition,* pp. 260–275. Tübingen: Narr.
MICHAEL, I. 1987, *The Teaching of English: From the Sixteenth Century to 1870.* Cambridge: Cambridge University Press.
OBUCHOWSKI, K. 1982, *Kognitive Orientierung und Emotion.* Cologne: Pahl-Rugenstein.
OCHS, E. and SCHIEFFELIN, B. B. 1984, Language acquisition and socialization. In R. A. SHWEPER and R. A LEVINE (eds) *Culture Theory: Essays on Mind, Self, and Emotion.* pp. 277–320. Oxford: Oxford University Press.
ONG, W. J. 1982, *Orality and Literacy.* London: Methuen.
PIEPHO, H. E. *et al.* (eds) 1987, *Polnisch-deutsche Gespräche über interkulturelles Lernen und Fremdsprachenunterricht.* Giessen: Universität.
SCHIEFFELIN, B. B. and OCHS, E. (eds) 1986, *Language Socialization across Cultures.* Cambridge: Cambridge University Press.
SCHUMANN, J. H. 1978, The acculturation model for second-language acquisition. In R. C. GINGRAS (ed.) *Second-Language Acquisition and Foreign Language Teaching.* Washington: Center for Applied Linguistics.
SEELYE, H. Ned 1984, *Teaching Culture: Strategies for Intercultural Education.* (rev. edn). Lincolnwood: National Textbook Corporation.
SIXT, D. (ed.) 1985, *Comprehension as Negotiation of Meaning.* Munich: Goethe-Institut.
SMITH, L. E. (ed.) 1987, *Discourse across Cultures: Strategies in World Englishes.* New York: Prentice-Hall.

STEINBERG, J. 1987, The historian and the *questione della lingua*. In P. BURKE and R. PORTER (eds) *The Social History of Language,* 198–209. Cambridge: Cambridge University Press.

STERN, H. H. 1983, *Fundamental Concepts of Language Teaching.* Oxford and London: Oxford University Press.

STREVENS, P. 1987, Cultural barriers to language learning. In SMITH (ed.) pp.169–78.

VALDES, J. M. (ed.) 1986, *Culture Bound: Bridging the Cultural Gap in Language Teaching.* Cambridge: Cambridge University Press.

WIERLACHER, A. (ed.) 1987, *Perspektiven und Verfahren interkultureller Germanistik.* Munich: Iudicium.

WUTHNOW, R. *et al.* 1984, *Cultural Analysis: The Work of Peter L. Berger, Mary Douglas, Michel Foucault, and Jürgen Habermas.* Boston and London: Routledge & Kegan Paul.

ZARATE, G. 1986, *Enseigner une culture étrangère.* Paris: Hachette.

2 Teaching Culture and Language: Towards an Integrated Model

MICHAEL BYRAM

Linking Language and Culture

Although there have been attempts in British secondary schools to teach children about European cultures without teaching a foreign language, traditions of secondary education have usually taken for granted that language and culture teaching must be clearly linked. A frequent metaphor of language as the 'key' to a culture embodies this link and at the same time reveals an implicit separation. The language shall 'unlock the door' to the culture. Once learnt, the language becomes less significant as the learner's efforts are focused on the artistic, philosophical, historical or scientific endeavour of the culture enshrined in its 'great works'.

Although originally applied to the opening of the works of high culture, the metaphor still has influence on thinking about broader, more inclusive definitions of culture. It is apparent in the documents of Her Majesty's Inspectorate (HMI) who consider that a division can be made between the 'linguistic and literary' aims of language teaching on the one hand and the 'human and social' aims on the other. They then argue that although the two aspects are of equal importance the latter are dependent on the former; the human and social aims are dependent on 'success in mastering the linguistic objectives' (HMI, 1987: 4).

The separation of language and culture is even more apparent in those textbooks which divide their units or chapters into language work and, appended as a gesture rather than integrated, a few pages of 'background information' or '*Landeskunde*' at the end of the chapter. In practice this leads the teacher to treat these pages as supplementary and optional, something to talk over if there are a few minutes free from the real business of language learning. Such textbooks were common in the period of audio-lingual methodology but can still be found today despite the sociological dimension of communicative language teaching. Communicative competence is too frequently interpreted — especially in beginners and intermediate stages — as a capacity to fit appropriate language to specific transactions.

The by now hidden metaphor of language as a key is both theoretically untenable and educationally unsound. Language is not simply a reflector of an objective cultural reality. It is an integral part of that reality through which other parts are shaped and interpreted. It is both a symbol of the whole and a part of the whole which shapes and is in turn shaped by sociocultural actions, beliefs and values. In engaging in language, speakers are enacting sociocultural phenomena; in acquiring language, children acquire culture. (The case is made at greater length in Byram, 1989: Chapter 6.) Given this theoretical viewpoint, it follows that to teach culture without language is fundamentally flawed and to separate language and culture teaching is to imply that a foreign language can be treated in the early learning stages as if it were self-contained and independent of other sociocultural phenomena. The consequence is that learners, rightly unable to accept this isolation, assume that the foreign language is an epiphenomenon of their own language, and that it refers to and embodies their existing understandings and interpretations of their own and the foreign cultures. Where this arises, as it does so frequently in the early years of secondary education, the pupils cannot be said to be learning a foreign language in the proper sense; they are learning a codified version of their own.

On the other hand it would be misguided to teach as if learners can acquire foreign cultural concepts, values and behaviours as if they were *tabula rasa;* just as it is misguided to teach language structures as if there will be no transfer from the first language. Equally it would be short-sighted to assume that the first language cannot be used to help learners grasp aspects of the foreign culture. Just as ethnographers interpret a foreign culture by using, modifying and expanding the first language of their readers (Agar, 1985) so the teacher can draw upon and modify the language of his or her learners. This process is simply part of pupils' expanding understanding of the world. In primary and secondary socialisation, their schemata (Rumelhart, 1980) are modified, their capacities for understanding and dealing with new phenomena are increased. If, however, their learning is to be experiential too, and some schemata are to be recognised as inadequate to deal with phenomena in a foreign culture, then their learning must be a clear approximation to first language and culture acquisition. They must understand and experience the culture from within, by acquiring new values and behaviours in a non-mediated form through direct experience.

There are, therefore, two possible approaches: first, the use of learners' first language as the medium of study of a foreign culture interpreted ethnographically, although without the intention of introducing the learner to the totality of the culture. Second, the integration of language and culture learning by using the language as a medium for the continuing socialisation of pupils is a process which is not intended to imitate and replicate the socialisation of native-speaker peers but rather to develop pupils' cultural competence from its existing stage, by changing it into an intercultural competence. This is in sharp contrast to the widespread current practice of providing pupils with a consumer-tourist competence which offers them the opportunity to reach a critical threshold, enabling them to survive in the foreign and, by implication, hostile environment of the foreign country. What is at issue here is a modification of monocultural awareness. From being ethnocentric and aware only of cultural phenomena as seen from their existing viewpoint, learners are to acquire an intercultural awareness which recognises that such phenomena can be seen from a different perspective, from within a different culture and ethnic identity.

Language and Culture Teaching Combined

In practice the two possibilities ought to be combined. The use of the learners' mother tongue for comparative analysis of own and foreign cultural meanings can be combined with the teaching of the foreign language both as a subject and as the medium of experience of foreign cultural phenomena. This would involve, first, language learning in the current sense of skill-acquisition, enriched by the study of the nature of language as a social and cultural phenomenon (Language Awareness). Second, the study of language would in turn be combined with a study of culture, both of these carried out with comparative techniques using the learners' mother tongue (Cultural Awareness). Thirdly, the direct experience of selected aspects of the foreign culture from the viewpoint and within the ethnic identity of the foreign peer group would be in the foreign language, and this would in turn contribute to the language learning process. The whole process can be represented as a circle of techniques and experience (see Figure 2.1).

The mutual support of each quarter of the circle with the two adjacent quarters is represented by the double-headed arrows. Cultural Awareness

MEDIATING LANGUAGES AND CULTURES

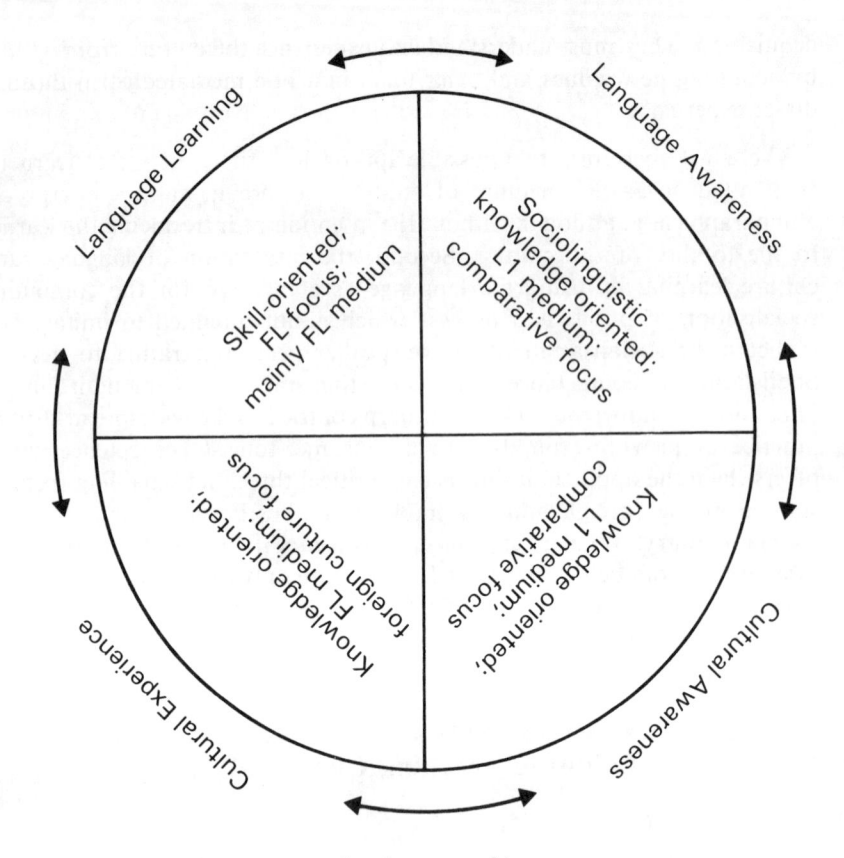

[Circular diagram with four quadrants, divided by "Language Learning" (top-left arc), "Language Awareness" (top-right arc), "Cultural Awareness" (bottom-right arc), and "Cultural Experience" (bottom-left arc). The four quadrants contain:]

- Top-left: Skill-oriented; FL focus; mainly FL medium
- Top-right: Sociolinguistic knowledge oriented; L1 medium; comparative focus
- Bottom-right: Knowledge oriented; L1 medium; comparative focus
- Bottom-left: Knowledge oriented; FL medium; foreign culture focus

FIGURE 2.1 *The language and culture teaching process*

develops out of and parallel with awareness of the sociolinguistic dimension of language study by comparative analysis of, for example, the semantic fields of the two languages, and their relationship to cultural meanings. Cultural Awareness is also mutually supportive with the direct experience in the foreign language of selected cultural phenomena by allowing for L1-medium analysis of that experience and of the relationship between the language and cultural meanings of the experience. Language Awareness will also have beneficial effects on the acquisition of linguistic skills by allowing learners to reflect on their learning, but in turn will be supported by the experience of learning if the language learned is made the focus of comparative analysis. Finally the relationship between Language Learning and Cultural Experience is mutually supportive in that Language Learning may well be largely rehearsal-oriented, with some communicative teaching techniques shifting the learner towards performance, for example by information gap exercises. This shift can be made more realistic by using the language as a medium and for experiencing and talking about cultural phenomena presented from the viewpoint of native-speaker peers and adults.

So far the four sectors of the circle have been represented as being of equal size, implying the same amount of time devoted to each; this will, however, be determined by the stage of learners' development and the emphasis and time allocated to any one sector will vary as learners advance. This point will be considered again in the detailed discussion of the various aspects of the model.

Language learning

The advances in language teaching made under the banner of Communicative Language Teaching are welcome because they have switched emphasis to active use of the language as a technique for learning and acquisition, and have taken some note of the social character of language embodied in the notion of a speech act. Furthermore, Communicative Language Teaching has stressed the use of 'authentic' language as the material from which pupils learn, providing them with experience of language produced by native-speakers, even though in the initial stages it may have to be carefully selected if it is to remain accessible. The conception of language competence in terms of know-how or skills which have only a tenuous relationship with knowledge about the language in question has led to a re-emphasis of language use as a form of language learning. Provided these various shifts in emphasis do not become exclusive of, for example, the ego-centred use of language in imagination and thought or the conscious manipulation of language which does undoubtedly benefit from knowledge about its structure, whether rhetorical or grammatical, the Communicative Approach provides pupils with a satisfactory process of language learning. There is no need here to add to the considerable literature on its refinements and developments.

The Communicative Approach provides pupils with immediate experience of the language both in those activities which emphasise rehearsal and practice of skills and in those which, by dramatising language use in role-play and simulations, introduce learners to language as social action. None the less, despite 'authentic materials' imported into the foreign language classroom, the experience is a restricted and limited version of using the language in the foreign culture and society, and the principal focus remains on the language, and on learners' fluency and accuracy in language use.

Language awareness

The development in Britain of language awareness teaching (Donmall, 1985; Hawkins, 1987) has stressed both the need to educate children in one of the fundamental characteristics of being human and, secondly, the benefits in language learning of having a general understanding of the nature of language and positive and realistic attitudes towards language learning. The potential range of topics on which to construct a language awareness course is so large that selection has to be made both with a view to restricting the extent of a course and with regard to the learners' age and cognitive capacities. In general, courses have introduced pupils in the early secondary years to topics in the sociology and psychology of language, with some forays into philological and grammatical issues. Lessons on first language acquisition, on dialects and other language varieties, on historical and contemporary relationships between different languages or on social attitudes towards speech and writing can all contribute to the two principal purposes of educating about language and preparing the ground for language learning. Illustrations are usually taken from pupils' own linguistic environments. In some instances this means drawing on the languages spoken by bilingual pupils from ethnic minorities; in other cases the emphasis might be on dialectal varieties spoken by the pupils. The aim is to arouse curiosity in their linguistic environment, to make them aware of their own linguistic competence.

In the model proposed here it is in the analysis of sociological and structural aspects of language that the language awareness component will contribute most directly to the whole. For, by presenting learners with the opportunity to understand the relationship between language and other cultural phenomena, this component allows them to link their acquisition of language skills with their understanding of the foreign culture. In so far as the study of first language acquisition also includes the relationship between language acquisition and culture-specific socialisation, the psychology of language is also directly pertinent. Since selection is inevitable, one new criterion should be the contribution which a particular topic can make to this linking function between language learning and cultural awareness.

For example, in language learning pupils acquire the skills and some linguistic formulae needed to greet and take leave. These may be practised in role-play, and be acquired through experiential learning. The language awareness component would draw conscious attention to the similarities with and differences from the learners' first language, perhaps focusing on different degrees of formality and the appropriate linguistic formulae. Yet this issue of formality is inextricably linked with cultural knowledge of social structures. The linguistic formulae are the surface indicators of native-speakers' cultural knowledge, which is itself largely unconscious and difficult to articulate. In order to help pupils to understand that cultural knowledge, the teacher would compare it with their own unarticulated cultural competence and begin to make them aware of the nature of cultural behaviour in general, as well as how to act acceptably in the specific foreign culture in question. This would differ from much current practice which would keep the focus on fluent and accurate use of the language while providing simple recipe-like recommendations on when to put the linguistic formulae into operation. Cultural awareness teaching thus shares with language awareness a dual purpose of supporting language learning and extending general understanding of the nature of culture.

The proposal for a new selection criterion would probably mean a greater concentration in the language awareness component on the particular language of the language learning component. In many language awareness courses, the net is cast widely to include examples and illustrations from many languages. Although this has many advantages — not least the possibility of drawing on the languages spoken by bilingual pupils — the new criterion would mean a new focus in the available time, without entirely excluding opportunity for wide-ranging lessons. This would, however, be offset by a greater cohesion between the two components, overcoming some of the problems of current courses, and would introduce more opportunity for using and simultaneously analysing the particular language in ways not available within the Communicative Approach. The dominant teaching medium would remain the learners' mother tongue, as in current language awareness courses, as the demands of abstract discussion and the kind of learning which will change attitudes and schemata of concepts require use of learners' first language.

Cultural awareness

The similarities in purpose between the language awareness and cultural awareness components have already been mentioned. Both are concerned with specific and general learning. Both are concerned with the relationship between language and culture. The cultural awareness component is also concerned with non-linguistic dimensions of culture and more focused on the question of change from monocultural to intercultural competence.

In an off-beat account of anthropological fieldwork, Barley recounts how an African chief offered him a drink of beer in a calabash and how, his own training notwithstanding, he foolishly imported a custom from his own culture:

> Possibly I was infected by his own courtliness. Whatever the reason, instead of simply draining the cup as would have been expected, I held it up and proclaimed Zuuldibo's name in a toast. Immediately a deep and shocked silence descended upon the gathering. The boys stopped talking. Zuuldibo's smile froze upon his face. The very flies seemed hushed from their buzzing. I knew, as everyone knows who works in an alien culture, that I had made a serious mistake. (Barley, 1987:58)

To rectify the damage he is forced into a role-reversal, where Zuuldibo becomes the ethnographer and Barley himself 'the confused and hopeless informant'. For he finds it very difficult to explain the custom of toasting one's host and Zuuldibo is understandably doubtful about how saying someone's name can prolong a person's life and make them happier. Eventually he seizes on a concept he knows is familiar to Zuuldibo and says toasting is 'like the opposite of cursing', thus rescued after all by his ethnographer's training and his ability to make coherent comparisons which they layman might not be able to do.

> It was the famed 'comparative method' of anthropology in action, an enlightening example of a way in which we both had half a picture that was meaningless until put together. I was also discomfortingly aware of how Zuuldibo had forced my thought into paths that were not their own. Until I discussed it with him, I had no clear thoughts at all about toasting, about why we did it, what we expected its effects to be. It was very disconcerting. (Barley, 1987:59)

It is the feeling of being disconcerted which is an indication of a change of attitudes and concepts, of a modification of culture-specific schemata, which cultural awareness teaching should bring about. Barley's comparative method differs from practice in foreign language classrooms precisely because of the reversal of roles. Current practice is more akin to the attitude of the ethnographer who seeks to understand and explain the culture, although foreign language teachers and learners seldom go to the lengths of trying to understand the cultural phenomena they notice from a viewpoint within the other culture. Cultural awareness teaching should, however, involve both viewpoints, making learners both ethnographer and informant, allowing them to gain a perspective through comparison which is neither entirely one nor the other. In the process of comparison from two viewpoints there lies the possibility of attaining an Archimedean leverage on both cultures, and thereby acquiring new schemata and an intercultural competence. Hurman, in her attempt to introduce anthropological knowledge and ethnographic methods into the school curriculum, has a similar formulation:

> I have had three aims in writing this book: first and most important, to help us to see how we, as odd and amusing or irritating foreigners, are seen by other peoples; second, to help us see how other peoples see themselves; third, by building on this double understanding, to be able to look at and understand ourselves more clearly than before. (Hurman, 1977:1)

Although foreign language teachers may resist the emphasis on the learners' own culture and selves, it should not be dismissed without more ado. For an intercultural competence and a deeper self-understanding are far from being mutually exclusive. The particular value of Hurman's book, however, is that it is practical, has been piloted in schools and demonstrates how the most abstract of concepts can be made accessible to young people. Through newspaper articles, stories, pictures and illustrations from daily life, she introduces the notions of stereotype, category and role within our own society. She then expands the horizon to compare categories within different societies, taking her examples from kinship terms, a crucial area of anthropological study. She then deals with racial stereotyping and prejudice and moves on to problems which arise – not unlike Barley's – when two cultures meet.

Foreign language teaching, on the other hand, is traditionally concerned with only one language and culture and the teaching of general concepts would normally be seen as incidental. Even were this to change in favour of teaching more than one language and culture during the period of secondary education, it is unlikely, although none the less desirable, that the scope will be extended beyond the languages spoken in the developed world and Western Europe in particular – possibly including the new immigrant languages from the Third World. Moreover, the emphasis on the link of languages and culture and experience of the foreign culture in and through the language means that Hurman's explicit framework of social science concepts illustrated by whatever ethnographic material seems appropriate – from British newspapers to Evans-Pritchard's studies of the Nuer –

would have to be reversed, with the emphasis on introducing pupils to one specific, usually Western European, culture and the use of social science concepts as a means to that end. However, since Western European cultures are in themselves complex and multi-layered, there is still opportunity for selecting material from a wide range of sources. The advantages Hurman gains from being able to select from markedly different cultures is that the fundamental contrasts are very clear, whereas comparisons across European cultures can easily stop at the level of superficial customs and habits whose significance as symptoms of underlying beliefs is not explored. It is assumed that beneath the surface all Europeans have essentially the same culture and 'civilisation'.

To summarise, the cultural awareness component would examine the phenomena of, say, French culture and by so doing would have a number of purposes. It would provide a further opportunity for comparative study of French and the learners' mother tongue by examining the use of French in French culture, for example by concentrating on key concepts and their linguistic manifestations. It would cause learners to reflect on and explicate their own key cultural concepts, however disconcerting this may be, thereby making them see themselves as others do and modifying their existing schemata and cultural competence. The content of this component would be in part drawn from the Language Learning and Language Awareness components and in part dependent on the Cultural Experience component of the model. For the Cultural Experience component would of necessity give little opportunity for reflection, both because the emphasis would be on immediacy and directness of experiential learning and because, taking place in the foreign language, learners would need the chance to stand back from the experience and reflect upon it in their first language.

Cultural experience

The fourth component of the model serves as a bridge between study of the culture and learning of the language, but it is not simply an opportunity to apply or put into practice the abstract cultural study and the rehearsal of linguistic skills. For this fourth component introduces another kind of learning, through direct experience, of the relationship between language and culture, of the way in which language is part of culture and also embodies the whole.

Cultural experience is widely available already to pupils in secondary schools, through exchange holidays, educational visits, contact with native-speaker teachers and assistants, family holidays and so on. In the best cases, links with language learning are made incidentally and deliberately, for example by giving pupils tasks to carry out 'for real' which they have many times practised in role-play and simulation. The emphasis on linguistic survival in a foreign environment which such exercises may imply, however, is inimical to the link with Cultural Awareness which is also desirable.

If this link is to be made, direct experience of the foreign culture needs to be structured in such a way that it gives learners insight into the culture from the native-speaker's viewpoint. It is not the intention or hope that, by some undefined process of immersion, learners will become native-speakers culturally any more than linguistically; they shall not change identity and abandon their own cultural viewpoint. It is rather a question of suspension of disbelief and judgement for a period of experimental learning, which is prepared for in the Cultural Awareness component and later analysed there too. Learners need to be prepared for experience of the daily rhythm of the foreign culture, of the behaviours which are different and those which are the same but have a different significance. Such phenomena are verbal and non-verbal, and learners need both the skills of fluency and accuracy in the language and the awareness of the cultural significance of their utterances and behaviours. Direct experience of the foreign culture is therefore not the culmination of language and cultural learning, not the final performance for which all else is rehearsal, but rather an integral contribution to the whole process which is prior to, simultaneous with, and subsequent to other components.

Furthermore, not all cultural experience need take place in the foreign country. That aspect of a stay abroad which consists of using the foreign language to cope with new experience by modifying existing schemata, can also be found in the classroom when pupils are taught through the foreign language. This is most evident and best known in Canadian immersion programmes but is also apparent in '*sections bilingues*' or '*internationaux*' where pupils are taught part of their normal curriculum in the foreign language. When pupils are introduced to new concepts in geography or new foods in home economics lessons in the foreign language, their new experience is embodied in the language.

Were this kind of teaching to take as its subject matter the particular culture associated with the language used as a medium, then the learning involved would be similar to that in the stay in the foreign country. It would not be as complex and rich, but learning to cook the food in a home economics lesson which is focused on the specific culture would be comparable with cooking and eating the food in the foreign country. Similarly, being introduced to new concepts in geography through study of the particular country in the foreign language would involve a non-mediated learning of the foreign viewpoint provided the geography were taught as it is in the country itself. As with cultural experience in the foreign country, this kind would need preparation and subsequent analysis in both Language Learning and Cultural Awareness components. It would, however, also serve as a bridge between these two by providing opportunity to turn language rehearsal into performance and by creating experience on which to reflect in more abstract terms in the mother tongue. This notion, which might be called a *'section biculturelle'*, would be different in scope and purpose from existing *'sections bilingues'*, but the success of the latter is an indication of the feasibility of this aspect of the Cultural Experience component.

Balance and cohesion of the four components

It was stated earlier that the four components are mutually supportive and integral to the whole, and that the balance and proportion allocated to each will vary within the period of learning. It will also be evident from the preceding discussion that the components are not separate entities to be taught exclusively of each other. It is particularly the case that language and cultural awareness overlap in content and teaching method, and there is a different kind of mutual dependence between language learning and the *'section biculturelle'* dimension of cultural experience. The change of emphasis and allocation of time to each component will to some extent occur in detail from week to week within a course. However it is possible to establish theoretical guidelines as to appropriate emphases over larger periods of time.

In order to make the discussion more concrete, let us consider a five-year course of secondary school foreign language learning. This is about the usual minimal length in European countries. In the first year, approximately 60% of the time should be spent on language learning, 20% on language awareness and 10% each on cultural awareness and cultural experience. In this first year pupils are keen to make swift progress in the foreign language and this can be supplemented by language awareness work which draws extensively on the particular language they are learning, dealing largely with sociological and psychological dimensions.

In the second year the language learning component can be reduced (50%) to benefit cultural experience (20%) and the first moves towards *'section biculturelle'* teaching. Similarly, language awareness and cultural awareness can be given equal proportions (15%) although, with more emphasis on structural and semantic issues in language awareness, there will be increased overlap between the two. This pattern can be held through the third year too, although the '*section biculturelle*' proportion of cultural experience may increase from year to year.

In years 4 and 5, there will be a decrease in language learning and a marked increase in cultural experience, particularly through *section biculturelle* work, since the practical difficulties of providing long periods in the foreign country will in most cases preclude what might be theoretically desirable. Thus by the end of the fifth year, in the optimum case, language learning will be reduced to about 20%, cultural experience increased to 40% and language and cultural awareness components will be allocated 40%, divided approximately equally. Table 2.1 summarises this scheme.

TABLE 2.1

Year	L.L.	L.A.	C.A.	C.E.
	%	%	%	%
1	60	20	10	10
2	50	15	15	20
3	50	15	15	20
4	20	20	20	40
5	20	20	20	40

Yet it has been argued that 'language learning' should not and cannot be understood in the narrow way in which cultural experience, language awareness and cultural awareness are considered to be separate and different from language learning. In terms of the effectiveness of teaching and in terms of the educational values and aims of language teaching, they are mutually supportive elements of a whole.

As implied by the title of this collection of papers, the language teacher has the task not simply of presenting another language and culture to be acquired as a complex of skills and behaviours. The language teacher is not merely an instructor but an educator. Like other teachers this task as 'mediator' is to help pupils — and here the term is more appropriate than 'learners' — to understand themselves and the world about them. The specific task as a teacher of language and culture is to help pupils realise that that world is not monolingual and monocultural. He or she has to encourage them to take that step outside their monocultural world which can be likened to a further, tertiary stage of socialisation. Those who are successful gain a viewpoint which is not merely a widening of their existing horizons, but allows them to see new and quite different horizons.

References

AGAR, M 1985, *Speaking Ethnography*. Beverly Hills: Sage.
BARLEY, N. 1987, *Plague of Caterpillars*. Harmondsworth: Penguin.
BYRAM, M. S. 1989, *Cultural Studies in Foreign Language Education*. Clevedon: Multilingual Matters.
DONMALL, B. G. (ed.) 1985, *Language Awareness*. London: CILT.
HAWKINS, E. W. 1987, *Awareness of Language,* 2nd edn. Cambridge: Cambridge University Press.
HMI 1987, *Modern Foreign Languages to 16*. London: HMSO.
HURMAN, A. 1977, *As Others See Us*. London: Arnold.
RUMELHART, D. E. 1980, Schemata: the building blocks of cognition. In R. J. SPIRO *et al.* (eds) *Theoretical Issues in Reading Comprehension*. Hillsdale, N J: Erlbaum.

Part II

Towards a Social History of Language Teaching in Europe

Like all other aspects of education, foreign language teaching is the product of its time. The five chapters in this section trace the development of cultural studies in several European countries and demonstrate that this element in particular of foreign language teaching must be considered in its historical and political context. Language teaching is a political activity and the nature and presence of cultural studies at any given moment is the clearest indicator of the kind of political activity involved.

Risager describes the international influences on the debate on language teaching in Scandinavia. Despite the close ties between the three countries she surveys, each has its own traditions. The role of the Danish tradition as a mediator of ideas from Germany is particularly striking, but the opening of Norway and Sweden to influences from North America and Britain makes Scandinavia an especially rich ground for tracing the fortunes of cultural studies since World War II.

Buttjes and Kerl each deal with perhaps the most influential tradition of cultural studies, *Landeskunde* and its variations in Germany. It is in Germany that the politicisation of cultural studies and foreign language teaching in general has been most clearly evident, and Buttjes's account shows how significant this is both historically and contemporaneously. In post-war years the divergence of traditions within the two Germanies has brought criticism of developments in the Federal Republic from scholars in the German Democratic Republic. It is therefore particularly appropriate to have Kerl's account of the debate in the GDR in which clarity has been sought over the purpose and status of cultural or area studies.

Byram's chapter deals with change in English schools and the failure to take advantage of new educational structures in order to develop cultural studies on a firm foundation. The introduction of comprehensive schools was a political decision wholly within British politics. Mariet's account of language teaching in France brings us to the point where the politics of Europe as a whole impinge on the traditions of a single country. Mariet also stresses the importance of a sound disciplinary base for cultural studies, a theme which runs through the other chapters, in particular Kerl's, and which underlines the importance of a continual review of the debate over time and across frontiers. The chapters in this section are thus not just accounts of individual and separate national histories but also the basis for the internationalisation of the debate necessary for future developments.

3 Cultural Studies and Foreign Language Teaching after World War II: The International Debate as Received in the Scandinavian Countries

KAREN RISAGER

Introduction

This chapter deals with cultural studies and foreign language teaching in the three Scandinavian countries Denmark, Norway and Sweden. It comprises the subjects English, German and French in the general school system since the 1950s, paying special attention to the ways in which the international debate is represented in the countries under consideration. The central point of view is that diversity to be found within cultural studies and the cultural studies debate should be related to the broad social history of the respective countries. Thus this chapter offers a preliminary investigation of that relationship.

In Scandinavia the need for foreign language qualifications is generally accepted, which is natural, considering that Scandinavian languages have no appreciable distribution outside Scandinavia. Thus since the early nineteenth century, modern language teaching has been obligatory in secondary schools (grammar schools), at first German and French, then, from the early twentieth century, English as well. The three countries have had close relations with the rest of European culture, not least with Germany, and since the mid-nineteenth century foreign language teaching has been considered as an activity contributing to the development of general education, including knowledge of important cultural traditions in Europe.

Scandinavia often appears as a unity, perhaps especially Denmark – Norway – Sweden. The languages of these countries are closely related, and with a little practice people in the countries in question understand each other's languages, especially when written. There are many common cultural features too, and politically and constitutionally the countries are quite similar. Today there is an extensive co-operation in many areas, economic, political and cultural. But there are many differences as well, connected with the different security policies, the different economic resources and international economic relations, and the somewhat different traditions concerning cultural relations and orientations. These will be briefly described in the following paragraphs.

The Historical Background: Before the 1950s

Historically there is a close connection between Denmark and Norway: from 1380 to 1814 they were united in the Kindom of Denmark-Norway, with Denmark as the dominant part. Today, one of the two offficial written languages of Norway, the Bokmål, is based on Danish, whereas the other is based on Norwegian dialects. In 1814 Norway got her own constitution, but had to enter a union with Sweden, independent but with a common king and common foreign politics. Complete independence was not reached until 1905.

Norway has ancient commercial relations to Britain, notably by her export of timber in the seventeenth and eighteenth centuries. Sweden has ancient relations to the countries around the Baltic – for instance during the period 1323–1803 Finland was annexed to Sweden – and to Britain, her chief market for iron and steel. Moreover there are certain historical connections with France, among others dynastic; the French marshal Bernadotte became King of Sweden in 1818 after the Napoleonic Wars. The French influence has resulted, for instance, in more French loanwords in Swedish than in Danish.

During the period 1850–1905 emigration to North America was especially large from Norway and Sweden, larger than from Denmark (in proportion to population figures). This has created an interest in American history, particularly in Norway, and after World War II a tradition of research on American history has developed there, supported by the USA.

In general, German influence has been strong in Scandinavia, particularly in Denmark, by virtue of her geographical position. Through Germany Denmark has received impulses from Central European culture. But Denmark has close connections to England too, England being her chief traditional grain market.

For centuries Denmark-Norway and Sweden-Finland have been rivals in the struggle for power in Scandinavia. Since 1814, however, they have not made war against each other. But to this day the three countries have fundamentally different military and economic interests that impede the creation of a regular union.

During World War II Sweden was neutral, whereas Norway and Denmark were occupied by Germany; and after the war Norway and Denmark joined NATO. Moreover, Norway made special agreements with the USA, because she is contiguous to the Soviet Union at the Norwegian Sea; and Denmark made agreements with the USA as well, concerning military installations in Greenland. Sweden kept neutral, in accordance with her principle of non-alignment (which is considered to be one of the reasons that Sweden, as the only country in Europe for which this can be claimed, has not been at war since 1814).

Economic, Political and Cultural Development since the 1950s

Since the 1950s, the Scandinavian countries have experienced a general national economic, political and cultural development that is common in many ways, and parallel to that of the other Western European countries, except that the Scandinavian countries have been marked by the comparatively egalitarian politics of the Social Democratic parties. But as mentioned above, the international relations are somewhat different. Beside the differences of military politics, two areas should be mentioned.

Economic relations

There are obvious differences in national resources, which are expressed in different industrial structures, and different import-export relations: Denmark has a large agricultural and fishery sector, and has developed into an industrial country dominated by food industry and the manufacture of machinery and chemicals. The Norwegian production structure is dominated by a large fishery sector, food industry, wood and paper industry, generation of energy from water power, and, since the

1970s, extraction of oil and oil industries. She has a large merchant fleet. Sweden is characterised by metal ore extraction, motor car industry, wood and paper industry, heavy industry (among others, armaments), and in the south agriculture and some food industry. The overall capital concentration is more pronounced in Sweden than in Norway and Denmark (cf. the population figures: Sweden 8.3 million, Denmark 5 million, Norway 4 million.)

These differences have been important for market policies. After the breakdown of negotiations in the late 1960s concerning Nordic economic co-operation (the Nordek), Denmark entered the European Economic Community in 1973. It was Danish agricultural interests in particular that made Denmark enter the EEC, together with Britain, her chief export market for food. Norway stayed outside, and Sweden is not a member either (Norway and Sweden being members of the European Free Trade Association). But Sweden still considers seriously a close co-operation with the EEC, and in recent years Norway has drawn nearer to the EEC through oil agreements with a number of Western European countries.

Cultural relations

All three countries are clearly oriented towards the West, and open to Anglo-American culture, industry and general cultural influence, especially from the USA. But some differences of orientation have to be mentioned. (It should be added here that the description of the varying cultural orientations of the countries concerned is somewhat tentative, as there is practically no research in the area that is of the broad character needed.)

By virtue of her geographical position, Denmark is especially marked by the confluence of Anglo-American and West German/European cultural currents. Although Anglo-American currents dominate mainstream social and political sciences, German philosophy, humanism and social science are still much represented and developed in Denmark. The German critical and Marxist tendencies of the 1970s influenced the Danish educational milieu quite widely. One expression of the traditional connections to the neighbours in the south is the organisation of the school system, which bears resemblance to the Central European model with coherent curricula and relatively few options.

Culturally, Norway resembles Denmark more than Sweden (remember their long political connection in the past), and orients herself a little more towards Denmark. But compared with Denmark, Norway is more oriented towards the USA (Lundestad, 1982) and Britain, thus being still more receptive of Anglo-American pragmatic and empiricist impulses. The strong Norwegian interest in American Studies has been mentioned above. One expression of this westward orientation is the school system, which bears a resemblance to the American model, characterised by a system of modules with many options.

Sweden looks southward a bit less than Denmark, though this is not as pronounced as with Norway. The orientation towards North American science and technology is strong, which is due to Sweden's greater integration into international capital, and her greater interest in problems of internationalisation – the debate on internationalisation occured in Sweden in the 1970s, in Norway and Denmark not until the 1980s. In Sweden, the humanistic and social tradition is comparatively weak, and very little influenced from West Germany. For instance, the academic circles of the 1970s were much more interested in French structural Marxism (Althusser, Bourdieu) than in West Germany tendencies. On the other hand, the pragmatic tradition is relatively strong in Sweden. As for the Swedish educational system, it resembles the American model, as in Norway (the Swedish educational reforms of the 1960s were famous in Europe for their creation of a broad standardised system for all categories of pupils).

These differences of cultural orientation are reflected in the translation practices of the countries in question. There is a clear tendency that in Denmark more German and French books are translated than in Norway and Sweden: see the figures in Table 3.1 (based on the *Yearbook of Nordic Statistics*, 1986).

The Status of Foreign Languages in the School Systems

The pattern in translations corresponds to the relative status of English, German and French in the school systems.

After World War II, foreign languages were introduced in primary schools. Step by step, English attained a privileged position as the only obligatory foreign language in primary schools (comprising nine years), first in Sweden, then in Norway, and finally in Denmark:

- in Sweden from 1962 (from the 4th year of school. Until 1969 it was optional in the 8th and 9th years. From 1969 English started in the 3rd year; from 1980 schools may choose to wait until the 4th year);
- in Norway from 1974 (from the 4th year);

TABLE 3.1 *Translation practices in Scandinavia*

Country/Year	Languages translated from	No.	%
Denmark, 1985	English	937	53.8
	German	196	11.2
	French	157	9.0
	Norwegian/Swedish	278	15.9
Norway, 1985	English	485	59.8
	German	54	6.7
	French	32	3.9
	Danish/Swedish	159	19.6
Sweden, 1985	English	1,716	71.5
	German	151	6.3
	French	127	5.3
	Danish/Norwegian	170	7.1

- in Denmark from 1976 (from the 5th year. During the period 1958−70 English or German were obligatory from the 6th year, but the majority chose English. In 1970−6 both English and German were obligatory, one from the 5th year, the other from the 7th year).

Formally, German and French have been put on an equal footing as alternative options, first in Sweden, then in Norway, and more recently in Denmark as an experiment:

- in Sweden from 1962 (from the 7th year). Here about 66% of the pupils choose a second foreign language; of these, about 43% choose German, and about 23% French;
- in Norway from 1974 (from the 8th year, alternating with Russian, Spanish, Finnish, and Samian (Lappish)). Here about 60% of the pupils choose a second foreign language; of these, about 48% choose German, and about 11% French;
- in Denmark German maintained its position until the late 1980s. After having been obligatory during the period 1970−6, it became an optional subject from the 7th year, while French was optional in the 10th (optional) year of school. On the other hand, French had a strong position in upper secondary school (the *Gymnasium*), being obligatory in all branches for three years. In 1987 French was about

to be put on an equal footing with German (from the 7th year, and throughout secondary school). Up to 1987 about 90% of the pupils chose German in the 7th year. However, the relative status of the two languages is still under discussion.

In general, German and French have a weaker position in Norway and Sweden than in Denmark. As the school systems of Norway and Sweden are marked by many options and consequently a great many problems of co-ordination and time scheduling, German and French are in a rather difficult situation, which is only just appearing in Denmark. In Denmark, moreover, either German or French is still obligatory if you want to enter the *Gymnasium*. Another factor is the relatively pluralistic second foreign language policies of Sweden and Norway, which offer more languages alternative to German and French than are offered in Denmark.

Foreign languages and general education

With regard to language teaching at secondary schools, there are traditions in the Scandinavian countries to consider it as an activity contributing to general education, i.e. an activity furthering among other things some insights into foreign cultures, even if there are differences as to priority of dimensions and types of texts. As for the primary school level, this idea was generalised in the 1960s and 1970s, valid in principle for all pupils. Thus cultural studies (or cultural orientation, and the like) entered the official guidelines:

- in Sweden in 1962 (among the goals);
- in Norway in 1974 (not formulated as a goal, but mentioned in passing in the text describing the subject. From 1985 formulated as a goal too);
- in Denmark in 1975 (among the goals).

In the 1960s and 1970s, general education changed focus, as in other Western countries. From being primarily a literary and historical education aiming at the national cultures of European countries, it changed into a more sociological and global education, aiming at current problems of culture and society at regional, national and global level. This new content of education is mediated partly by literary texts, partly by other types of texts and other sources.

The Professional Debate

In connection with these changes in the role and content of foreign languages – which concerns also the linguistic content, an aspect not treated here – the professional debate was intensified. A number of periodicals were created, the most central of these being *Sproglaereren* (Denmark), *Språk og språkundervisning* (Norway), and *LMS-Lingua* (Sweden). And some common fora were created by the Scandinavian countries, among others the Nordic Conferences for Language Teachers (from 1977).

National and Scandinavian discussions have focused primarily on problems of foreign language pedagogy and educational policy. To date, discussions of cultural studies have chiefly been limited to national fora, and they have very seldom shown knowledge of parallel discussions in the other countries, except that Norway has received some impulses from Denmark, and vice versa. But as we shall see, the Scandinavian countries have received impulses from the international debate, although people have rarely referred explicitly to foreign discussions until recent years. Generally speaking, the development of ideas corresponds to the West European transition from tendencies of social and ideological criticism in the 1970s, to more culturally oriented tendencies in the 1980s. While the critical tendency is best represented in Denmark, the more cultural tendency is quite widely accepted.

Parallel to the debate, a great many teaching materials have been developed in the Scandinavian countries, mostly in Sweden, least in Norway. It is important to include these materials, as they can be taken as expressions of unpronounced, but widespread, views on cultural content.

Main trends in the international debate

In describing the Scandinavian discussions, I shall distinguish between the following trends in the international debate:

1. The justification of cultural studies, a trend focusing on the role of cultural studies in relation to various types of general and professional education.
2. The content of cultural studies, sometimes divided into three sub-trends:
   – the social and historical trend, focusing on pupils' ability to comprehend the structure, development and mutual relations of

societies. Thus it starts from the macro-level of society. (see for instance: Buttjes & Kane, 1978; Baumgratz et al., 1980; Michaud & Marc, 1981.)

– the anthropological trend, focusing on pupils' ability to gain a sympathetic insight into socially and culturally different conditions. Comprising such themes as the daily life of social groups, or the political and ideological struggle of minorities and grass-root movements, it starts from the micro-level of society. (see for instance: Buttjes & Kane, 1978 (who, like many others from West Germany, combine the macro- and micro-levels); Keller, 1978; Firges & Melenk, 1982; Seelye, 1985; Zarate, 1986.)

– the pragmatic trend, focusing on pupils' ability to communicate in the foreign culture. It starts from the utilitarian perspective of the learner, (see for instance Erdmenger & Istel, 1973, and many proponents of communicative language teaching, though these often have a rather restricted view of cultural content.)

3. The history of cultural studies, a trend focusing on the development of cultural studies, and on meta-scientific aspects.

Denmark

The most common Danish term for cultural studies is *kulturformidling* (= cultural transmission). A characteristic feature of Danish discussions is that they cover a wide spectrum of problems: all the above trends, and all levels of teaching. Besides, many contributions deal with cultural studies at a general level (i.e. covering all foreign languages), a fact that may enhance the development of theoretical considerations. Thus in Denmark, unlike in Norway and Sweden, there has been a debate on foreign language teaching and general education (Geist, 1979; Harder, 1982; Oehrgaard, 1984).

The social and historical trend is represented among others by a project on the integration of cultural teaching and language teaching at the elementary level, starting from French, but covering in principle all foreign languages (Andersen & Risager, 1978). It comprises discussions on the possibilities of combining the macro- and micro-levels. The views are influenced by the West German debate on *Landeskunde/Frankreichkunde* (Buttjes & Kane, 1978; Baumgratz et al., 1980), but also by France (Debyser, 1973; Fichou, 1979). Other representatives include Séférian, 1979 (French); Specht, 1985 (English); Lammers, 1987 (German); and a number of editors/authors of anthologies/compendiums on Britain, West Germany and France. Sevaldsen (1986) discusses the need for further Anglo-Scandinavian comparative studies.

The anthropological trend is represented among others by Elbeshausen & Wagner, 1982 (German), who refer to the thinking about *Alltagswissen* (cf. for instance Firges & Melenk, 1982). And in recent years, the interest in intercultural studies has started discussions on intercultural attitudes and stereotypes, especially within English (Sevaldsen & Djursaa, 1988) and French. More general aspects are treated by Séférian, 1986, and Risager, 1987a.

During the 1970s and 1980s many materials were produced, especially for the intermediate level: anthologies on various themes of current sociocultural interest. Some of these are used in Norway as well — Norwegians read Danish without great difficulty.

As communicative teaching is expanding, especially within English and German, the pragmatic trend is represented as well, though not much discussed. A contribution related to this domain is Phillipson & Skutnabb-Kangas, 1983, who discuss the content of the concept of intercultural competence.

The history of cultural studies has been treated in recent years; see for instance Skydsgaard & Vesterholm, 1982; Kristiansen *et al.*, 1984; Risager, 1986; and Risager, 1988. Various dimensions of the concept of culture have been discussed by Specht, 1985, and Risager, 1987b. Here again, the considerations are mostly at a general level.

Norway

The most common Norwegian terms for cultural studies are *kulturkunnskap* (= cultural knowledge) and *bakgrunnskunnskap* (= background knowledge). It is characteristic of Norway that the major part of contributions on cultural studies are related to the teaching of English at all levels, particularly at the universities and other institutions of higher education (these have a common national forum: Working Papers in Civilisation (Trondheim and Oslo)).

The social and historical trend is mostly represented at university level, concerning the teaching of British and American civilisation. Many compendiums have been produced, and discussions have focused on the problem of content; some are in favour of teaching primarily the history of ideas (for instance Gulliksen, 1978), others prefer an approach focusing on contemporary institutions (Skårdal, 1979). It should be added that the Norwegian interest in American history has contributed to the creation of a Scandinavian periodical: *American Studies in Scandinavia* published in Oslo.

Cultural content at the elementary level of English has been treated too; for example Breidlid, 1979, who refers to Andersen and Risager's work (Denmark). The anthropological trend is represented among others by Brøgger (1980 and 1986), who, referring to the American anthropologist Geertz, is in favour of an anthropological semiological approach. The pragmatic trend may be said to be represented by the proceedings of a national seminar on the role of *Landeskunde* at universities and commerical colleges (Feigs & Kvam, 1986).

Sweden

The most common Swedish term for cultural studies is *realia,* possibly supplemented by *kulturorientering* (= cultural orientation).

Compared to Denmark and Norway, foreign language teaching in Sweden is characterised by a strong methodological and pragmatic tradition, and an extensive self-sufficiency with regard to teaching materials for the elementary level and the early stages of the intermediate level. A great many of these materials are used in Denmark and Norway (usually in translation). On the other hand, cultural studies are very little discussed (with some exceptions chiefly within German), possibly because of the relative weakness of humanistic and social traditions. It should be mentioned that particularly in Sweden, cultural studies are normally associated with the investigation of immigrant cultures; in this connection cultural studies are termed *kulturkunskap* (= cultural knowledge).

The social and historical trend has been represented by a politically tinted discussion on what to understand by post-war 'German reality' (cf. Hermodsson, 1972, 1973; Grass, 1973a and b). Quite recently, Svensson (for instance Svensson, 1986) has tried to develop the Swedish discussion along the lines of the international debate, stressing the importance of the teaching of cultural history and intercultural relations at the intermediate level. Thus his perspective covers the anthropological trend as well. He refers to West German and Danish work; although he starts from German, he discusses the problems at the general level too.

In Sweden, unlike in Denmark and Norway, it is stated in the goals of foreign language teaching that pupils should be able to describe Swedish society in the foreign language. Thus an English book on Sweden has been produced, supplied with exercises.

The pragmatic trend seems widely accepted, though not really discussed. It characterises the production of materials at the elementary and early intermediate levels, showing features of everyday life, seen with the traveller's eyes, putting an emphasis on material aspects of culture: street life, interiors and so on.

Conclusion

With regard to teaching practices, based on teaching materials widely used, the Scandinavian countries show many similar features. The elementary level in particular, and to some extent the early intermediate level, are marked decisively by materials produced in Sweden. The cultural content of these is mostly characterised by the pragmatic trend, yet the materials are of a quality that can easily compete with non-Scandinavian materials. At the intermediate level, teaching in Denmark, and to a certain degree in Norway, is influenced by materials produced in Denmark, with a cultural content characterised primarily by the anthropological trend, often with a critical perspective. Danish materials have the reputation of being 'engaging'.

With regard to pedagogical discussion, differences appear, that are to a certain degree attributable to the different cultural orientations of the respective countries, although institutional factors and pure chance have to be considered as well. Denmark is essentially a mediator of impulses from West Germany, the centre of international debates. On the other hand, Norway and Sweden, more monopolised by English than is the case in Denmark, receive impulses mostly from the USA and Britain; Sweden in particular is influenced by the pragmatic tradition of the teaching of English as a foreign language, originating in Britain. Thus the Scandinavian countries form an excellent field for the investigation of the diversity of cultural studies within foreign language teaching.

References

ANDERSEN, H. and RISAGER, K. 1978, The relationship between sociocultural and linguistic content in foreign language teaching. In K. GREGERSEN *et al.* (eds) *Papers from the Fourth Scandinavian Conference of Linguistics*, p. 73–78. Odense University Press.

BAUMGRATZ, G. *et al.* 1980, Landeskunde im Fremdsprachenunterricht – das Beispiel der Frankreichkunde. *East*, 1, p. 76–94.

BREIDLID, A. 1979, Om innhold i engelskundervisningen i grunnskolen. *Språk og språkundervisning*, 12, p. 6–12.

BROGGER, F. C. 1980, A cultural approach to American Studies. *American Studies in Scandinavia*, 12, p. 1–15.

— 1986, Vanlig språk er også 'figurige' greier: Om språk, litteratur og kulturkunnskap i språkundervisningen. *Språk og språkundervisning*, 1, p. 3–15.

BUTTJES, D. and KANE, L. 1978, Theorie und Zielsetzung der Landeskunde im Fremdsprachenstudium. *Anglistik und Englischunterricht,* 4, p. 51–61.
DEBYSER, F. 1973, Le rapport langue/civilisation et l'enseignement de la civilisation aux débutants. In A. REBOULLET (ed.) *L'enseignement de la civilisation française,* p. 58–75. Paris: Hachette.
ELBESHAUSEN, H. and WAGNER, J. 1982, Kontrastiver Alltag I – Die Rolle von Alltagsbegriffen in der Interkulturellen Kommunikation. *GIP* 32, p. 5–15. Odense University.
ERDMENGER, M. and ISTEL, H. -W. 1973, *Didaktik der Landeskunde.* München: Hueber.
FEIGS, W. and KVAM, S. (eds) 1986, *Deutsche Landeskunde im Fremdsprachenunterricht.* Trondheim: Tapir.
FICHOU, J.-P. 1979, *Enseigner les civilisations.* Paris: Presses Universitaires de France.
FIRGES, J. and MELENK, H. 1982, Landeskunde als Alltagswissen. *Praxis des neusprachlichen Unterrichts,* 29, p. 115–123.
GEIST, U. 1979, Fremmedsprog er også sprog. *Sproglaereren,* 5, p. 9–23.
GRASS, M. 1973a, Tatsächlich: die schwierige Wirklichkeitsbeschreibung. *Moderna Språk,* 67, p. 21–30.
— 1973b, Wirklichkeitsbeschreibung? *Moderna Språk,* 67, p. 352–58.
GULLIKSEN, Oe. 1978, Kulturkunnskapens plass i engelskfaget. *Språk og språkundervisning,* 4, p. 56–69.
HARDER, P. 1982, Sprogfag, almendannelse og fremtidens gymnasium. *Uddannelse,* 15, p. 82–91.
HERMODSSON, L. 1972, Über die Schwierigkeiten, die deutsche Wirklichkeit aufzuzeigen. *Moderna Språk,* 66, p. 369–80.
— 1973, Weiteres über die deutsche Wirklichkeit. Moderna Språk, 67, p. 151–159.
KELLER, G. 1978, Werden Vorurteile durch einen Schüleraustausch abgebaut? In H. ARND and F.-R. WELLER (eds) *Landeskunde und Fremdsprachenunterricht,* p. 130–150. Frankfurt Am Main: Diesterweg.
KRISTIANSEN, M. et al. (eds) 1984, *Umoderne sprog? – om fremmedsprog i gymnasiet.* Copenhagen: Gyldendal.
LAMMERS, H. 1987, Sprog–kultur–politik. De to Tysklande – faelles sprog og kultur, men modsatrettede samfundssystemer. In M.-A. SÉFÉRIAN and H.SPECHT (eds) *Sprog og kulturformidling,* p. 27–50. Copenhagen: Danmarks Laererhøjskole.
LUNDESTAD, G. 1982, History and politics: Research on the United States in Norway, 1945–80. *American Studies in Scandinavia,* 14, p. 69–98.
MICHAUD G. and MARC, E. 1981, *Vers une science des civilisations?* Bruxelles: Editions Complexe.
OEHRGAARD, P. 1984, Sprogfag er kulturfag. *Uddannelse,* 17, p. 533–37.
PHILLIPSON, R. and SKUTNABB-KANGAS, T. 1983, Intercommunicative and Intercultural Competence. *ROLIG-papir* 28, p. 43–77. Roskilde University Centre.
RISAGER, K. 1986, Cultural Studies and Foreign Language Teaching in Denmark. *ROLIG-papir* 41, Roskilde University Centre.
— 1987a, Fremmedsprog og nationalkultur. *Kultur og Samfund* 1, p. 1–17. Roskilde University Centre.
— 1987b, Kulturbegrebet i fremmedsprogsfagene i forskellige lande. In K. S.

JAKOBSEN and M. SVENDSEN PEDERSEN (eds) *Kultur og kommunikation i fremmedsprogsundervisningen*, p. 15-45. Roskilde University Centre.
— 1988, Nye veje i kulturformidlingen i Vesteuropa og USA. In *Tvaersproglige Blade,* Copenhagen: Danmarks Paedagogiske Bibliotek.
SEELYE, H. N. 1985, *Teaching Culture. Strategies for Intercultural Communication.* Lincolnwood, Ill: National Textbook Company.
SÉFÉRIAN, M.-A. 1979, Samfundsorientering og fremmedsprogsindlaering. *Sproglaereren,* 8, p. 9-18.
— 1987, Sprog-kultur-identitet. For en fremmedsprogsundervisning der tager hensyn til identitetsdannelsen. In M.-A. SÉFÉRIAN and H. SPECHT (eds) *Sprog og kulturformidling,* p. 101-116. Copenhagen: Danmarks Laererhøjskole.
SEVALDSEN, J. 1986, Cross-Cultural Studies and Anglo-Scandinavian Relations. In *Working Papers in Civilisation. Topics and Research,* III, p. 142-172. University of Trondheim.
SEVALDSEN, J. and DJURSAA, M. 1988, *England og englaenderne – en kort praesentation for danske besøgende.* Copenhagen: FUHU (Foreningen for unge handelsmaends uddannelse).
SKYDSGAARD, N. J. and VESTERHOLM, B. 1982, Om tekstvalget i nysprogligt gymnasium. *Meddelelser fra gymnasieskolernes engelsklaererforening,* 92, p. 8-28.
SKÅRDAL, D. B. 1979, Kulturkunnskapens plass i engelskfaget. *Språk og språkundervisning,* 3, p. 46-54.
SPECHT, H. 1985, Kulturkendskab som begreb og som fag. Hvilke mål og hvilke midler? *SELF* (Seminariernes engelsklaererforening), Supplement 1.
— 1985, Kultur- og samfundsforhold: en kritisk oversigt over nyere laerebogsmateriale I og II. *SELF* (Seminariernes engelsklaererforening), 2, p. 8-23, and 3, p. 8-19.
SVENSSON, S. E. 1986, Kulturorientierung als Ziel des gymnasialen Unterrichts in Deutsch als Fremdsprache. *Didakometrie and Soziometrie,* Lärarhögskolan i Malmö.
Yearbook of Nordic Statistics, 1986. Stockholm: The Nordic Council of Ministers and the Nordic Statistical Secretariat.
ZARATE, G. 1986, *Enseigner une culture étrangère.* Paris: Hachette.

# 4 Culture in German Foreign Language Teaching: Making Use of an Ambiguous Past

DIETER BUTTJES

Introduction

The historiographic approach followed in this chapter can be justified against the backdrop of a specific German heritage of language teaching and the peculiar role culture has played in it. The main focus will be directed to those eighty years from the beginnings of foreign language teaching at the time of the modern language reform, to the 1960s when foreign languages finally became a normal and regular part of any school curriculum. Within this period of less than one hundred years, the foundations were laid for foreign languages as a school subject and for culture as part of the foreign language curriculum.

In addition, earlier developments in the history of language teaching and parallel movements in Europe and the USA are noted that may have contributed to the definition of culture within foreign language teaching. Finally, the state of intercultural studies in West Germany is presented as an overview of recent debates and tendencies in the 1970s and 1980s. The results show that culture has lost its ambiguity and is gaining priority in German foreign language teaching.

Towards a History of Culture in Language Teaching: Motivations and Directions

The sociocultural direction of foreign language teaching

We are working in an underdeveloped field of language teaching theory. The theory of foreign language teaching 'still lacks a well-defined sociocultural emphasis', and the 'possible contribution of social sciences to language pedagogy' remains less than clear (Stern, 1983: 246, 242). Why, under these circumstances and in this specific field, should historical studies be useful? In fact, an observer might reject the current and increasing interest in the past of our disciplines as an indication of escapism from more urgent needs in the practice of present language teaching. Yet, some of our problems in 'giving language teaching a sociolinguistic direction' (Stern, 1983: 262) may be related to narrow working concepts of language teaching as much as to an attitude of neglect regarding traditions of language teaching. There is no simple returning to the roots, but the rapid turnover of established teaching practice following changes in linguistic or educational theory may in itself betray a lack of confidence and direction in our disciplines. Even though the hope of learning from history may be futile and the danger of imposing our concepts on history may be inevitable, making use of the past by recreating a usable past may be a worthwhile attempt towards providing that sociocultural orientation which has been found missing in the theory of foreign language teaching.

At present, certain political and educational developments seem to enhance the need for intercultural communication via foreign languages. The cultural survival value of national languages is emphasised, but there is also a growing awareness of dependency across linguistic and political boundaries. At the same time, the social value of language learning for the individual and the chances of global education for all are being recognised. Such changes in the international constellation and intellectual climate can only be appreciated by a social history of language teaching transcending the limits of the classroom and the narrow language curriculum. Looking thus at the social and historical context of language teaching may reveal lost opportunities and recover a hidden past which may help us to gain a sense of continuity and a purpose for continuation in the effort of realigning language and culture in foreign language teaching. Finally, looking back upon a national heritage in language teaching may allow us to be more sensitive to specific cultural restrictions as well as to general transcultural developments affecting the continuing reform of foreign language teaching.

The peculiarity of German Landeskunde

The traditions of teaching culture and language in Germany have raised both irritation and expectations. Especially from British and American points of view the practice of integrating culture within foreign language teaching has often appeared as a specific German, or at least Continental, predilection. As an officer of the British Council commented in a 'personal overview' of the English Language Teaching scene:

> Indeed, in the countries of the EEC English Studies has become a subject in its own right aimed not only at imparting the language but also at filling in the background to British life and institutions as part of the process by which member nations get to know each other better. At any rate, this aspect of training is really part of the general teaching of English for social and cultural purposes and has no independent impact on the state of the art in UK. (Pickett, 1979: 93)

And Stern's well-informed voice from Canada raises similar reservations regarding the peculiar German tradition of *Kulturkunde*: 'This sophisticated historical, literary, and philosophical approach, expressed in the slogan *"Kulturkunde* as history of ideas" (*"Kulturkunde als Geistesgeschichte"*) has maintained itself in Germany until today' (Stern, 1983:248). Both observers view background and cultural studies as basically alien to Anglo-American concepts of language teaching. However, a more recent voice from Britain seems to have put high hopes in 'the long history of academic interest in *Landeskunde* in Germany', only to discover – after an analysis of textbooks – that he did not find 'all he hoped for in the well-established tradition of *Landeskunde* in Germany' (Byram & Schilder 1986:168).

Within the German foreign language teaching profession, attitudes towards their own traditions of teaching culture – either as *Kulturkunde* or as *Landeskunde* – have been ambivalent. During the first half of the twentieth century culture was never doubted as part of foreign language curricula. Aiming at an elite education for the German-Prussian nation-state, modern language teachers found themselves squeezed between the traditional demands of the classics and the modern requirements of a 'national culture'. Both these conservative roots made foreign language teaching in Germany susceptible to educational misuse in those periods when imperialist expansion and military aggression called for ethnocentric affirmation in teaching.

Some time after World War II, critics in both East and West Germany deplored the cultural heritage of foreign language teaching as an 'aberration of philology' causing the ideological dispossession of literature and the totalitarian instrumentalisation of language teaching. These attacks in the 1960s and 1970s represented the climax of deconstruction of culture in language teaching. In Germany, too, culture came to be discredited as alien to the true purposes of language teaching. At that time no effort was made yet to find the causes for failure in either the foundations of the cultural concepts used or the political intentions for which they were misused.

The reintegration of cultural studies

It took a difficult and sometimes painful process of isolating the specific German ideological contexts of schooling and foreign language teaching before a new and unbiased view of culture in language teaching became possible. In the course of this re-evaluation important predecessors were discovered in the modern language reform movement and in various minority positions since then (Buttjes, 1984). These cosmopolitan concepts of teaching culture – which had been either forgotten or suppressed – could now be restored in order to initiate the new cultural studies debate in West Germany. This discussion in both English and French as a foreign language was reopened in the 1970s and has provided new foundations and directions after decades of conservative and nationalist domination.

In some ways the early *Kulturkunde* debate can be seen to reflect a general 'ambivalence towards modernity' in Germany (Eisenstadt & Curelaru, 1976:16). In foreign language teaching the drive for modernity – even in the nineteenth century – seemed stronger in Germany than elsewhere, with an expanding market for utilitarian language courses and the deep changes caused by the modern language reform movement (Howatt, 1984: 130, 170). This reform, the introduction of foreign languages as a school subject and academic discipline, and the beginnings of the early cultural studies debate coincided with the appearance of the German-Prussian nation-state after 1870. The separate, belated and aggressive development of Germany has been attributed to the weakness of the less self-confident bourgeois classes and the exclusion of the working classes. Foreign language teaching and the teaching of foreign cultures were bound to be affected in many ways, especially in the rejection of Western democratic values and of sociology as an alien discipline (Lepenies, 1985:285).

Viewed against this backdrop of separation and alienation, German foreign language teaching and the German cultural studies debate need to be reintegrated into the European and international discussion. The examples from German history show that perhaps no other discipline suffers more from ethnocentric isolation than the profession of teaching foreign languages and cultures.

The Stages of the Cultural Debate (1880–1960): Traditions and Contradictions

In the history of foreign language teaching and foreign language pedagogy in Germany, the issue of culture and cultural studies has been debated again and again. The debate was opened in the 1880s when foreign languages were accepted into the curricula of German schools. In the 1960s that debate was slowing down, but was taken up at the end of that decade when English became a school subject for all social classes. The late 1960s were also characterised by political changes in West Germany when the first non-conservative government (*sozial-liberale Koalition*) was installed and non-aggressive foreign policies (*Ostpolitik*) were implemented.

The beginning and the renewal of the cultural studies debate reflect not only important political and educational changes within Germany, but can also be related to broader movements like the modern language reform in Europe and the student unrest in Western Europe and the USA. In this respect, the German cultural studies debate can be seen to confirm the impression that changes in foreign language teaching objectives have generally been related to changing intellectual climates (Stern, 1983: 81) besides reflecting the social and political history of a country (Hüllen, 1979: 3). In the case of cultural studies in German foreign language teaching the most productive debates occurred in the 1880s, the 1920s, and the 1950s and can therefore be clearly attributed to the Prussian-German *Kaiserreich,* the Weimar Republic, and the West German *Bundesrepublik* (for East German perspectives see chapter by Kerl in this volume). In retrospect, the contradiction becomes obvious. The teaching of foreign cultures and languages in Germany has developed in a climate of chauvinism in thinking and aggression in politics. This paradoxical association – noted by more than one critical observer – needs to be resolved.

Cultural content in early foreign language teaching

Even before the modern language reform movement summarised and criticised the established teaching practice at the end of the nineteenth century, foreign language teaching had evolved under various circumstances and for different purposes. These language teaching programmes from the Renaissance period on did not always indicate any cultural orientation; but some of them began to relate language form and cultural content in interesting ways. The earliest examples of combining language and subject skills seem to have originated in commerical trading centres. Thus, German trading apprentices were sent to foreign offices of Hanseatic towns in Russia, Italy and Britain in order to acquire trading knowledge along with language skills (Meyer, 1980:63). Much later, in the Flemish trading centres, the need for double-manuals arose in order to facilitate commerical communication between English- and French-speaking traders (Howatt, 1984:6). Their content as well as their specific language seems to have been geared to subjects that would enable people of different language groups to communicate within the worlds of trade and commerce.

Another early example of close interrelations between language and content can be found in the teaching traditions initiated by Comenius. It is in this context, too, that the term 'realia' gains significance. Comenius, though not concerned with either foreign languages or language teaching as such, developed an educational philosophy that would introduce the child to 'the great common world' by a combination of visual and linguistic representation. In the late seventeenth century, his famous Latin textbook appeared in both Germany and England allowing an early form of an 'audiovisual course' in Latin or in the German or English vernacular (Howatt, 1984:39).

Up to the nineteenth century these early examples of commerical or educational motivation towards a cultural orientation in language teaching seem to have been forgotten. However, both the commercial orientation and the cosmopolitan outlook were to reappear during the modern language reform movement. The school and language policies in nineteenth-century Germany were not favourable either to modern languages or to cultural objectives in language teaching. On the one hand, the school reform connected with Humboldt's name concentrated on the classical languages for the educated elite. And on the other hand, the numerous textbooks and methods for self-instruction and school teaching were not primarily concerned with content. Only when contents and topics could no longer be ignored, for example in dialogues or in texts for the advanced, did the specific cultural setting gradually replace vague general or literary themes.

The foreign language teaching theory proposed by Mager around the middle of the nineteenth century seems to have been the only modern language concept expressly incorporating reality (*'Sprachunterricht ist Sachunterricht'*) and aiming at some knowledge of the contemporary European cultures and civilisations. His foreign language teaching theory integrated language, literature and culture and hoped for a new world-view that would transcend the 'barriers of the merely nationalistic, particularistic consciousness' (Mager, 1843 in Flechsig, 1965:69–154). In a recent re-evaluation of Humboldt's philosophy of education both Mager and Vietor appear as those who realised Humboldt's true intentions of humanistic education (Meyer, 1986:64). It is true that the modern language reformers – in a curious mixture of emulation and rejection – were to refer to basic concepts of classical cultural studies as proposed by Humboldt and others.

Realia and the modern language reform

With their emphasis on the oral quality and the communicative function of foreign languages, reformers like Vietor, Palmer and Jespersen are recognised as having laid the foundations of modern language pedagogy. But Vietor's call for reorienting language teaching was accompanied by a redefinition of the cultural content, too. Within the German context of modern language reform, the emphasis on some knowledge of the foreign realia (*Realienkunde*) can certainly be considered as one of the key demands of the reformers. This programmatic point can be derived from the core theory of modern language reform and from the models of language teaching available at the time, but should also be related to commercial and political interests of the new German nation-state, as well as to the professional interests of the emerging new group of foreign language teachers.

The biannual conferences of foreign language teachers (*Neuphilologentage*) most clearly presented their new self-image and professional ethos. Competing with the established and highly prestigious disciplines of Classical Studies and German, modern language teachers asked for realia and culture to be included in foreign language teaching. It was teachers and school officials from the ranks of the reform movement, like Klinghardt, Waetzoldt and Wendt, who shaped the new self-concept of foreign languages. Around 1900, after less than twenty years, the cultural objectives of foreign language teaching had become widely accepted among the teaching profession. Against the growing resistance of university philologists even chairs for cultural studies were considered self-evident for teacher training in modern languages.

At the time when modern languages became established school subjects and opened up teaching careers at the universities, their cultural dimension was questioned by minorities only. Within the foreign language rationale, culture had come to occupy a central and crucial position. Foreign language teaching was seen to concern itself with 'the real life expression of modern peoples' (so said Klinghardt in 1886), and foreign language teachers were considered 'experts of the material and intellectual culture of foreign peoples' (Waetzoldt in 1892). The term' realia' was at the time expanded beyond merely visible objects for demonstration to include any aspect of the foreign social reality.

Foreign language skills as well as literary and linguistic knowledge were considered subordinate and instrumental only in achieving such cultural and educational objectives. Wendt's classic formula in his 'manifesto of the modern language reform' of 1890 gave communicative competence high priority, but firmly linked this to the foreign cultural content (Flechsig, 1965: 179–189). English language teaching practice, as reconstructed from curricula and textbooks, from teaching handbooks and self-reported lessons shows some bias towards everyday life and social customs in Britain, but does not exclude topics like education, Ireland or the empire from advanced readers. Much of the material used betrayed ambivalent attitudes towards Britain, the admired rival in both constitutional and foreign policies. Like the authentic texts from British sources, visual representations increasingly became culture-specific, too. The cultural content of foreign language teaching at this period was aiming at a fair and realistic presentation of the foreign society.

Culture in the 1920s and after

It is not easy to identify those conditions and forces that retarded the initial impulse of the reform movement towards cultural content and cosmopolitan objectives in language teaching. There were, of course, the newly established modern language chairs at the universities which were exclusively concerned with phonetics and literature and which rejected the calls for cultural studies in teacher training. But it was the outbreak of World War I which effectively shattered the cosmopolitan dreams of foreign language teachers, thus demonstrating the gulf existing between educational ideas and economic interests. The political climate of the war led to some of the less noble statements about Germany's war opponents, even from philologists, and the cry for the abolition of foreign language teaching could also be heard. Yet it was the experience of war that led to a renewal of interest in the political and cultural function of foreign languages. In this respect, notable parallels can be drawn between the call for 'Modern Studies' in Britain and 'Foreign Studies' (*Auslandsstudien*) in Germany towards the end of the war.

In both countries government committees investigated the state of foreign language teaching and made suggestions for the time after the war (*Denkschrift*, 1917; Modern Studies, 1918). Both reports regarded foreign language teaching under pragmatic and educational aspects and suggested an expansion and modernisation of language teaching. Modern languages were considered useful for public service and for commerce, but were also to serve the cultural education of the citizens: 'Modern Studies are needed for the enlightenment of the nation no less than for practical purposes' (Modern Studies, 1918:50). Both Modern Studies and *Auslandsstudien* were to embrace subjects like history, politics and economics besides language and literature in order to gain historically enlightened, comprehensive views of the foreign culture. The cultural and political ignorance of foreign nations that had been apparent before and during the war could no longer be afforded.

In Germany, this unusual political support of foreign languages was taken up after the war when new institutes for area research and the first chair for American Studies were set up at universities. Teachers' organisations argued for the priority of cultural knowledge (*Kulturkunde*) in modern languages. However, this demand – familiar from the times of the modern language reform – was undergoing significant changes in the 1920s. Culture was set apart from the social realia and mystified as a people's soul and character as expressed in their philosophy, arts and literature. Any cultural expression was to be reduced to certain national traits of character. These characteristics would then have to be compared between the native and the foreign culture; this comparison would lead to a knowledge of weaknesses and strengths which would be for the national benefit. Finally, the German cultural values (*Deutschkunde*) were prescribed as the cross-curricular standard for all subjects in the Prussian school reform of 1924/25 leaving no room for any genuine interest in foreign cultures.

The speculative argumentation and the chauvinistic implementation of *Kulturkunde* was not accepted in all quarters of academic or professional foreign language teaching. Scholars like Schücking, Nohl and Litt severely attacked the ethnocentric assumptions and the manipulative reasoning of *Kulturkunde* and tried to defend international communication and cultural exchange as the objectives of foreign language pedagogy (Hüllen, 1979:144–80). The strongest opposition came from Schücking who claimed that culture was represented by such democratic and humanistic movements as women's liberation and the peace movement. Other critics deplored the lack of sociology in teacher training and suggested that cultural studies accept the sound methods of an 'applied' historical discipline. Yet the majority of foreign language theorists supported *Kulturkunde*, even under the perverted and paradoxical label of *Deutschkunde*. A great number of textbooks and anthologies presented foreign cultures to language learners, and more than one handbook was concerned with methods of *Kulturkunde*. Not all of them were openly hostile to the culture portrayed, but most of them offered proof of intercultural distortion and prejudice. Unfortunately, this need for devaluing foreign cultures could easily be taken up by Nazi education and eventually led to outright propaganda in textbooks, and also among the academic profession.

Literature versus Social Studies after World War II

World War II more than World War I discredited nationalism in Germany and with it those ethnocentric and aggressive tenets of *Deutschkunde* and its fascist counterpart, *Wesenskunde*, that had come to dominate *Kulturkunde* in the 1930s. In fact, even though Weimar representatives of *Kulturkunde* like Hübner and Hartig continued to be influential in post-war West Germany, the term *Kulturkunde* was avoided for a long time. Much of the philosophical and political thinking, however, returned in the period of the Cold War, when Western ideas and ideals appeared to be threatened by alien ideologies. This new international constellation emerging in the 1950s encouraged conservative culture concepts in Germany as well as the more patriotic tendencies within American Studies (Gleason, 1984).

In this period of widespread restoration it is difficult to find examples of renewal or reform within the foreign language debate. It is also difficult to separate these internal German professional developments from wider intellectual and political influences especially from Britain and the USA. The cultural void after 1945 was at least partly filled by the re-education measures of the Western allies. Originally these efforts aimed at exchanging the political elite and implanting new democratic values at all levels of the educational system. Despite considerable activity in the fields of cultural exchange and textbook revision before 1949, the practice of foreign language teaching was apparently not affected too much. As far as US-American initiatives and models were concerned, the concepts of Area

Studies developed during the war could not easily be transferred into the post-war situation even though the usual list of culture topics surfaced in some audiovisual courses of the 1960s (Angiolillo, 1947). The academic disclipline of American Studies was not promoted before the late 1950s and addressed universities and teacher training first. Most influential at the school level were Social Studies concepts which indirectly affected foreign language training, too.

In fact, the only comprehensive cultural concept for foreign languages in the 1950s was constructed by a teacher of Social Studies and English. The theory of contemporary and social studies (*Gegenwarts- und Sozialkunde*) accepted the social studies model for foreign language teaching and assimilated the realistic and cosmopolitan traditions from the modern language reform and the criticism of *Kulturkunde* (Fischer-Wollpert, 1956 in Flechsig, 1970: 147–59). Foreign language teaching was seen to contribute to democratic political education by offering social and international topics based on non-fiction texts and newspaper articles. Fischer-Wollpert was isolated within the profession whose conservative cultural outlooks were not concerned with problems of contemporary societies either at home or abroad.

The post-war curricula emerging in all regions of the new West German state kept alive idealistic concepts that were reminiscent of *Kulturkunde*. The experience in the 1930s had led many foreign language practitioners to retreat from the realities of political and social life into the realm of high literature and those human values that were said to transcend times and cultures. Language curricula and the teaching material of the 1950s show a clear bias towards the classics and aesthetics. Foreign observers of German textbooks deplored the continuing need for national clichés and the illegitimate and ineffective use of literature in portraying a foreign culture (Lütkens & Karbe, 1959). After the experience of the failure of *Kulturkunde* and in the emerging intellectual climates of the Cold War and of New Criticism, literature rather than culture was taught in most foreign language classes.

The State of Foreign Languages and Cultural Studies: Modernisation and Politicisation

The modernisation of foreign language teaching

The 1970s and 1980s saw an expansion of foreign language teaching in West Germany. When in the late 1960s a foreign language became compulsory for each child after primary school, foreign languages had lost their marks of higher and elite education, but continued to serve as an instrument of social selection within the tripartite school system. Many new chairs of foreign language pedagogy (*Fremdsprachendidaktik*) have been created since then and have gradually been admitted into the academic discipline of modern language philology.

The introduction and expansion of English language teaching at the secondary technical school level (*Hauptschule*) was accompanied by the new structuralist and behaviourist approaches in international language teaching theory. The kind of modernisation symbolised by the language laboratory seemed to leave no room for cultural content in language courses. Content objectives could be accepted only under the condition that they proved to be beneficial to the actual language learning process. Since language was conceived of as a purely behavioural code only, any element of foreign cultural content could only be admitted in terms of tourism and consumerism. Therefore textbooks continued to teach pupils how to ask their way and how to buy things. More ambitious forms of culture were not completely banned from language courses, but were relegated to marginal positions of a pragmatic, minimal or immanent *Landeskunde* (Erdmenger & Istel, 1973). These concepts were motivated by the attempt to simplify language requirements for the average and the lower ability levels. But they also betrayed a dogmatic rejection of political and ideological implications of language learning and cultural studies.

The communicative competence approach to language teaching emerging in the 1970s was not restricted to the latecomer in English language teaching, the *Hauptschule,* and was also less obviously influenced by American linguistic and teaching rationales. In principle, it recognised the sociolinguistic setting of language and language teaching and considered communication a basically social event. Some spokesmen of communicative competence theory extended language learning to include 'participation in the sociocultural reality' of a foreign language (Piepho, 1979). Yet, communicative teaching was in practice primarily concerned with roles and behaviour and therefore tended to neglect the speaker's and listener's social background. Cultural references could thus be deleted from communication. Only in the late 1980s was the attempt made to reconcile communicative and cultural objectives in foreign language teaching (Melde, 1987).

A third development in West German foreign language pedagogy has been less concerned with details of language teaching methodology, but with modernising the language teaching profession as such. Both

Finkenstaedt and Schröder have been influential in criticising language teaching traditions and adapting them to the perceived needs of the modern West Germany society. They have supported the reform of 16+ curricula (*Sekundarstufe II*) allowing for modern contents such as English for special purposes and non-fiction texts. Traditional concepts of *Kulturkunde* with their emphasis on the high arts are viewed with similar suspicion as the 'pseudo social studies' proposed by the New Left. However, these modernisation concepts have always implied that the heyday of literature was over and that culture would in some way have to take its place in school and university courses (Finkenstaedt, 1983). This new place that culture would take in advanced language teaching is being explored in the context of combining academic and commercial training (cf. chapters by Meyer and Kordes in this volume).

The politicisation of cultural studies

Two historical studies of cultural traditions in German foreign language teaching appeared around 1970 which seem to have cleared the ground for the present revival of interest in cultural studies. The East German critique of *Kulturkunde* up to 1945 exposed the philosophical and ideological weaknesses in the specific context of German ideas and politics (Apelt, 1967). The West German revaluation of language teaching concepts after 1945 showed that they were indebted to contemporary concepts of political education and could not claim to be politically neutral (Langer and Schurig in Hüllen, 1979). These studies made the point that if language teaching was to have a cultural dimension and an intercultural objective, the choice of cultural content would have to be both conscious and explicit and could not evade basic decisions concerning educational and political values.

A view of French language teaching since 1970 may illustrate the way in which the expansion of cultural studies has been a process of both modernisation and politicisation in Germany. Starting out under the influence of the student movement as an internal critique of the current practice and unresolved academic heritage of university courses, the cultural and political emphasis of French as a foreign language gained momentum and reached the West German public beyond the teaching profession. Under the impression of flourishing French-German relations within Europe and increasing personal contacts between French and German families and communities, French language teaching was accorded a crucial role in preparing for transnational communication (Bosch-Stiftung, 1982). Although the academic discipline remained reluctant, a growing number of anthologies and textbooks for teaching cultural studies in French as a foreign language have been published.

American Studies have always been committed to more comprehensive cultural concepts in research and teaching, thus paving the way for combining literary and cultural studies in English language teaching. When 16+ courses allowed for thematic specialisation and cultural foci, a new generation of readers came out offering selections of fiction and non-fiction texts dealing with topics of American society such as education or racism. The 'dialogue of texts' between literature and culture has been one of the productive approaches in cultural studies even though frictions and rivalries between literary and social studies persist (Kuna & Tschachler, 1986). In practice, cultural studies courses for the advanced often have a bias towards the immediate aesthetic effect and the transcultural value of literary texts, thus keeping alive the traditional predominance of literature in philology and teacher training. Other attempts at realigning literature and culture have pointed to the 'foreignness' of both of them in language teaching and the general need for intercultural emphathy. Finally, the domains of everyday reality may offer a common vantage point for both literary and cultural studies in language teaching (Sauer, 1986).

English is at present the most widely taught foreign language in West Germany and has for more than a century been associated with modernising foreign language teaching. That is perhaps why English language teaching has been most receptive to worldwide changes in foreign language teaching theory. Structuralist and communicative approaches continued to dominate English teaching methodology even after French and American Studies had discovered culture. At the same time, English language teaching took closer notice of changes in general educational theory, especially in the New Social Studies in the 1970s. With its interdisciplinary approach towards society and its awareness of social problems and international politics, this new teaching rationale found its way beyond history and social studies into foreign language teaching, too (Buttjes, 1981 and 1987). In a similar manner, British Cultural Studies have been adapted to the needs of German language classes (Kramer, 1983; Lehberger & Lange, 1984). The topics and texts of both culturalist tendencies in West German language teaching focus on social problems and human rights in foreign cultures. They are not only intended to arouse empathy and solidarity with members of another culture, but also to offer alternative models for the orientation and identity within the native culture.

Conclusion

The basic ambiguity of German language teaching consists in the shifting and contradictory roles culture has played in its history. Whenever the foreign languages suffered from crises of legitimation in times of political and educational transition, culture has played a crucial role, yet has never reached a firm and sound position in language teaching theory. This is true for all the periods under question from the 1880s to the 1980s although the modern language reform and the present intercultural studies debate have come closest to a cultural rationale for language teaching.

With the legacy of *Kulturkunde* dominating great parts of the German language teaching history, the faults and contradictions of narrow culture concepts have been exposed. Such a view of culture has not only discredited cultural studies, but has also counteracted language teaching in several ways. It was used for the national distinction between foreign and native culture rather than serving international objectives. It was committed to idealistic speculation rather than social observation and focused on the high arts rather than on comprehensive concepts of culture. Finally, it was reserved for a social elite and the advanced learner only, rather than addressing all pupils at all stages of language learning.

The language teaching profession in Germany did not find it easy to break with their nationalist cultural learning traditions after World War II. But even critical outside observers of the West German cultural studies scene concede that profound changes have occurred in the recent past (Fischer, 1988). There is growing concern among many German teachers, scholars and adminstrators that foreign language teaching must and can serve international understanding. At times of threatening global crises on the one hand and shifting political frontiers on the other, intercultural objectives are becoming more important and urgent every day in the practice of language teaching (Bausch *et al.*, 1989: 112–19).

References

ANGIOLILLO, P. F. 1947, *Armed Forces Foreign Language Teaching*. New York: Vanni.
APELT, W. 1967, *Die kulturkundliche Bewegung im Unterricht der neueren Sprachen in Deutschland in den Jahren 1886 bis 1945*. Berlin: Volk & Wissen.
BAUSCH, K.-R. *et al.* (eds) 1989, *Handbuch Fremdsprachenunterricht*. Tübingen: Francke.
BOSCH-STIFTUNG (ed.) 1982, *Fremsprachenunterricht und internationale Beziehungen*. Gerlingen: Bleicher.

BUTTJES, D. (ed.) 1981, *Landeskundliches Lernen im Englischunterricht*. Paderborn: Schöningh.
——1984, *Fremdsprache und fremde Gesellschaft*. Dortmund: Universität.
——1987, *Panorama. English Cultures Around the World*. Dortmund: Lensing.
BYRAM, M. and SCHILDER, H. 1986, As others see us. Reflections on English textbooks in Germany. *Praxis des neusprachlichen Unterrichts* 33, 167–73.
DENKSCHRIFT, 1917, Über die Förderung der Auslandsstudien. *Internationale Monatsschrift für Wissenschaft, Kunst und Technik* 11, 513–32.
EISENSTADT, S. N. and CURELARU, M. 1976, *The Forms of Sociology – Paradigms and Crises*. New York: Wiley.
ERDMENGER, M. and ISTEL, H.-W. 1973, *Didaktik der Landeskunde*. Munich: Hueber.
FINKENSTAEDT, T. 1983, *Kleine Geschichte der Anglistik in Deutschland*. Darmstadt: Wissenschaftliche Buchgesellschaft.
FISCHER, G. 1988, Zum Kulturbegriff in fremdsprachendidaktischen Konzepten der BRD. *Deutsch als Fremdsprache* 25, 143–8.
FLECHSIG, K.-H. (ed.) 1965/1970, *Neusprachlicher Unterricht* (2 vols). Weinheim: Beltz.
GLEASON, P. 1984, World War II and the development of American Studies. *American Quarterly* 36, 343–58.
HOWATT, A. P. R. 1984, *A History of English Language Teaching*. Oxford: Oxford University Press.
HÜLLEN, W. (ed.) 1979, *Didaktik des Englischunterrichts*. Darmstadt: Wissenschaftliche Buchgesellschaft.
KRAMER, J. 1983, *English Cultural and Social Studies*. Stuttgart: Metzler.
KUNA, F. and TSCHACHLER, H. (eds) 1986, *Dialog der Texte: Literatur und Landeskunde*. Tübingen: Narr.
LEHBERGER, R. and LANGE, B. P. (eds) 1984, *Cultural Studies: Projekte für den Englischunterricht*. Paderborn: Schöningh.
LEPENIES, W. 1985. *Die drei Kulturen. Soziologie zwischen Literatur und Wissenschaft*. Munich: Hanser.
LÜTKENS, C. and KARBE, W. (eds) 1959, *Das Bild vom Ausland*. Munich: Oldenbourg.
MELDE, W. 1987, *Zur Integration von Landeskunde und Kommunikation im Fremdsprachenunterricht*. Tübingen: Narr.
MEYER, M. A. (ed.) 1980, *Fremdsprachenunterricht in der Sekundarstufe II*. Königstein: Athenäum.
——1986, *Shakespeare oder Fremdsprachenkorrespondenz? Zur Reform des Fremdsprachenunterrichts in der Sekundarstufe II*. Wetzlar: Pandora.
Modern Studies, 1918, *Report of the Committee on the Position of Modern Languages in the Educational System of Great Britain*. London: HMSO.
PICKETT, D. 1979, A personal overview of the British ELT scene in late 1978. In *The Use of the Media in ELT*, pp. 85–95. London: British Council.
PIEPHO, H.-E. 1979, *Kommunikative Didaktik des Englischunterrichts*. Limburg: Frankonius.
SAUER, H. (ed.) 1986, *Amerikanische Alltagskultur und Englischunterricht*. Heidelberg: Winter.
STERN, H. H. 1983, *Fundamental Concepts of Language Teaching*. Oxford: Oxford University Press.

5 Area Studies in the German Democratic Republic: Theoretical Aspects of a Discipline in Evolution

DIETER KERL

Social Practice and Scientific Progress

In order to determine the scientific character of area studies, it is necessary to consider the important question of its justification in societal terms. The evolution of new scientific disciplines is only the specific expression of the continual progress made in the human understanding of reality. Therefore, the fundamental propositions concerning the motive forces and natural laws involved in the human action of acquiring this understanding must also necessarily apply to the process by which new scientific disciplines evolve.

In contrast to idealistic philosophy, which claims to find the motive forces for understanding in a genial individual, who acts independently of society, Marxism takes social practice as its object of investigation. The word 'practice' is understood not in the sense it is normally given, but rather as the whole social process of materially re-forming objective reality.

Along with practice, which is the most significant external motive force behind progress in scientific understanding, there are, however, also other impulses, internal to the scientific discipline itself. These are, in contrast to practice, relatively self-contained and independent, and are the result of the particular level reached in the evolution of the scientific discipline. They are the product of the understanding that the scientific tools available are no longer sufficient to solve new problems that have recently developed. It is only through the joint action of these factors, both internal and external to the scientific discipline, that scientific investigation can be carried out. For the reasons mentioned, the scientific development of area studies must be investigated with respect both to the demands of social practice and to the changes that take place within the system of the science.

It goes without saying that it is necessary to provide knowledge in the field of area studies and to teach it to others. It is above all the result of the ever-increasing internationalisation of social life, as well as of the fact that most of the problems that concern human kind can only be solved by international co-operation. This is especially true in the case of the most fundamental question which the world faces − that of ensuring peace − but also as regards questions dealing with the world economy, the securing of a basic supply of raw materials, the protection of the environment, human health and many more besides. The increase in the real danger of the human race destroying itself in an atomic war has given rise to qualitatively new ways of thinking about the form international relations should take. This involves primarily the realisation that security can no longer be achieved if forces remain opposed to each other; instead, they must work together on the basis of complex co-operation. It follows that area studies is presented with an important task. By means of a programmed study of a country, it should attempt a more precise understanding of those social forces that may potentially influence the possibility of peaceful coexistence. Furthermore, the increased interdependence of all states demands that we should be in a position to comprehend these global processes, for they may affect us to a much greater extent than ever before. This presupposes, however, the availability of such a basis of knowledge as makes such understanding possible. Area studies therefore develops into a 'need' of society; it affects almost every person, involved both actively and passively, as a subject or an object, in the internationalisation of social life. It is unthinkable to be able to develop international relations in the direction of peaceful co-existence, unless something is known of the economic, political, social and cultural relations in foreign states.

Area studies, in contrast to other disciplines, takes as the object of its research the 'country' itself; thus it is to a great extent appropriate to provide the information required. It describes not only the 'visible' political situation, but also this situation in terms of its being a result of historical, ethnic and above all economic developments. A new interest in area studies is therefore developed which is qualitatively new, in that it aims towards an understanding of social relations in foreign countries for the purpose of better comprehending present-day processes. To facilitate an understanding of political and social processes in other countries, including those which have different social orders, is not a purpose in itself; rather, it is of paramount importance in helping people to coexist peacefully. Besides these external social demands made on area studies, factors internal to the scientific discipline, as mentioned at the beginning, must also be investigated for they promote the evolution of area studies as a science. Here it is apparent that the evolution of area studies represents the result of a process of differentiation within the traditional philological disciplines.

The status of area studies

Despite a growing social need for area studies it remains the case that its status as a discipline at a theoretical level is generally denied or at least questioned. The reason for this, we repeatedly hear, is the eclectic, 'polyhybrid' nature of this type of academic work, which cannot be reduced to a single discipline. Thus area studies tends to be seen, at best, as interdisciplinary work, or as an activity which is properly carried out as an 'added extra' to fully established disciplines. As things currently stand, we do not seem to have developed a position which would allow us to respond to such arguments with a convincing defence of area studies as a discipline in its own right, and consequently the likelihood of such a status eventually being conferred is something which is itself in some doubt.

Such a state of theoretical insecurity does have serious consequences:

- for the further development of area studies as a field of advanced academic study (for instance obtaining funding for the production of suitable teaching materials);
- for aspects of academic policy-making (for instance the question of levels of qualification and the definition of the degree award; the training of a new generation of area studies lecturers; the establishment of lectureships and Chairs in Area Studies);
- for the creation of adminstrative and organisational support for academic work in area studies (for instance the funding of library collections in an area studies field, and the cataloguing of such collections in relation to the field rather than to the separate contributory disciplines).

What we must now attempt to do, therefore, is gradually to move from this clear contradiction between the social recognition and need for area studies and the as yet inadequate theoretical foundation of this academic field towards some form of resolution. This is all the more urgent because in the long term area studies can only fulfil its aims effectively through the dialectical unity of empirical work and disciplinary theory. But we should also bear in mind the broad experience of intellectual history, namely that the establishment of academic disciplines does not in general 'keep pace' with the pattern of academic enquiry.

The Problem of Area Studies in Context

In the GDR at the beginning of the 1970s there were some rather rash attempts to construct a Marxist-Leninist disciplinary model for the study of national areas. These did offer some useful and important stimuli for the fusion of theory and practice in area studies, but were not at that time yet able to provide any unified and theoretically convincing pattern of argument. However, it would be quite wrong to conclude from this that we should give less attention to the theoretical aspect of our work in the future. On the contrary, what must be done is to develop a theory of area studies in parallel with the empirical teaching work, and examine each practical step that we take with a view to discovering its significance in relation to a developing theory. Nevertheless, it cannot be denied that at the moment the theoretical foundation of area studies is in a state of retarded growth; to overcome this the first step must be to identify the reasons for the difficulties involved in its development. The following points examine and discuss some of these.

Firstly, our professional 'need' for an identifiable discipline pushes us to arrive at a clearly defined theoretical foundation for our work as quickly as possible. Yet if we look at studies in the sociology of knowledge, we find that, paradoxically, the laying of such foundations often occurs only after a long developmental period in a particular subject area, after a wide-ranging experience of the field and a relatively profound level of practical enquiry into the object of study (Kosing, 1964:781). Whilst recognising this historical pattern, we should still be prepared gradually to 'build' a theory, or record our theoretical insights, as the more practical definition of the aims and objectives of our work becomes defined.

Secondly, the 'object of study' of area studies work appears to be limitless in extent. Many of the questions and problems which it must deal with are 'occupied' by other academic disciplines. The crucial problem occurs here of differentiating, in qualitative terms, between the specific approach of the area studies practitioner and that of colleagues in other academic disciplines who investigate in their own way the culture and society of a particular national area.

Thirdly, in contrast with the natural and applied sciences, which have long been the object of systematic disciplinary definition, many gaps can still be found even today in the methodological and theoretical framework of the social sciences. Given this background it is hardly surprising that particularly in the case of area studies, with its controversial and insecure status, there has been considerable reluctance to engage in theoretical discussion about the social sciences out of which area studies has emerged.

Fourthly, a further problem lies in the fact that the science of science is itself an academic realm which is in the early stages of development, and there are a number of varying opinions about its object of study and its precise place in the hierarchy of the social sciences. But despite these differences of opinion it can be assumed that this activity has as its main aim an enhancement of disciplinary self-awareness and self-definition, and that this aim cannot be realised without some level of empirical enquiry into the practice of particular disciplines, in the form of case studies. The insights from these specific studies will form the building blocks of a more embracing theory of intellectual history, and, conversely, these theoretical advances in the sociology of knowledge will in turn need to be used in the analysis of individual disciplines – a dialectical process.

Fifth, it appears that the way in which area studies has been constantly put in question as a discipline, and only very tentatively accepted as an independent academic subject, has led to a level of insecurity amongst the academics and teachers involved in working in this field. In place of a readiness for theoretical reflection on the issues raised by the subject we frequently see a marked tendency to retreat on to the 'safe ground' of empirical, factual teaching. This attitude is reinforced in particular wherever we find doubts about the independent character of area studies and a clinging adherence to traditional disciplines which are socially and politically sanctioned by institutional structures. A further problem here, notably in the German historical context, has been the political exploitation of the area studies concept, especially during the fascist period with its studies into the 'essence of national character' (*'Wesenskunde'*). This and other similar politically coloured perversions in the history of the subject have had the effect of making its academic aims appear to many as somewhat suspect and ambiguous, blackening it with the label of un-academic self-prostitution.

A sixth point concerns attempts at building a theoretical foundation, which have often foundered in the early stages because of a one-side concentration on the issue of disciplinarity. Such a narrowing of the focus of discussion on area studies has as its result a position where the denial that area studies is a discipline in its own right is equated straightforwardly with the verdict that it therefore lacks proper academic rigour, and can thus be dismissed as 'non-academic'. The unspoken premise here is that the concept 'discipline' has, *per definitionem*, a recognised place in the theory of knowledge. The fact of the matter, however, is that so far such a generally accepted definition of the concept 'academic discipline' simply does not exist; at best we have only a series of working definitions, which characterises the qualities of a discipline in very different ways.

A seventh point is the problem that area studies work lacks a theoretical basis which extends outside the academic context of foreign language study. As long as area studies was understood merely as a component or a guiding principle in the study of a foreign language, there was no need to see it as an independent discipline in the making, and to analyse it accordingly. But the more we find other areas of social activity and need (international relations, foreign policy, marketing, business, tourism etc.) making demands of the subject, the more we find that its importance grows within the totality of the social sciences. It is in the course of this process that the disciplinary features are becoming increasingly clearly marked, thus placing upon us the requirement to reflect upon the whole pattern of development in a more thorough way.

Those attempts which have so far been made to apply the current findings of a broad theory of knowledge to area studies unfortunately have to be described as inadequate. The aims and interests of this field of theoretical work, concerned as it is with questions relating to the historical development and typology of new academic subjects, with the dialectic of disciplinarity and interdisciplinarity in the process of creating new knowledge, are however clearly of relevance to us. It would now seem to be urgently necessary to aim for a close collaborative dialogue between those thinking about the structuring of academic knowledge in general and the practitioners of area studies as a particular field of work.

Finally, the contemporary debate on area studies is notably lacking in an ability to relate the developmental processes taking place in our own academic area to those which are present in similarly structured academic fields. If we do not register such parallels, we allow area studies to be considered as the anomalous case in the pattern of disciplinary development. That in turn leads to a blinkered viewpoint which inhibits the recognition of general structural principles which may be operating here.

To repeat at this point: our urgent need now is to put the discussions concerning the theoretical basis for area studies into the context of the wider study of academic disciplines, and to examine the findings of this general disciplinary theory (as it occurs in the history and sociology of knowledge) with a view to applying them to area studies.

Differentiation and Complexity in Academic Disciplines

The present level of the debate has not yet arrived at any conclusions about the definition of area studies as a discipline; therefore any theoretical engagement with the activities of area studies is intervening in an as yet unfinished or undetermined process. We can only attempt to fix with any precision the position which we have now reached, and to make prognoses about possible lines of development from it. Such a coincident form of study has to face a series of problems which the analysis – usually retrospective – of already established disciplines is not likely to present; these problems occur precisely because of the uncertain status of the discipline in its embryonic form – '*in situ nascendi*' – and the uncertainty concerning its future development. But despite these problems it is an important and necessary task in contemporary society to answer these questions. The analysis of the early stages of the discipline 'area studies' has its place among the more general attempts of many disciplinary areas, including the established ones, to put questions and seek solutions concerning their own pattern of formation and theoretical foundations.

The necessity of some measure of distanced, 'metatheoretical' reflection both for the development of intellectual life in general and for the formation of new disciplines in particular has indeed been widely recognised. It is therefore all the more surprising that this aspect of area studies work scarcely figures in national or international discussion of the subject. What we most frequently find is simply the expression of the desirability of a theoretical foundation for the subject, without any attempt at all to provide it. It is also difficult to understand why those academic subjects such as regional studies or local studies, whose genetic relationship with area studies is unmistakable, have made such a small contribution to any theoretical consolidation of the insights which they have achieved.

We have to assume that one of the main reasons for the currently unsatisfactory situation regarding area studies theory lies in its being seen as an anomaly in terms of disciplinary development, and furthermore one which is located mainly in the context of the debate on foreign language study. But practice shows that the case of area studies in fact demonstrates numerous parallels to other subject areas that are in the developmental stage. One of the most important of these parallels is the current tendency of area studies to examine complex aspects of social reality in a unidisciplinary academic approach.

It is self-evident that at the root of the theoretical questions thrown up by area studies there must also lie the question of the complex nature of reality and its reflection in a discipline or pattern of disciplines. Certainly area studies work has to focus upon an extraordinarily complex range of phenomena, of which the analysis and interpretation by one single academic area alone – i.e. area studies – must appear open to challenge.

But developments seem to have proven correct those who have argued that area studies must be understood as an integrative discipline – and taught as such (*'integratio in persona'*). Such a view has its basis in the recognition that area studies is related to the many other contemporary ways of attempting to grasp reality as a totality. We therefore consider that our subject in particular is predestined to impart the techniques of interdisciplinary work and to develop cross-disciplinary perspectives. In emphasising this complex, i.e. integrative, nature of area studies we must also remember to note that the development of this subject has been the result of a process of differentiation within the traditional discipline of philology. At least since the beginning of the twentieth century this older discipline area has included, alongside the study of language and literature, the area studies aspect – at first under a variety of different labels and activities. From this perspective it is all the more astonishing that there has hitherto been no substantial theoretical debate within the established philological subjects concerning the realisability of the 'Life and Society' type of work which preceded area studies as a subject formation.

The differentiating division of the established philological discipines into language, literature and area studies work can therefore be understood as a logical reaction. Both for reasons internal to the structure of the discipline and for reasons stemming from external social pressures, the ever-increasing sum of knowledge has in fact required a level of specialisation and thus a more effective differentiation between these sub-disciplines. As far as the gradual establishment of area studies is concerned, it is clear that the subject matter with which it deals can no longer be adequately encompassed, understood and theoretically handled by the philological disciplines in their traditional form. This then provided the impetus to work on area studies material in the more systematic and academically satisfying context of an independent but related academic area, embracing both teaching and research. Such a development also coincided with and sought to respond to the increased social needs which demand a closer understanding of the complex social reality of particular states or national/regional groupings.

Evolution and Consolidation in Area Studies

In general it seems that precise definition of the nature and subject of integrative disciplines is an extremely complicated matter. However, the pressure on higher education to play its part in the analysis and understanding of social as well as natural phenomena is one which is growing – the need to give formulation to a complex understanding of reality is not a problem specific to area studies alone. It is also indubitably the case that Marxist thought and the theory of knowledge which is built upon it can provide substantially more favourable methodological premises for the realisation of such a synthesising function. This fact is also recognised by non-Marxist academics. For instance Holt, in a discussion of area studies work in Great Britain, comes to the conclusion that:

> Anyone who is a Marxist has no problem, because he has been given a science of society that touches all the main areas of life ... Other theories in the social sciences, even in sociology, are not usually as interdisciplinary as Marxism and do not attempt to relate history so precisely to the contemporary scene. This is not because non-Marxist social scientists believe history is not so related, they simply find the connections too complex to systematize. (1981:2)

Finally, if we consider the general process of the formation and development of academic disciplines, it has been argued that it is characterised by the following main stages, which can also be applied to the case of area studies:

1. On the basis of the development of the necessary material and ideational social conditions, the production of a higher level of intellectual reflection in a particular context.
2. The linking together of various intellectual activities and findings; the development of a coherent explanatory theoretical frame.
3. The separating out of those academic elements which have been occupied by the newly developing discipline from their original formative context, and the creation of an independent academic area.
4. The establishment and development of a specific institutional framework.
5. The consolidation of the new discipline on the basis of a stability of social interests and demands (both material and intellectual) in relation to its further existence (Guntau, 1978:16)

It is clear that if we compare the developmental process of area studies with the five stages outlined here, similar patterns emerge. In particular we can see the intensification of new intellectual activity in response to social changes which is mentioned under (1). The boom in area studies type of work generally, and the increasingly numerous language text books at all levels which, implicitly or explicitly, now use this approach are both external expressions of a clearly defined increase in social interest relating to the development of this disciplinary area. Another parallel is seen in the increase in the publication of metatheoretical studies which can be characterised as attempting to establish 'a coherent explanatory theoretical frame'. And as we have already seen above, the separation of the elements of area studies from their original context as well as the creation of a new academic area have been necessary steps on the path towards the consolidation of this discipline.

The five stages referred to here are, naturally, abstractions of a process which in academic practice takes a more complex course. But taken as a whole they are useful in marking out positions which have either been reached or which must be occupied in the future. In this way, perhaps, a comparison of the emergent disciplinary characteristics of area studies with the insights of the theory of knowledge may offer some productive starting points for a further theoretical grounding for our subject.

References

GUNTAU, M. 1978, Zur Herausbildung wissenschaftlicher Disziplinen in der Geschichte (Thesen). *Rostocker wissenchaftshistorische Manuskripte* 1, 11–24 (Rostock: Wilhelm-Pieck-Universität).
HOLT, S. 1981, Purposes and problems in European Studies. Supplement to *Journal of Area Studies* 4, 51–2.
KOSING, A. 1964, Gegenstand, Struktur und Darstellung der marxistischen Philosophie. *Deutsche Zeitschrift für Philosophie* 7, 781–807.

6 'Background Studies' in English Foreign Language Teaching: Lost Opportunities in the Comprehensive School Debate

MICHAEL BYRAM

Foreign Language Teaching in Comprehensive Schools

The history of foreign language teaching is littered with discarded but, in their time, influential methods (Hawkins, 1981: 307–8). Yet the history of foreign language teaching in England in the second half of the twentieth century has been influenced more profoundly by politics than by methods and especially by one political decision: to introduce comprehensive schools throughout the state education system. Although the Labour Party's aim has never been completely fulfilled, the vast majority of English state-maintained schools are now comprehensive. The political desire initially was to provide grammar school education for all pupils, irrespective of social origins, and grammar school education included learning at least one foreign language: this was perhaps the most visible and obvious difference between the curricula of grammar and other schools. So, 'comprehensivisation' meant, for language teachers, that instead of teaching the best 20–25% of an age group they found themselves required to teach all the age group. That this often happened in mixed ability and co-educational classes rather than single-sex, ability-differentiated classes only compounded the complexity and difficulty of the change. It was a change which had a more profound influence on language teaching in England than all the developments of linguistic and psychological theories so frequently cited. More importantly, it was a change which not all members of the language teaching profession embraced with enthusiasm, seeing more often the problems rather than the opportunities.

The change to comprehensive schools coincided with the heyday of audiolingual learning and many a new comprehensive school boasted one, if not two, language laboratories. Irrespective of the political intention to introduce a grammar school curriculum for all pupils, language teachers had no choice. Teaching materials and methods until that point used with the carefully selected pupils of the grammar school were also used with those who would not have been selected; no other material or methods were available. The subsequent difficulties were doubtless not simply a consequence of inappropriate methods and material, but also part of the general problems arising from a fundamental change in all aspects of schooling. Schools became much bigger, new management structures were developed, curriculum innovations on a large scale were taking place in many subjects, the minimal school-leaving age was changing in practice and in law.

The detailed history of language teaching in this period remains to be written, but the developments are well known in the profession. Difficulties arose because many pupils found language learning difficult, lost their motivation and, if obliged to continue for the five years of secondary schooling, became difficult to teach. Yet it was one of the principles of comprehensive schools, for many people, that all children should have 'the same' curriculum. This widely held philosophy was important in the English education system where the headteacher of each school is responsible for deciding how the curriculum shall be composed. Even though, in principle, each school might have a unique curriculum, most schools are influenced by the same contemporary philosophies and have similar curricula. As a consequence all pupils have to have 'a foreign language' as part of their curriculum. This was the point at which 'background studies' – a term frequently used but rarely discussed – had a role to play.

Providing the Same Curriculum for All

If some pupils had difficulty in learning the French language – the most frequently taught first foreign language – then they could still have 'the same' curriculum by learning French 'background'. However, since audiolingual textbooks consisted mainly of carefully written dialogues and texts exemplifying grammatical structures, supplemented by just a page at the end of each chapter of 'background information', there was a need to find new materials. The information on the making of French perfumes, French transport, French sport, fashion, regions of France, French industries, French wines (all from Longman Audio-Visual French Stage B3) was insufficient in quantity and inadequate in appeal. The fact that it was arbitrary in content, with no theoretical foundation and of suspect educational value was probably not uppermost in many teachers' minds since their training for the profession had paid little attention to this dimension of language training (see below). It was necessary therefore to develop methods and materials *in situ*, relying on professional intuition and trial and error.

A related but different solution to the same problem was to extend the notion of 'French (background) studies' — in some cases the doubtful word 'background' was omitted — to a new concept of 'European Studies'. It was probably not without significance that Britain was at that time seeking entrance to the European Economic Community and the notion of being a citizen of Europe was an expedient justification for a solution to a practical problem; politics this time had a more indirect influence. European Studies was a more considered response to the desire to give all pupils 'the same' curriculum and was therefore more carefully justified in educational terms. There were theoretical writings as well as production of teaching materials (e.g. Freeman, 1970; CILT, 1973). Links with the philosophies of history, geography and social sciences teaching were evident and, in some cases, teachers of these subjects were called to the task. Languages teachers were, however, still 'responsible' for this part of the curriculum and had to teach the new subject too. Yet neither group felt that it was central to their professional identity and training and, together with the fact that it was obviously devised for pupils who had not succeeded in learning a foreign language, it is not surprising that European Studies had low status. The same problem of status was also present in the teaching of 'French Studies' or 'German Studies', for even though the language teachers involved could identify more with this kind of work its very origins in 'background' betrays the relationship to *language* teaching. One way to improve the status was through the examination system.

In the English education system, where the curriculum was until recently immediately controlled by the headteacher and his/her representatives, examinations determined by external bodies were a major influence. The content of examinations influenced the content of teaching. If there was no examination for a particular subject then the content could be freely determined by teachers but the subject had low status. This was the case for 'language' courses concerned mainly or exclusively with 'studies': it was not, however, an unchangeable situation. Examinations could be requested and bureaucracy set in motion. The most effective way to do this was for teachers to take over the role of examiner – contrary to British traditions – and to develop an examination which would be validated and certificated by the normal external examining bodies. Yet, though such examinations were officially deemed to be of equal status and value as existing examinations, they were widely regarded as of inferior value. 'Background studies' remained a low-status subject, despite having examination status.

Background Studies and 'Graded Objectives'

In the mid-1970s the problem of teaching pupils who had lost interest in foreign languages was approached from a new angle. By this time the notion of all pupils having the same curriculum for five years had been attenuated to allow choice of subjects in the last two years. This meant that for many pupils the third year was their last year of foreign language learning, and they did not complete the course or obtain any examination qualification. This was one factor which created a loss of interest in the third year. Another was the nature of the course itself, largely determined by and reflected in examinations which tested grammatical knowledge by means of translation. Such knowledge seemed irrelevant and uninteresting to many pupils, and to some teachers and theorists.

Opposition to this kind of examination came as a consequence of attempts to reform the examination so that all pupils – not only those who would have been selected for grammar schools – would be able to have a realistic chance of passing (Page & Hewett, 1987: 1–2). Opposition took the form of suggestions by theorists that examinations should test skills in communication, since language is primarily a means of communication. Although this view was intended to encompass all pupils, teachers faced with the de-motivated pupils in the third year saw it as a way of coping with this specific problem. Pupils might be made to see a new relevance if they could be persuaded that they would need to communicate in the foreign language. Secondly, if pupils were given clearly defined targets for the end of the third year, a test to determine that they had reached those targets and a certificate to attest their skills, they might find the idea of language learning more attractive. It appeared to work (Schools Council, 1981). What was the relation between this development and background studies? The answer lies in the notions of 'relevance' and 'communication'.

The most likely need of pupils for the ability to communicate in French, it was argued, would be as tourists in France. They had to be persuaded of the relevance of this by simulating situations in which they would need to speak French in order to 'survive'. 'Survival courses' in French did not only arise from the new development in examinations, as many teachers had already created their own materials for this purpose, but the new development helped to crystallise and clarify what was already happening. By simulating tourist situations in France, it became necessary to provide not just the appropriate language, but also some awareness of cultural difference, as perceived by a tourist. Nonetheless, this dimension was not recognised explicitly in the tests which were invented for the third year, and subsequently for younger and older pupils. Background studies remained of secondary importance in tests, and therefore in teaching. The Graded Objectives in Modern Languages (GOML) movement, as the development came to be known, did not change the basic approach to cultural knowledge. Instead of implicit information on selected aspects of economics and society – the characteristics of audiolingual methods – the GOML movement presented France as an environment which required survival skills. In order to obtain food and lodging or use public transport, pupils had to acquire appropriate linguistic and cultural behaviour; they had to adapt their own behaviour in so far as it would otherwise hinder their survival. Essentially, however, they would remain outsiders with limited behavioural skills, and would not be encouraged to seek an understanding of the foreign culture. Eventually this changed, and a decade later some courses and tests have been influenced in the meantime by other factors. One such scheme is described as follows:

> Linguistic aims are not the only ones in this scheme. There is a deliberate inclusion and description of cultural aims ('the intention is to make clear that linguistic transfer involves the understanding of meanings within the context of the foreign culture') and educational aims ('it is important that the process ... includes something of intrinsic educational value'). (Page & Hewett, 1987:14)

Background Studies and Communicative Language Teaching

Since the beginnings of the GOML movement in the 1970s, language teaching in Britain has come under the influence of work in the Council of Europe, of 'Communicative Language Teaching' and of general curriculum changes. The notion of survivial skills has been refined by theories of needs analysis and communicative competence, and the requirement that all language learners – irrespective of 'first', 'second' or 'foreign' – should use language in socially appropriate ways implicitly involves culture-specific knowledge. In his discussion of 'communicative competence', Hymes describes the relationship as follows:

> Within the developmental matrix in which knowledge of the sentences of a language is acquired, children also acquire knowledge of a set of ways in which sentences are used. From a finite experience of speech arts and their interdependence with sociocultural features, they develop a general theory of the speaking appropriate in their community, which they employ, like other forms of tacit cultural knowledge (competence), in conducting and interpreting social life. (Hymes, 1972:279)

In principle then the adoption of 'communicative language teaching' should mean the introduction of sociolinguistic competence, and there is no doubt that language teachers have at least adopted the rhetoric. There is ample evidence of that. The practices in classrooms are, however, much more difficult to evaluate. First, there are problems of feasibility: it may not be possible to develop all the dimensions of communicative competence in the classroom. This doubt has been raised about immersion programmes in Canada, particularly with reference to the sociolinguistic dimension:

> restricted learning contexts might produce unevenness in the development of the dimensions of language proficiency (against the standard of native speakers). Thus, for example, immersion students' sociolinguistic competence may lag behind their discourse competence because the classroom provides unequal opportunities for learning in these areas. (Hart, Lapkin & Swain, 1987:85)

Evidence from observations of a small number of British classrooms certainly suggests that the same doubt can be raised about foreign language methods (Byram, Esarte-Sarries & Taylor, 1990).

It is likely, then, that the introduction of communicative language teaching has not had a significant effect on classroom practices in this respect: 'background' still has lower status and priority. And again the examination system contributes to this situation. After almost two decades, the attempts to change examinations to make them appropriate for all pupils — opposition to which initially led to the GOML movement — have been realised in a form which was much influenced by the GOML movement itself. The notion of 'survival skills' has become more refined and sophisticated but the 'relevance' of the tourist view of the foreign culture remains a dominant feature. On the one hand the aims of the new examination include reference to cultural insight and tolerance and understanding of foreign peoples and cultures. On the other hand only the aim of equipping learners with the capability for 'practical communication' is included in the testing process. As with the earlier development in GOML, the simulation of survival situations in the foreign country implicitly involves some knowledge of cultural differences which might hinder 'practical communication', and the use of 'authentic' texts for teaching and testing inevitably introduces implicit culture-specific phenomena. Nonetheless, methods of assessment which are being developed and made known to teachers take no cognisance of cultural knowledge. There is assessment of grammatical competence and of success in transmitting a 'message'; the message is, however, treated as if meaning were independent of specific culture or as if there were some meanings common to the learner's and the foreign culture. It remains unclear which of these assumptions is used, since they are not made explicit. As a consequence, teachers too rarely concern themselves with such assumptions; the examination system is a powerful influence.

The Influence of the Textbook

The influence of the examination also extends over the writers of textbooks. Since the textbook is fundamental to much and probably most language teaching, teachers are again constrained by the 'practical communication' philosophy. There is one textbook which is most clearly linked to this philosophy since its author is also directly involved in developing examinations. The introduction to *Action!* (Buckby, 1980), cites the work of the Council of Europe and the aims of the new examination, including those which contain the notions of cultural insight, tolerance and positive attitudes. In the early part of the course, covering the crucial first three years, the tourist view of France is quite explicit. Pupils are introduced to Boulogne and Paris and given tips on how to cope with an alien environment, for example:

> Cafés are also useful as they nearly all have a public phone and lavatories. There are not many of either of these in the streets in France, but as you are never far from a café you can always find one in an emergency. Quite often, the same lavatory is used by men and women, so don't worry if you think you are going into the wrong one. One more thing: if you can't find a light switch, try shutting and locking the door – the lock often switches the light on. Remember though, that it is usual to buy something at the café if you use its services. (Buckby, 1980:89)

On the assumption that all pupils will visit France as tourists an assumption which is unfortunately without justification such tips are certainly useful. Where the course fails, however, in these early years is to invite reflection upon the relationship between the French and British ways of life. There is no doubt that pupils are able to discuss issues of cultural relativity since similar work is quite familiar to them in other subjects, such as English, Religious Education or Humanities. The textbook, however, offers only factual and essentially trivial information rather than contentious and debatable views. Similarly the teacher's manual, though very detailed in instructions on the teaching of language, has no suggestions about the teaching of culture. It is in this respect, however, no different from other teachers' manuals, and this is symptomatic of a general failure to include cultural teaching in the training of teachers (see below). Teachers therefore develop their own methods of teaching based on an imprecise philosophy of encouraging positive attitudes and 'broadening pupils' horizons', and use their common sense and intuition in their techniques.

As a consequence, comments on *Action*! collected from a small group of teachers (see Byram *et al.*, in this volume) are focused on the efficacy of the presentation of France, rather than on the appropriateness of the presentation and the lack of methodology. There is agreement that textbooks are limited in potential:

> But any textbook is really by nature limited in what it can tell you about France. You can't really put over the feeling of France in a book. Pictures help and letters and descriptions and tape recordings and things like that all help, but I think it depends an awful lot on the teacher as well to sort of add extra bits and talks about their own experiences.

or:

> I don't think it gives you any particular image of France to be honest. I find it very neutral, the *Action!* book. It's up to the teacher. It doesn't leave me with any particular impression about France. When it comes to the shops, it explains the shops but so briefly it is up to you to talk about how beautiful it is to look at the charcuterie or something ...

Acceptance of the tourist presentation is evident in the following comments:

> I think it is very good on the situational aspect of France. How to survive in this and that situation, what to say ...

and:

> Oh, I think this book is smashing because it tours a whole range of things. If [the pupils] follow the whole course they have picked up a very good notion of French life.

There is, however, a difference of opinion between the latter teacher and another who was observed to talk much more frequently about France in class:

> There is not really a lot, I don't think, in this. It's a shame actually that they haven't got this as part of the new GCSE. It isn't in at all. It's only a language subject. I think if you wanted to do a course which brought in background work, you would have to make your own up.

By implication this teacher also agrees with our earlier criticism of the influence of the examination system ('the new GCSE').

Teacher Training and the Lack of Theory

There have already been two references to the significance of teacher training. In this account of 'lost opportunities', teacher training and inspectors must take considerable responsibility. Like much else in the English education system, the independence of training institutions to determine the curriculum is highly valued. It means, however, that it is difficult to know what attention is given to specific issues. Language teachers are in effect trained in two stages. The first stage is an undergraduate course in 'French' or 'German', for example, which for the majority signifies a course in the literature in that language and in literary criticism. The study of the social sciences – including linguistics, social anthropology and sociology, and developmental psychology – which would be a more directly appropriate preparation for teaching, is available but only to a limited extent and, paradoxically, not often chosen by those who intend to teach. The second stage is a one-year course of 'initial training' in which emphasis is put on the practices and theories of classroom work. In the only detailed survey of such courses it was evident that the teaching of 'civilisation' took a low priority as the wording of the following indicates:

> Although, within the very clear limits of the total time available, much attention was properly paid to ways and means of developing pupils' performance in the Modern Language, the

> schemes of work also dealt with methods of imparting a knowledge of the foreign culture or 'civilisation' and, for work in secondary schools, of stimulating an interest in the foreign literature at levels appropriate to the pupils' progress in the Modern Language. (Spicer & Riddy, 1977:53)

Although the initial training course is not only theoretical in content, one factor which may explain the lack of attention to background or cultural studies teaching is the lack of theory in the British literature on language teaching. The two principal journals (*Modern Languages* and the *British Journal of Language Teaching*) have published very few articles which can be described as even tangentially concerned with cultural studies. In the 1980s there has been in *Modern Languages* one article on 'The use of foreign school atlases as an aid to modern language teaching' (Sandford, 1984) and another by the author of this chapter (Byram, 1984). The *British Journal of Language Teaching* has published nothing dealing explicitly with cultural studies.

The situation was no better in the 1970s. Unlike Germany and, to a lesser extent, the United States (Byram, 1986) British language teaching has no tradition of theoretical writing about cultural studies or *Landeskunde*.

The Way Forward

The lack of a tradition is, perhaps paradoxically, a hindrance to change. Because there is little theoretical concern with cultural studies, the practices of the classroom are seldom discussed. It may be that there are many teachers who would welcome serious theoretical and practical help for there is no doubt that many teachers would agree with the following statement by one of the teachers quoted earlier:

> You have got to be adding something to the kids' lives other than the ability to say 'Je suis anglais' ... they have got to be able to say at the end of it, yes well I have learnt this and that or that about French people or about France so that you have actually changed their concepts.

The critical issue is to ensure that these creditable aims are realised. At the moment, no doubt many teachers would agree with Her Majesty's Inspectors of education who claim that such aims are dependent on successful realisation of linguistic and literary objectives in language teaching (HMI, 1987). If this view is to be rejected and all aims treated equally, then it will be necessary to argue on both language learning and general educational grounds. It will be necessary to point out again and again that language learning necessarily involves learning culture and that neither is subordinate to the other. It will also be necessary to demonstrate that the value of foreign language learning as a part of young people's secondary education lies not in narrowly and exclusively preparing them for some possible future foreign travel but in giving them experience and knowledge in the present which contributes to their understanding and enjoyment of themselves and the world around them.

Note added in proof

It is encouraging to note that, as this manuscript goes to press, new proposals for a national curriculum for foreign languages are expected. The interim report recognised the significance of cultural learning as part of language learning, even though it did not acknowledge that cultural learning could and should be assessed as part of the new system. Perhaps the opportunities missed in the past are about to be realised and in a few years' time a second version of this chapter will be able to trace a distinct change.

Acknowledgement

I am very grateful to Mr David Westgate of the University of Newcastle on Tyne for helpful comments on this chapter.

References

BUCKBY, M. 1980, *Action! Graded French.* London: Nelson.
BYRAM, M.S. 1984, Cultural studies in language teaching. *Modern Languages* 65, 4, 204–12.
—— 1986, Cultural studies in foreign language teaching. *Language Teaching* 19, 4, 322–36.
BYRAM, M., ESARTE-SARRIES, V. and TAYLOR, S. 1990, *Cultural Studies and Language Learning.* Clevedon: Multilingual Matters.
CANALE, M. and SWAIN, M. 1980, Theoretical bases of communicative approaches to second language teaching and testing. *Applied Linguistics* 1, 1, 1–47.
CILT, 1973, *Modern Languages and European Studies.* London: CILT.
FREEMAN, P. 1970, *European Studies Handbook.* Brighton: Centre for Contemporary European Studies, University of Sussex.
HART, D., LAPKIN, S. and SWAIN, M. 1987, Communicative language tests: perks and perils. *Evaluation and Research in Education* 1, 2, 83–94.
HAWKINS, E.W. 1981, *Modern Languages in the Curriculum.* Cambridge: Cambridge University Press.
HMI, 1987, *Modern Foreign Languages to 16.* London: HMSO.
HYMES, D. 1972, On communicative competence. In J. B. PRIDE and J. HOLMES (eds) *Sociolinguistics.* Harmondsworth: Penguin.
PAGE, B. and HEWITT, D. 1987, *Languages Step by Step: Graded Objectives in the U.K.* London: CILT.
SANDFORD, I. 1984, The use of foreign school atlases as an aid to modern language teaching. *Modern Languages* 65, 2, 104–6.
SCHOOLS COUNCIL, 1981, *Graded Objectives and Tests for Modern Languages: An Evaluation.* London: Schools Council.
SPICER, A. and RIDDY, D.C. 1977, *Initial Training of Teachers of Modern Languages.* Leeds: Arnold.

7 Interculturalising the French Educational System: Towards a Common European Perspective

FRANÇOIS MARIET

> Ill est bon de savoir quelque chose des moeurs de divers peuples, afin de juger des nôtres plus sainement, et que nous ne pensions pas que tout ce qui est contre nos modes soit ridicule, et contre raison, ainsi qu'ont coutume de faire ceux qui n'ont rien vu. [It is advisable to know something of the customs of various peoples in order to better judge our own and to ensure that we do not think that anything contrary to our own practices is ridiculous and unreasonable, as do those who have never seen anything]. (Discours de la Méthode)

In 1637, Descartes had already set the goals of intercultural teaching. He who is considered the most representative of French philosophers wrote, at the beginning of the classic era, the best plea for intercultural training; this plea associated the apology of travelling and tourism with the apology of foreign language studies. Whether the message came through clearly is not certain: there is still a long way to go before France offers its youth, as well as to all people in training, an intercultural approach to the subject matter under consideration.

A new factor, however, has been introduced which will thoroughly change the educational landscape: Europe and the single market of 1992. By the end of this historical year, Europeanisation will have become a major consideration behind each decision, be it economic or cultural. Instead of trying to invent a new discipline to add to the already heavy workload of our students, it is more realistic to establish ways of interculturalising all aspects of our school system. Some disciplines are already highly internationalised: music, for instance, transcends customary divisions and brings together Segovia and Stockhausen, Varese and Mariner. Some disciplines, such as law or management, adapt easily: for them Europeanisation goes without saying, they simply follow the trend set by companies and European institutions. On the other hand, when it comes to maths, chemistry or economics, interculturalisation is much slower and limited. As for sports, things are headed in the worst possible direction: international competitions have become the most horrible opportunity for blatant exhibition of nationalist feelings, flags and intolerance.

Of course interculturalisation is considered here only in its European dimension: it is not a theoretical choice but a pragmatic one. One day, hopefully soon, it will include other more distant cultures (although some aspects may already prove to hold an important place in our everyday life) such as that of the Berbers or the Chinese. Let us be realistic and efficient: Europeanisation is the first step to a more complete and future interculturalisation.

In this chapter we will address the situation of intercultural teaching in France in four points: first, we will examine the meaning of 'intercultural' throughout the history of the French teaching system; secondly, we will examine the scientific conditions of intercultural teaching; thirdly, we will treat a more classic but very sensitive point: the teaching of history; and finally we will try to predict the consequences of interculturalisation on modern language teaching methods and objectives.

Traditions Affecting Intercultural Teaching in Europe

Intercultural teaching in France can only succeed if it conforms to the major principles of French educational philosophy: universalism and secularism. It will also have to deal with the powerful lobbies of diverse disciplines which have opposed any form of school reform in France over the years.

Intercultural education as an art of synthesis

With the exception of a limited number of intercultural classes which temporarily take in the children of migrant workers or political refugees, intercultural teaching *per se* does not currently exist at the high school or university level in France.

The division of pedagogic labour following that of scientific research is reinforced by the lobbies of the different discliplines, each protecting its own field against incursions from other disciplines while concurrently claiming to be the best equipped to provide an intercultural synthesis. A clear illustration of this is found in the recent rivalries between historians and geographers, or between historians and economists or social scientists. Even Braudel, despite his very powerful and legitimate position, did not succeed in overcoming such divisions in his effort to give an intercultural dimension to the teaching of history (1987).

For many years philosophy claimed the role of the synthesis builder, a role facilitated by its situation: at first, because this discipline is taught only during the last year of high school and is considered the crowning touch of cultural training (a traditional image found throughout the history of philosophy and emphasised by Descartes), and secondly because it is a requirement for graduation. Traditionally, the philosophy class is where Valéry meets Einstein, Kant confronts Mauss, Newton converses with Unamuno, Marx encounters Croce, and Montaigne debates with Euripides. The syllabus is so enormous and the final dissertation so formalist that philosophy naturally becomes an art of synthesis touching on all major topics of our society: art and revolution, psychoanalysis and science, economy and justice, epistemology and technology, politics and human rights, etc. As Bourdieu remarked, this philosophical exercise is so typical of French society that its effects can be seen in the way newspaper articles of political speeches are written (Idt, 1979). The very image of the 'total intellectual' is shaped by this philosophical model; its most recent exemplification is Jean Paul Sartre (Bourdieu, 1980); Gaston Bachelard, in a more ironic and critical way, spoke of philosophers in the French university as being 'specialists in generalities'. Any intercultural teaching will have to contend with philosophy both as a lobby and as a thinking habit (Fabiani, 1988) or, as Erwin Panofsky would call it, a 'habit-forming force'.

A trade-off between identity and universality

In the past, many disciplines took upon themselves the responsibility of teaching about cultures and civilisations. According to the legislators and theoreticians of the Third Republic, (like Fernand Buisson, whose *Dictionary of Pedagogy* was a classic for generations of French teachers) ethics and civics would have been the most appropriate disciplines for an intercultural approach. In any event, school was more directed at that time towards universal behaviour and concepts than towards the diversity of cultures. Colonialism, the other major project of the republican policy, was presented as the means of civilising the savage mind, just as the Romans and the Greeks had civilised the Gallic tribes. When Jules Ferry, the founding father of the republican school system in France, addressed his famous letter to teachers, he insisted that nothing said in the classroom should shock any student's father. He meant to promote a tolerance of all religions (himself a Protestant in a Catholic-dominated country) but did not necessarily take into account the different cultures, regional or otherwise. The Republic believed in the existence of 'barbarism': it considered itself responsible not only for the abolition of the ignorance and prejudices of the peasant children but also for the civilisation of the children in Africa or the Far East. The Republicans considered Human Rights to mean the right to share the only true culture, scientific, classic and cartesian, a culture necessary to becoming both a citizen (and soldier) and a worker. In many ways this concept is still the implicit philosophy of the French school system as well as that of French politics, as can be seen in the recent difficulties encountered by any of the decentralisation or regionalisation laws.

At the high school level, Latin and Greek literature celebrated other cultures: but these cultures were considered as superior, exemplary models for art, politics and engineering. Based on universal values they were meant to be emulated: French citizens could do no better than to imitate the virtues of Ulysses or Socrates. Given the universal nature of this culture, it was certain to triumph above all others, able to transcend any military or economic defeat suffered by the country: 'Graecia capta ferox victorem cepit'. In this way the intercultural approach was limited to the more universal productions of the Greek and Latin cultures: law, literature and the arts. At the time there was no question of applying an ethnological approach.

This was also the philosophy of the Renaissance and it is not too surprising to encounter the same feelings about Italian art from this period: Leonardo de Vinci or Petrarch were not regarded as simply Italian, the universal nature of their art enabled the French to adopt it in the name of humanism.

As modern languages gradually replaced ancient Greek and Latin, they nevertheless followed the same path. Goethe, Shakespeare, Cervantes and Dante succeeding Homer, Virgil, Lucan, Plutarch and Plato. Like Racine or Pascal, they are realisations of the universal, their work gives concrete expression to the eidetic essence. Even now the pedagogy of modern languages is still viewed more as an introduction to classic literature (to which a preparation for the average tourist activity has been added) than as a reflection on the diversity of cultures, with the exception of comparative literature as understood by Etiemble (1988;13).

Respect for other cultures came mainly from nationalism and romanticism (there were some foreshadows in the Pléiade's reaction to the Italian cultural domination, as can be seen in 'la défense et illustration de la langue française'). National cultures began to take on a noble status in the works of Hugo and Byron (cf. the Greek cause) as well as in those of Pellico or Manzoni. But regionalism has been associated chiefly with conservative movements ever since the French Revolution; it even went so far as to develop compromising links with fascism during the Petainist years. Because of its dubious past it necessarily engenders doubt about its values: its slogans often sound more particularist or nationalist (and often both) than humanist.

It is clear that the cult of the region, of the roots, of the fatherland or of the mother tongue presents a real danger for a school system which is supposed to prepare citizens for a single European market. Slogans like 'volem viure al pais' ('we want to live in our home region'), which one can hear in some regions of southern France, are not only counterproductive, they often disguise certain modern forms of conservatism (often supported by catch-all or sometimes ecologist parties fishing for voters). Such slogans have the suspicious smell of 'petainism' and are nothing but the first step towards xenophobia. Indeed, as James Baldwin says, 'Even the most incorrigible maverick has to be born somewhere', but this does not mean that nostalgia for our childhood should be transformed into a celebration of the past, of 'the good old days'. These strategies of preservation are incompatible with the single market of the 12 European Community members: flexibility and geographical mobility are the keys to success. The unified European labour market towards which we are moving is only the generalisation of what European migrant workers have done over the past centuries; what is new is the fact that everyone (and not only the poorest or the unemployed) will experience it and, moreover, will benefit from it under incomparable socio-economic conditions.

According to the French tradition, school should not be a party to the philosophies which celebrate the past or the homeland even in the most euphemised form (as in Heidegger's works). Such philosophies are nothing but generalised luddism; a source of comfort for people afraid of progress in these modern times and a means of exploiting their fear of competition, they harbour a conservative spirit and often degenerate into anti-semitism or racism. History has proven in many a bloodbath that such ideology provides the most fertile ground for the growth of fascism: one thing that Hitler, Mussolini, Franco, Salazar and Petain had in common was the cult of 'natives' and the fatherland. Some French politicians make use of that concept today, and it does not take long before it becomes hatred of the '*métèques*', the foreigners, the cosmopolitans. Nothing is more debatable than the notion of 'cultural identity'; nothing could furnish a better pretext for racism and xenophobia.

The culture taught in school must necessarily be universal and supranational. Better than the image of 'the melting pot', the concept of common rights and values reflects this necessity; intercultural education should stress what unifies people and not what divides them. With this in mind, less cultural identity in the public education system means more intercultural identity. Cultural differences and traditions belong to the private sphere.

Inevitably intercultural

An intercultural dimension does exist, however, in the teaching of foreign languages and is even more extensive in the fields of history, geography and economy. Some disciplines are necessarily multicultural, such as management: marketing is more and more international as is business law, finance or accounting. Here intercultural teaching goes without saying since, in order to be efficient, these disciplines necessarily interact with the real world, a world in which interculturalisation is a factor whose importance increases daily. There is no need to convince a management professor to open his or her class to intercultural reality: reality probably already did a good job of that, especially, as is often the case, if the professor does outside consulting for companies.

Everyday life itself is already intercultural in many ways: when people demonstrated in 1987 for the respect for new migrants and foreigners in France, they yelled slogans like 'Couscous, muscadet, paella, même combat', or 'First, second, third generation, we are all migrants' children'. They were only chanting what anyone can observe in everyday French life: popular grocery stores run by people born in North Africa, restaurants serving food from all over the world, Mexican and Moroccan, Italian and Chinese, Indian and Greek, American and Lebanese. A stroll down the aisles of our local supermarket reveals more and more spices, a multitude of various goods imported from Spain, Germany, Italy, Portugal; even the cheese store presents products from the Netherlands, England or Italy. More and more families spend their vacation in other European countries,

Europeans from every region come on holiday or business to France: travelling is easy and will be even easier after 1992. Even marriages in France are becoming more and more intercultural, giving birth to children having a mother tongue, a father tongue and, sometimes, even French as a school tongue.

These are only picturesque and obvious results of the interculturalisation of the European economies. The same demonstration could be made with cars, clothing, newspapers or magazines. What is a national identity in such countries? Our TV sets are made by Phillips from the Netherlands, our suits by Hugo Boss of Germany or Benetton of Italy; olive oil comes from Spain or Greece, a well-known brand of nappies is controlled by a Swedish company, couscous is the most popular dish in cafeterias, and that is not even to mention movies or rock and roll music which are completely internationalised. Airbus planes are European and Berlusconi and Maxwell own shares of French television companies. What is French? The currency? Not really since it belongs to the European Monetary System which regulates the currency rates. There remains the language and, before it too is given European status, the citizenship which determines where one pays taxes, votes and is drafted into the army in a specific country. A Frenchman is now, first, a European who speaks primarily French and more and more often other languages (Portuguese or English, for instance, learned in school or at home); he is then a French citizen, and finally he might claim to be from a region and even from a village.

Intercultural Teaching Should be Based on Social Sciences

Against folklorisation

More than the 'domestication of the savage mind' (Jack Goody), the major risk of intercultural teaching lies in the folklorisation of the cultural mind. There are numerous examples of such a danger whose explanation lies in demagogy: the desire to please and not to disappoint students, happy to see their prejudices confirmed. Despite all the spontaneous expectations of French students, the Spanish banking system is more open to international banking cards than the German one (one can understand why the slogan of the Spanish tourist bureau for its advertising campaign in France is 'Spain is not a common place'). Despite all the representations of other European students, the French buy less and less bread and when they do, they buy it more often in supermarkets than in bakeries. Despite all that we may believe, only 31% of the Spaniards still go to Mass regularly, and

INTERCULTURALISING FRENCH EDUCATION 91

French companies are among the most computerised in Europe. We could draw up a long list of the misrepresentations we all have of other cultures, preconceptions which are reinforced by approximate journalism or language teaching. Precisely because of their convenience should clichés be systematically rooted out from any intercultural teaching.

Against chatter and opinion

Teachers should stay as far as possible from what Nietzsche called '*die Journalistik*', i.e. a very superficial way of treating social facts. This precaution is especially important if teachers are to use the media to teach intercultural facts. No newspaper is free from bias: using newspapers could prove to be either a boon or a bane. A boon if they are used to demonstrate the different points of view or the various preoccupations in other countries, a bane if they are used as a textbook or as a reference document. This particularly holds true for foreign language teachers who are often led to overestimate their understanding of the foreign culture. Granted, their knowledge is often updated thanks to tourism and newspapers; it should not be forgotten, however, that newspapers and magazines are only the reflection of opinon and not a source of rigorous knowledge. Articles are often written by people who have no scientific training in the field, although there are some exceptions now in specialised publications, such as medical or economic journals.

In order to use the press in class, teachers need a strong background in statistics (so they will be able to comment correctly on the polls and other quantitative data); they need training in sociology in order to avoid 'hot air' and what Charles S. Peirce called 'philosophical soup' about social trends or social classes. Valid training in this field will keep them from the temptation of prophesying (which is, as Weber showed, endemic to teaching), cure them of any psychologism and guard them from their own intellectual interests.

Scientific training is necessary to fight against any kind of spontaneous evidence, lazy ways of thinking, and the prejudices and partisanship of the teacher. Following Bachelard's recommendations, intercultural teaching should break with opinions and 'common sense', and leave the pleasures of cultural tourism to others. A 'dictionary of interculturally received ideas' could be written and updated on a daily basis. Teachers should be conscious that an intercultural approach requires that affirmations be made with prudence unless proof is available (proof in the scientific sense). The most important danger in intercultural teaching is the absence of doubt, especially in the fields where goodwill easily takes the place of demonstration. To paraphrase Nietzsche again, we had opinions, it is now time to have ideas.

In his Letter to the Academy (1714), Fenelon wrote that historians inevitably belong to their own epoch; Hegel repeated this and we can now claim the same in what concerns teaching. Teachers belong to their own epoch and to their own country: that is precisely what they have to fight against. Teachers must not remain too close to their roots so that they may be more universal and, at least to start with, more European. Secularisation of teaching, which began in France with the separation of school and religion, should continue by keeping the school separate from nationalism and ethnocentrism.

From the cultural facts to the cultural grammar of behaviour

Jack Goody and Pierre Bourdieu described the magic of the transformation operated by social research and then by the teaching process. The logic of school is different from the logic of life. Every teaching process inevitably transforms what is taught. This is particularly true of culture: cultural practices become objects, what is complex is over simplified, everything is organised, classified, hierarchised by the presentation strategy chosen by the teacher. Everything is turned into statistics, charts or text; whatever the teacher chooses to teach is automatically considered legitimate whereas whatever is not covered in class falls into the realm of the illegitimate. Game theory might often be an intellectual game instead of an explanation of the choices made when actors in cultural life do not have the time to calculate the advantages and drawbacks of every single possibility. By way of example: when questioned by pollsters, migrant workers in European countries say they intend to go back to their country of origin. Even though they continue to affirm this return, most of them never do leave: the representation of this alternative enables them to stay in a country which will always remain a little foreign to them. They are not lying to themselves: although it may seem paradoxical, the logic of their life is different from the logic of the way their life is represented by researchers or journalists.

In order to avoid that risk, the description of socialisation institutions should be placed at the beginning of syllabi. Schools, family and the media are the most important since they are the institutions which teach how to become Belgian, French or Italian while inculcating values and roles. Learning how the life of a child is organised by different cultures, what he or she learns in school, what is taught by both partners and schools and how, watching TV, news or game shows on different European channels might make the specific *Weltanschauungen* of different countries much clearer and more understandable. For instance, understanding how Spanish textbooks for *'Ciencias Sociales'* combine national and regional history might indicate to a French person exactly what *'Las Communidades Autonomas'* means to a Spaniard.

European History Revisited

Despite many efforts, French teachers still teach history from a French point of view; they will soon have to delete all nationalist references from their speech. In an intercultural surrounding, Austerlitz can no longer be considered a victory, Napoleon cannot be presented as a hero conquering Spain but rather as a tyrant responsible for massacres of Spaniards, and perhaps the literature teacher should tone down the famous autobiographic verse from Victor Hugo: 'Mon père, ce héros au sourire si doux ...' because that gentle smile was on the face of a general in the Napoleonic Spanish army. And thus will we treat every episode of our history: Louis XIV will have more shadows than sun, and coming a little closer to home, we will have to mention the hostility of French peasants towards a single-market Europe, De Gaulle's opposition to the entry of Great Britain into the Common Market, the resistance of Chirac and the Communist Party to the entry proposals of Spain and Portugal because both hoped to win the support and the votes of the French agricultural lobbies.

At the end of this process, politicians and warriors will have lost a major part of their grandeur; the next logical step will be to replace their names currently found on our squares, streets and stations. In his novels, Boris Vian already named the streets after great jazz musicians: Europe will have to fulfil his dream. I suggest a Metro station be named after Django Rheinardt, in tribute to his music and to the gypsies who have been so badly treated in Europe, and who obviously suffer from lack of a strong lobby. It is probable that novelists, philosphers, musicians and scientists alone would survive such a necessary historical laundering: if the Avenue Foch were to be called Shakespeare Avenue, it would certainly not tarnish the memory of people who lost their lives at Verdun, especially when every one of them, whether German or French, would surely have preferred staying at home with their families. Furthermore, renaming the Austerlitz station the gare d'Espagne (the 'Spanish station') would also help most of the French travellers who do not always know which train station serves which region; and in return, Waterloo station could be rechristened after Adam Smith. All the 'rues Victoire de la Marne' could be named in tribute to Renoir's movie, 'Rue de la grande illusion' and the Metro station Solferino could be changed to 'Fellini'. One thing is sure, designating the name of a place should not be the responsibility of any politician.

History has to be taught from the loser's point of view as well, but what is more important, it should be examined from a European point of view. This does not imply sophisticated research: it is only a question of making sure that no European citizen could be offended by the discovery that a street somewhere in Europe carries the name of someone who at one time menaced his region of origin. Let us apply the rule dictated by Jules Ferry to the French teachers, and replace 'any French father' by 'any European person'.

'Babel es una benedición'

This sentence was purposely pronounced by Rafael Conte, a journalist from the Spanish daily paper *El Pais* (25 March 1988), in front of French teachers: language is only the most obvious sign of the differences between cultures, a fact which should convince people to learn that international understanding requires a real intercultural effort.

Language teaching can find a new dimension and expanded roles in an intercultural Europe only if it can adapt to this challenge. Language teaching cannot remain as inefficient as it has been until now: learning a language is no longer an intellectual luxury, it has become primarily an economic necessity. A single-market Europe is strong motivation for the students: teachers should be sure not to disappoint their hopes.

Languages as tools of mobility

Pedagogic research in the intercultural field usually emphasises a gratuitous dimension of language teaching: learning a language in order to better understand the cultures of other people. There is, however, a trivial and more profit-oriented argument in favour of languages: the mobility of workers throughout Europe as well as the internationalisation of most professions. The main objectives of language teaching should be establishing the ability to work in more than one European language.

Instead of simply designating language classes as 'Italian' or 'German', many steps and diverse skills corresponding to different objectives should be isolated: the ability to read technical literature in a specific field, the ability to understand speeches in a professional field, the ability to translate bio-medical literature, etc. In any case, language teaching should not aim at only one (and a very sophisticated) ability: mastering the language as natives do. Many people will have to use more than two foreign languages and this at different levels: setting only one goal, as is the current practice in most of our courses, is not only unrealistic but also a deterrent for many students, young or old.

Language teaching should become fast, cost-efficient and geared primarily towards short-term results (which does not exclude long-term efficiency). It seems that language teaching is too often now a self-perpetuating activity in which teachers produce mostly teachers. Instead of traditional language teaching, we should perhaps talk about learning German in order to read maths, French for understanding business, or English for working in the British chemical industry, etc.

Then the question arises, as to the type of teacher needed: within a single European market, can we still afford to have French people teaching German or Italian? From an economic point of view, it is clearly counterproductive since so many German or Italian students would be more than happy to come to teach their mother tongue in France while, at the same time, taking advantage of the occasion to learn French, or medicine or music in the French language. The intercultural dimension would in this case be greatly enhanced with the learning and teaching of language acting as an intercultural investment accelerator. It is to be expected, of course, that another lobby, that of language teachers, would probably oppose such a proposition and work to delay its accomplishment (Mariet, 1986).

Economics as a culture shared among Europeans

In order to build Europe people need to be convinced of the advantages of the single market which will be the basis of any intercultural activity. Since the major arguments are economic, economy should become a sort of 'koiné'. The study released by the EEC in March 1988 shows that the elimination of internal EEC frontiers will save billions of ECUs. Increased competition, integration of the financial markets and economies of scale will result once the trade barriers, quotas and different kinds of standards (how many sorts of plugs, of TV sets, etc.) are dropped. Not everyone, however, possesses the competence required to understand this quiet revolution, and lacking an adequate intellectual training they might be receptive to demagogic arguments (nationalist are the most frequent). Intercultural education should lean on what makes it necessary and possible. Economics should be that cultural consensus if combined with human rights. Once people are able to understand the advantages of being European citizens, they will be more predisposed to supporting the idea: more convincing than any cultural or humanist arguments, reasoning must first be based on economic facts.

A few things people should learn about economics in order to have a set of thinking tools are:

1. The comparative advantage and the opportunity cost
2. Economies of scale

These ricardian concepts will help explain the advantages of the specialisation of countries and regions as well as the interest of concentration. The multinational logic of takeovers, mergers, and more generally of multinationalisation of companies will also be clearer. A good understanding of these topics is necessary in order to avoid any dubious overtones of nationalism, so easily provoked by the growing internationalisation of our economies: for example, the opposition brought by the French Ministry of Finances when it learned that Pearson, which owns *The Financial Times*, intended to build an 'international chain' of financial newspapers, including the French *Les Echos* and the Spanish *Cinco Dias*. Those who would profit most from such an endeavour would most certainly be European readers and companies.

3. Protectionism does not protect consumers

We are all consumers; protectionism protects only the few producers, and only in the short run: thus any sort of protectionism which guards the interests of the few producers is contrary to the majority of the people's interests.

4. Cultural goods are products too

Every period of social change provokes resistance on behalf of the people who lose their protected privileges: Spanish soccer players oppose the opening of the soccer market in 1992, as do, to some extent, the French insurance companies and German breweries. I would not bet that the very same fears cannot explain the position of those who are in favour of barriers protecting French movies, French television or the French language. In centuries past, French people have spoken other languages throughout their land (Latin, Occitan, Breton, etc.); there is therefore no valid reason to equate the defence of the French language with the defence of French cultures. Languages are historical productions, too; they appear, develop and die. Our countries survived the death of ancient Greek and Latin, they will surely survive other deaths in the language market. An argument which is often used to counter this reasoning claims that culture is not an economic field like any other, that it is something which needs to be protected. Protected against what? Against other cultures? We cannot transform our countries into museums filled with past cultures; where other regions of Europe hold the comparative advantage, there will follow the production and employment markets. No argument could be more convincing to encourage the development of a European cultural industry in publishing and printing, television production, recording, and so on.

Intercultural information

Satellite and management requirements have made the European media more and more intercultural. Over the next years cable will generalise what Eurovision started: European TV in every home. Newspaper stands all over Europe already offer the press from each European country, in every European language. Recent experience in Belgium, however, where cable has an already long history and supplies many foreign TV channels, shows that the spontaneous consumption of foreign television is very limited.

How to improve this situation and take advantage of a wonderful opportunity of interculturalisation? The first step is to equip schools and universities with cable or dish antennas so that they receive all the European channels available through satellite (if not encoded). Satellite Television guides are published in different languages (for example, *Satellite TV Europe* is published monthly in Spanish, French and English) which could help in choosing the appropriate programmes for different classes or which could simply be recommended (or required) for students.

Furthermore, the installation of modems would permit communication between the different data banks established through universities or schools, thus creating the possibility of networking which could constitute another opportunity of engraining concrete European reflexes in intellectual work. Any gain in productivity which is yielded from the interculturalisation of Europe will prove more convincing than a multitude of generous speeches.

Let us give a word all its intercultural meanings

May I suggest a more Europeanised semantics which would protect our tourists and travellers from some of the most frequent surprises? Take the word 'café' (coffee, *Kaffee*) for example: it can mean many things depending on whether it is uttered by a Greek, an Italian, a German, a Frenchman, or a Spaniard. A German will picture a cup with a pitcher of condensed milk on the side (*'Kaffee Sahne'* or *Milch*), whereas the Spaniard might think of a glass of coffee mixed with milk (and maybe even some *churros* to dunk into it!) to be drunk standing at a counter; the Greek will think of a 'Turkish coffee' and a glass of cool water, while the Frenchman might have in mind *'le petit noir'*, that tiny cup of black coffee you drink at the café at practically any time of the day. For Americans the word coffee evokes a mug of transparent liquid, burning hot, that they carry everywhere in their home, their car, their office. And Italians believe the entire world shares their taste for expresso or cappucino. We all think 'coffee', and we are all often disappointed to find that another culture associates another texture, another taste, another presentation to what we take for a given.

This 'European semantics' emphasises the richness and the fortunate necessity for a mixture of cultures. It demonstrates that one word may have various implicit meanings for different regions of Europe, and will hopefully prepare Europeans to be more culturally tolerant: intolerance is too often triggered by the small details of everyday life: unconscious habits concerning meals, courtesy, schedules, vacations, etc. It could help in changing the spirit of tourists, too often prone to ethnocentric reactions when confronted with the little peculiarities of everyday life in a foreign region. Without going through all 'the metaphors we live by' (Lakoff & Johnson, 1980), such an endeavour could lead to a more sophisticated ethnological reflection on our cultures and on the way we are unconsciously both French (for example) and European. An insufficient amount of scientific results are available in this domain, however, to authorise any serious training for students, let alone a complete course. Improvised ethnology based on a few advertisements and some sociological concepts can be really disastrous: it is worth noting that, in general, those people involved in international marketing or advertising have been more prudent than teachers in drawing conclusions from the research in sociolinguistics or comparative ethnology.

Conclusion

'Imagine there is no country': John Lennon's dream might come true at last, at least in what concerns Europe. Interculturalisation is an inevitable consequence of the single market in Europe. The school system must be ready for that new step: but being ready does not only imply establishing some international collaboration. The issue is far more serious and complex: teaching will change with that new step. School prepares students for the market-place and for the real world, and both are changing very quickly in Europe. Effectiveness of the school system will be measured according to its ability to meet new needs of the European population. Interculturalisation is not folklore nor simply another 'academic hobby' as it is sometimes depicted by company executives when speaking of pedagogical ideas: it is the new European way of life. Are teachers and professors trained for this new challenge?

Are they conscious of the changes that will necessarily be wrought in their work and their career? I doubt it, and I am afraid that government and unions will approach the subject in too conservative a manner. How many of the European teachers correctly master a foreign language? How will French maths teachers react when required to learn Spanish or German? Are they ready to work with an Italian teacher on second derivations? Are language teachers prepared to leave behind familiar literature and conversation classes in order to work on accounting or chemistry? A new profile for language teachers must be drawn: a major in language with minors in the sciences, technology or economics, or vice versa.

Will schools and governments grant the same salary to teachers with different language skills? Many teachers in Europe are already leaving the teaching profession for more lucrative positions in business. Once maths or biology teachers are bilingual their market value will increase. Which salaries or fringe benefits will be necessary to keep them in the school business? The answers to these trivial questions will also be a determining factor in the success of interculturalisation.

References

BOURDIEU, P. 1980, Sartre. *London Review of Books* 2, 22, 11–12.
BRAUDEL, F. 1987, *Grammaire des Civilisations.* Paris: Flammarion.
ETIEMBLE, F. 1988, *Ouvertures sur un comparatisme planetaire.* Paris: Christian Bourgeois.
FABIANI, J.-L. 1988, *Les Philosophes de la République.* Paris: Editions de Minuit.
IDT, G. 1979, Modèles scolaires dans l'écriture sartrienne. *Revue des Sciences Humaines* 174, 83–103.
LACKOFF, G. and JOHNSON, M. 1980, *The Metaphors We Live By.* Chicago: University of Chicago Press.
MARIET, F. 1986, Le marché interdisciplinaire et le discours de la didactique des langues. *Etudes de Linguistique Appliquée* 61.

Part III

Towards a Research-based Theory of Intercultural Communication

The history of language teaching was shown in the previous section to be closely tied to general social and political history. It has also been influenced by developments in the social sciences. As previous chapters show, attempts to establish a sound theoretical base for cultural studies have drawn widely on anthropology, sociology and psychology, turning away to some extent from the traditional links with literary history and criticism.

As the social sciences themselves have changed towards an increasing emphasis on empirical research, this too has had an effect on foreign language teaching scholars. They have found themselves adopting new research paradigms, initially in experimenting with methods of language teaching, more recently adapting the resurgence of interest in qualitative research to the investigation of intercultural communication.

The four chapters in this section reflect these recent concerns. They share a desire to establish some empirical evidence which will help clarify both contemporary practices and potential developments in those practices. Byram *et al.* describe a project which attempts to trace effects of language teaching on learners' views of other peoples and cultures and also to describe the process involved. Their focus on the classroom process is complemented by Keller's investigation of that most crucial experience, the visit to a foreign culture. Both chapters draw their methodology from the social sciences and are concerned to describe and analyse their informants' experience with as little intervention as possible.

Meyer and Ertelt-Vieth are concerned to clarify the complexities of intercultural communication arising where advanced language learners meet people from another culture. Linguistic difficulties might still be present but, as both authors show, the major need is to overcome different, culture-specific understandings of 'the same' phenomena. Teasing out those contrasting interpretations and understanding the other person's perceptions of the world are, as Ertelt-Vieth demonstrates, complex enough for the researcher. Meyer shows how learners are often hindered in their communication by those complexities but can nonetheless attain a level of understanding which is fundamental to successful intercultural communication.

The contributions of empirical research to cultural studies teaching are as yet limited by the number and range of projects. Further work will depend both on levels of finance and status – another indicator of change within disciplines which reflects differing national traditions – and on the development of appropriate methods. The four chapters presented here are among the first signs that empirical research will play an increasingly important role in theoretical debate and classroom practice.

8 Young People's Perceptions of Other Cultures: The Role of Foreign Language Teaching

MICHAEL BYRAM, VERONICA ESARTE-SARRIES, SUSAN TAYLOR and PATRICIA ALLATT

Introduction: The Aims of Foreign Language Teaching

Foreign language teaching in general education aspires to high and noble aims which are not only linguistic. In England one very cogent expression of aims is in a discussion document from Her Majesty's Inspectorate (HMI), the body of national inspectors of education who have a significant influence on education policy. Their definition of the aims of foreign language teaching suggests that it contributes to pupils' experience in two areas, the linguistic and literary and the human and social. Their description of aims in the second area of experience is as follows:

Human and social [aims]
to increase social competence by promoting an awareness of and sensitivity to differences in social customs and behaviour:

to foster positive attitudes towards other countries and those who live in them and to counter prejudice;

to enable learners to meet foreigners in this country and to travel abroad with confidence, enjoyment, interest and advantage;

to awaken an interest in foreign cultures and life-styles and to foster a willingness to see one's culture in a broader context;

to develop a capacity for understanding and accepting the unfamiliar;

to encourage tolerance and a willingness to work together. (HMI, 1987)

The process of induction into the social world beyond the national boundaries which these particular aims of language teaching embody might be termed 'tertiary socialisation'. HMI assert, however, that these aims are dependent on 'success in mastering the linguistic objectives', and after this initial discussion the rest of the document is focused on how these linguistic objectives might be attained.

The same tendency to pay lip-service to social aims but to ignore them in discussion of objectives and assessment is evident in the documents for the first public examination, taken after five years of language learning. The new General Certificate of Secondary Education lists seven aims but proceeds to ignore all but the first, 'practical communication', for assessment and examination purposes. This is probably symptomatic of attitudes and practice in general. Most teachers consider that language learning has a wide range of aims – including creating tolerance of and insight into other cultures – but how those aims are realised in daily practice remains unclear. It may in fact be that the emphasis on the assessment of the linguistic aim and its associated objectives leads to little or no attempt to realise the human and social aims in daily practice. The essential purpose of this chapter is to describe a research project which begins the empirical investigation of whether and how language teaching within general education in secondary schools does in fact contribute to 'tertiary socialisation', does realise the human and social aims.

The Durham Project: Aims and Methods

Two important fields of this dimension of language teaching are the notions of 'tolerance' and 'insight'. They are part of the rhetoric of the General Certificate of Secondary Education, for example:

> The aims of a course in French leading up to a G.C.S.E. examination should be ....
>
> 3. to offer insights into the culture and civilisation of French speaking countries ....
>
> 6. to encourage positive attitudes to foreign language learning and to speakers of foreign languages and a sympathetic approach to other cultures and civilisations. (DES, 1985)

The Durham project attempts to explore the effects of French teaching on pupils' tolerance of French people and insight into French culture, (the latter is understood in the social anthropological sense of 'way of life'). 'Insight' is operationalised in terms of pupils' knowledge about French culture and perceptions of the values and viewpoint of French people. 'Tolerance' is operationalised in terms of pupils' level of ethnocentricity with respect to French people. Both of these are then related to the teaching of French and other potential influences through the notion of 'change', in quantity or quality of knowledge and in level of ethnocentricity before and after a period of learning French in a secondary school.

The research is based on case studies of two secondary comprehensive schools where children begin French at age 11 in the first year and continue for a minimum of three years. The decision to work with case studies was taken because of the exploratory and intensive nature of the combination of research techniques chosen. The three fundamental concepts of 'insight', 'tolerance' and 'change' are observed and 'measured' by a combination of qualitative techniques. 'Knowledge about France' as an operationalisation of 'insight' is examined through semi-structured interviews with pupils in the year before they begin French (the last year of primary school) and in the third year of learning French (secondary year 3). 'Attitude to French people' is measured by a semantic differential test (Osgood et al., 1967) of pupils' level of ethnocentricity before and after learning French. Two separate cohorts of approximately 200 pupils each were tested and about 100 from each cohort interviewed. 'Change' as an effect of learning French, and of other external influences, is measured in terms of associations between the dependent variable of 'level of ethnocentricity' and independent variables of exposure to French teaching, socio-economic status, visits to foreign countries, parents' knowledge of foreign languages, gender and so on, collected by questionnaire.

Furthermore, the process of French teaching is analysed by in-depth non-participant observation of French classes over a period of eight months. The purpose of this is to provide detailed case studies of French teaching with specific emphasis on methods of realising the human and social aims of 'tertiary socialisation'. These case studies are valuable in themselves, given the lack of research knowledge of this dimension of language teaching, but also serve to explain differential effects of language teaching on pupils' knowledge and attitudes should these be discovered.

The Durham Project: Analysis of Data

The amount of data available (for example, interviews lasting on average 40 minutes with almost 200 pupils, and field notes from classroom observations over eight months) is too vast to allow summary. We propose to select some aspects which represent the main focus of the research: i.e. to relate 'insight' and 'tolerance' to methods of teaching foreign languages. This can be seen in three roughly defined stages:

1. statistical analysis of the associations between the dependent variable of level of ethnocentricity in respect of French people and the independent variables of exposure to French teaching and other factors;
2. qualitative analysis of attitudes towards French people expressed in interviews by pupils in the three different levels of ethnocentricity rating: this also serves to validate the measure of ethnocentricity;
3. qualitative analysis of the specific contribution of language teaching to pupils' knowledge and attitudes, first through the analysis of observations and second through analysis of pupils' accounts in the interviews.

This selection gives no account of the nature of pupils' knowledge about French culture or the relationship of attitudes towards French people with attitudes towards other nationalities. Even this selection has to be summarised, in the space available, and results of the analysis will be presented without the detail of method and supporting evidence, such as statistical tables or detailed collections of transcript quotations, or detailed descriptions of lessons observed.

Statistical analysis of attitudes

The independent variables found to be most strongly associated with attitudes tended to be those measuring pupil background rather than experience of other countries and languages. Gender, membership of a particular school class, age and socio-economic status are more significantly related to attitudes than are experiential variables. Of these, having foreign relations, language learning experience in the family and experience of countries other than France have some small association with attitudes, but only in interaction with other variables.

Gender was found to be one of the variables most frequently associated with variance in attitude scores. Whether in primary or secondary school, girls have a more positive attitude towards French people than boys. Of three groups, the French, the German and the Americans, only the latter are mainly positively perceived by boys. Given the preponderance of girls studying languages in Britain (Powell, 1986), the fact that girls have positive attitudes towards foreign peoples before they start learning a foreign language is particularly interesting.

Being in a particular class at school – both primary and secondary – appears to associate significantly with attitudes. As school class serves both as a descriptor of a collection of pupils receiving similar teaching and as a descriptor of an aggregate of individuals having a variety of backgrounds and experience, interaction amongst factors is likely to be present. Gender is one factor to be considered, as is foreign travel. Two secondary classes with the highest positions in the rank listing both have high proportions of girls in them. Further, classes rated highest in achievement in French are highest in their regard for the French, although general achievement in French does *not* covary with attitudes to the French.

With respect to age, the younger age group (both boys and girls) showed generally more negative attitudes towards one people – the Germans. The corollary of this was that the younger age group perceived the Americans, who have a similar linguistic background, even more favourably than did the older age group. It is evident from above, however, that the relations between age, school class and gender are so complex that no firm conclusion as to the significance of French teaching can be drawn from statistical analysis alone. The latter simply suggests ways in which the analysis of interview transcripts and field notes might be best pursued.

Qualitative analysis of attitudes

The majority of pupils interested were asked about their attitudes towards French people at some time during the interview. For both age groups the correspondence between scores on the semantic differential test and attitudes expressed in interview was reasonably clear, bearing in mind the breadth of the categories used. The greatest correspondence was found amongst those categorised as non-ethnocentric, only one pupil being unequivocally negative. In the other two grups – 'ethnocentric', and 'medium ethnocentric' – pupils expressed both positive and negative views about the French. Perhaps more importantly, where extremely negative and hostile attitudes were expressed, these came exclusively from those in the ethnocentric group. An illustration of the latter point in a most vehement form is the following:

'Have you met any French people over here or when you were in Spain?'
'I didn't meet any when I was in Spain but when I was in –

when some of the French people came over here they all like walked around the school, lashing out with dirty looks and everything. I just don't like the way they look at you, they look at you as to say what are you looking at — I don't like them.'

On the other hand the range of views within the ethnocentric group is represented in the following two quotations:

'The people, they are not very polite, not very sociable.'
'When you say "they are not very polite", how do you mean?'
'Like when I was in Boulogne we went into a café and asked if we could go to the toilet and they snapped at us and told us that we couldn't go in because with it being a café and that. It wouldn't have been so bad if they had told us politely we couldn't go but they snapped at us and we had to go out.'

This incident contrasts with another from a school trip. The pupil here had a different view of what had been interpreted as harassment by others. He also noted the use of trying to make verbal contact:

'All he wanted to do was see who they were 'cause they were English, they were different and sort of he started talking as we walked past 'cause we were lost and told us where the hostel was and took us back to the hostel, all helpful. Just if you talk to them not if you sort of shout at them in a loud voice and try and get over in English they ignore you but if you try to talk to them in French they'll help you as much as they can.'

Amongst the medium or neutral ethnocentric group there was a marked increase in the number of favourable comments made about the French and a diminution in the number of clearly negative comments; almost one third of the comments were, however, ambivalent. The same kinds of issues were as important for this group as for the most ethnocentric group. The principal concern was with whether French people were generally impatient, unfriendly and unhelpful or their opposites; opinions were roughly equally divided.

The influences upon the formation of the more negative attitudes in this group were chance occurrences and the media. The most strongly expressed opinion in this group came from a boy with no experience of France. In the estimation of the interviewer the general tone of the interview suggested that this participant was something of a 'character', who sought consciously to amuse and referred to himself as having his 'own theories'. His opinions are quoted, however, as being illustrative of a particular kind of reaction which, if left undetected, could militate against class teachers' efforts to ameliorate pupils' views of other peoples. The second extract in particular indicates the persistence of stereotypes and is an exemplar of how they can become evident in the most unexpected places. He had met French people on holiday in a different part of the country:

> 'And they always used to pretend they used to own the place and things like that.'
> 'Yes?'
> 'So I didn't get on very well with them.'
> 'No?'
> 'They seemed as if they wanted to look as if they owned the place.'
> 'Yes. What did they do?'
> 'They used to boss you around and things like that and say don't go on there and like boss you around.'

Later, discussing housing he concluded that few French people had 'very good gardens':

> 'I don't reckon they'd have much patience with it. Like with England like nearly every house has a garden so they're much more like patient so they're always like plodding over it but the French would like get sick after a couple of minutes, hard digging and things like that.'
> 'Why do you think they're impatient?'
> '... It's like when they do have a traffic jam over in France like, all these people blast their horns where we just take it, like 'cause we're used to it but over there they get impatient.'
> 'Do you think most people are impatient?'
> 'No, not really. Like if you're used to traffic jams you can take it like. Say like when they have like traffic jams over there they're not used to it see so they like just miss each other but when they do have one they get impatient and that and drive around like maniacs and the police are trying to undo the traffic jams and that.'

The final statement is a deduction from an earlier premise that as France was large there were few traffic jams, a contrast to the habituation of the English to traffic jams.

Amongst the interveiwees' responses drawn from the non-ethnocentric group there were no extremely hostile comments, whilst there were a few ambivalent or mixed responses. The majority were clearly favourable and well disposed towards the French. The majority of the comments were again concerned with friendliness, helpfulness and so on, but for this group it was the positive end of the spectrum which was represented. One boy with family visit experience saw the people as 'more friendly' and recommended an outgoing strategy which contrasted with the reactions of some pupils who on school visits had admitted to keeping themselves to themselves:

> '... Well just expect friendliness from people and advice like don't be afraid to ask people where to go, things like that.'
> 'What about being in a family, a French family?'
> 'In a French family? ... Join in a little bit like some people are sort of shy, aren't they, sort of get like in there and be freindly with them.'

and later:

> 'Yes. I got along when I was there like. There was lots of French people that spoke English. That was like helpful but even when the people didn't speak English it was good. I didn't feel left out or odd. I felt, well I will have a go and I can only try my best.'
> 'Yes. They were friendly when you did that?'
> 'Yes.'

Family holidays could also influence attitudes:

> 'They are quite friendly, because I have been to France before and enjoyed it. My Mam and Dad didn't though because we were camping, and they were helpful, came round all the time and helped us clear up. They were just nice in all the shops and that.'

One girl's unhesitating response to being asked what France is like was:

> 'If you had to tell someone what you think France is like.'
> 'It would be OK, nice there, nice people and the shops and that will help you to get what you want, and it's nice and hot there.'

Qualitative analysis of the contribution of language teaching to knowledge and attitudes

In-depth observation of language teaching over eight months was reported as an ethnographic study. It dealt both with case studies of four teachers and classes and with the representation of French culture embodied in the textbook. The significance of the latter in guiding teachers' accounts of France was very evident from the case studies.

Four features relevant to cultural teaching were identified as common to the four teachers, despite the range of styles and the complexity of the phenomenon. The first takes us back to the question of aims expressed by teachers, irrespective of whether and how they are realised in classroom practices. The views expressed concerning the role and importance of cultural study can be divided roughly into two kinds: those which relate to the personal development of children, and those confined to the conduct of the lesson. When asked if and why cultural learning is important the teachers generally talked about how it is important for children to know about other ways of living which may or may not be better than their own. Through such knowledge they may become more tolerant of other peoples and less restricted in their own lifestyle.

One teacher says:

> You have got to be adding something to the kids' lives other than the ability to say 'Je suis Anglais' ... They have got to be able to say at the end of it, yes well I have learnt this and that or that about French people or about France so that you have actually changed their concepts, especially around here ....

Another says:

> I always tell them straightaway that there is more to life than Newfarm because they honestly can't see more and that one way out is to travel and see what other possibilities there are, and that they will improve as people if they can see how other people are and they needn't be wasting their time say not knowing what to do in Newfarm. This helps me of course because I say 'Have a language, do something with it and off you go'. Obviously plugging my subject. But I feel the quality of life differences should be stressed because children like them miss out and don't realise it.

So there is a general philosophy among these teachers of positively developing children's personalities. In addition, cultural information is seen as a pedagogic device for capturing the interest of pupils, contextualising their language learning, giving light relief or filling in lessons where language learning ability is believed to be limited. This second function is briefly expressed in the second teacher's description above. Other teachers talk about how important it is for the country to be made real to the learner rather than 'a nondescript place' or 'never never land'.

The third common factor was the extent and nature of teachers' experience of France. It was all centred first on visits to, or work in, schools in France, or secondly, brief holidays; it was usually a combination of the two. Their personal experience of France as a source or stock of knowledge on which to draw is therefore quite limited in range, despite the large number of visits made by some teachers. The significance of the fourth factor – the textbook – is therefore all the more marked. Even the most independent of the teachers charts a course through the three volumes of the textbook topic by topic. At the very least it provides a strong core around which he or she builds his or her lessons. Very few lessons are conducted without opening the textbook and many lessons consist of a series of exercises from the book. The textbook provides an overall structure to the information children receive about the language and culture in terms of topics, such as 'Au restaurant' and 'Le camping en France'.

The individual case studies cannot be reported in their entirety and to summarise would be contrary to the ethnographic methods used. From the studies, however, the concept of a teaching 'style' with respect to cultural teaching was developed; a 'style' is the specific combination of teacher A with class X. The factors which comprise a style reflect the open-ended definition of culture used and are not intended to be all-inclusive. The aim was to identify those factors most salient in differentiating teaching styles. They were the result of observations rather than being predetermined, and the ratings of the teachers on these factors are based on observed activity rather than expressed intention or attitude. In the first instance they serve the ethnography, as a means of systematising observations. The question of generalisation to other 'styles' in other schools remains to be tested. Secondly, the factors are the basis of descriptive models of cultural teaching linked to pupil perceptions.

Pupils' perceptions of the significance of the textbook and the teacher in their knowledge of France were probed through the interviews. As an illustration, the views from one particular class – and therefore one particular style – can be reported.

Seen from the pupils' viewpoint the function of the teacher is to supplement and enrich the information provided by the textbook. Twelve pupils were interviewed in total. All but one of the eight pupils who were asked about what the teacher had told them agreed that they did receive supplementary information. The one exception contrasted German lessons where 'every so often we will read a bit about the German family' with French lessons where 'I don't think I have learned anything about France' but says the French teacher talks about France 'not very often' which suggests that it is the contrast with German which influences her reply, not the absolute lack of teacher information.

YOUNG PEOPLE'S PERCEPTIONS OF OTHER CULTURES

In pupils' views, then, the teacher first of all supplements the textbook:

'It tells you everything, you just get more bits from the teachers who have been to France.'

but also improves on the textbook:

'... probably learn a lot more from the teacher than I do from the textbook because they've usually had like more experience and that and they're easy to understand than just reading it 'cause if somebody tells you it sticks in your mind rather than just reading it.'

Furthermore the teacher can provide experience which the textbook cannot. Three pupils spontaneously referred to a lesson in their first year of French which had clearly stuck in their minds, as was suggested above. The teacher had provided a cheese-tasting occasion:

'Yes, they tell us like about the different foods and Mrs X brought in a lot of cheeses and that ...'
'Is this in addition to what you learn from the textbooks?'
'Yes, we were just, just when we'd started learning about how to ask for food and how to go into cafés she brought all, about 15 different French cheeses in.'
'You found that interesting then?'
'Yes, never realised there was so many – there's about hundreds of different types.'

However, the textbook remains the guide in the sense that it determines the topic and the order in which topics are taken. Within the textbook guidelines, the acquisition of language is determining:

'Do you do more language than about France?'
'We do about France and then it mingles with about France when we learn about the language, the vocabulary and that.'
'Do you do about the country without bothering about the language and learning the words?'
'No, not really.'
'It's all connected with learning the language is it?'
'Yes.'

One of this group of pupils was also asked whether she had any preferences within the dichotomy which the interviewer had established between 'language' and 'France':

'Which do you prefer?'
'... Learning about it better, 'cause I'd like to find more about

the place rather than how to say where's the toilet and things like that, I'd rather learn about the place.'

Although it is the interviewer's distinction, the pupil appears to recognise it even though she puts it in terms of language functions ('how to say') which have a specific realisation ('where's the toilet and things like that').

If we now turn directly to pupils' perceptions of the textbook, they demonstrate both how dominant the book can be and how some pupils are able to take a critical view, apparently without the help of the teacher. First, the general view of the book is summed up by one pupil as follows:

'And how do you learn about the things you've been telling me about, the food and so on, how's that done?'
'Well, we have 'Action!' group French and different chapters are on different subjects, like one chapter could be on the sort of food they have, another chapter on how to pay the round on a bus and another chapter would be about the table and what to expect on the table, and it's mostly either meal times or transport.'
'When you say "one chapter is on", what does it consist of then, the chapter on transport say?'
'It consists of the vocabulary that you would use, the phrases translated into English as well and then there'd be some pictures and there would be a conversation or some facts about it and then there would be say another conversation but with some bits missing bits about it and then some more information and maybe a game, an educational game sort of thing, that you can play and ...'
'When you say information what kind of information is there?'
'It tells you in English what to expect sort of thing on the bus and how to say things and sort of thing you would say on the bus and wanting to go – just generally telling you about the thing.'

The reference to pictures is confirmed as significant by others who mention the pictures when asked about their sources of information:

'So that is one source. And in the book, what sort of things are there in the book?'
'Well it shows you the French houses and everything and then there is a section of objects in the house and the different meals and everything. It shows you a lot of pictures in the books.'
'Do you also discuss these things in class?'

YOUNG PEOPLE'S PERCEPTIONS OF OTHER CULTURES

> 'Yes we discuss like we compare them both from English to French and see what the differences are between them.'
> 'Does your teacher then talk about France herself?'
> 'We had Miss X, she talked from her own experience of being in France and taking part in exchanges and that and the same thing with Miss Y now.'
> 'So that adds a lot more to it does it?'
> 'Yes.'

Again the teacher's own experience enriches the textbook image.

The relationship of textbook image to reality was pursued particularly with one pupil who had just returned from a holiday in France:

> 'Well that is interesting as well because what I am interested in is because you have just been, what you thought you were going to see from what you had learned from your textbooks.'
> 'I expected a lot of buses and trains but there wasn't. I hardly saw any trains and I hardly saw any service buses. I think I only saw a couple of bus stops as well.'
> 'Anything else that you were surprised about?'
> 'I knew I would see them carrying French loaves about but I didn't expect carried them about like on the backs of bikes and they were just walking down the street with them. Things like that.'

Here it is evident that particular images ('carrying French loaves') differ and also that the choice of topic, the emphasis given and the ordering of topics within the book are significant. The emphasis on means of transport, confirmed in the summary above, has an effect on expectations about the whole 'street image', not just on knowledge of how to function linguistically, and especially as a tourist, on French transport.

One interview theme was particularly revealing. Pupils were asked about how people earn their living in France:

> 'Do you have any impressions from your textbooks about what people do in France? What the men do in your textbook?'
> ... [silence]
> 'I mean there are presumably characters in your textbook?'
> 'Yes. They just like work – the first year book we had characters, a family, but I can't remember what the man did.'
> 'What about the women, what do they do?'
> 'They seem to be just housewives.'

'So do you get any real impression of what work is like in France from the textbooks?'
'The men seem to do most of the work.'

In fact, since the topic 'work' had not been treated as such by the textbook — and therefore not by the teacher either — pupils have a less conscious stock of 'information' about work, but nonetheless an awareness of what people do is present:

'Do you get any impression of it from your textbook again?'
'Work?'
'About what people do for work.'
'No, we haven't done anything on work.'
'There are presumably people in the textbook, I mean characters in the textbook.'
'Yes, like the shop workers that's about all, then the youth hostels and so on that's about it that we've done about.'

One pupil explained what kind of impression was available, simultaneously pointing to the cause of the particular image — the 'tourist' view, propagated by the textbook:

'The other thing that interests me is what people know about the work that French people do. For example your textbooks, the jobs that are described there is there are any?'
'No.'
'No? What do you see people doing for work?'
'From what we saw, it was more as if you were a tourist. There was more in department stores and everything so the only jobs there were like shop assistants and everything. That's about it.'

The particular issue of women's occupations was discussed with pupils and it is already evident from an earlier quotation that they are thought of by some only as housewives because of the textbook image. One pupil was critical:

'What about men going to work?'
'I don't think there's many go to work as they do here.'
'The women in your textbooks, what do they do?'
'They're all perfect housewives and that sort of thing.'
'The fact that you're smiling about that obviously implies that you're not too impressed by that.'
'No, it doesn't show you real life like really ....'

In general, it is clear that pupils can learn French for three years — after which some will not continue — and are given no firm knowledge about how French people earn their living. They have to draw conclusions from their experience of their own culture and tend to assimilate French culture to their own, despite the underlying uneasiness about the relationship of textbook to reality.

Conclusion

As implied at the beginning, the question of generalisability from this exploratory study of highly complex issues in two case study schools remains unresolved. The significance of the study lies both in the combination of techniques of data collection and analysis and in the results themselves. The data presented here are selective and, more important, do not illustrate the detailed cross-referencing and synthesis which is necessary if any insight into the precise contribution of language teaching is to be realised. It is not simply a question of triangulation, although that too is significant. It is in the synthesis of statistical analysis, interview data and ethnography that the fuller picture of the effects of language teaching on young people's perceptions of other cultures will be found.

Nonetheless a number of interesting points are evident from the analysis so far. They are presented here to provoke thought rather than lead to immediate conclusions for application to practice. Since the nature of the project is in any case that of 'basic' rsearch, recommendations and applications will have to be tentative. The following points are therefore aspects of the knowledge developed in the course of the project which, assuming they are generalisable, should be brought to the attention of teachers for their own reflection and action. The points are presented in no order of priority, irrespective of whether they arise from aspects of the project already described.

The first point is that children in primary schools have definite and clear expectations of what they will learn in foreign language lessons. They think they will learn 'words' and what to say and write. They do not expect to learn about the foreign people or country. Secondly, they already have, in many cases, a much wider personal experience of foreign travel than their language teachers appear to believe. In general their attitudes towards language learning are positive, they look forward to this new subject with pleasure. Some are, however, less enthusiastic and a few are negative in attitude. The third (quite striking) point is that girls are more positive towards foreign people than boys, particularly if the foreigners speak a language other than English. This is the case before they begin to learn a foreign language and continues to be so after three years of learning. The relationship between this and the fact that more girls than boys choose to continue their learning of foreign languages remains open to speculation.

After these three points concerned with pupils, the next three relate to the conduct of foreign language lessons. It is, first, very clear that the textbook is the determining, dominant factor in what teachers choose to offer pupils. The influence of the textbook on the range and depth of cultural information to which pupils are exposed is perhaps a cause for concern. It is all the more so, since there is evidence that pupils value highly teachers' accounts from their own viewpoint and experience. Pupils recognise a difference in quality between teachers' accounts and the information provided in the textbook. The next point is closely connected with the last. It is clear that approaches to or 'styles' of teaching about the foreign culture vary considerably. Teachers' contributions above and beyond the range of the textbook differ in manner and extent. The differences seem to depend on a teacher's individual philosophy of language teaching, the nature of his/her experience of the foreign culture and, thirdly, his/her perception of the language-learning ability of the class. The final point is that pupils' knowledge of and attitudes towards the foreign culture are much influenced by visits organised by teachers. The influence is, however, not always positive: pupils sometimes return with negative attitudes reinforced, or perhaps even created, by their individual experiences. But it is also evident that these visits and other sources of knowledge and experience are not drawn upon to any noticeable degree during lessons. Pupil contributions to discussion of the foreign culture are limited to the asking of occasional questions.

In summary, the general pattern of teaching of and about the foreign culture has not followed the trend towards pupil-centred learning apparent elsewhere. Despite the development of pupil activity in the learning of the foreign language — under the general banner of 'communicative language learning' — the teaching of culture remains didactic, oriented towards the transmission of information. It is, however, largely unsystematic, guided only by the textbook, even though some pupils recognise the weaknesses of an approach which does not, in the words of the pupil cited above, 'show you real life'.

It is clear that there is much to be done. Textbook writers must be more aware of the burden they carry. Teachers must be aware of the value pupils place on their personal contribution. And both teachers and teacher-trainers must consider whether the present techniques are adequate to fulfil the noble aims of language teaching to which we all aspire.

Acknowledgement

This research was funded as Project No. C00232177 the Economic and Social Research Council from April 1985 to March 1988: 'The effects of language teaching on young people's perception of other cultures'. A full report of the research is to be found in: Byram, M., Esarte-Sarries, V. and Taylor, S. 1990, *Cultural Studies and Language Learning* (Clevedon: Multilingual Matters).

References

DES 1985, *General Certificate of Secondary Education. The National Criteria. French.* London: HMSO.
HMI 1987, *Modern Foreign Languages to 16.* London: HMSO.
OSGOOD, C.E., SUCI, G.J. and TANNENBAUM, P.H. 1967, *The Measurement of Meaning.* Illinois: University of Illinois Press.
POWELL, B. 1986, *Boys, Girls and Languages in Schools.* London: CILT.

9 Stereotypes in Intercultural Communication: Effects of German-British Pupil Exchanges

GOTTFRIED KELLER

It is a widespread belief that a pupil exchange is the best way to achieve international understanding because the pupils experience the complexities of a foreign culture at first hand. In the host family, the school and in public life they get to know the host country from within, which might modify and differentiate their presuppositions. The accompanying teachers, however, very often realise that pupils find their prejudices confirmed and that they tend to express their views with greater conviction than before their stay abroad.

This observation could lead to the assumption that prejudices are not reduced by an exchange, and a better understanding of the host culture is not achieved. On the other hand, however, objective judgements about a culture are not possible, because we do not have an absolute knowledge of our world. Social psychologists have proved that we rely on stereotypes which enable us to understand the complexity of the world and to communicate with foreigners. What we perceive is filtered, simplified and modified by our own concepts, attitudes and perspectives. Therefore a correct knowledge of a culture is not available, and we can neither verify nor falsify stereotypes. The best way to understand a foreign culture is to see it from within and to get to know the different perspectives which are shown in the habits, value judgements, characteristics, beliefs and attitudes of the people in the target culture. In this process the pupils might give up, generalise, modify or differentiate stereotypes, find others confirmed or gain new ones.

What is important for international understanding is the acquisition of a new perspective and the differentiation of general judgements. This is revealed in a comparison between auto- and heterostereotypes. The more the heterostereotype of the foreign visitor is modified to the level of the autostereotype of the people in the host culture the better is the mutual understanding. There will of course always be differences between the two perspectives, but they are necessary in order to compare the native culture and the target culture critically. The research reported here is part of a long-term series of enquiries into what effect exchanges do in fact have on pupils' understanding.

In order to find out if a better understanding of the target culture is achieved we gave pupils a questionnaire before and after their stay abroad. They were asked to rate the foreign people on a wide range of characteristics (See Appendix). Social psychologists in America, Great Britain and Germany had done relevant research in the theory and methods which we were able to use in our questionnaire (Jahoda, 1962 and 1963; Katz & Braly, 1933; Sodhi & Bergius, 1953; Wolf, 1963). In addition to that we extended the enquiries to several schools in both countries (Keller, 1969a). These gave the results shown in Tables 9.1 and 9.2.

TABLE 9.1 *The British image of Germany* (E − D)

Characteristic	%
national pride	74
hard-working	71
skilled craftsmen	68
well-built	62
conscious of duty	60
intelligent	60
proud	60
good scientists	55
strong willed	51
extremely patriotic	50
good technicians	49
sport-loving	48
progressive	48
clean	46
military nation	43
glory-seeking	42
hardy	42
musical	42
anti-semitic	40

TABLE 9.2 *The German image of Great Britain* (D-E)

Characteristic	%
bound by tradition	76
national pride	75
polite	68
class-conscious	65
disciplined	63
gentlemen	62
reserved	58
correct	56
freedom-loving	55
tactful	50
cultured people	49
unemotional	48
conventional	47
reserved with foreigners	45
self-confident	45
conscious of duty	44
sport-loving	44
good politicians	43
proud	43
hospitable	41
nation of businessmen	41
class distinction	41
good democrats	40
snobs	40

German pupils had the widely held opinion that in Great Britain tradition was very important; this was shown by the fact that German pupils described the British people as being bound by tradition, conservative, conventional and class-conscious. A second important feature in the picture German pupils had of Britain was the 'gentleman ideal' with characteristics such as being polite, disciplined, reserved, correct and self-confident. A number of further characteristics – sport-loving, hospitable, good politicians, freedom-loving – complete the generally very positive picture which they had of Great Britain before their departure.

The British picture of German people is also characterised by a number of positive traits; predominantly those referring to technical skill and scientific ability – skilled craftsmen, good scientists, good technicians, musical, conscious of duty, hard-working and progressive — are here the dominant traits ascribed in Britain to German people. On the other hand the British image of Germany also contains preconceptions with which our young people do not identify: thus national pride seems to influence the British view of Germany since more than 40% of the pupils questioned considered Germany to be a militaristic nation characterised by a desire for glory, by obstinacy, pride and anti-semitism.

How is the German View Changed by an Exchange Visit?

In order to find out whether a better mutual understanding arises from a visit abroad we compared the pupils' image of the foreign country (heterostereotypes) with the image that nation has of itself (autostereotypes) (Keller, 1970). This comparison gave surprising results. In many respects German pupils acquired a different image of Britain, an indication of the fact that their experience in the host country proved their prejudices to be unfounded. At the same time, however, the pupils' judgements developed in different ways, summarised in Table 9.3. On the other hand some high expectations of Britain were modified to the level of the British self-image, such as the still widespread ideal of the reserved unemotional self confident 'gentleman' (Table 9.3a). The same applied to the image of the thrifty and mean Scot, which was held by 76% of the group before the journey but by only 10% afterwards. The following opinions illustrate the change:

> 'Before the journey I believed the Scots were economical or even mean, but this prejudice simply is not true. Anyone at home who claims that the Scots are mean should be flogged.'

> 'They are more friendly, helpful and hospitable than I had ever imagined.'

On the other hand some low expectations changed to the higher level of the British self-image, as for example 'home-loving' and 'TV fans.'

It would be wrong, however, to believe that all judgements came to resemble the self-image of the other nation. Our findings show that big differences remain. Thus after the stay one is still struck by the markedly low evaluation of professional ability (good housewives, good educators, skilled craftsmen, good doctors), which could possibly be due to the fact that pupils had no chance to gain experience in this area. At the same time the pupils rate other features much more highly than the British themselves and thereby idealise them (polite, bound by tradition, cultured people, disciplined). If the list of categories can give only a rough indication of the

TABLE 9.3 *The German image of Great Britain after the exchange*

Characteristic	D–E (before) (N=38) %	D–E (after) (N=38) %	E–E (British autostereotype) (N=169), %
(a) Slight distance from the British autostereotype			
correct	63	23.5	24.5
reserved	60	44	48
hospitable	36.5	70	64
TV fans	15.5	84.5	78
conscious of duty	49	52.5	46
conservative	76	65.5	57
gentlemen	76	49	40
national pride	76	76	86
anti-communists	39	34.5	45
unemotional	54.5	20.5	9
self-confident	55.5	28.5	14
home-loving	49.5	84.5	68.5
sense of humour	31.5	33.5	50.5
uncommunicative	41.5	23.5	8
good politicians	23.5	31.5	50
class-conscious	63.5	52	70
thrifty	76	10.5	30
(b) Large distance from the British autostereotype			
good doctors	7.5	2.5	61
intelligent	10.5	7.5	60
decent	2.5	0	51
skilled craftsmen	2.5	0	50
good educators	12.5	10.5	60
good housewives	2.5	5	53
sport-loving	60.5	34	80
disciplined	73.5	55	10
freedom-loving	63	24.5	65
sentimental	14	12.5	53
nation of businessmen	37	8	48
good scientists	10.5	5	44

Table 9.3 continued

Characteristic	D−E (before) (N=38) %	D−E (after) (N=38) %	E−E (British autostereotype) (N=169), %
reliable	18	12.5	52
sociable	7.5	15	48
conventional	47.5	31	63
just	28.5	26	57
comfort-loving	14	31	61
cultured people	60	45	19
liberal family upbringing	5	45	21
animal-loving	23.5	42	65
reserved with foreigners	45	21	41
bound by tradition	84	87	67
polite	68	76	55

changes of opinion the pupils' essays reveal the underlying reasons. We may quote examples to show that the pre-judgements were corrected by their experience abroad and by comparing this with their own experiences at home:

> 'We were welcomed in Scotland with a warmer hospitality than we had ever expected. At home we think the English are reserved towards foreigners. That is not true. People in Britain are much more friendly than I had ever thought. I used to believe the Scots and English were gentlemen but I didn't find any, at least not in the sense I had imagined.' (Keller, 1970)

How is the British Image of Germany Changed by an Exchange Visit

To answer this question the British pupils on the exchange visit were given the same questionnaires as their German contemporaries. The first thing that was revealed by the questionnaire was very surprising: the pupils who wanted to go to Germany already had, before setting out, a much more positive view of Germany than their contemporaries in Britain, indeed one that largely corresponded to, or even surpassed, the Germans' view of themselves. As Table 9.4 shows, this applied particularly to features of social behaviour, such as being hospitable, polite, sociable, family-conscious and community feeling.

TABLE 9.4 *Differences between the British pupils' image of Germany and the exchange groups' image before the journey*

Characteristic	E–D (N=339)	E–D (exchange group) (N=75)	D–D (N=246)
(a) *higher rating by the exchange group*			
hospitable	28	67	42
polite	32	69	24
good housewives	23	57	59
sociable	18	50	14
home-loving	28	54	57
family-conscious	27	53	28
clean	45	71	56
sport-loving	45	68	57
community feeling	21	42	48
(b) *lower rating by the exchange groups*			
glory-seeking	41	13	10
military nation	50	30	16
anti-semitic	41	20	16
skilled craftsmen	68	51	40
well built	62	50	29
good scientists	55	41	53

On the other hand Table 9.4 shows that negative characteristics were far less widespread with the exchange pupils than with other British pupils even before the journey. These include the characteristics glory-seeking, military nation and anti-semitic. It is interesting to note that German pupils think of these features as typical of the Germans during the Nazi era (Keller, 1969a). Thus they try to distance themselves from the past by having two distinct self-images, whereas the British pupils seem to have a concept of Germany as a single entity.

The differences between the views of Germany held by the exchange pupils and other British pupils may be explained in three different ways:

1. It is possible that the exchange pupils adopt a positive attitude towards the host country before they leave.

STEREOTYPES IN INTERCULTURAL COMMUNICATION

2. Since the exchange was voluntary it may be that the participants were predominantly pupils who already had a positive view of Germany.
3. The form of the test itself could have affected the results, as the pupils, in spite of their anonymity, were reluctant to underline negative traits when they were intending to visit the country.

The test revealed another surprise: after the journey the Scottish pupils' image of Germany had hardly changed. The only significant increases were in the percentage of pupils who thought that the style of education in German schools was liberal and of those who saw Germans as avid television watchers. In many other respects (talent for languages, polite, proud, hospitable, sociable, strong-willed, national pride, musical) the Scottish pupils rated the Germans more highly after their visit than the Germans did themselves (see Table 9.5).

TABLE 9.5 *Large distance between the British heterostereotype and the German autostereotype (after the journey)*

Characteristic	E−D (before) (N=75) %	E−D (after) (N=75) %	D−D (N=246) %
(a) *through lower dissemination of the British heterostereotype (E−D <D−D)*			
bureaucratic	17	8	62
beautiful women	13	5	59
poets and thinkers	11	5	52
good scientists	40	8	53
TV fans	8	30	68
anti-communists	38	33	69
tolerant	19	9	43
good doctors	21	13	43
brave	19	15	41
materially minded	15	23	53
(b) *through higher dissemination of the British heterostereotype (E−D>D−D)*			
talent for languages	57	70	28
polite	69	63	25
proud	56	49	17

Table 9.5 continued

Characteristic	E–D (before) (N=75) %	E–D (after) (N=75) %	D–D (N=246) %
hospitable	67	72	42
sociable	50	46	16
family-conscious	53	63	35
extremely patriotic	42	30	3
self-confident	40	55	28
strong-willed	58	46	22
national pride	76	54	31
hardy	44	42	20
musical	47	43	21
sport-loving	68	78	57

For the characteristics listed in Table 9.6 (skilled craftsmen, conscious of duty, liberal education, freedom-loving, hard-working, progressive) the British view of Germany and the German self-image were almost identical. The fact that there was evidence of only two significant changes should not lead one to the conclusion that school exchanges do not contribute to international understanding. Since fourteen features already differed significantly from the British view of Germany, the exchange had the effect of confirming the positive expectations about German social behaviour (e.g. hospitable, polite), while the negative traits were not observed.

Differences between the British view of Germany and the German self-image after the stay, however, suggest that there are still misunderstandings between the two nations. Some of them are due to the different views of characteristics that the British pupils see as typically German, such as strong-willed and self-confident. On the other hand only 9% of the pupils had gained the impression that the Germans were tolerant. In addition, the British pupils found that national pride was a typical German attitude – not part of the German self-image (Keller, 1969a).

Are Prejudices Reduced by an Exchange?

The tests carried out with a list of categories merely indicated certain trends in pupils' judgements, and did not enable us to establish whether

TABLE 9.6 *Little distance between the British heterostereotype and the German autostereotype (after the journey) (E−D=D−D)*

Characteristic	E−D (before) (N=75) %	E−D (after) (N=75) %	D−D (N=246) %
skilled craftsmen	51	39	40
well-built	50	36	38
conscious of duty	56	49	53
liberal education in schools	26	55	59
good housewives	57	55	59
community feeling	42	43	48
home-loving	54	63	57
clean	71	48	56
freedom-loving	32	45	57
progressive	40	28	41
intelligent	71	57	42
hard-working	82	63	48
cultured people	48	43	60

judgements about the foreign countries really became more discriminating. The accompanying teachers have always been struck by the fact that pupils who had just returned from an exchange visit too readily generalised their observations and held to their view with great conviction. In order to find out whether this phenomenon could be proved statistically the pupils were given a questionnaire in which they were asked to say whether they believed certain features to be typical of few, many, most or even all inhabitants of the foreign country (Keller, 1978).

The test gave us interesting insights into the development of the judgements during the stay abroad. As Table 9.7 shows, those pupils who observed correctly before the stay that it is impossible to make a judgement about *all* the people in any country unthinkingly tended to do so after the stay. They did so especially when they had noticed particular patterns of behaviour which conflicted with their expectations. Thus, for example, 51% of the German pupils thought that all the British were TV fans. Similarly, characteristics such as polite, disciplined, hospitable and national pride were generalised as can also be seen from the following quotations:

TABLE 9.7 *Numerical generalisation of the German heterostereotype by an overseas exchange (D−E)*

Characteristic	Most Before (N=101) %	Most After (N=93) %	All Before (N=101) %	All After (N=93) %
TV fans	28	31n.s.	6	51***
hospitable	43	60**	6	34**
good housewives	17	51***	1	0
home-loving	37	52n.s.	6	16***
sociable	36	59*	2	0
polite	48	52n.s.	4	14**
bound by tradition	45	52n.s.	12	23*
national pride	51	52n.s.	13	25*
class distinction	10	23**	7	4n.s.
animal-loving	42	44n.s.	7	14n.s.
disciplined	42	53n.s.	8	6n.s.

Significance levels: *** = 0.1; ** = 1.00; * = 5.0

TABLE 9.8 *Differentiation of the German image of Britain through an exchange visit*

Characteristic	Few Before (N=101) %	Few After (N=93) %	Many Before (N=101) %	Many After (N=93) %
gentleman	9	16n.s.	48	50n.s.
reserved	19	65***	42	29n.s.
reserved towards foreigners	48	76**	31	18**
uncommunicative	47	72*	42	24**
snobs	54	67n.s.	34	22*
thrifty	17	35**	53	45n.s.

Significance levels: *** = 0.1; ** = 1.00; * = 5.0

'The great hospitality of the Scots surprised me most of all. I used to have a completely different idea of them because in jokes and stories we think of the Scots as very thrifty.'

'Before I visited Scotland I had already heard a lot about British discipline but I had never imagined it would be so extreme. I had never thought it was possible that people queued like that for the bus or at the counter at the bank.'

Such generalisations often stem from misunderstandings as in the following:

'The national pride of the Scots was new and baffling to me. We were never allowed to use the word English, they would immediately tell us to call them British or Scottish. The ultimate goal of the Scots is to be independent from England. This struggle for independence and for a government of their own sometimes brings out an incredible hatred for the English, which I find difficult to understand'.

A different type of development, however, was evident in certain cases where prejudices seem to have been overcome. This occurred whenever participants' expectations of certain forms of behaviour had not been fully confirmed. From the German point of view, it happened particularly with relation to the 'gentleman ideal', as the following example illustrates: 'Before you visit Britain you always think the British are gentlemen. This was not confirmed for me; they were certainly no more polite than the people at home.' Other characteristics such as 'reserved towards foreigners' and the proverbial Scottish 'thriftiness' were similarly reduced in the Germans' eyes, as seen from the following judgements:

'"All Scots are very economical" – that's the typical German view of Scotland. Well, if it is true, they are economical in such a way that no-one notices. I didn't meet a single mean Scot; in fact, everywhere I found a generosity that is unknown at home.'

As a whole, however, the evidence shows that, contrary to widespread belief, there is a tendency to make even more generalised judgements after a trip abroad than before.

Perspectives for the Future

The work which has been presented here in English has been described and discussed in greater detail in the German articles cited in the text.

Conclusions drawn from this kind of enquiry can only be summarised here as a number of points for consideration by teachers and others who arrange foreign pupil exchanges:

1. In order to avoid unjustified generalisations abroad, pupils should be given the chance to meet representatives of different social groups (political parties, trade unions, age groups, denominations).
2. The foreign pupils should be integrated in the home school for a longer period of time so that they could learn to adjust to the foreign culture, and learn to understand it from its own perspectives (Keller, 1969 and 1964).
3. They need to acquire cultural competence which makes them aware of the fact that stereotypes are necessary to understand a culture but as they do not describe the complexity of modern societies adequately, the pupil should learn to modify them in accordance with his/her experience.
4. International empirical research on pedagogical decision-making and its influence on the attitudes of pupils is needed in order to promote a greater understanding of this significant dimension of foreign language teaching.

References

HOFSTÄTTER, P.R. 1960, *Das Denken in Stereotypen*. Göttingen: Hogrefe.
HOLZKAMP, K. 1959, Das Erlebnis des Verstandenwerdens von anderen Völkern. *Psychologie and Praxis* 169–78.
JAHODA, G. 1962, Development of Scottish children's ideas and attitudes about other countries. *Journal of Social Psychology*, 91–108.
—— 1963, The development of children's ideas about country and nationality. *British Journal of Educational Psychology*, 143–53.
KATZ, D. and BRALY, K.W. 1933, Racial stereotypes of 100 college students. *Journal of Abnormal and Social Psychology*, 280–90.
KELLER, G. 1964, Kulturkunde und internationale Erziehung im Dienste der Völkerverständigung. *Die Neueren Sprachen* 283–92.
—— 1968, Grundlegung der kulturkundlichen Didaktik durch ein sozialpsychologisches Modell der Völkerverständigung. *Die Neueren Sprachen* 617–26.
—— 1969a, Erkenntnisse der Sozialpsychologie als Grundlage der kulturkundlichen Didaktik. *Praxis des neusprachlichen Unterrichts* 261–81.
—— 1969b, Integration deutscher Schüler in den Englischunterricht britischer Schulen. *Die Neueren Sprachen*, 381–93.
—— 1969c, Die Funktion von Stereotypen beim Erkenntnisprozeß im kulturkundlichen Unterricht. *Die Neueren Sprachen*, 175–86.
—— 1970, Die Änderung kognitiver Urteilsstrukturen durch einen Auslandsaufenthalt. *Praxis des neusprachlichen Unterrichts*, 352–74.

―― 1979a, Die Auswirkungen eines Deutschlandaufenthaltes auf das Deutschlandbild britischer Schüler. *Die Neueren Sprachen,* 212–31.
―― 1979b, Werden Vorurteile durch einen Schüleraustausch abgebaut? In H. ARNDT & F.R. WELLER (eds) *Landeskunde und Fremdsprachenunterricht. Schule and Forschung.* pp. 130–50. Frankfurt: Diesterweg.
SODHI, K.S. and BERGIUS, R. 1953, *Nationale Vorurteile.* Berlin.
WOLF, H.E. 1963, *Schüler urteilen über fremde Völker.* Weinheim.

Appendix: List of Characteristics Used for the Questionnaire

1. talent for languages
2. good politicians
3. reliable
4. glory-seeking
5. decent
6. poor democrats
7. generous
8. cruel
9. well-built
10. conscious of duty
11. tolerant
12. materially minded
13. conventional
14. revanchists
15. unfaithful
16. exploiters
17. dirty
18. skilled craftsmen
19. cultured people
20. home-loving
21. not persevering
22. master nation
23. reserved
24. brave
25. polite
26. nation of farmers
27. boastful
28. quick-tempered
29. avoiding hard work
30. obstinate
31. mistrustful
32. animal-loving
33. top military nation
34. reserved with foreigners
35. community feeling
36. sport-loving
37. unreliable
38. over-industrious
39. religious intolerance
40. inhospitable
41. overestimation of foreigners
42. easy-living
43. poets and thinkers
44. artistic
45. love for children
46. just
47. servile
48. hardy
49. primitive
50. envious
51. charming
52. family-conscious
53. bureaucratic
54. unrestrained
55. vain
56. people of the future
57. gentlemen
58. intelligent
59. lazy
60. miserly
61. hypocrites
62. unaffected

63. national pride
64. unsophisticated
65. unsociable
66. world citizen
67. flatterer
68. conservative
69. credulous
70. uncultured
71. tactful
72. poor politicians
73. herd instinct
74. pleasure-seeking
75. hard to please
76. organisers
77. overeager to hold records
78. culture-conscious
79. beauty-loving
80. corruptible
81. persevering
82. cowardly
83. carefree
84. little courage of conviction
85. class-conscious
86. heroic
87. too trusting
88. slim
89. accepting authority
90. good democrats
91. zealous
92. idealists
93. good doctors
94. good technicians
95. philosophical attitude to life
96. affected
97. good educators
98. race-consciousness
99. poor
100. uneducated
101. comfort-loving
102. unemotional
103. easy to please
104. fanatical
105. individualists
106. rich
107. impulsive
108. anti-communists
109. thrifty
110. religious
111. inferiority complex
112. superstitious
113. clean
114. shrewd
115. people of extremes
116. stolid
117. extremely patriotic
118. willing to make sacrifices
119. wit
120. arrogant
121. hospitable
122. timid
123. intolerant
124. anti-semitic
125. fashionable
126. inconsiderate
127. belligerent
128. sociable
129. thorough
130. uncommunicative
131. comradeship
132. faithful
133. gallant
134. freedom-loving
135. lively
136. self-confident
137. petit bourgeois
138. easy-going
139. deceitful
140. unfathomable
141. liberal education in schools
142. loyal servants
143. dogmatic
144. snobs
145. good scientists
146. military nation

147. shallow
148. liberal family upbringing
149. slack
150. good housewives
151. brutal
152. sentimental
153. radical
154. disciplined
155. effeminate
156. nation of businessmen
157. without purpose
158. men of the world
159. awkward
160. unmilitary
161. emotional
162. vengeful
163. correct
164. class distinction
165. revolutionary
166. following instinct
167. dainty
168. strong-willed
169. decadent
170. TV fans
171. bound by tradition
172. proud
173. hard-working
174. progressive
175. sense of humour
176. beautiful women
177. musical
178. grateful

10 Developing Transcultural Competence: Case Studies of Advanced Foreign Language Learners

MEINERT MEYER

Introduction

In this chapter I will start with a definition of intercultural competence, and then identify three levels of intercultural communication and present some examples of how students of the German upper secondary stage behaved in communicative tasks which were offered them in a research project on foreign language learning (cf. Kordes in this volume). The presentation of the examples will fill the larger part of the chapter, but the reader should realise that they rely on more extensive case studies which cannot be presented here (cf. Meyer, 1986: 359–521). In my conclusion, I will try to show that intercultural competence is not a 'natural' or 'automatic' by-product of foreign language learning.

Definition of Intercultural Competence in Foreign Language Teaching

Wittgenstein asks in his *Philosophical Investigations:*

Denke, du kämst als Forscher in ein unbekanntes Land mit einer dir gänzlich fremden Sprache. Unter welchen Umständen würdest du sagen, daß die Leute dort Befehle geben, Befehle verstehen, befolgen, sich gegen Befehle auflehnen, usw?
[Imagine that, as a researcher, you were to go to a foreign country with a language totally alien to you. Under which circumstances would you say that the people there give orders, understand orders, follow them, revolt against them, etc?]

In the next sentence, he presents an answer himself:

DEVELOPING TRANSCULTURAL COMPETENCE

> Die gemeinsame menschliche Handlungsweise ist das Bezugssystem, mittels welchen wir uns eine fremde Sprache deuten. (Wittgenstein, 1960, 206)
> [The common human way of acting is the system of reference with the help of which we interpret a foreign language]

Wittgenstein is right. Whatever we do when we speak, our speaking is an integrated part of what we do non-verbally. And yet, if this were a simple thing, if our common human actions were a simple clue for foreign languages, there would be no intercultural misunderstanding. We would see what people do *and* say, and through this understand them. Obviously, this 'theory' of understanding is wrong, and foreign language teaching (FLT) has to cope with a more complex reality. We have to learn foreign languages *and* the cultures of the speakers of these languages, if we want to be successful in international communication.

I define intercultural competence as follows. Intercultural competence, as part of a broader foreign speaker competence, identifies the ability of a person to behave adequately and in a flexible manner when confronted with actions, attitudes and expectations of representatives of foreign cultures. Adequacy and flexibility imply an awareness of the cultural differences between one's own and the foreign culture and the ability to handle cross-cultural problems which result from these differences. Intercultural competence includes the capacity of stabilising one's self-identity in the process of cross-cultural mediation, and of helping other people to stabilise their self-identity.

In accordance with Wittgenstein's dictum, as I see it, definition of intercultural competence implies that action (*'Handlungsweise'*) and interpretation (*'Deutung'*) go hand in hand. The definition implies criticism of normal German *'Landeskunde'* (the study of the geography, history and institutions of the country concerned as part of FLT; cf. Kane in this volume). Normal foreign language teaching concentrates on the cultural differences between mother country and foreign country (countries) on a cognitive level. It fosters the students' awareness of cultural differences, but it does not systematically allow the students to learn to *act* in cross-cultural situations.

To some extent, the definition implies a criticism of *Landeskunde* and 'intercultural studies' as areas of research as well. Action is normally left out in these studies. But I find quite a few positions I can agree with. Take Baumgratz's recent paper on 'Transnational and cross-cultural communication as negotiation of meaning', for example. Baumgratz demands that pupils should learn to 'negotiate' *meaning* and that a good learning programme should 'not only develop mental capacities but should also provide learners with opportunities for participating successfully in real situations' (1985: 119). I believe this is right. One could even claim that students have to get these opportunities *in order to* develop their mental capacities. Baumgratz's definition of negotiation of meaning, however, does not explicate this aspect of intercultural understanding: 'Negotiating meaning ... is an emotionally influenced cognitive and communicative strategy accompanied by cultivated empathy on the part of a person or group of people really trying to get in touch with foreign reality' (1985: 121).

It may be that my criticism is just a quarrel over words. Most probably, Baumgratz would accept that communication means communication in real intercultural situations. You have to have something to bargain about, you have to have a real problem, you have to come along with a result. The inclusion of action as an integrated part of learning is in accord with a long tradition in educational theory. Take, for example, John Dewey's definition of learning as the growth of experience. Dewey criticises the 'fundamental fallacy' in instruction which lies in supposing that experience on the part of pupils may be assumed. He demands actual empirical situations as 'the initiating phase of thought' (Dewey, 1916: 153). So let us turn to this aspect of FLT.

Communicative Tasks for Students of the Upper Secondary Stage

In the College School (a vocational and general education institution for 16- to 19-year-old students) foreign language project of North Rhine-Westfalia, we constructed semi-formal, interlingual and cross-cultural scenarios in which German students of the upper secondary stage were asked to take over the role of a mediator between a German and a foreigner. The German students were asked to interpret between the Germans and their guests, to show their partner where they saw cases of misunderstanding and to find solutions for the problems they were confronted with.

The communicative tasks which we gave to the students consisted of a written and an oral part. The written part was to be done in about four hours. The oral part proper took from 20 minutes up to one hour, depending on the communicative competence and co-operation of the students, not counting the preparation time and the feedback after the performance. The performance itself was copied on cassettes, and evaluated. All the examples of student performance which I give below are taken from the oral part. Table 10.1 gives information concerning the tasks

DEVELOPING TRANSCULTURAL COMPETENCE 139

the students were given. There was a test in the 11th, and in the 12th, and in the 13th grade of the College School, and in other types of schools which we studied for comparison.

TABLE 10.1

	Written part	Oral part
1st year	Writing letters etc. in preparation for the invitation of a German class to the 30th anniversary of an English school.	Mediating between the mother of a German host family and an English student visiting the family. Topics: School uniforms, military service and conscientious objection, and others.
2nd year	Preparing business letters and private correspondence between a German and an American business partner. Topics: A wine deal breaks down; the partners quarrel about bussing and de-segregation in the USA and Germany.	Mediating between the German mother and the English guest student. Topics: School life and German and English food.
3rd year	Producing a text for a German school magazine. Topics: The North–South conflict and problems of Nigeria in particular; integrated tasks such as selling an advertisement in order to raise money for the magazine, etc.	Mediating between the head of the German school and a Nigerian exchange student who does not want to modify an interview he has given for the school magazine. Topic: The exploitation of the South and the role of the missionaries in colonialisation.

One might argue that the scenarios did not produce 'real' intercultural situations because they took place at school. I would admit that, but I would stress that the scenarios were very realistic in so far as the German players and their English-speaking guests were native speakers of different languages who did play their parts convincingly. So the German students whose intercultural competence we wanted to evaluate had to play *themselves*; they were confronted with real situations of intercultural conflict. Thus they had a real chance for intercultural mediation.

The evaluation of the written and oral parts of the communicative tasks of the students relied on the definition and distinction of four dimensions of foreign language competence: an *interlingual dimension* proper, identifying the command of linguistic material and the use of this material in communication; the *intercultural dimension,* which we discuss in this paper; a *professional dimension* concentrating not only on commerical correspondence, but on action in language in general; and an *analytic dimension* concentrating on what is normally done in the German upper secondary stage – text interpretation, analysis, grammar, argumentation, and so on.

Using Keller's (1987) concept of cultural hetero- and autostereotypes as a starting point, we built in the following intercultural problems in the three oral mediation tasks:

1st year: British and German stereotype of the hard-working and disciplined German; German heterostereotype of the conservative, old-fashioned English student, wearing school uniforms, etc.
2nd year: Heterostereotype of the well-behaved German and heterostereotype of the English student who cannot come to terms with life in a German family.
3rd year: Autostereotype of the good German missionary and heterostereotype of the uncivilised black African.

Let me point out two things relating to our use of Keller's approach. Firstly, as we see it, his methodology allows us to identify only a cognitive and – to some extent – a reflective dimension of intercultural understanding (see, for example, Keller, 1987 and his chapter in this volume). If students are confronted with a list of 'qualities' which they have to apply both to their own and to foreign countries, this allows a broad influence of uncontrolled associations on the evaluative results. Words are not yet sentences, they do no yet reach the level of thought and sentences are not yet communicative acts. So we could not accept Keller's methodology, though we did make explicit use of his concept of auto- and heterostereotypes.

Secondly, let me anticipate a possible criticism by Keller concerning our approach. We did not depend on a solution of the question whether the stereotypes brought in by us were the 'correct' ones. I can imagine that Keller would ask whether there really is a heterostereotype of the English student as one who cannot behave abroad, or he might question whether there really is a German autostereotype of a good missionary. However, this does not devalue our scenarios because we brought in 'real', living English, American and Nigerian role players. They had to try to win the Germans over to their side. For example, the German mother in the second oral scenario tried to convince the students that the English guests must eat German food, while the English guests tried to convince the German students that they couldn't accept this. The German headmaster in the third oral scenario had to convince the German students that the Nigerian's interview in a school magazine was biased and had to be changed, while the Nigerian student explained why he could not change a single word of his interview.

As we see it, intercultural behaviour and cross-cultural understanding cannot be separated.

Levels of Intercultural Performance

If intercultural action and understanding are tasks one has to learn, it is necessary, both for evalutive research and for learning programmes, to identify levels of performance in intercultural tasks. The evaluative questions steering such an evaluation may be: To what degree does a learner manage to understand a foreign way of life, foreign institutions, a foreign culture? Does he manage to clear up misunderstandings in intercultural transactions? Can he reduce biased or prejudiced conceptions concerning other people, and can he build up a more adequate conception of his own culture in contrast to foreign cultures? Can he build up the role of a mediator without coming in conflict with his own cultural identity? Is he able to realise that his own behaviour may come in conflict with the norms and everyday convictions of the people he has to deal with? Can he develop communicative strategies which are sensitive to cultural differences?

If we ask for degrees and levels of intercultural performance in this way, we must accept a zero-level, a starting point, for behaviour and for learning. On such a level, learners will communicate, but they show no awareness of the fact that they communicate with people who belong to a foreign culture. Consequently, they are not able to solve intercultural problems. We can then contrast this zero-position with what we consider to be the ideal, a highest level of intercultural performance. Between zero and the optimum of thinking and behaviour, we have the long road of intercultural learning, ways of thinking and behaviour which demonstrate that students build up an understanding of foreign cultures which goes beyond simple realisation of differences and which demonstrate techniques of intercultural negotiation and mediation.

I therefore define a monocultural, an intercultural, and a transcultural level of performance (once more, compare Kordes in this volume for a parallel approach):

> *Monocultural level*: The learner uses behavioural schemes and demonstrates ways of thinking which are merely adequate for his own culture, and he does so in situations which demand cross-cultural activity and understanding. The learner's concepts relating to foreign cultures are stereotyped, cliché-ridden and ethnocentric. Problems arising in interaction are solved in ways adequate among fellow countrymen and women, not in intercultural situations.

The identification and definition of a monocultural level is comparatively easy. Such a level must exist if intercultural competence is something one has to learn. The concrete evaluation of a particular case of interaction and communication as belonging to this level is much more difficult. It might well be that at the very moment of the interview, the student does something else which makes sense for him in interaction and that he is well aware of an intercultural problem without explicitly stating it as such. Therefore it should be clear that the identification of levels of competence depends on *more than one* demonstration of performance at a particular level. It demands a complex system of evaluative findings.

> *Intercultural level*: The learner is able to explain cultural differences between his own and the foreign cultures because he can make use of information he has acquired concerning his and the foreign countries, or because he is able to ask for information in relation to cross-cultural differences. The information he has may be of historical, sociological, psychological or economic nature, etc. Putting it metaphorically, one could say that the learner stands between the cultures.

The learners' method of solving intercultural problems can be best characterised as *sic-et-non method*. Here, in Germany, things are such and such (*'sic'*), but over there, in Great Britain, or wherever, things are different (*'non'*). The method refers to a famous medieval scholar, Petrus Abelardus, who thus described a means of scholastic argumentation and

DEVELOPING TRANSCULTURAL COMPETENCE

learning (compare Henningsen, 1974: 43–54). The learners realise differences of behaviour and attitudes between the cultures they are confronted with, the foreign as opposed to their own culture, and they are able to explicate these differences, at least to some extent. But a strategy of problem-solving by mediation and negotiation does not yet exist. If the students are successful in solving the tasks they are confronted with then their solution depends on good luck, on trial and error, or on empathy and good will on their part and that of the players, the Germans and their foreign counterparts.

> *Transcultural level*: The learner is able to evaluate intercultural differences and to solve intercultural problems by appeal to principles of international co-operation and communication which give each culture its proper right and which allow the learner to develop his own identity *in the light of* cross-cultural understanding. He is able to negotiate meaning where negotiation is possible. Speaking metaphorically, one can say that the learner stands above both his own and the foreign culture, but it should be clear that this does not mean a 'cosmopolitan neglect' of his own culture.

The highest level of intercultural performance can be formulated and understood with reference to Kohlberg's stages of moral consciousness. Here the principles of behaviour and understanding and the norms of interaction and justice are involved (Kohlberg 1981, 1984).

Principles of cross-cultural activity might be:

- Be tolerant concerning deviant world-views and conceptions!
- Be co-operative concerning the resolution of misunderstanding!
- Be undogmatically universalistic!

All three principles pose problems. The first principle demands that you be more tolerant to a foreigner than to your neighbour. The second tends to camouflage the fact that misunderstanding is often the result of substantial conflicts of economic, political or historical nature. The last principle is the most problematic one. Does one have to have a 'global' view in order to be on a level of intercultural understanding and behaviour which we can consider to be desirably high? I'm not sure about that. The principle may be culturally prejudiced. Americans might take it for granted while smaller nations might oppose it, for example. Americans are more willing to accept a world-view with them as world power number one in the centre while the Dutch and the Danish, to mention two smaller nations, tend to foster diversity and difference. Yet, there must be something universally 'humane' even if we have problems in defining it. Otherwise, intercultural understanding would be nothing but a dream.

Let me add that Kohlberg has been criticised because levels of moral consciousness do not necessarily identify levels of moral performance. It should be clear from my argumentation that intercultural understanding without appropriate performance cannot be accepted as performance at the highest level.

Student Performance in Intercultural Tasks

Presumably, the reader of this chapter has been convinced by now that I present my case in a typically German, monocultural way: a system of definitions, propounded and defended. Let me therefore back up my definitions by some case studies.

Ruth Kick (all names are pseudonyms) was an upper secondary stage student who had considerable problems. She nearly failed the A-level (*Abitur*) although she had made very considerable effort to learn English. In the first year of the sixth form, she had many interlingual and intercultural problems, but while the interlingual problems lessened in the course of time, the intercultural problems remained. So, in a sense, one could have left out the intercultural dimension in the analysis of her development, without any problems arising in the analysis of the other dimensions. Ruth understood intercultural tasks as tasks which had to be solved monoculturally.

In the first task, for the 11th grade, one of the problems discussed was military service and conscientious objection, as indicated above. We linked this problem with 'school uniforms'. The Germans had school uniforms – at least school caps were normal – at grammar school, in the Weimar Republic, and before. But they were completely abandoned in West Germany after World War II. A normal youth of the 'Gymnasium' will most likely be insensitive concerning the intercultural difference. He or she will consider school uniforms not to be fashionable. They are out-dated. They stand for British tradition. Furthermore, he or she will consider conscientious objection as something normal, as legitimate, even as necessary. And many girls will tend to avoid the topic altogether. They are not involved. Therefore, if a West German grammar school student is to be interculturally competent he/she should be sensitive concerning the fact that such a position is not normal, is not considered legitimate in many other countries, among them the United States and Great Britain. We do

DEVELOPING TRANSCULTURAL COMPETENCE 145

know that the Nazi regime and the outcome of World War II are closely connected with this cultural difference. We, the Germans, have been the attackers, while the British and the other allies could understand themselves as the people under attack.

In her argumentation, Ruth did not respond to this problem. One could say that she managed to produce a 'pragmatic' solution to her problem in the dialogue with the German mother and her English guest student: school uniforms are something she does not like. But she could only state this fact; she could not give reasons.

Remaining at a monocultural level

In the following extract, one can see this student behaviour. Conversation starts when the English student says she wants to go to the German school, together with her German partner.

English student: Oh, he will certainly notice me. I have only my ordinary street clothes and no uniform.
Ruth: Sie meint, ah, sie hat nicht die die Schuluniform, ne, weil in England da ah müssen die ah Schüler Uniformen tragen in der Schule.
German mother: Wieso Schuluniform? Der Lehrer wird dich höchstens bemerken, wenn er dein gutes Englisch hört, was in dieser Klasse 'ne Seltenheit ist. Aber was meint sie mit Schuluniform?
Ruth: Ah, soll ich erst jetzt übersetzen?
German mother: Ja frag sie mal!
Ruth: What do you mean with school uniforms?
English student: In England we all wear uniforms and it's easy to see to which school the pupils belong by the school uniform.
Ruth: Hm, in England tragen sie alle Schuluniformen und so ist es auch einfacher zu erkennen, ah, zu welcher Schule man gehört.
German mother: Ah so ja, in Deutschland ist das ganz anders. Hier kann jeder so zur Schule gehen, wie es ihm gefällt.
Ruth: Ah, in Germany it's, ah, it's not so strict like in England, ah, here, ah everybody can go to school like, ah, how he wants.
English student: Oh really?
Ruth: You can wear what you wants [want]!

Ruth's solution of her mediating task is inadequate because her communication partners cannot understand why there are school uniforms in one country but not in the other. We do not learn what the reason for this difference is though, of course, Ruth is aware of the difference.

One year later, in the 12th grade, Ruth's attitude and behaviour is unchanged. The intercultural problem is defined as a problem of 'pressure', of teacher–student interaction:

English student: Aha, yes I can see how that would be, how she would connect that, but how do you feel about it?
Ruth: I don't know, but, ah, I think I wouldn't like it to wear uniforms, because I never did it and it would be, ah [Pause], I think *it would be a little bit pressure*, because, ah, you, ah, you have to, em ah, with the uniforms, ah, to show, ah, from which school you are and if you do something wrong everybody can see it, ah, that it's someone from that school, ah and ah, the school becomes, ah, the school gets a, ah, a bad, ah, call.
English student: A bad reputation ...
Ruth: Ja, reputation.
English student: Aha, yes it does, it ah ...
Ruth: I'm talking only with you, she doesn't know anything.
English student: Yes, em, tell her ah what you said.
Ruth: Ah, also ich würd' nicht gern 'ne Uniform tragen, weil, ah hm, jetzt weiß ich nicht mehr, was ich gesagt hab, ah, *weil ah, es wohl irgendwie em, irgendwie ein bißchen Stress würd' ich sagen*, ich hab' das auch vorher noch nie gemacht, ne, und das ist auch ungewohnt dann für mich und, ah, was hab' ich denn noch gesagt? [Pause]
[Author's note on italicised text: the intercultural difference treated as teacher–student conflict]

The problem of intercultural difference becomes more urgent in a later part of the scenario where the dialogue partners ask the German student to explain her/his attitude towards military service and conscientious objection proper. Ruth's monocultural way of thinking and problem-solving does not change:

English student: You know, I was surprised to see that you don't wear uniforms at school. Why not?
Ruth: Yes, in Germany there are other, em, it's not like in England, em, because we don't have to wear, eh, uniforms and, eh, I think it's not, it's only popular eh, in England to wear school uniforms.
English student: But I always thought Germans like uniforms?
[Note: presentation of a British hetero-cliché]
Ruth: Why?
English student: Well, eh, you know, in the army or in the navy, a friend of yours told me this morning that your boys have to join the army

when they are 18 and we don't have that in England. I think that's a lot better. If someone doesn't like to wear uniforms then they still have to when they join the army.
Ruth: Yes, in the army they have to but I think *they don't like it very much*.
[Note: monocultural interpretation]
English student: Eh, what did the boys do, eh, in Germany when they don't want to join the army?
Ruth: Yes, they can, em, hm, they don't have to go to the army. They also can, em, do other things, like working in a hospital, or, em, in a house for old people.
English student: Hm, what do you think is the best thing to do?
Ruth: Oh, I don't know.
English student: To join the army or to work in a hospital?
Ruth: Em, I don't like to, eh, *I wouldn't like to go to the army because*, eh, most people, em, come from school or are eh, don't have worked for a long time in a, eh, in a factory and, eh, *they lose a lot of money* by going to the army because, em, they only get, eh, two hundred Marks there per month.
[Note: Ruth demonstrates a 'financial solution' for a moral question.]
English student: I see, they get paid. Em, but if they, if they don't join the army and they work in a hospital like you said did they still get paid?
Ruth: Yes, I think so but I don't know that.
English student: I see. I still think the situation in England is better where they don't have to go to the army if they don't want to.
Ruth: Yes, that's the same opinion like mine.

One could argue in Ruth's favour that she did not know about British schools, but the German topic *Bundeswehr* and military service is something she should have been informed about. But here, too, her role in the mediating task is inadequate. Though it is true that one cannot earn much money in the German army, this fact is not the real problem when one talks about military service and conscientious objection. The real problem is whether we, as Germans, have a right to let other people, the British among others, do the military 'work' leaving us out; the real problem is whether NATO and the Warsaw Pact are the best means for peace in Europe or not.

If we could go through all the tasks which Ruth did in our evaluation, it would become obvious that she could only formulate a personal opinion *in the light of* the opinion expressed by her dialogue partners. She always looked for the position of the others in order to ask herself whether she could agree or not. And whenever she did not know what to say, she tried to reduce her mediating role to the role of a simple translator (interpreter in the technical sense) of what was going on. Sometimes she even went below this level by cheating a little. This became obvious at the end of the second oral interview when her English guest student asked her: 'I hope I wasn't too impolite. Do you think I said the wrong thing?' And Ruth's answer was: 'Oh, I think, it wasn't e, em, not everything was very nice you said but *I didn't translate everything.*' Ruth tried, in vain, to solve her intercultural task with the help of omissions and corrections. She was not competent enough to analyse the intercultural differences. She could not develop and communicate her own position to her partners, she could not negotiate meaning because she always tried to understand and accept the position of her partners. In spite of her urgent desire to be in agreement with them, she could not show them *how* they could come to an agreement with her. She could not show a self-profile which would allow her partners to accept her as a person. This becomes clearer when we contrast Ruth's behaviour with the role other students played in the same communicative tasks.

Moving towards intercultural level

Nichol-Udo Bock, a comprehensive school student, tried to compare the German and the English tradition. He points to the fact that prefabricated, stereotyped pictures of the others have to be rejected, but he is not yet able to explicate his position in the foreign language in such a way that the English guest student can understand him. This becomes clear when we hear his own interpretation of what he has said in English, in his mother tongue:

Nicol-Udo: Er meint also, die Deutschen wären also die, die meist disziplinierten und am härtesten arbeitenden Leute auf der ganzen Welt.
[Note: introduction of stereotype by the English student in preceding conversation]
German mother: Na, wenn das so ist, dann sind die meisten meiner Freunde aber Zugewanderte, von meinen Kindern erst mal ganz zu schweigen. Aber was er da gesagt hat, halte ich fur ein Vorurteil.
Nicol-Udo: Ah, she thinks, ah, that the most of her friends and her family members have to, ah, are not from Germany, they've come from abroad or something like that, because they don't like very much working and discipline.
English student: I see!
Nicol-Udo: And she thinks that, ah, only what you just said *it's only the*

German out of a book. You can read of him as disciplined and he's always working and . . .

English student: What do you mean with 'out of a book?'

Nicol-Udo: You can read that in history books or something like that. This people say so, ah, your father said the Germans are disciplined and work all day and so on.

English student: But you're saying it's not true?

Nicol-Udo: It's not true. *You've also in England such types of people.* Ich hab 'also gerad' gesagt, also, es gibt, ah, also *praktisch so'n Bilderbuchdeutscher,* wie man also in Geschichtsbüchern nachlesen kann, vielleicht in England, und daß das also so überliefert wird, vielleicht der Vater sagt, die Deutschen sind so und so, und, ah, das versteht er jetzt so langsam.

English student: So well, she thinks it's some preconception and, but – ah, do you agree with that?

Nicol-Udo: Yeah, I think so, because there are always different people. Ah, some people like to work and others like to have free and so on, and sleep all day. *I think this type of people is always also in England . . .*

English student: In every country, yes.

Nicol-Udo: *I've seen such people in England.*

[Note italicised text: Rejection of stereotype and differentiation]

Nicol-Udo himself uses metaphoric language which his English guest cannot understand when he says that the 'disciplined and always working German' is 'out of a book'. But he has a clear understanding of a difference between reality and prejudice, and he has his own opinion; he can show self-identity which allows his partner to respond to him.

Another student in our sample, Judith Kick, shows a behaviour and understanding similar to that of Nicol-Udo Bock, but she goes one step further. When she is confronted with the cliché that the Germans are disciplined and hard-working, she reacts with a counter-argument.

Judith: Ehm, she can't believe that German pupils are more disciplin*ate* than eh Eng. . .

English student: Disciplined, yeah!

Judith: Yes, than, ehm, English pupils and, ehm, as far as I *knew* [know] *each German thinks that,* ehm, *the English pupils are more disciplined because they are very conservative and ehm old fashioned.*

[Note: identification of a heterostereotype]

English student: Yes but there is a little bit much to say. The Germans, right, are meant to be, are said to be the most disciplined and most hard-working people in the world. It's a fact, isn't it? It's well known.

Judith: Also er meint wiederum, daß die Deutschen das eh am härtesten arbeitende Volk überhaupt wären and daß sie sehr diszipliniert und ordentlich und all so was wären, also *die ganzen Vorurteile tischt er uns jetzt hier auf*, nicht?

German mother: Ja, das ist also richtig, wenn das so ist, dann sind die meisten meiner Bekannten Zugewanderte – von meinen Kindern ganz zu schweigen! Also, ich halte das Ganze auch für ein Vorurteil.

Judith: Yeah, she agrees with me that this are only prejudices because ehm as far as we can see the whole situation most Germans we know wouldn't be German if they have to be the way you think. There are the children and ehm all the pupils are very, eh, loud and ehm funny and *I think the whole school situation is not so strict as in England.*
[Note: intercultural comparison]

At the end of the interview, Judith gives a comment with which she shows she has made more out of the conflict between the different cultures – school uniforms there, no uniforms here – for herself. She reaches a self-reflective, transcultural level of argumentation:

> Ehm, eh she thinks that it's only ehm, a sort of a possibility of *compare* [comparing] it but ehm, she can't explain what she *mean* [means]; it's not so easy for us and eh then she asked me what I think about the whole situation and if you ask me I ehm have to tell you that I wouldn't like to wear a school uniform because I don't like being uniformed! Is it possible? Because, ehm, everybody looks like, eh, the others and, ehm, I don't like that everybody wears the same clothes outside. *If you look outside you can see that most teenagers wear the same clothes and this is also a form of being a soldier.*

Judith realises that the German students reject school uniforms with the argument that they don't want to be 'uniformed'. However, they themselves are 'uniformed', as far as their clothes are concerned, and – of course – in their behaviour in general. She draws the conclusion that she herself has a right to dress individualistically; she justifies her individuality in intercultural comparison.

Demonstrating intercultural competence and performance

My last and longest example for intercultural performance is an interview with a College School student, Silvia Kick, in her last year.

DEVELOPING TRANSCULTURAL COMPETENCE 151

The conflict she is confronted with is the North–South conflict; to be more precise, it is a dispute between a German headmaster and a Nigerian exchange student who has given an interview for the school magazine which the headmaster cannot accept. The German student, Silvia, is asked to find a compromise. Being the school magazine editor, she wants to have the Nigerian's interview printed, but the headmaster rejects this because he is convinced that it is very one-sided and full of prejudice concerning the role of the white missionaries in black Africa. A solution of the conflict can only be reached if the German student, the interpreter, develops and expresses her own position in the conflict. She must do this because the headmaster and the Nigerian student do not give any help in finding a solution; they stick to the instructions they have in their scenario. The student has been given the information that the headmaster doesn't understand English and that the Nigerian student doesn't understand German.

Silvia starts with an *ad hoc* translation of a letter in which the headmaster, Dr Kirchmann, expounds his position concerning the disputed interview for the school magazine. The missionaries were not the forerunners of the colonists who exploited Africa. They did not 'steal the African's gold', it was just the opposite, they were full of good will and they helped the Africans. After that, Aka Amuam, the Nigerian exchange student, reinforces his own position:

Amuam: Well, your headmaster wrote my, that my position was rather biased and one-sided ...
Silvia: ... yes, in a way ...
Amuam: ... in a way ...
Silvia: ... perhaps.
Amuam: Let me say something in a, for a moment. I rather say it's realistic. I remember the interview for your school magazine 'The Machtwächter'. You asked me if I had a grudge against Christianity.
Sylvia: Yes.
Amuam: And I told you 'yes' as well as 'no'!
Sylvia: Yes.
Amuam: Could you please translate to him?
Silvia: Ja, also er sagt, ehm, er kritisiert 'n bißchen, daß Sie meinen, er wäre absolut einseitig und undifferenziert in seiner Ansicht. Er findet es absolut realistisch, was er gesagt hat, weist aber auch darauf hin, daß er zu der Frage, ob er jetzt 'n Vorurteil gegen Christentum hat, gesagt hat, 'ja' *und* 'nein'.
Kirchmann: Ja, em, gut, aber er hat ja behauptet, die Missionäre hätten den Afrikanern ihr Gold gestohlen. Das ist eine Aussage, die ich nicht verstehen kann.

Silvia: Ja, ehm, he, ehm, asks again about your opinion or about your statement that the missionaries have stolen, yes, stolen your, eh, gold, ah, you had. And this is a statement, eh, he doesn't hm ...
Amuam: ... understand ...
Sylvia: ... yes, understand, is allright.
Amuam: Yes, you know there was a quotation from a novel ...
Silvia: Yes.
Amuam: ... which say, education is like gold ...
Silvia: Yes.
Amuam: ... for gold is never found on the surface of the soil.
Silvia: Yes.
Amuam: The missionaries were the first people who came to Nigeria but it was the European in general who exploited us and are still exploiting us. *Could you please translate.*
Silvia: *So you see the missionaries* as, ehm, *messengers in a way for the exploitation which came afterwards?*
[Note: Silvia's first rejection of her job as mere translator]
Amuam: Yeah.
Silvia: Oh, I see. Also, ehm, er setzt Reichtümer, Gold und so, wenn ich das richtig verstanden habe, so mit Erziehung gleich, und er sagt, die Missionare wären die ersten, die jetzt gekommen sind, ehm, sind, die nach Nigeria gekommen sind und danach kamen eben die Ausbeuter, europäischen Ausbeuter, wie er es sieht, die sie ausgebeutet haben und das auch heute noch machen. Er bezeichnet also die Missionare oder betrachtet die Missionare als Vorläufer oder auch Boten ...

After this introduction, many aspects of the topic are discussed. Silvia manages to build up her own position in this discussion; she soon abandons the role of a simple translator (interpreter). She accepts the headmaster's position that one should not identify the missionaries with the other whites who colonised and exploited Africa. A long discussion about the qualities and deficiencies of the school system which the missionaries brought to Africa follows. The headmaster stresses that the missionaries gave their best, while the Nigerian student points to the fact that the missionaries' schools destroyed the African culture and that they did not bring what the Africans needed most: technical know-how in order to make use of the natural resources which Africa has.

The last minutes of the interview then pass as follows:

Amuam: Well, I'm sorry to say it, *my forefathers were slaves,* now it's no more open slavery but industrialising us, using us, exploiting us. I am the new generation who's to change everything. For this very reason *I*

can't change a single word from my article, because if I allow it, then I'll become the same generation who is still under exploitation. It is now in my own generation whereby I have to see that things are changing. You see, from slavery, no more slavery.
[Note: Amuam brings in his final and toughest argument]
Silvia: Oh, but I think, eh, it's easy . . .
Amuam: I have to, I have to stick to my opinion. I can't change a single word.
Silvia: *Yes, you can tell your opinion.*
[Note: Silvia accepts Amuam's position and defines herself as independent mediator]
Kirchmann: Es tut mir furchtbar leid. Ich muß Sie unterbrechen. Ich muß in 'ner viertel Stunde zu 'ner Konferenz, und, eh, wir müssen schon schnell zu 'ner Einigung kommen.
Silvia: Ja (lacht), ich versuche mein Bestes, ihn zu überzeugen, weil ich Ihren Vorschlag, sich vorsichtiger auszudrücken, also, auch für gut halte. Vielleicht könnte man, ehm, den Text, den er jetzt, das Interview, das Original, eh, vielleicht trotzdem behalten und für Oberstufe als Diskussionsstoff geben, dann käme er also dazu, seine persönliche Meinung ohne Abstriche zu sagen und für die Schülerzeitung kann man's ja eventuell 'n bißchen sanfter formulieren, damit eben die Kleinen nicht so einseitig da gepolt werden.
Kirchmann: *Gut, wenn er dazu bereit ist.*
[Note: the headmaster accepts Silvia's compromise.]
Silvia: Das wäre vielleicht . . .
Kirchmann: Das finde ich ja wunderbar.
Silvia: . . . 'ne Möglichkèit.
Kirchmann: Ja.
Silvia: Ja, so the proposition is . . .
Kirchmann: Hm, dann kann ich mich verabschieden, wenn das alles klar ist.
Silvia: Ja, wenn Sie damit einverstanden sind, gut.
Kirchmann: Wunderbar, gut. Herr Amuam, vielen Dank, es hat mich sehr gefreut, Sie kennenzulernen. Fräulein Kick, auf Wiedersehen. Sie können gern noch 'n bißchen bleiben, wenn Sie wollen, sich 'n bißchen unterhalten.
Silvia: Ja, ehm, I proposed now that you, ehm, *this interview will be kept in his original form* as it is with your words, with your opinion all this, but, eh, and this interview will be given as subject for discussion for the elder people, who are able to differentiate, who certainly understand your position but who also take other, eh, positions into consideration, and for the little children . . .
Amuam: *Okay, I accept that.*

Silvia: We, ah, ...
Amuam: Well, well Silvia, that was a hard discussion ...
Silvia: [laughing]
Amuam: ... wasn't it?
Silvia: Yes.

Silvia is able to find a solution to the conflict. This solution has to be a compromise, but this compromise is the result of an analytic, argumentative evaluation of the problems under discussion. It is not the result of one-sided argumentation, and of course, it is not the result of her telling one side something different from what she tells the other side, or of simply leaving things out as Ruth did. Silvia manages to combine two tasks, the task of finding the truth and of finding a compromise in a conflict which is intercultural.

A task which she could not accomplish in her interview (or of which we do not know to what extent she was successful) is the last and final consequence of our definition of transcultural competence. If she manages to help the German headmaster to find *his* identity as educator responsible for a German school in the light of the North–South conflict, and if she helps the Nigerian exchange student to find *his* identity, this would be excellent. One can see, however, how difficult this task would be. Aka Amuam, the Nigerian student, rejects the Western influence in his country, and at the same time he comes to Europe because he has to accept that the Europeans are superior to his countrymen in many questions of schooling, university education, technological development etc. His self-identity is extremely unbalanced, compared with the identity the headmaster reveals. But the headmaster is at home. So his rejection of the African's position doesn't have pressing consequences for him. He cannot accept that the Africans want their own, un-Christian, culture. It is apparent that Silvia is well aware of this intercultural conflict. When Aka Amuam says that his forefathers were sold as slaves and that he therefore has to see to it that things are changed, she accepts his position. 'You can tell your opinion', and we could add, in brackets: 'because this is necessary for your identity as an African studying in Europe'.

I can come now to my final point.

Developmental Tasks and Intercultural Competence

The case studies I have presented show that Ruth has not managed to solve the *developmental task* which she was confronted with in our evaluation, as far as the intercultural dimension of this task is concerned. One can say that Nicol-Udo and Judith followed the right path and that Silvia has demonstrated an intercultural competence which fulfils the definition of the highest level we wish to adhere. But, it is an open question whether the learning process, the development, which the four students reveal is the result of formal instruction. I have my doubts in this respect. It would appear that developing intercultural competence depends on learning situations and qualifications which cannot be taught, as long as school itself does not provide the learners with 'opportunities for participating successfully in real situations,' as Gisela Baumgratz has put it.

This makes it necessary to offer a few final comments on the concept of developmental tasks introduced by Havighurst (1972) in educational theory. Learning is not defined as the acquisition of isolated skills and knowledge of a subject, but as the development of the ability and readiness to solve *subjectively meaningful assignments* in the light of the *objective demands* society has to make on the next generation. Havighurst assumes that learning takes place in the tug-of-war between objective demands and subjective possibilities. Society presents the students with demands they cannot master at their current levels of competence; nor with the objectives they already know. They try to meet these demands, and exactly this is their learning process. They reach higher levels of competence. Therefore, it is most important that the assignments and tasks they are given are personally acceptable to them, and that they are at the same time subjectively meaningful to them and adequate from the adult point of view.

One important developmental task in adolescence is the preparation for an economic career (Havighurst, 1972: 43ff.). Students will start to learn once they see that what they have to do is good for this career, not because it fosters their selfishness, but because this is what society expects them to do. Some students will see a professional opportunity in foreign languages. They like them and they have previously had success in these subjects in school. They will identify with this part of the adult world. But this identification process is difficult and risky: think of unemployment, think of the uncertainty of long years of study. The conflicts and controversies of society are reflected in the developmental tasks of the students and in their subjective courses of education.

What then is the developmental situation for students of the German upper secondary stage who decide that they want to prepare for an economic career in the field of foreign languages? How can they bring together the demands of society relating to international communication, business activities, etc., with their own subjective perspective of meaningful studies?

A positive answer to this question is difficult. But there is a much easier negative answer concerning the status quo of the upper secondary stage. The curriculum which such students are confronted with, in the different types of the upper secondary stage, demands that they deal with a host of problems in *all* dimensions of a global foreign language competence throughout their learning time. They have to develop interlingual competence, cross-cultural understanding, professional competence and the ability to analyse language and to interpret texts, all at the same time. This is so because classroom instruction is dominated by the so-called direct method – instruction using the foreign language throughout – and because the teachers embody for the students the ideal competence of a near-native speaker, even in those cases where the teacher's competence might be criticised as deficient by more experienced and further advanced colleagues.

Our findings concerning the College School curriculum suggest that in this learning situation, the majority of the students try to identify fixed tasks or isolated dimensions of the complex whole as a starting point. Our students did not accept the overall approach as demanded by the curriculum and presented by the teachers. They isolated the learning task into 'handy bits', quite in accord with Havighurst's model, and by that developed their individual profile:

- Students understood their foreign language course of education as a demand to develop their own interlingual abilities as far as possible. In striving for accuracy in the foreign language, however, they for the most part separated the language and difficulties in learning it from those problems and questions in the texts that they were supposed to discover and work out. They took the means as an end.
- Other students were enthusiastic about the real confrontation with the ways of other countries, a confrontation which was always reinforced by contact with 'real' speakers of the foreign language and by trips abroad. They defined the course of education as a demand to develop intercultural competence and thus critically to overcome prejudices and things taken for granted within their own language and culture.
- A third group was mainly interested in the foreign language and culture as the achievements of the culture, and not as an instrument of real communication to overcome language barriers. Basically they regarded this educational course as a course in literature, to some extent in linguistics and as an analysis of the language. Working with language in order to decode texts fascinated them. They gladly sacrificed intercultural communication and especially petty insistence on linguistic accuracy.

- A fourth option was that of the mediating, professionally relevant skill of foreign language correspondence. This was an obvious choice for the College School students whose course of studies ends with the acquisition of a professional certificate in commercial correspondence *and* the general university entrance examination, the *Abitur*. The rigid and standardised demands for accuracy in commercial correspondence and the clarity of business transactions as taught at school were identified as fixed points of reference, particularly in the case of students who developed little creativity in intercultural communication and in literary and linguistic text analysis.

It is therefore not surprising that only a few students managed to achieve what the curriculum intends: the integration of various dimensions of competence, the combination of foreign language communication with the understanding of foreign cultures, the intertwining of analytic argumentative communication, aimed at truth, and professional mediation and negotiation in a variety of roles, aimed at successful action. Silvia Kick was one rare example of this type of learner.

I therefore conclude that intercultural competence is not a 'natural' or 'automatic' result of foreign language teaching. Students with low linguistic competence may be excellent in intercultural mediation, and vice versa. Intercultural competence is closely related to self-identity. One could even say that intercultural competence is the expression of self-identity in communicative situations which transcend national barriers. If my conclusion is right, we have further legitimation for intercultural studies as an integrated, but independent part of foreign language teaching. And we have to develop an interlingual and intercultural FLT programme which does justice to the fact that students of the upper secondary stage build their own model of foreign languages and cultures, and by so doing reduce the complexity of the learning task offered by school and society.

References

BAUMGRATZ, G. 1985, Transnational and cross-cultural communication as negotiation of meaning: objectives, sociological and psychological implications and methodological problems. In Goethe-Institut/Ralf Eppeneder (ed.) *Comprehension as Negotiation of Meaning.* Munich: Goethe-Institut.

DEWEY, J. 1916/1966, *Democracy and Education. An Introduction to the Philosophy of Education.* New York/London: The Free Press, Collier Macmillan Publishing.

HAVIGHURST, R.J. 1972, *Developmental Tasks and Education,* 3rd edn. New York: McKay Company.

HENNINGSEN, J. 1974, *Erfolgreich manipulieren. Methoden des Beybringens.* Ratingen: Aloys Henn Verlag.
KELLER, G. 1987, Auto- und Heterostereotype amerikanischer und deutscher Schüler in einer neuen Kulturkunde. *Die Neueren Sprachen* 86, 1, 63–79.
KOHLBERG, L. 1981–4, *Essays on Moral Development,* vols I and II. San Francisco: Harper and Row.
MEYER, M.A. 1986, *Shakespeare oder Fremdsprachenkorrespondenz? Zur Reform des Fremdsprachenunterrichts in der Sekundarstufe II.* Wetzlar: Verlag Büchse der Pandora.
WITTGENSTEIN, L. 1960, *Philosophische Untersuchungen.* Frankfurt a.M.: Suhrkamp Verlag.

11 Culture and 'Hidden Culture' in Moscow: A Contrastive Analysis of West German and Soviet Perceptions

ASTRID ERTELT-VIETH

Introduction

The term 'hidden' culture in the title of this chapter alludes to the research of the American anthropologist E.T. Hall (1966) who investigated the perception and formation of space (proxemic behaviour) as a culture-specific 'hidden dimension' of living together. The term 'hidden', as opposed to open and conscious, denotes the unconscious end of the scale that applies to cultural and intercultural analysis of behaviour, perception and feeling. The work described here introduces the dimension of axiologic lacunas for differences in symbolic meaning in intercultural encounter as opposed to differences on a factual or verbal level.

In the title concepts are related which traditionally have stood for clearly separated fields of knowledge and correspondingly separated methodologies: culture versus perception of culture, descriptive knowledge of realia versus cultural psychology, evaluative description of foreign political facts versus socio-psychological understanding, cognitive learning objectives versus humanistic learning objectives, e.g. toleration or solidarity. The recent debate about intercultural learning in foreign language teaching has tended to downplay such rigorous dichotomies, replacing them by more holistic concepts. In this discussion, relations are reconstructed between linguistic and social meanings, between the world of ideas and the profane everyday reality, between the political and cultural identity of people, between academic knowledge and common-sense experience in everyday life (Piepho, 1986; Buttjes, 1987; Davids, 1981; Ehlich, 1980; Schwerdtfeger, 1987).

The discussion is bringing to light deficits and discrepancies in both theory and practice of intercultural studies. We lack a consistent theoretical model as well as systematic empirical research in this field:

1. Social pschological studies of intercultural learning focus on the learners' cognitive structures (Keller, 1983; Byram, Escarte-Sarries & Taylor, 1988). However, the actual foreign cultural objects that tend to arouse certain perceptions and cognitions on the part of the non-native learner must also be considered as such.
2. Political concepts of intercultural learning have tended to employ culturally neutral concepts, e.g. class-specific social experience (Lange & Lehberger, 1983; Schüle, 1983). However, we have to find out which are the crucial prerequisites in the individual person and in a specific foreign culture that lead to misunderstandings in intercultural learning, name them and explain them.

Thus the claim for intercultural studies must not be based merely on moral appeals for understanding and solidarity, but rather on empirical grounds, on empirical analyses of cultural errors. After defining areas of misunderstanding, explaining them and reducing them would be the precondition of intercultural understanding.

Analysis, naming and explaining, of cultural errors must include both everyday life – specifically, the practical performance of everyday life, everyday life common sense, knowledge and communication – and academic perspectives, both theoretical and empirical, and should be applied both within a given culture as well as between different cultures. Thus in addition to everyday life experience the academic discourse itself, which is the aim of this book, would also be included as locations and objects of intercultural communication. In this way the comparison between foreign and native cultural realities would be related to the comparison between foreign and native ways of viewing and explaining them.

Such an empirical study will be described here. The project approaches the reshaping of the object of intercultural studies by empirical means, at a time when neither a sufficient theory nor an adequate method seem to be available. (For detailed technical and theoretical background, see Ertelt-Vieth, 1990).

The Project

Assumptions

1. Cultural studies are operational: they seek to gain information on facts and factors that prohibit or further intercultural understanding and intercultural behaviour.
2. It is only via the brains of people that (foreign cultural) reality ends up as an obstacle to (intercultural) communication.

The goal of the project could be expressed as follows. Reality understood as psychological reality should be recorded in order to find out what (i.e. which material and ideological phenomena) functions how (i.e. by means of which meanings) in influencing feeling, thinking and deeds of individual foreigners as well as individual Muscovites.

Procedure

In Moscow in 1984, I interviewed 30 West German scholars and postgraduates who had been staying there from two to ten months. I asked them about their experience of everyday life in Moscow and recorded the interviews on tape. I ensured that the interviews were held in an informal, freely colloquial atmosphere, thus approaching the kind of conversation usual and typical for foreign students in this residence. Specifically, choosing and naming the topic of any intercultural object was little influenced or limited.

I introduced the interview by posing the problem: what, how and how much learners of Russian at schools and universities in the Federal Republic of Germany should be instructed about everyday life in the Soviet Union, the way of living, the common sense experiences. I told them that I was not primarily interested in facts and figures, dates and deeds or situations, rather in their experiencing of strange behaviour, strange processes on the part of Muscovites. For orientation I proposed the following questions: What do you consider interesting? What do you like particularly? What is strange? What is unpleasant? In what respects did you change your conceptions as compared to the beginning of your stay or to earlier visits? What aspects of everyday life would you consider expecially rewarding for research? The resulting 20 hours of audiorecording were transcribed into 800 pages of typescript, analysed, evaluated and arranged for a contrastive analysis by Muscovites. In this process of primary analysis and primary preparation I tackled the problem of giving preliminary answers to the questions stated above as the goal of this project, while at the same time preserving and condensing the inconsistencies and complex multiformity (which resides partly in the seemingly trivial act of commenting on reality).

Characteristics of the transcripts

In the interviews we notice conspicuously few direct comparisons of the following type:

'... also wenn die Marburger Schlangen (in der Mensa) hier abgefertigt werden sollten, dann würde das'n Tag dauern' (If the Pushkin Institute they had to cope with queues for lunchtime as in the Mensa of Marburg University, it would take them a whole day)

'... wie die Menschen sich kleiden hier, nich' so bunt wie wir in Westen' (... the way they dress here, not as colourful as we in the west)

'... und die kommen viel näher auf einen zu als in Deutschland' (and they approach you much closer than in Germany)

Similarly there were few explicit (positive or negative) judgements, for example:

'... was mir immer noch hier gefällt, is' das bißchen Mystische, nich' so Rationelle' (what I still like here is the rather mystical, not so rational)

'was mir besonders gut gefällt, das öffentliche Transportsystem' (what I like very much, the public transport)

'was mich shon stört, daß alles so unheimlich lange dauert' (what does annoy me, they take so exasperating long in everything)
(talking about cultural studies, the way they are taught at Puskin Institute:) '... das is' auch ... Verarschung irgendwie' (this also somehow is a lot of bullshit)

Thus little could be gained by any quantitative assessment. Rather more rewarding is explicating the implicit comparisons and judgements, and in this way finding out just why a particular phenomenon, a particular episode, was considered worth telling.

CULTURE AND 'HIDDEN CULTURE' IN MOSCOW 163

The process of explicating and signifying constitutes a way of parsing implications specific for a given culture (cultural variants) which pertain to intercultural understanding and intercultural behaviour. The process indicates that the researcher's knowledge about (culture-specific) everyday life is an important precondition for scientific analysis of international communication. For practical purposes of this analysis a most convenient step was to select narrations and exemplifications interspersed in the interview; here, phenomenon and significance of a phenomenon are open for systematic deduction. Take the following examples:

- The narration of the behaviour of a porter at a restaurant is supposed to underline that contrary to what we read in Russian textbooks there also are unfriendly Russians ('nich' freundlich').
- The narration of the behaviour of a teacher and an Intourist guide (calling each other by their first names) is supposed to be an example of cordiality amongst Russians.
- The narration of how Russian friends brought a thermos flask of non-sugared coffee to a meeting in a *Pel'mennaja* is supposed to allude to the statement that Russians have spontaneity ('Spontaneität') and to underscore that the way Russians treat you is great ('Wie die mit einem umgehen ist echt ganz toll').

A *pel'mennaja* is a simple inexpensive restaurant or snack bar. In small restaurants, snackbars, canteens and cafeterias, black tea is the main drink. If coffee is served at all, it is usually premixed with sugar and milk and is served in glasses with (and not after) the meal.

Pre-arranging of the German narrations for comment by Muscovites

Cultural differences between German narrator and Muscovite commentator might arise with respect to the *core of the narration* (where is the point?), with respect to the *qualitative meaning* of this core (what does this mean?), and with respect to its *quantitative meaning* (is it typical of Muscovites or not?). In order to arrive at predicaments that are comparable, the core of the narration was elaborated and the German meaning of the episode explicated. For this a linguistic system of analysis by Quasthoff (1980) was studied and modified: the core of a narration is a semantic and interactive entity. (For further information see Ertelt-Vieth 1990: 47–81.)

Here is an example (referring to one of the 52 narrations analysed):

(A) *Context of the narration within the interview:*
The narrator reflects on what she likes in Moscow: the city, the people and the fact that she is able to talk to them ('in der Lage zu sein, mit den Leuten zu reden.')

(B) *Wording of the narration (slightly abbreviated):*
'Gestern, ei, das ist ganz interessant, gestern ham wir im Zug-da sind wir 'n paar Stationen zu weit gefahren. Und da war so 'ne ältere Dame, saß uns gegenüber. Und. Da fing die plötzlich an, mit uns politische Diskussionen zu führen ... wieso wir denn nicht für den Frieden wären, und was der Reagan da machtet das wär' ja ganz fürchterlich. Und dann ham wir ihr erst mal erklärt, daß wir ... begriffen hat sie's bestimmt nich', aber – sie hat sich jedenfalls damit mal befaßt. Das fand ich ganz gut. Mm.'

(Yesterday, eh, that's quite interesting, yesterday in a train we – well we missed a couple of stations. And there was this old lady, sat in front of us. And. So suddenly she started and got us into political arguments ... How come we were not in favour of peace, and what this Reagan was up to [this was in 1984: E-V.], how terrible that all was. And so we set out to explain to her, that we ... I'm quite positive she hasn't got it straight, but – anyhow she had spent a couple of thoughts on that matter. I thought that was quite good. Mm.

(C) *Core:*
The narrator and other German scholars were addressed by an elderly Russian lady in a train and engaged in a discussion about peace policy.

(D) *German meaning:*
(a) It is unusual for elderly ladies to be interested in politics.
(b) It is unusual for elderly ladies to address foreign young people in public for a discussion about peace policy.
(c) The narrator approves of this elderly lady dealing with politics.

Comments of Muscovites – Analysis

In 1986, Muscovites were provided with context (for their background information), core and German meaning of the episodes. They were asked to tell if a given episode was 'typical' or 'not typical' and if they share the evaluation described as the German meaning or what divergent evaluation they offer. For every episode there are 5–8 comments by Muscovites.

Prejudices against groups of different social status or different ethnic background are often explained and criticised as stemming from undue generalisation of singular information and experiences (c.f. 'Generalisierung' and 'Typisierung' in Keller, 1983: 14). In view of this the result of this project is astonishing. Relatively seldom did Muscovites name an episode as 'not typical'. Differences arose instead with regards to the German meaning or some aspects thereof. Let me explain this by three examples which serve to elaborate systematic comparison of episodes, German meaning and Russian comment.

Example 1

The above episode of the elderly lady in the train is deemed 'typical' by four out of six Muscovites. And only one Muscovite stated it was 'not typical', yet specifying that this pertained only to the political subject of the discussion and not to the situation of an elderly lady engaging young foreigners in a discussion. The diversion of opinion between different Muscovites is thus merely gradual, concerning the number of typical elements that make up this episode.

This example demonstrates that in cultural contrastive analysis there must be the possibility of distinguishing and qualifying intercultural differences as interrelated to intracultural differences and vice versa.

Example 2

With another episode, all five Muscovites agree in naming it 'typical' and also agree in their criticism of the German meaning, and yet the very wording of their criticism supports – from a German viewpoint – that German meaning. Thus we have a twofold source of error: the situation in itself (as seen from a heterocultural viewpoint) and talking or writing about the situation by natives of this cultural surrounding (again seen from a heterocultural viewpoint). In the example, a West German scholar tells of children in a nursery school singing 'soldiers songs'. As the German meaning of this episode, I had explicated as follows: 'If songs praise the defending of one's mother and one's native country this stands for praising war in general. Topics of war, whether defensive or otherwise, are political topics unsuitable for children of this age. (Correspondingly the narrator used the word 'soldiers' songs' – *Soldatenlieder* – even though in all probability technically speaking they were childrens' songs.) To occupy children with political topics is exercising an undue influence, is manipulation ...'

The Muscovites commented: 'By no means are these soldiers' songs. They just refer to phases of the history of this country ...'; '... it is self-evident that children admire the heroism of Soviet man'; '... these songs defy the sequels of war. Heroes are only sung about as heroes of magnanimity, friendship, cordiality and patriotism — as heroes that gave their lives for a cause'; '... this isn't any praise of war. What it says is that "native country" and "mother" are holy notions to a human being which he should tend and protect for all his life ... there is nothing in it about war at all, just about love of one's country, which should be taught from childhood on. War is not merely a political topic. In our country there is not a single family that did not suffer in the years from 1941 to 1945. And all the children, without exception, do not want to have it repeated. They know about war from the tales of the elderly, from films and books.' Even if these Muscovite comments give important additional information for assessing the given episode, they hardly serve to ameliorate the evaluation of the actual situation in the nursery school. Quite on the contrary, to West Germans, they reinforce it. As opposed to Muscovites, for a large number of West Germans, words like 'native country' (*Heimat*), 'love of one's country, heroism' and the line of thought 'mother — native country — holy notions (*heilige Begriffe*)' function in an exact opposite way from what Muscovites think they do: to the listener they are indicative of a speaker's right-wing conservative attitude.

In addition to differences in meaning of single words and phrases, here we note the importance of differences in connotation or symbolic meaning. This symbolic meaning is convention. It functions correctly only within the respective collective. I prefer 'symbolic meaning' over 'connotation' as these are manifestations which, though described in philological terms, transcend this level of analysis as might be illustrated by the following example.

Example 3

This episode was deemed 'typical' by four out of five Muscovites, and by the fifth as 'typical of the Pushkin Institute': A scholar recalls filing an application at the administration of the institute regarding an excursion for her learners' group. At the end of her conversation with an administrative clerk, the clerk came out to show her precisely which button she had to push in the elevator in order to arrive at the right floor. The narrator, and also her German listeners, took this as a sign of over-protectiveness, underrating of their capability and spoon-feeding. 'Facts-oriented social studies' would stop and be content at finding out from the Muscovite comments that indeed this episode is typical.

At the level of the symbolic meaning, however, grave differences appear.

CULTURE AND 'HIDDEN CULTURE' IN MOSCOW 167

Muscovites interpret the behaviour of the clerk in the following way: '... basic form of being polite ...', 'basic form of politeness and attentiveness ...', 'this situation is quite typical indeed, but we disagree with the rating it got and are very much astonished at how this act of pointing to which button to press might evoke such a peculiar and unfitting reaction.' This example shows how trivial matters in foreign cultural everyday life lead to problems or misconceptions not necessarily only because of discomfort or adaptational difficulties of other sorts, but also because of their (diverging!) symbolic meaning.

Conclusion

German as well as Russian evaluation of an episode depends on several elements which make this episode 'typical' for Moscow (from the respective point of view), and which constitute its intra- and/or intercultural meaning (i.e. they are in each case relative and viewpoint-bound). Differentiating and interpreting these elements in direct discussions with Muscovite academics served to explicate the intercultural situation the narrator of an episode was involved in, as well as the later verbal communicative acts (German narration and Russian comment). At the same time this method serves my purpose of step-by-step illumination of cultural differences or peculiarities as they gain their respective relevance in particular intercultural encounters. As was stated at the beginning, this empirical method helps to reshape into tangible forms the object of intercultural studies. Difficulties in depicting these peculiarities arise from their being connected with the viewpoint of the individual, and from the manifold connections and interactions of so-called primary and secondary meanings which are relative, in that primary may become secondary and vice versa. Thirdly, difficulties arise from the variable, procedural context of such cultural peculiarities: for example, some are initially related causally and then acquire a momentum of their own, as when one behaviour incites an attitude which may in turn lead to a further behaviour.

As conceptual apparatus for systematic depiction of these specifics I use Sorokin and Markonvina's 'lacuna' system (Sorokin, 1977, 1982; Sorokin & Markovina, 1983; Markovina, 1982; Ertelt-Vieth, 1988). In the context of the research outlined above this system was further elaborated and its efficiency proven, especially with regard to further differentiation and with regard to the unevenness of the available empirical material.

The lacuna system

Using the term 'lacuna', Sorokin and Markovina continue certain traditions of Russian/Soviet textual science and traditions of comparative linguistic and cultural sciences. By way of definition, it can be said that lacunas:

- are elements of national cultural specifics of a text or context, which for a heterocultural recipient prohibit or hamper understanding of this text or context;
- do not describe stable meanings, but depend on the respective conditions of the actual encounter of two cultures at a given moment in time;
- are historic in the sense that they are raised, changed or annihilated by differences in time or development;
- do not constitute rigid classifications, but make up a dynamic system that necessitates consideration and differentiation of changing attitudes towards and different aspects of a course of events;
- are not applicable to realia only but also to specific processes and situations which are in conflict with certain experiences of a bearer of a certain other culture.

Explanatory exemplification

Using the second example above ('soldiers' songs' in nursery school) let me explain how, by means of the lacuna system, culture-specific 'realia' and culture-specific psychological artefacts can systematically be differentiated:

1. *Ethnographic lacuna* for the Germans: in Soviet nursery schools they sing songs that deal with war.
2. *Lacuna of positive national autostereotype* for the Soviets: regarding their conduct in the face of German fascism, and in World War II in general, Soviets have a positive national autostereotype (we defended our native country and helped other peoples to defend theirs). With Germans a comparatively strongly anchored positive national autostereotype regarding resistance against fascism is non-existent (interestingly enough – to clarify this point – this does exist with Italians, who till today cherish traditions of anti-fascist resistance). This positive autostereotype of the Soviets is contrasted with a *negative national heterostereotype* of Germans against Soviets: many

CULTURE AND 'HIDDEN CULTURE' IN MOSCOW

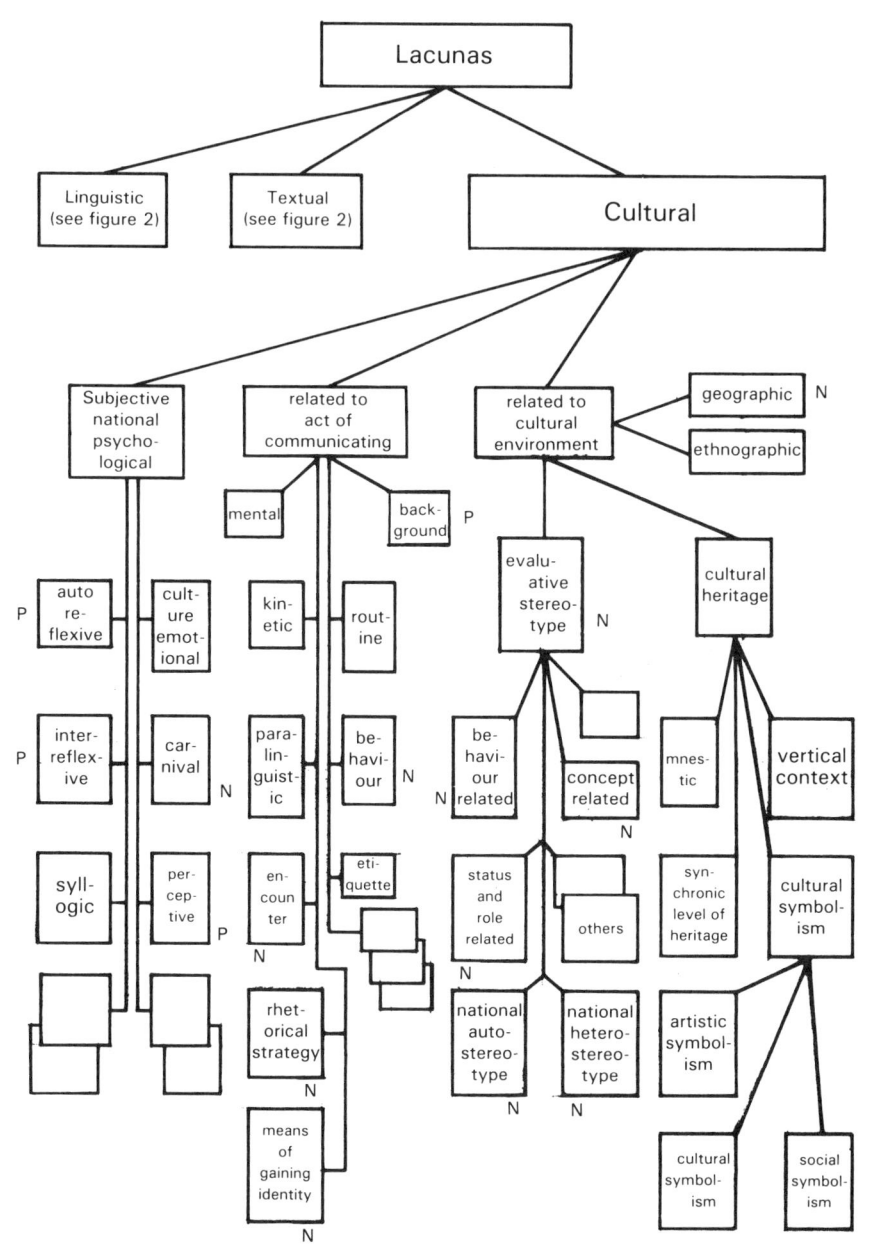

```
                        ┌─────────┐
                        │ Lacunas │
                        └─────────┘
         ┌──────────────────┼──────────────────┐
  ┌─────────────┐   ┌─────────────┐      ┌──────────┐
  │ Linguistic  │   │  Textual    │      │ Cultural │
  │(see figure 2)│   │(see figure 2)│      └──────────┘
  └─────────────┘   └─────────────┘
```

Subjective national psychological / related to act of communicating / related to cultural environment — geographic (N), ethnographic

- mental / background (P)
- auto reflexive (P), culture emotional, kinetic, routine
- evaluative stereotype, cultural heritage
- inter-reflexive (P), carnival (N), para-linguistic, behaviour (N), behaviour related (N), concept related, mnestic, vertical context
- syllogic, perceptive (P), encounter (N), etiquette, status and role related (N), others, synchronic level of heritage, cultural symbolism
- rhetorical strategy (N), national auto-stereotype (N), national hetero-stereotype (N), artistic symbolism
- means of gaining identity (N), cultural symbolism, social symbolism

☐ P the position of this kind of lacuna was changed as compared to Sorokin and Markovina
☐ N a kind of lacuna I have added to the system

FIGURE 11.1

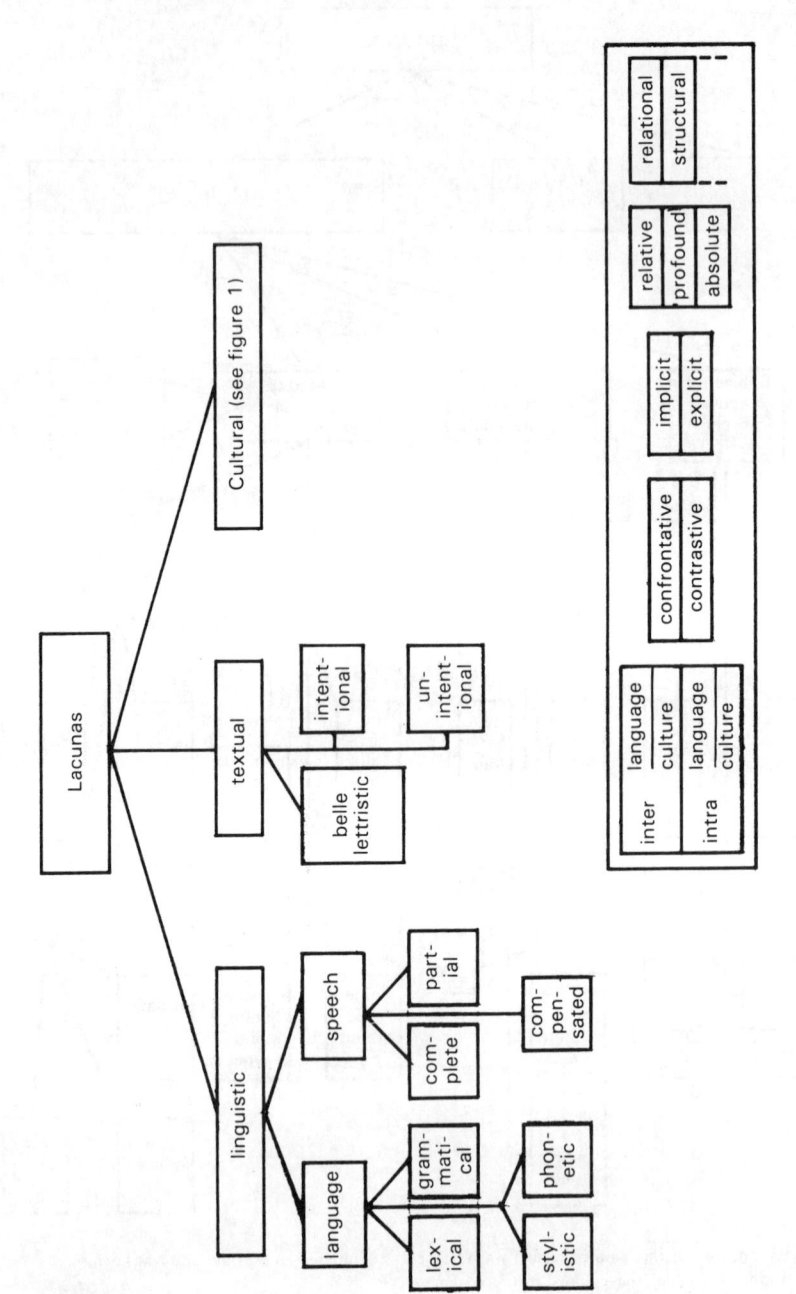

FIGURE 11.2

West Germans think that the Soviet army is basically an aggressive army. Generally the question of who started World War II is seldom asked in this context.
3. *Lacuna of evaluative stereotype* (notion-oriented): the notions of 'native country, love of one's country, heroism' etc. (explained above).
4. *Culture-emotional lacuna:* The notions 'heroism' and 'love of one's country' not only are negatively tinted for West Germans – and not for Russians – but they also react to them spontaneously with annoyance.
5. *Mnestic lacuna* (historic remembrance) for West Germans: The amount of death, loss and destruction in the Soviet Union during the invasion and retreat of German fascism are no longer recalled or are unknown to many West Germans.

Further development of the lacuna system

Using the third example described above (button in the lift) let me explain an important enlargement of the lacuna system that I invented and that was subsequently discussed with Sorokin. A behaviour is deemed spoon-feeding and patronising by the West German narrator, while several Russian commentators regard it as politeness, even as a basic form of politeness. This is what I call a difference in social evaluation or in symbolic meaning of an act or circumstance, an *axiologic lacuna*. Axiologic lacunas arise only from a combination of several lacunas. In this case the difference (= lacuna) between German narrator and Russian commentators primarily stems from different ways of realising politeness or of being patronising. This is overlaid by the national auto- and heterostereotype of or against Russians. The different symbolic meanings of the above-mentioned behaviour of a Russian can be described in opposing terms as in Table 11.1.

TABLE 11.1

German meaning		*Russian meaning*
patronising	≠	good manners
patronising	≠	elementary form of politeness
patronising	≠	being sociable, pastime of the elderly
patronising	≠	incorrect assessment of a person
general restriction	≠	occasionally annoying

A precondition for these differences in meaning is a *lacuna of etiquette*. For Russians, being polite means extending optimal helpfulness to a person; that is, giving most detailed explanations to a stranger asking for the right way, even accompanying him if possible in order to make sure that he or she does not lose their way. German etiquette does not warrant this . Quite on the contrary, German etiquette sets a limit to helping a person at the point where there might be the faintest idea of restricting that person's freedom of choice and freedom of movement. So if a German informant thought of his relations of interfering or distance as being on a continuum:

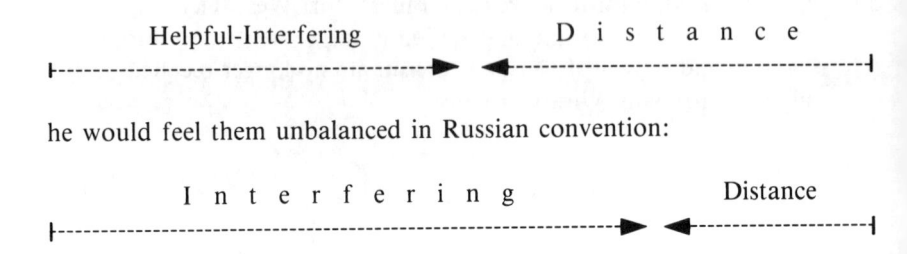

```
            Helpful-Interfering              D i s t a n c e
|----------------------------------►  ◄----------------------------------|
```

he would feel them unbalanced in Russian convention:

```
               I n t e r f e r i n g              Distance
|----------------------------------------------►  ◄------------------|
```

So in actual situations, for the German informant, the convention of distance will be violated much more often than for the Russian. Conversely, for the Russian informant the convention of helpfulness is more often in danger of being violated.

It does not necessarily follow, however, that violating the convention of distance is automatically taken for being patronising – this appears so only in view of additional lacunas typical for German–Russian relations. First, a German has a deep lacuna with respect to the Russian national autostereotype. Russians have, as an important positive autostereotype, being polite and helpful to foreigners, demonstrating a special interest in them. Thus in one of the Russian comments cited above there is indignation over the German interpretation of the behaviour described. Secondly, there is a culture-emotional lacuna. For Russians, especially Russian women, it is nearly 'tragic' (as stated by one commentator) if a person is far away from home. Similarly, Russians have a deep lacuna with respect to the German national heterostereotype of Russians. They don't realise that many Germans – possibly the majority of Germans – consider being patronising and restricting the individual in all social spheres to be a typical Russian behaviour and attitude.

Relativity of intercultural differences in meaning

Developing the axiologic lacuna above, I gave oppositions of several different German and Russian meanings for a particular behaviour. The behaviour of the old lady in the train (first example) also provokes different interpretations by Russians and Germans (see Table 11.2).

TABLE 11.2

German meaning		Russian meaning
interest in politics	=	interest in politics
self-confidence	≠	0
0	≠	general Russian eagerness for information, especially on foreign countries
0	≠	typical for Russian pensioners, their sociability and willingness to have conversation or: whims of the old

The last group of notions (typical for pensioners/whims of the old) denotes a fluent transition between evaluations among Russians: from the understanding that this behaviour is − still − within the framework of convention to the supposition that it is not (whims of the old = negative). This behaviour and its evaluation thus also constitute an *intracultural lacuna of behaviour* and *intracultural axiological lacuna*, depending on the sociological and psychological viewpoint of an informant within his/her own culture, depending on the personal experience of the informant.

A decisive aspect regarding these intracultural oppositions in meaning is, however, that they are valid within this culture, and that (in spite of partial or more than partial correspondences or analogies) combined they differ from the German system of meanings and the German framework of intracultural oppositions. Let me emphasis this by way of the following *lacuna of social and cultural symbolism*: West German scholars decribe in one episode, how in the provincial town of Sagorsk a woman asked them why they had beards. From the Russian commentaries on this episode it is clear that having a beard in the Soviet Union is still considered special (contrary to the FRG = *ethnographic lacuna*) and associated with a series of intracultural oppositions in meaning, as listed in Table 11.3.

TABLE 11.3

Russian meaning			German meaning	
Beard	Non-beard		Beard	Non-beard
foreigner	resident	≠	0 (complete lacuna)	
townsman	provincial	≠	0 (complete lacuna)	
intellectual	non-intellectual		(1960s – early 1970s)	
0 for the actual informants in the past but in rural areas still today:			(19th century, in rural areas till beginning 20th century)	
old men	other men		0 for the actual informants	
westerner	Russian	≠	0 (complete lacuna)	
priest	layman	≠	0 (complete lacuna)	
0 (complete lacuna)		<	(1960s – early 1970s)	
			progressive	conservative
			politically left	politically right

Historicity of inter- and intracultural differences or specifics

To the objection that intercultural differences are 'only' relative, I suggest that relativity is the very principle of science. In doing so I also stress that there is no use in contrasting permanent intracultural changes (as in the above example of the changing implications of wearing a beard) with allegedly stable intercural differences. Quite on the contrary, only by noting their historicity do we arrive at ways and means of understanding and handling them.

With respect to the characterisation of axiologic lacunas we might envisage them as a second dimension of the lacuna system. Diagrammatically they could be visualised as a mirror (see Sorokin & Tarasov, 1984) or a superstructure. Thus we illustrate that they depend in their appearance, existence and disappearance on the other lacunas, and yet have a certain autonomy, comparable to that of language and other semiotic systems.

Summary

Landeswissenschaft (cultural studies) should study all material and spiritual phenomena among two different cultures that achieve significance in the process of their encounter. The project described here set out to redefine the object of *Landeswissenschaft* in its own right, based on empirical studies, using empirical techniques, answering empirical needs. What are the actual intercultural stumbling blocks explicitly and implicitly relevant to the foreigner or the learner of a foreign language, from his/her own point of view and from that of readers/listeners in either cultural surrounding?

Principles of research in a *Landeswissenschaft* defined in this way are:

1. Contrastivity: phenomena of intercultural relevance are pointed out and described from the point of view of both the foreigner and the native.
2. Meta-communication: research projects are planned and carried out in intercultural co-operation, and at the same time this intercultural co-operation is taken into account as a source of intercultural conflicts and misunderstandings, and is as such part of the study.

As a systematic tool for this research, the lacuna system fills important needs:

- it takes into account the fact that national 'prejudices' not only have something to do with the individual and his/her socialisation but also with the foreign cultural reality that helps to create them;
- it not only reflects the development of suppositions and attitudes from natural or social circumstances but also their repercussions on these;
- it allows for the fact that in intercultural encounter (and also in cultural studies as long as they are not narcissistic), as in any research that is tied to the researcher's perspective, any odd fact or circumstance may become a sign or symbol (axiologic lacuna);
- it is operational, as the approach of starting with concrete empirically proven intercultural differences or conflicts, implies their inversion, their detection and exposure, and finally their solution and avoidance.

Acknowledgement

I am grateful for the helpful contributions of the 'group for psycholinguistics and theory of communication' (E.F. Tarasov, N.V. Ufimceva, Ju. A. Sorokin and I.Ju. Markovina) at the linguistic institute of the Academy of Sciences of the USSR, Moscow.

References

BUTTJES, D. (ed.) 1981, *Landeskundliches Lernen im Englischunterricht*. Paderborn: Schoñingh.
—— 1987, Amerikanische Alltagskultur als Gegenstand landes- und kulturwissenschaftlicher Forschung. *Anglistik und Englischunterricht* 31.
BYRAM, M., ESARTE-SARRIES, V. and TAYLOR, S. 1988. The effects of language teaching on young people's perception of other cultures. Interim paper. Foreign languages project, School of Education, University of Durham.
DAVIDS, J.-U. 1981, Orientierung und Identität. Stichwort zu einer emanzipatorischen Landeswissenschaft. In D. BUTTJES (ed.) 1981, pp.30–49.
EHLICH, K. (ed.) 1980, *Erzählen im Alltag*. Frankfurt: Suhrcamp Taschenbuch Verlag.
ERTELT-VIETH, A. 1988, 'Die sowjetische Ethnopsycholinguistik und das Modell der Lakunen in der landeswissenschaftlichen Forschung. *Die Neueren Sprachen*. Frankfurt a.M.: Peter Lang.
—— 1990, *Kulturvergleichende Analyse von Verhalten, Sprache und Bedeutungen im Moskauer Alltag. Beitrag zu einer empirisch, kontrastiv und semiotisch ausgerichteten Landeswissenschaft*. Frankfurt a.M.: Peter Lang.
HALL, E.T. 1966, *The Hidden Dimension*. New York.
KELLER, G. 1983, Didaktische Analyse eines neuen kulturkundlichen Unterrichts auf lern- und sozialpsychologischer Grundlage. In A. RAASCH, W. HÜLLEN and F.J. ZAPP (eds) *Beiträge zur Landeskunde im Fremdsprachenunterricht*, pp.142–57. Frankfurt: Diesterweg.
LANGE, B.-P. and LEHBERGER, R. 1983, Neue Tendenzen in der Landeskunde. In *Landeskunde und Didaktik. gulliver. Deutsch-Englische Jahrbücher Band 13*, pp.5–12. Argument Sonderband AS 97. Berlin: Argument Verlag.
LEONT'EV, A.A., SOROKIN, Ju.A. and TARASOV, E.F. (eds) 1977, Nacional'no-kul'turnaja specifika rečevogo povedenija (National-cultural specifics in language behaviour). Moscow: Izdatel'stvo Nauka.
LEONT'EV, A.A., TARASOV, E.F. and SOROKIN, Ju.A. (eds) 1982, Nacional'no-kul'turnaja specifika rečevogo obščenija narodov SSSR (National-cultural specifics in verbal communication of the nations of the USSR). Moscow: Izdatel'stvo Nauka.
MARKOVINA, I.Ju. 1982, Vlijanie lingvističeskich i ekstralingvistieskich faktorov na ponimanie teksta. (Influence of linguistic and extra-linguistic factors on comprehension of texts.) Dissertation at the Institute of Linguistics at the Academy of Sciences in Moscow.
PIEPHO, H.E. 1986, Didaktisches Denken und Handeln im DaF-Unterricht. In R. EHNERT and H.E. PIEPHO (eds) *Fremdsprachen lernen mit Medien*, pp.122–32. Munich: Hueber.
QUASTHOFF, U. 1980, *Erzählen in Gesprächen. Linguistische Untersuchung zu Stukturen und Funktionen am Beispiel einer Kommunikationsform des Alltag*. Tübingen: Gunther Narr.
SCHÜLE, K. 1983, *Politische Landeskunde und kritische Fremdsprachendidaktik*. Paderborn, Munich, Vienna, Zürich: Schöningh.
SCHWERDTFEGER, I.C. 1987, *Alltag und Fremdsprachenunterricht. Eine Streitschrift gegen die Schweigsamkeit*. Munich: Hueber.
SOROKIN, Ju.A. 1977, Metod ustanovlenija lakuny kak odin iz sposobov vyjavlenija specifiki lokal'nych kul'tur (chudožestvennaja literatura v

kul'turologičeskom aspekte). (Method of determining lacunas as a possibility of unfolding the specifics of local cultures (belles-lettres from a cultural point of view). In LEONT'EV, SOROKIN and TARASOV (eds) 1977, pp.120–36.
—— 1982, Lakuny kak signaly specifiki lingvokul'turnoj obščnosti. (Lacunas as signals of the specifics of linguo-cultural communities.) In LEONT'EV, TARASOV and SOROKIN (eds) 1982, pp.22–8.
SOROKIN, Ju.A. and MARKOVINA, I.Ju. 1983, Opyt sistematizacii lingvističeskich i kul'turologiceskich lakun. *Metodologičeskie i metodičeskie aspekty.* In V.P. VOMPERSKIJ, V.G. KOSTOMAROV, N.J. TOLSTOJ and E.V. KLJUEV (eds) *Leksiceskie edinicy i organizacija struktury literaturnogo teksta,* pp. 35–52. (Trial to systemise linguistic and cultural lacunas. Methodologic and methodic aspects. In: *Lexicalic units and the organizing structure of the literary text.*) Kalinin.
SOROKIN, Ju.A. and TARASOV, E.F. 1984, Otobraženie 'teksta' v tekste. *Izomorfizm na raznych urovnjach jazykovoj sistemy,* pp.38–43. (Picturing of 'text' in the text. In *Isomorphism in different levels of language system.*) Moscow.

Part IV

Towards a Revision of Intercultural Teaching Media

The power of the textbook as a reflection of theory and a determiner of practice is well known to teachers and theoreticians alike. Not only does it embody theories of language learning and methods of teaching dependent on them, it also portrays an image of other cultures which is none the less significant for being largely implicit. The need to take a critical view of the images teaching materials transmit underpins the four chapters in this section. Two themes are common to them all: the insistence on a true or faithful image which gives a new significance to the call for 'authenticity' in texts, and the critique of the point of view taken up by many materials writers, who may not give sufficient thought to the influence they unwittingly wield.

Risager provides a new view of textbook analysis, based on a notion of realism, and points out some of the tendencies which have developed in recent years. On the one hand, she notes the increase in attention to cultural studies after the dominance of concern with finding ways of teaching linguistic structures. On the other hand, her criteria reveal inconsistencies and misrepresentations of the people and cultures most often portrayed in European textbooks.

Kubanek also takes a radical look at the content of textbooks and suggests that a wider view must be taken of what is appropriately associated with particular languages. By linking foreign language teaching with development education, she challenges the claim of language teaching to introduce learners to other ways of life by suggesting that it must shift from a Euro-centred to a global perspective. Starkey also takes this wider perspective by linking foreign language teaching with world studies. He is, however, concerned not just with textbook content but with the lessons about teaching processes which can be learnt from world studies curricula. His account of a new textbook based on these principles goes some way towards satisfying the demands of the other two authors.

Finally, Baumgratz-Gangl describes another experiment in materials development which introduces a new perspective and a concern for a true image of the foreign culture. By the use of video, the capacity to capture a more complex image is much enhanced. This is then combined with a new concept of the materials writer or producer, by placing the task in the hands of the learners themselves. It is the pupils who visit the foreign culture and, in a context which is already familiar to them − life at school − they bring a new kind of authenticity to the materials produced.

12 Cultural References in European Textbooks: An Evaluation of Recent Tendencies

KAREN RISAGER

Introduction

Textbooks as we know them from the elementary level of institutionalised foreign language teaching have a long development behind them. But since the 1950s in particular, the rate of change has increased considerably, so that the social functions of the textbooks and the demands made upon them have become much broader than ever before.

During the long period before the 1950s, textbooks primarily served linguistic purposes, containing on the whole examples of linguistic or grammatical matters: isolated sentences, dialogues, proverbs, anecdotes, fairy tales, journey accounts, and extracts of literature. But from the 1950s they have been ascribed an increasingly important cultural role as well: linguistic examples have been dramatised to a larger extent, interlocutors have become flesh and blood by the way of drawings and photos, and the everyday life, the social context, and the natural environment of the foreign countries concerned have been gradually introduced. Today the pedagogical milieu considers it a *sine qua non* that a modern textbook for beginners contain some references to the foreign culture taken in a broad sense.

This means that foreign language teaching textbooks no longer just develop concurrently with the development of foreign language pedagogy in a narrow sense, but that they increasingly participate in the general cultural transmission within the educational system and in the rest of society. They thus receive impulses from cultural trends originating outside the discipline itself, and as cultural texts they can be compared with other types of texts and other media participating in cultural reproduction: travel brochures, photographical reportage in newspapers and magazines, museum displays of life and culture, and so on.

However, even if foreign language teachers since the 1950s have attached a growing importance to sociocultural content, it is still often considered as secondary in relation to linguistic content, at any rate at the elementary level. Thus the socio-cultural domain is characterised by a widespread amateurism. Normally, teachers and authors have not had the education and the materials needed to deal systematically with the sociological and anthropological field, and to clarify what themes and approaches are suited or necessary at the elementary level. This predominantly secondary status has presumably had some specific consequences for the character of the sociocultural content, as we shall see later.

In the following paragraphs I shall identify and discuss some important trends in the sociocultural content of the textbooks. Later I shall describe the development in the light of broad cultural trends characterising Western societies today.

Analytical Categories

The analysis of the content of textbooks, their universe, starts from a model comprising a series of categories. Many models have been elaborated for the content analysis of foreign language teaching textbooks (see for instance Krauskopf, 1985). Here we shall make use of one originally based on the analysis of realistic prose (cf. Jørgensen, 1972), but adapted to the actual appearance of textbooks and the actual pedagogical needs (Andersen & Risager, 1978; Risager, 1987).

Among other things, foreign language teaching textbooks are characterised by a major change with regard to genre: in the 1950s and 1960s they were dominated by a kind of realistic fiction, in the 1970s and 1980s they are rather mixtures of ultra-short (realistic) fiction (mini-dialogues) and many types of non-fiction. Thus these textbooks offer an example of the general tendency of mixture of genres in the media.

The categories can be distributed into four groups:
1. The micro level – phenomena of social and cultural anthropology:
    a. the social and geographical definition of characters
    b. material environment
    c. situations of interaction

d. interaction and subjectivity of the characters: feelings, attitudes, values, and perceived problems.
2. The macro level – social, political, and historical matters:
   a. broad social facts about contemporary society (geographical, economic, political etc.)
   b. broad sociopolitical problems (unemployment, pollution etc.)
   c. historical background.
3. International and intercultural issues:
   a. comparisons between the foreign country and the pupils' own
   b. mutual representations, images, stereotypes
   c. mutual relations: cultural power and dominance, co-operation and conflict.
4. Point of view and style of the author(s).

Below I shall present a general description of the development since the 1950s, using the above categories. The description is based primarily on experience with textbooks for the elementary level used in Scandinavia, which for a major part have been produced in Sweden. But the overall tendencies seem generalisable to the whole of Western Europe.

Micro level: Life and Activities of Textbook Characters

The social and geographical definition of characters

In the whole period, the middle class has preponderated. However, from the 1970s some representatives of the working class have appeared, and a few Black or Arabic immigrant workers, especially by the way of photographs. As for the textbooks aiming at young learners (of about 11), social characteristics have been more indefinable, since we are seldom told about the occupation of the characters, and the occupation cannot be seen in the pictures. Thus, for youth and adult learners, we see a certain spread concerning social or occupational affiliation. But quite a few occupations occur very rarely: top directors and politicians, farmers and fishermen, not to mention unemployed people.

One characteristic of recent textbooks is that the thematic organisation of the intermediate level is coming into the later stages of the elementary level. Some sociocultural innovations are introduced in this way. That goes for some social categories, for instance immigrant workers.

During the whole period, elderly persons of more than 50 years, and small children, have been almost non-existent, but a few appear in recent textbooks (from the late 1970s and the 1980s), sometimes introduced in a thematic unit. So we see a moderate spread concerning age groups, but at the same time a growing specialisation, as the age focus of the textbook is clearly adapted to the age group of the intended pupils.

In the 1960s the central characters were almost always gathered in a nuclear family group, consisting of a mother and a father with two or three children, ranging from some 10 to 15 years. But since the early 1970s, this family orientation has been toned down or completely disappeared (with some exceptions, as for textbooks aiming at young learners). In the textbooks for youth learners (of about 13) the focus is almost exclusively on young people, together with friends, or isolated. And in the textbooks for young adults or adults (from about 15) it is the isolated adult who dominates the picture. So people have extremely weak social networks. Very few people meet each other more than once. Thus we see a strong tendency towards individualisation in the modern textbooks. Furthermore, in so far as there are no central characters at all, we see a fragmentation of the social universe in relation to that of the textbooks of the 1960s.

Sex roles have changed a lot, as the old family-centred textbooks always depicted housewives working at home, whereas textbooks from the late 1970s and the 1980s are careful to represent women having out-of-home occupations (but female unemployment is hardly touched upon).

The early textbooks normally showed native residents, whereas modern textbooks very often show tourists or visitors, and the content is then built up around their practical needs. The family-centred textbooks showed middle-class residences with a house and a large garden; in the later textbooks it is often hard to define the residence socially, as it is described in a very vague way. In textbooks where the content is characterised by the perspective of the adult tourist, we do not see people's residences, only the reception desk of hotels. In these modern textbooks the tourist's occupation or purpose of travel is often not told. Thus we see a certain marginalisation of native everyday life.

As for the geographical environment, it has during the whole period been dominated by life in urban centres, not any longer to be identified with the capital (which has characterised textbooks in French in particular). Whereas textbooks up to the mid 1970s only mention centre countries, for instance England, West Germany, or France, they have changed a lot, so that they now stress other countries where the particular language is spoken. In some cases, the scenes are transferred to these countries. Thus there is a geographical spread concerning the choice of towns and — to a lesser extent — countries.

Material environment

The primitive drawings of the early textbooks have been replaced by a large amount of realistic drawings and photos, showing persons, environments, and articles and texts for everday use (coins, signs, menus, timetables etc.). It is characteristic that isolated pictures prevail, perhaps gathered in collages. Connected pictures, for instance strips, were used for a short period, but seem to have been dropped again. So, even if the visual materials are of great value, representing everyday life, their arrangement tends to represent the universe in a very fragmented way. Very few pictures are used to illustrate social and geographical contrasts, for instance. At any rate, the heavy emphasis on photographs tends to stress the objectifiable, material aspects of culture — though photos may occasionally illustrate affective aspects too, for instance certain atmospheres.

Situations of interaction

In the earlier family-centred textbooks the situations were mostly activites of the families at home (in the sitting-room, in the garden), and outside the home (shopping, in the bus, holidays in the country), and the activities of the children at school, mostly in the classroom. These might be described as scenarios where conversation took place. The later textbooks are largely dominated by dyadic service situations: at the reception desk, in the restaurant, at the booking office, and so on. That has to do, of course, with the fact that the teaching material is increasingly directed towards communication situations, stressing linguistic routines that are situation-dependent. However, there are still conversations between young people or adults, always in situations of spare time. Situations at work did not exist in the earlier textbooks, but do appear, though rarely, in the newer ones. But it is certain that situations of spare time and consumption prevail during the whole period.

Interaction and subjectivity

In terms of linguistic function, it is the informative and phatic functions that prevail in the newer textbooks. The dialogues are usually very short, and one jumps abruptly from one situation to the other. Thus one might speak of 'a tendency to linguistic fragmentation', which is of course, to some extent at least, inherent at the elementary level, due to the necessity of simplification.

During the whole period human relations have been quite smooth, neutral and friendly. There is very little anger, love, disappointment, hatred or fear. It is true that feelings are to some extent being introduced into the textbooks by way of short poems, placed here and there between the dialogues. Although this is in itself a positive thing, it still does not attribute the feelings to the characters who serve as models with regard to communicative activities. The preoccupations of the characters are typically pragmatic and trivial.

The attitudes, values and personal opinions of the characters are very rarely expressed in the early textbooks. In the newer ones they exist, as the basic categories of language functions include expressing an opinion, and expressing sympathy or antipathy, and the functional approach is coming into the textbooks. Typically characters express personal opinions in interviews, i.e. in rather impersonal situations. Religious attitudes or activities are generally absent, as are all other philosophical and moral questions. Perceived problems are very rarely shown, and they are seldom of a serious type. In good cases the problem may be about pocket money, or pupil participation. There are only a few more problems represented in the newer books compared to the earlier ones. We see here a strong under-representation of the subjective aspects of culture.

Macro-level: Social, Political and Historical Matters

Broad social facts about contemporary society

In some textbooks since the late 1970s, short texts give information on sociocultural facts, placed at the end of each lesson (if necessary in the mother tongue). Usually, it is information that might in a broad sense be practical to the visitor. This kind of information is finding its way into textbooks in general. Geographical information was almost absent in the early textbooks, but in the newer ones many towns are mentioned. However, only some names are given, and there is practically no information on cultural geography. As mentioned above, the newer textbooks are anxious to tell where English, German, French and so on are used in the world, but there is no mention whatsoever of the global historical background, problems of bilingualism etc. Thus we see an initial interest in the orientation to sociocultural facts.

Broad sociopolitical problems

Broad sociopolitical problems have not been touched upon until the most recent times, neither in the texts nor in photos and the like. Since the late 1970s textbooks for youth and adult learners have shown problems like women's work out of the home, or immigrant workers, but only in passing. In the very newest textbooks, problems like youth unemployment, violence and racism are sometimes mentioned or treated briefly in thematic units. Thus we see some recent attempts at problem-orientation.

Historical background

There are practically no passages giving historical background, though this should be possible in the mother tongue. Still, thematic units have in some cases given way to historical information, for instance a theme on 'la Bretagne'.

International and Intercultural Issues

Comparisons between the foreign country and the pupils' own

As foreign language teaching textbooks are not only produced in order to be used in the country of production, but are also made for export to various other countries with similar needs, it is in principle impossible to elaborate a sociocultural content that is based on a contrastive analysis of the two countries originally involved. Nevertheless the actual interest in intercultural matters has resulted in some invitations in recent textbooks to make comparisons with facts related to the pupils' own country. Sometimes national editors present some figures for discussion.

Mutual representations

Here too it is not possible to elaborate materials that are directly based on the existence of mutual representations, as for instance national stereotypes, but in some recent textbooks one can find examples of invitations to discuss the stereotypes that different nationalities are supposed to have about the country and the people in question.

Mutual relations

Such questions are practically not touched upon. The target country or countries are still considered as isolated units. This state of affairs can among other things be related to the absence of a historical perspective.

Point of View and Style of the Author(s)

Expressions of attitudes – positive, negative, critical – towards the country and the people are extremely rare, especially in the textbooks from the 1970s and the 1980s. There are no hints at connections or contradictions, or invitations to critical analysis, not even in the mother tongue. The pedagogical focus in the modern textbooks is to show how individuals get along linguistically without outside assistance, and mini-dialogues normally demonstrate success in the enterprise. So the predominant style is objective, pragmatic, tending to avoid expressions of attitudes towards sociocultural issues.

Some Explanations and Some Evaluation

First of all it must be stressed that an evaluation of textbooks is not directly an evaluation of the teaching and learning process that is associated with them. Naturally, the actual practice in the classroom is mostly pragmatically oriented, linguistically simple, and it relates primarily to the life and experiences of the pupils themselves, which is preferable, as far as oral production is concerned. The general function of the sociocultural content of the textbooks is to go beyond this self-centred perspective.

Some characteristics are the same for all the textbooks, whatever the time of production. Firstly, they share a definite sociocultural focus: people from the middle class, or socially indefinable, of both genders, living in an urban environment, who carry out rather trivial linguistic interaction in situations of spare time and consumption. The age of characters is more or less adapted to the age of the intended pupils. Maybe this sociological focus should be interpreted as being characteristic of the typical learner? But it is a fact that since World War II, the group of learners attending foreign language teaching has greatly expanded in terms of both age and social affiliation: originally covering young people within secondary education, the group now also covers children within primary education, and highly different categories of adults (including elderly people lately) within adult education. This goes particularly for English, the typical first foreign language in many European countries. So it is increasingly difficult to speak of typical or perhaps average learners. This is especially so with regard to adult learners; but young people today have many different lifestyles as well, in spite of the homogenisation of Western youth culture. So the middle-class focus seems partly to be a cultural lag today.

The preponderance of situations of spare time and consumption may be legitimated by referring to linguistic needs, as these situations are mostly characterised by common language, whereas situations at work are often (but not always) characterised by special languages, not appropriate at the elementary level. But situations of work should nevertheless be better represented, especially with adult learners.

The triviality of dialogues at the elementary level is a great problem, as well as the tendency of infantilisation. Probably this is necessary to a large extent at this level, but still it seems that some efforts should be made to create dialogues that are somewhat more imaginative.

Secondly, in all the textbooks, the subjectivity and feelings of characters are under-represented. In a way they are half-persons. This state of affairs, which is certainly not easy to change at the elementary level, has been underscored by the growing pragmatic orientation of foreign language teaching. However, it might be counteracted by the extended reference to authentic persons already known by some, and by the use of mother tongue texts and portrait photos.

Thirdly, all the textbooks are characterised by the objective, neutral style. Everything that might be provocative or cause conflict is avoided. This is related to an important underlying ideology, acting together with pragmatic language teaching: cultural relativism, which has influenced foreign language teaching since the 1960s, not least at the elementary level. As is known, it stresses that all national cultures and other cultural matters are of equal worth, and have equal rights to exist, but also that one should not interfere with them, evaluate or criticise them, or engage in political action in relation to them. The dominance of cultural relativism is perhaps attributable to the fact that the specific sociocultural content has presumably seldom been reflected from a pedagogical point of view. For cultural relativism is in fact damaging to pedagogical aims of discussion and engagement.

These three constants serve as background to some profound changes in the universe of the textbooks. Firstly, though the sociocultural focus is still the middle class, we have seen an overall spread of social and professional groups, age groups, towns, and countries, especially in the visual material. Even if the picture is not representative in a quantitative way — this is hardly practicable — it is much more realistic than the social narrowness of the 1950s and 1960s. However, this realism is not socially and culturally structured, it is fragmented. Reality is described in flashes.

At the same time, a radical individualisation has developed, particularly with (almost) adult learners. The only stable social function left is that of the customer. This is accentuated by the stronger pragmatic orientation, which has furthered the choice of tourists or visitors as models of identification. Here too we may speak of fragmentation.

Thirdly, advances in reproduction techniques have made possible the introduction of a large amount of photos in the textbooks. Thus the under-representation of subjectivity is increasingly accentuated by an orientation towards visualisable aspects of culture. Moreover, the aesthetic dimension in general (pictures, lay-out etc.) has become another motivation factor, apart from the practical linguistic motivation. This is a sharp contrast to motivation factors that focus on the psychological content, all widespread outside the pedagogical context: violence, death, terrorism, magic, or agonising love dramas.

The above-mentioned tendency to a somewhat greater sociocultural and geographical variation clearly corresponds to the general widening of the scope of interest of Western populations since the 1960s. The other changes that have been mentioned — fragmentation, individualisation, pragmatism, and objectivisation by visualisation — also correlate with some lines of development of Western societies.

It should be added that the attempts to introduce social and historical information, as well as contrastive and intercultural considerations, sometimes by way of thematic units, is a response to a general tendency within institutionalised foreign language teaching: a greater emphasis on the elementary level. The generalisation of language teaching to a large public means that pupils who have chosen a second or a third foreign language — typically German/French/Spanish as optional subjects in many European countries — stop after one, two, or three years, according to the possibilities offered by the different educational systems. So often pupils are acquainted only with the elementary level, and the textbook is then likely to be the only material they get. This means a greater responsibility as to what is basic and minimal, both linguistically (cf. the Threshold-level discussions of the European Council concerning the definition of minimal communicative capabilities) and socioculturally. So sociocultural elements of more advanced stages tend to 'sink' into the elementary level. It is not unlikely, by the way, that separate thematic units will supplant traditional textbooks even at the elementary level.

Textbooks Between 'Modernism' and 'Post-Modernism'

There are many demands made upon modern textbooks. Beyond the demand that they be good instruments for language learning, they are gradually acquiring a new role as instruments of culture teaching. One may say that they should 'present the country in a nut-shell'.

As the importance of textbooks for the development of a cognitive and affective structure increases, one has to insist on a growing emphasis on social realism (construed in such a way that it is of relevance to the pupils). This can be interpreted as the beginning of a modernisation of textbooks, a modernisation which has come about late at the elementary level because of language teaching traditions. But at the same time textbooks can be said to be influenced by another trend that to a certain extent counteracts the modernisation process: the broad trend within Western culture production that some call *post-modernism*. Many features of recent textbooks can be ascribed to this trend: fragmentation, objectivisation and interest in the bright surface, the absence of expressed values and personal feelings, and the lack of a historical perspective. However, the juxtaposition of styles, which is an important characteristic of post-modern culture, is insignificant. This is presumably to be attributed to the modernisation trend, which for textbooks favours a comparatively realistic style, depicting contemporary everyday life, without great artistic extravagances.

Thus textbooks are quite advanced aesthetically and formally, but from a pedagogical point of view the fragmentation in particular is to be criticised. It is possible that textbooks have been influenced so much by the post-modern trend exactly because of the traditionally secondary status of the sociocultural content. However, the pedagogical milieu is beginning to reflect on the didactic and methodological dimensions of the sociocultural content. One central task of future textbooks, is to contribute to 'cognitive mapping' (Jameson, 1985), i.e. give a structured insight into culture and society. The present interest in national identity may be – among other things – a symptom that the disconnectedness of culture is being felt and questioned.

Away From the Secondary Status

The sociocultural side is thus in the process of being developed pedagogically, and is obtaining a status equal to that of the linguistic side. This entails among other things a more pronounced interdisciplinarity in the production of textbooks, involving for instance a foreign language teaching specialist, an anthropologist, a historian, an illustrator, actors (for photos), and most important: a professional writer who can contribute to a more imaginative, but still realistic, dramatisation of everyday communication.

One of the characteristic features of foreign language textbooks is the great anonymity of the author(s). Though their names are known, they traditionally act as mere mediators with regard to sociocultural issues, at least at the elementary level. This tradition ought to be revised; the point of view of the authors should be open to discussion, so that one might derive some more motivation from the sociocultural content, in addition to those motivation factors associated with the aesthetic form and the language in a narrow sense.

References

ANDERSEN, H. and RISAGER, K. 1978, The relationship between sociocultural and linguistic content in foreign language teaching. In K. GREGERSEN *et al.* (eds) *Papers from the Fourth Scandinavian Conference of Linguistics*, p. 73–78. Odense University Press.
JAMESON, F. 1985, Post-modernismen og den sene kapitalismes kulturelle logik. *Kultur og klasse* 51, p. 82–104 (Copenhagen).
JØRGENSEN, J. Chr. 1972, *Realisme. Litteratursociologiske essays*. Copenhagen: Borgen.
KRAUSKOPF, J. 1985, *Das Deutschland – und Frankreichbild in Schulbüchern*. Tübingen: Gunter Narr Verlag.
RISAGER, K. 1987, Cultural studies and foreign language teaching in Denmark. *ROLIG-papir* 41, Roskilde University Centre.

13 Presenting Distant Cultures: The Third World in West German English Language Textbooks

ANGELIKA KUBANEK

Introduction

West German English-language textbooks have traditionally focused on Great Britain and the United States. In comparison to these 'classic' countries the Third World is far more distant and unfamiliar to the average German student and, as may be contended, the textbook author as well. The Third World is less close in the literal geographical sense which means that it wouldn't be chosen as readily as England for direct cultural contacts like a weekend trip, a language course or a student exchange. It is also less close if we interpret closeness in terms of mass media coverage. In contrast to the pervasive presence of Americana on TV and in everyday life, which seemingly turns us into participant observers of US culture, the quantity of information reaching us from developing nations is rather insignificant. Above all, the Third World is less close because it is not Western. This chapter tries to describe this cultural distance somewhat more precisely, especially its impact on the making of textbooks and on the comprehension of the students working with them. These remarks are to be seen in the context of what may be called a hermeneutic approach to intercultural education and to foreign-language teaching in general. The fact that the Third World has been considered a peripheral and difficult topic in the English-language classroom proves advantageous for an analysis: it allows us to see many of the dimensions of mediation as well as its limitations.

If one looks at English lessons in German schools, the circumstances admittedly are not very favourable for approaching the Third World. Unlike in geography, topical texts appear sporadically only, project teaching is rare, there is a tension between linguistic and cultural aims and the learners are made to discuss an emotional subject in a language which is not their own. Whenever they are presented with a text from or about the Third World, they are actually confronted with three cultures, namely that of the Third World country, that of Great Britain (via the medium of the English language) and their own. The intellectual effort expected from them is even higher if they are to understand the situation of a Pakistani immigrant in Britain in relation to a Turkish worker in West Germany, as reference is made to four cultures. How and to what extent West German post-World War II textbooks have coped with this situation is pointed out below.

The emphasis of this chapter on the concept of distance, thus the 'otherness' of the foreign culture, does not denigrate universal standpoints or educational considerations that have led to representing other countries in an idealised form, especially for younger children (cf. Wright, 1987). On the way towards a world view, however, it might be more sincere not to gloss over existing differences or anticipate a political utopia. A phrase like 'we are all human', which was chosen as a chapter heading in a recent English-language textbook, would lose its vagueness and become an enlightened statement only *after* the learners have become aware of cultural diversity and its positive potential. For a hermeneutic approach to intercultural education, understanding comes by way of seeing the limits of understanding (Hunfeld, 1990).

The method of media evaluation adopted here is reader-orientated in that it focuses on the reader's reception of the texts and illustrations. Thus it places the pupils' comprehension at the centre of attention. It attempts not only to consider teaching resources in terms of bias – which educationists have done in the period since World War I – but to keep in mind the interpretative processes during the making and reading of the textbooks. They include, for instance, what Donald Massey has called 'pre-publishing censorship' that 'directly determines the view of reality allowed in the texts' (1987:130) or the attitudes towards the Third World which the students have acquired before dealing with the subject matter in school. Even if much of this can only be arrived at by means of a construct here it is regarded to be an important complement to a media analysis on the descriptive level.

A Note on Terminology

'To them, we are the Third World.' ('Für die sind wir schon die Dritte Welt'.) This quotation was used by a recent *Der Spiegel* feature to highlight the feelings of the Ruhrgebiet steelworkers and coalminers faced with yet another series of lay-offs. The speaker quoted does not express concern about the Third World but about his own situation. He is using the term figuratively to denote a state of poverty and political powerlessness. It can be seen that he gives the Third World only those attributes he presently finds relevant to his own condition. As to the Third World, he is generalising.

Some 15 years ago a slogan was made up in adult development education which bears some resemblance to the steelworker's statement quoted above: 'The Third World begins in Germany'. ('Die Dritte Welt beginnt bei uns'). In this case it is the expression of a theory that assumed that an awareness among the West German population for the Third World proper might be awakened only if people were shown everyday situations where they felt powerless themselves (Gronemeyer & Bahr, 1977). This chapter keeps to the established geopolitical meaning.

'Third World' is an umbrella term, covering the least developed and newly industrialising countries, urban conglomerations and deserts, Westernised elites and slum dwellers, nuclear research in Brazil and Stone Age ploughing methods. If one is to use distance as a key concept one would then have to be clear first of all about the specific *degree* of distance manifest in each text selected for the classroom. As cultural distance is a very complex phenomenon, some examples may serve to illustrate the range of points a teacher might consider before examining the texts proper. A West German 16-year-old might, due to his exposure to American TV programmes, music and popular trends, feel quite at home in his fictitious version of American reality and not be aware of any distance at all. The same German might, depending on his socio-economic background and upbringing, feel as uneasy in a Soweto Kahawa shack (i.e. a Nairobi slum area) as in the manor house of some aristocratic Etonian his age. And the business traveller might not be able to tell Nairobi from La Guardia right away (or even care to) as a consequence of the internationalisation of many sectors of life.

Germans and Foreigners

A German student's image of the Third World, thus one of his frames of reference when understanding a text, has been shaped to some extent by the foreigners in his own country. As in the classroom his encounter with the Third World is doubly indirect — he is reading and he is in a Western country — he will draw on any points of comparison he can find anchored in his own experience. The following demographic data[1] will be somewhat detailed to give an idea of one sociocultural factor that influences the interpretation of texts about other cultures. West Germany has a total population of 61 million, of which 4.5 million are foreigners according to the Federal Bureau of Statistics (31 December 1986). The eight largest ethnic minority groups are listed in the following order: Turks (1.4 million), Yugoslavs (600,000), Italians, Greeks, Austrians, Spanish, Dutch and (Portuguese (78,000). Some 58% have lived in Germany for more than 10 years (Statistisches Bundesamt, 1987). In addition, there are some 850,000 members of the allied forces and their families. Of the eight countries afore-mentioned seven are European; Turkey is an associated member of the EEC and a newly industrialising country which is classified as a European developing nation by the OECD, whereas in the list of UN member states it is entered under Asia. The majority of Turks, though, are trying to feel at home in Germany, and to some of the second generation, Turkey might seem stranger than Germany once did to their parents. In 1985, some 34,000 people were granted German citizenship, though only 850 of them were Turks.

As to registered foreigners from Third World countries, the highest numbers are given for Iran (73,000), Morocco (51,000), both Vietnams (31,000), India (28,000), Sri Lanka (28,000) and Lebanon (22,000) (Statistisches Bundesamt, Fachserie 1, 31 December 1986). A smaller group of foreigners and the one whose presence touches a sensitive political issue is that of the refugees applying for political asylum. In 1986, there were about 100,000 applications (Poles: 11,000, Iranians; 22,000; Lebanese: 11,000). At present, the quota of success is about 10% (*Suddeutsche Zeitung* Feb. 12, 1988). This number of 100,000 includes the ethnic Germans from Eastern Europe who arrive each year and who are considered German according to the Constitution if born within the German borders of 1937. The numbers of foreigners are highest in the big cities like Munich, Frankfurt and Hamburg, where 31 nationalities are having to co-exist in a certain district (*Zeit Magazin*, Dec. 12, 1987). In the light of these data, can Germany be called a multicultural society? An answer to this question would not only have to take numbers into account but also the attitude of the government and public opinion. The present Conservative ruling party does not seem all that favourable towards political integration of foreigners. It may be worthwhile to state in this context the view held by the influential Freiburg professor of politics Dieter Oberndörfer, himself a conservative. In his lucid and vehement pleading for a liberalisation of the legislation he contrasts the idea of the republic to which its citizens belong by act of will with that of the nation held together by the same language and heritage. He contends that the West German Constitution is outdated in so far as it adheres to the concept of the nation, and that not only Germany but also a future United States of Europe ought to open their borders to immigrants from the Third World countries, too, and grant them citizenship. He claims that the attitude of the average West German towards foreigners is, apart from pockets of extreme right-wing hostility, far more positive than that of the government (Oberndörfer, 1987). As to development co-operation in its present form, 74% of the population are in favour of it, an attitude which seemingly is irrespective of unemployment figures in Germany itself (Bundesministerium, 1985: 85).

If a reader's interpretation is guided by his experience and attitudes acquired before the act of reading, a comparative media analysis will be rendered rather difficult if not impossible in this respect, because the interpretation of the texts will vary both inside Germany and from one culture to the next, depending on the presence of foreigners in the students' neighbourhood and schools. Apart from the sociocultural background inside Germany, experience gained by travelling, i.e. by direct encounters with other ways of life, will bear on the understanding of texts read later on. Data on tourism ought to be taken into account even if the average 12 to 16-year-old most likely has not travelled to the Third World yet. The tourist approach is, however, rather common in foreign language textbooks, the coverage of Third World topics being no exception. Out of all the journeys made by Germans in 1986, 3% led to non-European countries; 1.7% of all Germans who travelled went to a Third World country which amounts to a figure of 840,000 persons. According to the World Tourism Organisation list of border arrivals (business and touristic), the seven Third World countries visited by most Germans were Mexico (120,000), Thailand (115,000), Hong Kong (115,000), Singapore (78,000), India (61,000), Sri Lanka (49,000) and the People's Republic of China (48,000). Developing nations north of the Sahara (Tunisia, Morocco, Egypt) are not included; here the figures exceed that of Mexico. In Tunisia there were, for instance, 6 million overnight stays by Germans in the year 1987 (*Die Zeit*, Feb 1, 1988).

Much criticism has been brought forward against the charter flight and the hippie-type tourist alike; on the other hand, tourism has become an important economic factor in many developing nations. It is argued that tourism can serve to reinforce existing stereotypes – a German will return as German as he was before (Hunfeld, 1984). Some stratagems to increase public awareness that are primarily addressed to multipliers like travel agents and tour guides have been devised by non-governmental development institutions (cf. Pfäfflin, 1985). So far, English-language textbook writers do not seem to have taken much notice of these suggestions. It may, however, be argued that awareness programmes aimed at outgoing foreign technical and business experts, like the ones gradually being implemented at the German Foundation for International Development, Bonn, will be much more consequential than any well-meaning efforts in textbooks, the contents of which will probably be forgotten by the pupils sooner or later (Punnamparambil, 1987).

Development Education and English Language Teaching Theory

As there is no accepted terminology, 'development education' will be used throughout this section even though teaching about the Third World has not always come under this title. In Germany one can read the terms *Dritte-Welt-Pädagogik*, *Entwicklungspädagogik* or *Entwicklungsbezogene Bildungs – und Öffentlichkeitsarbeit*; the 'world perspective' courses demanded by some British educationalists also belong to this context.

In their 1986 review of 30 years of development education in Germany, Treml and Seitz somewhat pessimistically write that it has come back to where it started, namely to the concepts of intercultural understanding promoted in the late 1950s (cf. p. 26). Most language teachers would agree that intercultural competence and tolerance towards members of other nations are indeed aims of their teaching, transcending linguistic and pragmatic competence. Are the two authors then playing down the role of foreign language teaching? Their statement is not directed against it, as one might think at first, for the simple reason that there has been no noteworthy interaction between the two fields, at least in the case of English. Whatever English-language textbooks since 1945 have had to say about the Third World has been far more influenced by the history of English didactics itself than by any impulses from outside. On a more general level, however, Treml and Seitz's criticism does not exclude English language teaching, as they are expressing concern about a return to non-political approaches noticeable for the 1980s. In West Germany, development education has basically been the domain of *Politikdidaktik*, the churches and other non-governmental organisations working at grassroots level. The *political* dimensions of consciousness-raising were first described around 1967, this shift in awareness being a consequence of decolonisation inside the Third

World, the students' movement and the reception of the dependency theories, to name some main factors:

> Jetzt erscheint die Dritte Welt nicht nur als Thema der Presse oder als Unterrichtsstoff ..., sondern im Mittelpunkt steht jetzt die (politische) *Beziehung* zwischen Industrieländern und sog. 'Entwicklungsländern' ... Weil Unterentwicklung jetzt als historisch und systematisch 'gemacht' erscheint, tritt die Forderung nach *Gerechtigkeit* ... in den Mittelpunkt der Entwicklungspolitik. Für die entwicklungspolitische Bildungsarbeit bedeutete dies eine Politisierung, d.h. die Dritte Welt erscheint jetzt nicht mehr bloß als ein Thema (unter anderen), sondern als normative Herausforderung globaler Verantwortung. (Treml & Seitz, 1986: 19)
> [Now the Third World appears not only as a topic in the press or as classroom material; instead, the (political) *relations* between industrialised and so-called developing nations are at the centre of attention. As underdevelopment is now being regarded as something created historically and systematically, the demand for justice is central to development policy. Development education thus became political, i.e. the Third World is no longer just one topic among others, but a normative challenge to global responsibility.] (Author's translation)

The period from 1968 to 1976 has been the most active phase of development education so far in regard to resources and reflections on concepts of mediation (Seitz, 1987: V, 41). Most of the approximately 800–1,000 materials and about 100 theoretical papers currently available were published during those years, which were followed by a sharp decline in the output of teaching notes and a stagnation of theory. The trends which have emerged since the middle of the 1970s are summed up by Seitz: there is an extended media coverage of ecological topics in answer to a more discerning public; non-governmental organisations are concentrating on supporting alternative strategies of development like adapted technology, basic needs and self-reliance projects; the 'human capital' theory which had placed high hopes in institutionalised learning and its effect on the socio-economic development in the Third World had to be reappraised; the general mood is described by Seitz as one of disillusionment about the potential of change which educational work might set free. There is too a shift of attention towards a world view; thus under- and overdevelopment, the effects of industrial civilisation on the ecological balance are placed in one common context, and there are some attempts to create a network between ecological and development education and teaching for peace

(*Öko-, Entwicklungs- und Friedenspädagogik*). Development education is propagated by persons living in industrialised countries ('*Erste Welt*') for target groups in industrialised countries. It starts out from phenomena in West Germany which are then viewed in their international dimension.

Development education has mainly been an out-of-school movement, even if the Third World became an obligatory topic in school syllabi during the 1970s, especially in geography teaching. Due to their conservative nature, schools were regarded with scepticism, as a change of the structural injustice in the relations between industrialised and developing countries would imply radical change within Western societies as well. The authors of a 1970 analysis of textbooks, for example, concluded that even the most thoughtful and advanced textbooks could not prevent a perpetuation of distorted images as long as these were being reproduced by socialisation (Fohrbeck *et al.*, 1971). Datta (1984) criticises schools because they lack interdisciplinary teaching and models allowing anticipatory and participatory learning. As many German teachers rely solely on their textbooks — which, incidentally, must be approved by the Ministry of Education of the respective constituent state — other possible perspectives and interpretations are kept outside the learner's horizon. Datta states, though, that some concepts originally designed for out-of-school education have disseminated into schools. In this context, the abandoning of curricular materials is viewed as a sign of insecurity among educationalists with regard to aims and methodology.

The trends in ELT theory have not run parallel to those in development education. In order to evaluate the approaches towards the Third World in ELT media one has to take a look at the history of English teaching in Germany (Kubanek, 1987: 10–13; 163–73). Firstly, English was established as a subject in German schools during the last quarter of the nineteenth century, thus in the heyday of imperialism when Germany's Emperor Wilhelm II also demanded a 'place in the sun' for his nation. Even if there is little information in those early textbooks about the regions that today comprise the modern Third World it can be contended that the textbook image was distorted to begin with. Secondly, English language textbooks seem to perpetuate standard approaches to their contents (e.g. London) from one generation to the next until there is open controversy, such as on the image of women. After World War II, German textbooks were only approved for use after having been purged of nationalistic and racist passages. In the course of 1946 and 1947, responsibility was handed back to German commissions. Most attention was devoted to history and German textbooks, and it may be assumed that in the case of English textbooks the sections on Britain and the United States were handled most carefully. Because of re-education these two countries were now presented as model democracies. Third World countries were still unfamiliar and unimportant (decolonisation was only just beginning) to textbook makers. Thus tendencies expressed in previous textbooks were not fully eliminated because of a lack of awareness. Thirdly, as a consequence of Britain's exemplary image the British figures featuring in the texts were endowed with positive characteristics. This positive attitude extended to British colonial and Commonwealth history, or rather the German textbook authors' interpretation of it. Thus it was possible for instance to print texts on the white Cecil Rhodes and the black Matabele warriors which today would be considered as being openly racist. Because of German anglophilia, decolonisation the British way would in general be regarded positively, the 'family of nations' metaphor being one example. Fourthly, most of the articles written about the Third World as a topic in the English classroom (not a large number as yet) are of rather recent origin, namely the late 1970s and the 1980s. This is partly due to the time lag with which English didactics quite often reacts to trends in related academic disciplines; partly it follows from the role of English didactics at universities. Tenured chairs were established as of the late 1960s only, and the new discipline in certain respects tended to take up trends first set by English Literature (*Anglistik*). There, however, Commonwealth literature including that from English-speaking Third World countries was deemed worthy of academic scrutiny rather belatedly, too, i.e. towards the end of the 1970s only. If one goes by the number of publications, the year 1980 seems to mark a change towards a more discerning perception of phenomena related to the Third World. The fact that many of the newer articles in English didactics have been devoted to (mediating) Third World literature ought not to be considered as a handicap; on the contrary, the attempts to come to terms with literary texts provide plenty of food for thought on mediation and intercultural dialogue in the foreign language classroom in general.

The Textbook and the 'Reality' of the Third World

The encounter with the Third World taking place in the English classroom is of an indirect nature. Basically, the student learns by reading and then talking about what was read. The meaning of texts is negotiated during classroom discourse. Access to the foreign culture is gained by means of resources (print media, or, for that matter, films or oral history cassettes) which serve as a substitute for living informants from the Third World. This means that the Third World is not really tangible; the learners' experience is secondary, imaginative and rather cognitive. In comparison to multi-racial classes there is less potential conflict but also less potential insight which would be made possible by the presence of pupils of non-western nationalities. Due to Germany's demographic structure (pointed out before) there are few classes with non-European pupils.

Thus it is up to the media to bring some glimpses of foreign reality into the classroom. If one goes by checklists for textbook evaluation, the quality of a textbook is partly determined by whether it provides a realistic image of a foreign country, the keyword being 'authenticity'. Publishers do not fail to emphasise the amount of authentic material when they are promoting new books. However, after considering how a textbook is made one is led to conclude that 'authenticity' is a criterion with little if any validity; first of all, every text about the Third World is already an *interpretation* of reality, whether it was written by a native novelist, a favela dweller like Carolina Maria de Jesus from Sao Paulo, a Western journalist or a German teacher putting together a background commentary. The most authentic document would be the one the learner cannot understand because it is written in a native dialect. If one thinks of the oral tradition in many Third World cultures, even the recording and writing down of recited poetry, for instance, would be a stepping away from authenticity. English lessons have one advantage over German classes in so far as the teachers do not need to draw on translations if the Third World author has used the medium of English.

By the time the learner finally looks at the chapter on the Third World in his book, further moves away from authenticity have taken place. The texts have been transformed from a non-Western to a Western culture, they have been screened, abridged and simplified by textbook makers and editors who have the German market and the ministerial stamp of approval in mind, the chapters are interspersed with tasks and exercises, and, in keeping with current trends, the pages are laid out as kaleidoscopically as possible. Textbooks are not written, they are assembled, to the effect that the learner is faced with many fragments of information. The texts have been deprived of their contexts. Much research is devoted to analysing the *image* of another society. Looking at recent English textbooks one may, however, contend that it would not be correct to speak of images, as the concept of image presupposes something that has discernible features and contours. What many textbooks are offering appears as a 'heap of broken images', to quote T.S. Eliot. The learner who is to make sense out of this is at a loss.

'Authenticity' is a political term too. It could be argued that an emphasis on aspects of underdevelopment is one-sided in so far as it subtly denigrates the dignity of people in the Third World, even if the opposite was intended by the textbook makers. In a paradoxical way, literary texts alone can be called authentic because they do not pretend to depict reality. The foreign world is recreated by the reader's imagination and is authentic as long as the act of reading continues.

The Third World in West German English-Language Textbooks

It was said before that English didactics in West Germany became aware of the Third World rather belatedly, namely towards the end of the 1970s. This statement referred to the theory of English teaching, whereas in the textbooks themselves passages on colonies, later Commonwealth countries or developing nations were included long before. This factual evidence alone, however, does not allow any conclusion as to the quality of such texts and the value system manifest in them. What was lacking first was an interest in the Third World; later on, textbook makers and editors, though well-meaning and politically minded, have tried to muddle through. It can be seen from the German evidence that there needs to be a close interaction between practice and theory – especially a theory which takes into account the hermeneutic dimension of mediating texts on the Third World.

This section presents selected results of an empirical study of about 180 textbooks published between 1947 and 1986. The books examined were mainly made for learners in their first to sixth year of English (Sekundarstufe I), although some resources for sixth forms (Sekundarstufe II) were sampled as well as material from the 1920s and 1930s (Kubanek, 1987). Out of all Third World countries India has received most attention by far, for obvious reasons. It is a country confirming all popular clichés on poverty and the exotic; it was among the first nations to receive West German aid, and is the biggest recipient of aid today. Due to the German textbook maker's britocentric view, Britain's former 'jewel in the crown' was considered important enough to feature in German textbooks as well. The exemplary figure of Gandhi fitted in with education for tolerance as it was promoted in the 1950s. The article on Gandhi printed in the *Learning English* series of the 1960s (Klett Publishers) focused on Gandhi's personal achievement and not on what happened in India and Pakistan after his death. A preference for India can be noted in recent volumes, too. *Panorama*, a reader for sixth forms edited by D. Buttjes (1986, Dortmund), devotes one of its two chapters on the English-speaking Third World to India.

The highest quantity of texts is usually found in books for the fourth and fifth year of learning, Britain and the United States have been covered before. Many syllabi are leaving it open whether Canada, New Zealand or Australia or a non-Western Commonwealth country is dealt with. As a rule, there are more texts in grammar school books than in those intended for secondary modern, *Hauptschule,* or technical schools, *Realschule.* The two volumes with the highest percentage of passages devoted to developing nations (about 14% of all pages) were Klett Publishers' (1967), *Going Round the World,* the last volume in a series of four made for secondary modern schools, and the sixth volume of a series called *Yes* (1983, Dortmund, Mittlere Ausgabe).

The fact that contrary to what was just said a book for secondary modern schools dealt with the Third World so extensively can be explained by the year of its publication. Towards the end of the 1960s, English became a compulsory subject in this type of school after embittered discussions about more equality of opportunity in Germany's educational system. New books with new ideas were produced. This example quite obviously shows that a whole series of reasons is responsible for the way a topic is handled. As to *Yes,* one can see that the personal standpoint of the textbook makers bears on the treatment of a given subject matter. This is true for the series *Contacts,* too, jointly edited by Piepho and Bredella (Bochum: Kamp) which is the only one consciously trying to present a world perspective from the beginning.

If one examines the degree of activity ascribed to Western or non-Western figures inside the Third World the latter definitely lose out, which is in keeping with the results of related research on textbooks' images of the developing nations. An attempt to make out phases in the approach of the topic leads to the conclusion that a britocentric view was dominant up to the late 1960s. In the 1970s, the focus was on poverty, highlighted both by personalised though often fictitious accounts and factual texts including statistics. The 1980s gradually brought on a shift towards a global perspective, the emphasis now being placed on ecology and the future of the human race. These topics are undoubtedly important, but if one looks at the way the Third World has been approached so far it becomes clear that there has never been a time when it was presented in a direct way so that it could first be discerned by the learners as an object demanding interpretation in its own right, as a world which is different. In all the books examined there is only one sentence with striking unfamiliarity, namely a sentence in the Kikuyu language in a political fable by Jomo Kenyatta.

There is no evidence of racism in textbooks published since the 1970s. It is, however, worth mentioning in this context that even in all these more recent volumes only 10% of all texts dealing with the Third World are written by native authors. This clearly points to the eurocentric character of the books. Even if one grants that eurocentrism is inevitable because we cannot avoid thinking within our frames of reference originating in Europe, a different ratio ought to be possible.

As to other sources a teacher might draw on, very little is available for the English classroom. There are a radio play by the Black African poet Obi Ebuna (Klett), a sixth-form brochure called *Britain and India* (Schöningh), topical texts on tourism which basically amount to newspaper cuttings with vocabulary notes (Klett, Diesterweg), a booklet called *A Common Language* (Cornelsen – Velhagen & Klasing), and a 1988 sixth-form reader attempting to follow some concepts of a hermeneutic approach to intercultural learning (Bayerischer Schulbuch Verlag). Apart from this, a German teacher might consider the Dritte Welt Archiv run by W. Pfaffenberger, or he might turn to Heinemann's African Writers Series, for example, right away.

Suggestions and Issues for Debate

(1) It is assumed in this chapter that media evaluation ought to focus on contents and contexts equally. Some examples have been given of how the specific German context bears on the presentation of the Third World and, in turn, on the interpretation of data. Under these premises the value ascribed to comparative, cross-cultural studies appears to be somewhat limited, at least as regards English language textbooks.

(2) The concept of distance, some of whose facets were outlined, might be put to more practical use by a teacher assessing course materials. Four dimensions of distance were noted:

– the degree of distance between the pupil's European culture and that of the Third World, depending on which segment a given text turns to (Westernised elites, international conferences within developing countries, archaic traditions, Third World minorities in Western countries etc.)
– distance between the German pupil reading texts and the realities of the other cultures, due to the fact that neither authenticity nor, from the reader's position, total empathy are possible
– the degree of distance determined by the amount of knowledge and the attitudes a pupil has about the topic before the course begins (*Vorverständnis*)

- distance originating in the structure of the textbook itself which prevents the learner from gaining access to the foreign world.

(3) There is no lack of awareness of the problems of the Third World or of interdependence; what is striking, though, is the lack of an underlying didactic concept.

(4) The question of how the English classroom works towards a breaking down of stereotypes touches on a sensitive point in so far as beginner and intermediary level textbooks simplify both linguistically and contentwise; thus they use the mechanisms of stereotyping themselves for some time.

(5) Britain has lost much of her political power. In the light of this historical fact the traditional sequence of presenting English-speaking cultures in textbooks might be reappraised.

(6) Based on the evidence in 40 years of textbook production it is suggested that for future generations of textbooks, the following points might be considered. If the Third World continues to be a topic in textbooks, the ratio between texts written by native and Western authors ought to be 50:50. Another approach would be to leave out some of the cultural background sections in textbooks and devise country-study booklets similar to existing supplementary readers, one or two of which ought to be compulsory reading in a scholastic year. A third approach might place literary texts from the Third World at the centre of attention. Fourthly, the role of the German visiting the Third World has hardly been dealt with, even though it would seem rather natural to start out from there. His attempts at using the English language, culture shocks and misunderstandings would be topics to be presented in such texts.

(7) There is no lack of information about the Third World; the pupil is being overburdened with complex problems he is supposed to discuss in one lesson. The amount of texts ought to be reduced, leaving room for more questions critically guiding the pupil's comprehension.

(8) Current textbooks ought to be reappraised with regard to the way they shape a learner's view of the world. They appear as a compilation of fragments; to the eyes of the student, information about any given topic lacks coherence, there is no holistic approach, no *Gestalt*.

(9) In view of the sceptical assessment of achievements in development education, a closer contact with institutions working in the field of development co-operation seems necessary to reach such target groups that more directly determine the relationship between industrialised and developing nations.

(10) If foreign language teaching wants to approach the Third World more closely, the specific contribution of the foreign language classroom will have to be outlined more precisely.

Note added in proof

1. The manuscript was finished in 1988 and does not reflect political changes in Germany since then.

References

BUNDESMINISTERIUM FÜR WIRTSCHAFTLICHE ZUSAMMENARBEIT (ed.) 1985, 6. *Bericht zur Entwicklungspolitik der Bundesregierung*. Bonn.
——(ed.) 1987, *Journalisten-Handbuch Entwicklungspolitik*. Bonn.
DATTA, A. 1984, Theorie und Praxis der Entwicklungspädagogik. Lernprozesse und Krisen. *Zeitschrift für Entwicklungspädogogik* 7, 4, 3–9.
——1986, Pädogogische Vernetzung. Zum Zusammenhang von Öko-, Dritte-Welt- und Friedenspädagogik. *Zeitschrift für Entwicklungspädogogik* 9, 2, 11–17.
FOHRBECK, K. et al. 1971, *Heile Welt und Dritte Welt*. Opladen: Leske.
GRONEMEYER, M. and BAHR, H.E. (eds) 1977, *Erwachsenenbildung. Testfall Dritte Welt*.Opladen: Leske.
HUNFELD, H. 1984, *Geschichten vom deutschen Amerika*. Bochum: Kamp.
HUNFELD, H. 1990, *Literatur als Sprachlehre Ansätze eines hermeneutisch orientierten fremdsprachenunterrichts*. Berlin: Langenscheidt.
HUNFELD, H. KUBANEK, A. and MWAURA, B. (eds) 1988, *Approaching the Third World*. Munich: Bayerischer Schulbuch Verlag (Student Book and Teacher Handbook).
KUBANEK, A. 1987, *Dritte Welt im Englischlehrbuch der Bundesrepublik. Aspekte der Darstellung und Vermittlung*. Regensburg: Pustet.
MASSEY, D. 1987, Shaping textbook images. *Internationale Schulbuchforschung* 9, 2, 129–135.
OBERNDÖRFER, D. 1987, Die Bundesrepublik Deutschland, Europa und die Dritte Welt: Zum 'nationalen' Selbstverständnis der Bundesrepublik. In M. HÄTTICH (ed.) *Zum Staatsverständnis der Gegenwart*, 221–44 Munich: Olzog.
PFAFFENBERGER, W. 1987, Entwicklungspädagogische Überlegungen für Schule und Unterricht. *Zeitschrift für Entwicklungspädagogik* 3, 16–19.
PFÄFFLIN, G.F. 1985, *Tourismus und Entwicklung*. Stuttgart: Zentrum für Entwicklungsbezogene Bildung.
PRESSE- UND INFORMATIONSAMT DER BUNDESREGIERUNG (ed.) 1987, *Die alliierten Streitkräfte in der Bundesrepublik Deutschland*. Bonn (typescript).
PUNNAMPARAMBIL, J. 1987, Sprachunterricht für die Fachkräfte der Entwicklungszusammenarbeit. Einige grundlegende Anmerkungen. Bad Honnef: Deutsche Stiftung für internationale Entwicklung, 12 June (typescript).
SCHÜREN, R. 1985, Kulturkontakt und Lernerbezug. Zwei vernachlässigte

Dimensionen des fremdsprachlichen Unterrichts. *Englisch-Amerikanische Studien* 7, 2, 330–47.
SEITZ, K. 1986f., Steinbrüche, Bausteine, Impulse. Drei Jahrzehnte entwicklungsbezogene Bildungsarbeit. Serialised review in *epd-Entwicklungspolitik* no. 17 (1986), 20–2; no. 20 (1986), 21f.; no. 21/22 (1986), 28–30; no.2 (1987), 11–14 and 28; no. 5/6 (1987), 39–43; no. 14/15 (1987), 35–8.
STATISTISCHES BUNDESAMT (1986), Fachserie 1, Reihe 2. Ausländer 1986. Wiesbaden (Mimeo).
——(ed.) 1987, *Statistisches Jahrbuch für die Bundesrepublik Deutschland.* Stuttgart: Kohlhammer.
STUDIENKREIS FÜR TOURISMUS (ed.) 1974 ff., *Sympathie Magazine.* Starnberg.
TREML, A. and SEITZ, K. 1986, Geschichte der entwicklungspolitischen Bildung. 20 Jahre Dritte Welt-Pädagogik. *Zeitschrift für entwicklungsbezogene Bildung* 9, 2, 18–24.
WATTIE, N. 1983, Geographical, historical and cultural distances in the reception of literary works. In D. RIEMENSCHNEIDER (ed.), *The History and Historiography of Commonwealth Literature.* Tübingen: Narr.
WRIGHT, D.R. 1987, A pupil's perspective on textbooks – issues of motivation and racism. *Internationale Schulbuchforschung* 9, 2, 137–42.

14 World Studies and Foreign Language Teaching: Converging Approaches in Textbook Writing

HUGH STARKEY

In Austria, a class of 15-year-olds are writing letters in English to heads of government, calling for the release of prisoners of conscience. In Portugal, a class of 17-year-olds is preparing an exhibition for International Human Rights Day on the exploitation of child labour in nineteenth century England. In France, a class of 16-year-olds is studying a simplified version of the Universal Declaration of Human Rights. Two things link these examples: firstly pupils are learning about human rights, secondly they are doing so as part of learning a foreign language.

World Studies

For teachers of languages, the Council of Europe's important influence on foreign language teaching in the 1970s and 1980s is well known and well documented (Clark, 1987). Perhaps less well known to them, but also widely influential in Europe, is the Council's programme to promote teaching and learning about human rights in schools (Shafer, 1987). In Britain the major curriculum development initiative to include teaching and learning about other people and countries within an explicit values system of human rights is called World Studies (Hicks & Townley, 1982; Richardson, 1976 and 1979; Fisher & Hicks, 1985). The term dates from the early 1970s when the One World Trust, an education trust of the all-party Parliamentary Group for World Government, set up the 'World Studies Project'. Thanks to some imaginative and intellectually rigorous work by the project's director,

Robin Richardson, the innovative teaching techniques he pioneered were widely adopted, although as a curriculum subject World Studies has remained marginal. In particular, the suggestions contained in the project's first handbook, which is still in demand, enable teachers without first-hand experience of other countries to help children explore significant features of foreign cultures without stereotyping or simplifying absurdly.

Currently the project continues as the World Studies 8–13 Project (concentrating on work with 8 to 13-year-olds). The upper part of this age range is also when children start to learn a foreign language. The project has participating schools in nearly half of the education authorities in England and Wales. The first directors of the 8–13 project, Fisher and Hicks, define World Studies as 'studies which promote the knowledge, attitudes and skills that are relevant to living responsibly in a multicultural and interdependent world'. This will, of course, include 'studying cultures and countries other than one's own and the ways in which they are different from and similar to one's own' (1985: 8).

Selby and Pike, influenced by American usage, replace the term 'world studies' with 'global education'. This, they claim, has five irreducible dimensions, namely: systems consciousness, health of planet awareness, involvement consciousness and preparedness, process mindedness and perspective consciousness. The aims of this latter element are that students should 'recognise that they have a worldview that is not universally shared' and 'develop receptivity to other perspectives' (Pike & Selby, 1988: 34).

Both World Studies and global education insist on a child-centred, active learning and experimental pedagogy. Teachers adopting World Studies offer the following rationale:

- It builds on children's immediate curiosity so they work hard and learn basic skills.
- It uses active teaching methods such as discussion, simulations and co-operative games.
- Students learn to avoid ethnocentrism and false generalisations about others.
- It is useful for trade.
- Students start to think in terms of systems and structures as well as groups and individuals.
- Our interdependent but divided world threatens the existence of life itself unless it becomes an interdependent world based on solidarity.

Foreign Language Teaching

All the classroom activities proposed by the 8–13 project involve, it is claimed:

An approach to teaching and learning which begins from, though is certainly not limited to, children's own experience and interests. Active teaching methods such as role-play, discussion exercises or games are used in order to explore more graphically problems of perception, communication and action. Children are being stimulated and challenged; they are being invited to express their own opinions and their views are taken seriously. They are reflecting both on their own world and other people's worlds, and learning from each about both. (Fisher & Hicks, 1985: 7)

Surprisingly, it is only recently that teachers of foreign languages have made any links at all with these other labourers in the intercultural vineyard.

In many European countries, one important slot in the curriculum where human rights values are taught is foreign language teaching. The examples cited in the initial paragraph of this chapter are illustrative of this. In Great Britain, although the tradition of studying world issues and questions relating to human rights, such as sexism and racism, is well established in the final (sixth and seventh) years of secondary school foreign language learning, it has no explicit rationale nor any formal recognition. The values underlying the teaching of languages are rarely made explicit. Indeed, some textbooks are notoriously racist and sexist, whether by ignorance or design.

It is recognised, in Britain as in most European countries, that language learning should include cultural studies from the earliest age. Girard's (1987) survey for the Council of Europe reveals most national syllabuses to have cultural as well as linguistic and general educational aims. His survey of textbooks shows these cultural aims to be incorporated even though there was little evidence of attention to broader educational concerns. In Britain the 1988 official statement makes the following claim for the benefits of foreign language learning: 'It contributes to an understanding of the cultures, attitudes and ways of life in other countries which is important in a country with complex and extensive international relations' (DES, 1988: 2). Whilst not so detailed or impassioned as the statements from World Studies this statement is entirely compatible with their aims.

For such benefits to be delivered, syllabuses and textbooks need to bear this aim in mind as well as purely linguistic aims. However, one indirect result of the Council of Europe's pioneering work has been for the content of foreign language teaching to be defined in terms of transactional language and situations of supposed immediate relevance to an imagined Eurotraveller. As Clark (1987) points out, when groups of teachers in the late 1970s started to define language syllabuses in terms of graded objectives, they leant heavily on van Ek's 'Threshold level' (1975). For the first time syllabuses were constructed on the basis of situations in which a learner (an adult in the original version) might need to communicate in a foreign language and the kinds of language activity the learner might wish to engage in. The hegemony of a grammatically determined language learning sequence was broken.

However, the enumeration of situations and of linguistic functions is limited only by the imagination. Any selection of contexts and functions can be replaced by others. Each selection will be constructed after more or less careful thought. One common scenario upon which syllabuses are based is that of the young learner as traveller to the foreign country and guest in a family. The teachers compiling the syllabus then infer certain language needs, such as being able to introduce oneself, being able to make purchases, being able to accept or refuse invitations. The resulting syllabuses and their accompanying course books and examinations have tended to present a very circumscribed view of the world, both geographically and socially. The world presented tends to be white and classless, that is to say middle-class.

In a decentralised system such as that in England and Wales, developments in methodology occur through a partnership between, primarily, teachers, teacher-trainers and publishers. Changes in content are heavily influenced by the university-dominated examination boards. The priority of both groups through the 1980s has been to provide a teaching method and a content suitable for all pupils of secondary age. The stimulus to change arose from the fact that until the 1970s only selected students were offered a foreign language. The result of much hard work is that communicative methodology is now accepted in principle. It is, of course, only partially attained in practice.

Changing Content in Language Teaching

The content of foreign language teaching has also undergone changes, particularly in so far as there has been a move away from written forms towards spoken forms. However, the focus has been on a narrow range of content dominated by transactional language. The list of content areas provided by the inspectorate in England and Wales (DES, 1987: 9) is both illustrative and, to the extent that its publication influences teachers and course-book writers, prescriptive (though the inspectorate claim this is not the case):

> exchanging personal information
> family and home
> pastimes and hobbies
> weather
> school
> finding their way about town
> simple shopping
> food and drink
> daily routine
> sickness and health
> the foreign country
> travelling and holidays
> staying with a family abroad

For teaching and examining purposes these content areas are divided into individual tasks or exchanges. An objective is defined, such as: 'to be able to ask for directions to a destination in town'. An appropriate linguistic structure is then taught and the teaching is judged to be successful if the learner is able to produce a formula such as 'Pardon madame, pour aller à la gare s'il vous plaît?' given a recognised stimulus. As Clark observes, the fragmentation of the syllabus into small assessable units means that much foreign language teaching has a largely predetermined outcome. Students may, of course, use this knowledge and skill creatively for ends totally unforeseen by their teachers, but the situations proposed will often militate against imaginative variations. This largely predetermined, fragmented set of learning outcomes may be contrasted with a World Studies approach. In World Studies, enquiry-based learning and open-endedness are the essence. In language learning it is often only in the later stages that creative use of language becomes a goal, even though real-life communication is essentially unpredictable and therefore open-ended.

Because intercultural objectives are so much harder to define than linguistic ones they have been relegated to a mere appendage to mainstream foreign language teaching. As Byram (1984) has pointed out, Risager and Andersen's (1978) analysis of Danish textbooks for teaching French is equally applicable to most language teaching textbooks published in Britain. Imaginary and stereotypical middle-class families leading totally unproblematical lives, apart from the occasional car breakdown, serve to illustrate the more colourfully quaint aspects of their supposed home country. Byram's research reported in this present volume lends support to the clearly observable phenomenon that children learning a language learn little about its culture and that textbooks are often the source of misconceptions.

Textbook Content

To judge by most of the published courses, the basic values of foreign language teaching would appear to be materialism and consumerism. It is in fact quite possible that the rejection of foreign language learning by a large number of British students at 13 and at 16 is linked to their perception that the subject has very little to do with intercultural understanding and very much to do with fairly unenlightened forms of tourism.

However, even given the content categories specified by the inspectorate, alternative visions are possible. Conversations are likely to be very different if, under the heading of travel, the role-play is the traditional customs officer and tourist or if the roles are immigration officer and black tourist. The latter situation might offer some insights into immigration policy and an opportunity for raising some very open-ended questions. Food and drink are potentially interesting and controversial issues. Questions of health, of power, of advertising, of hunger and starvation in the world, hence of justice, are all areas of enquiry in this topic. Finding one's way around town may lead to all sorts of discoveries about life in cities that tourist boards and even governments would not wish to be revealed. Why are there people in London and Paris sleeping under bridges or in cramped hostels? Daily routine invites questions about lifestyle and its impact on the environment, for example. Alternatively the impact of working conditions and location on daily routine could lead to questions whose answers would need to be informed by a political analysis.

Authentic materials certainly help to provide insight into foreign cultures, but they can be treated as problematic and challenging rather than as simply given. Menus raise questions of who they are directed at, who can afford them, where the ingredients or dishes originate. Tourist brochures may be as interesting for what they do not say as for what they do. Indeed, the impact of tourism on indigenous people is itself a controversial issue. Authentic materials can include leaflets produced by pressure groups or cartoons conveying views on current events. The use of such materials can easily be justified on pragmatic grounds. Learners are likely to be much more willing to communicate and make an effort to understand if they perceive what they are talking about to be interesting and important. There are limits to the pretence that holidays and tourism are central concerns in life.

'Process' in World Studies Teaching

World Studies has emphasised process almost more than content. Certainly practitioners would argue that teachers or textbooks telling children about other cultures are likely to be far less effective in learning outcomes than experiences including simulations or, for that matter, personal or collective enquiry. The design of lessons and courses and the creation of conditions in the classroom in which learning and enquiry can successfully occur have consequently been a preoccupation of the World Studies project teams.

The World Studies or global teacher attempts to create a classroom climate of security and challenge for each student. Richardson (1979) identifies eight prerequisites for successful enquiry-based learning. Four of these create a sense of security and four give a sense of challenge and excitement, without which security may be merely apathy or complacency. They are summarised as follows:

Security for students is a question of:
- Getting to know and trust each other and respect each other as potential resources.
- Getting a sense of initial self-confidence through the successful completion of simple tasks.
- Getting a sense of the whole.

Teachers will further help this process by:
- Establishing and acknowledging the knowledge and experience which students already have.

Challenge is created by teachers who
- adopt a problem-centred and action-orientated approach

Students may challenge themselves (intrinsic motivation) when they:
- are stimulated (rather than overwhelmed) by their own ignorance, prejudice etc.
- realise that there are few absolutes or right answers and that people have different views.
- are able to take a measure of responsibility for negotiating and managing their course.

Converging Methods

The theoretical basis of language teaching and learning underwent a radical shift from the mid-1970s. Audio-visual courses based on behaviourist theories of learning and whole-class lock-step exercises gave way to decentralised communicative methods. When these methods are adopted, students talk not just to the teacher, but to each other. The climate of security and challenge is then precisely that required for effective foreign language learning. The creation of such a climate is not possible or even, perhaps, desirable, when using audio-visual and grammar-based courses. In such approaches the teacher controls the form of linguistic exchanges (e.g. asks a student a question; asks the class to repeat), and grammatical considerations (rather than truth or a desire to express something) control the range of acceptable answers. The teaching style is teacher-centred rather than learner-centred, authoritarian rather than democratic.

The stock in trade of communicative methodology, however, is active learning: discussion, role-play, games, problem solving, group work. In this respect writers on language teaching have been following a parallel and converging path with World Studies. Discussion and group work in any context need careful preparation and the advice is likely to be the same whether the context be management seminars or classrooms (Ur, 1982). The work of Prabhu has been an important insight for language teachers. His concern is with 'mind engagement', namely that students best learn language when they are concentrating on a problem-solving or other task. The language and the communication are generated by the demands of the task and the affective engagement of the student with that task (Brumfit, 1984).

In other respects, too, purely pragmatic considerations lead communicative language teachers towards a process compatible with a World Studies approach. The perhaps somewhat sterile 'information gap' now includes the potentially infinitely rich mine provided by personal opinion: the 'opinion gap'. In other words, language teaching now includes not only facts but ideas and opinions. It is possible to envisage learning about other cultures through the medium of the foreign language but with a World Studies type of enquiry-based, problematising methodology.

Classroom climate is also an important consideration in language teaching. Security needs to be quickly established. Tension and anxiety create an inhibition to language learning, which Krashen (1981) refers to as the 'affective filter'. Language is best acquired, he maintains, in relaxed conditions. Among other things, students must learn from the beginning those language strategies which will protect them from embarrassment, bewilderment and confusion. They need to know how to ask for an utterance to be repeated or explained, for example. Security without challenge is complacency, however, and a classroom climate of challenge must be created. Here again Prabhu's 'mind engagement' or the concept that form is best learnt when the learner's attention is on meaning is the guiding concept. Problem solving, discussion, role-play and creativity are all challenges which stimulate language learning. Brumfit (1984) draws a useful distinction between this kind of 'fluency activity' and the still important but more closely circumscribed 'accuracy activity'.

Converging Contents?

However, a convergence of teaching approaches does not necessarily entail a convergence of content as between foreign language teaching and World Studies. It is quite possible to use communicative methodology but for the cultural content of the lessons to be determined by the very limited demands of the examining boards. In fact the current syllabuses of the examining boards for the General Certificate of Secondary Education examinations at age 16, whilst encouraging active use of the language and role-play, have reduced the content to situations in which the student is invited to identify with a very limited number of roles. The role of tourist and consumer, possibly guest in a family, are the staple to the exclusion of all other interests, or indeed curiosity. Students are always, in a sense, playing themselves. There is, in most cases, an exclusion of empathy with people from another culture.

Empathy, or the capacity to understand the motivations of people from other cultural backgrounds, is an important educational objective in itself. The learning of a foreign language should provide the best possible opportunity for developing this. There is no more direct route to the heart of a culture than through its language. Other subjects and areas of the curriculum, such as history, geography, literature, personal and social education, also have the aim of development of the capacity to empathise. It is surprising to find that, in the UK, foreign language teaching syllabuses reflect this concern less strongly than, say history syllabuses.

Foreign language teaching has just emerged from a period during which teaching style has been inimical to anything other than a stereotypical two-dimensional representation of foreign cultures. The audio-visual revolution launched by the TAVOR course had as its major visual representation people drawn with stick bodies and pin heads. It is perhaps hardly surprising that this method, devised by behavioural psychologists for the American armed forces, should be authoritarian and based on 'drill'. The enterprise was essentially flawed. The very human activity of communicating through language is unlikely to be effectively promoted solely with a technological fix. Communicative methodology, on the other hand, has put the emphasis once more on learners and people rather than teachers and technology. The humane approach is gradually coming to terms with a more humane content.

The lack of appropriate content for language teaching has been a contributory factor to the low level of motivation of many learners. Brumfit sees only two 'ideal alternatives'. These are: 'either to use immersion and claim that the language is being learnt incidentally while another equally worthwhile subject is being taught; or to find subject matter which can arguably reinforce the understanding of the language. This is the attraction of literature and culture courses.' (1984: 134). Either way, appropriate content is a key to successful teaching and learning.

Baumgratz usefully distinguishes 'two tendencies in communication in international and cross-cultural communication'. There is, she maintains, an *instrumental* tendency where the language learning serves 'the political and economic interests of a given society or multi-national organisation'. Tourism, as an economically important activity, comes under this heading. The other tendency is a *human rights* tendency. The aims of this strand involve a positive effort to put human rights into practice. 'This means taking into account our partner's political, social and cultural situation as an individual as well as the relations between his [sic] country and our own on the international scene.' Language learning can be a means: '(1) of improving the social conditions of foreigners living in our own societies, as well as (2) of supporting national and international activities aimed at the peaceful solution of conflicts and the abolition of oppression, injustice, exploitation and poverty' (1985: 113).

Such aims, of course, command widespread and non-partisan support. They are similar to those found in the Recommendation R(85)7 of the Committee of Ministers of the Council of Europe on 'Teaching and learning about human rights in schools'. Since it has proved difficult to mobilise school students to embrace enthusiastically an approach to foreign language teaching based on the instrumental tendency, perhaps pragmatism is now leading teachers to adopt the World Studies approach and the human rights tendency which have a record of high levels of student motivation.

'Orientations' – A New Textbook

Appropriate materials, using aspects of a World Studies approach for the teaching of foreign languages, are starting to become widely available as commercial publishers become convinced that there is a demand from teachers. Klippel's (1984) book of ideas for teachers, *Keep Talking*, for instance, introduces material taken from the World Studies Project's earlier publication *Learning for Change in World Society* (Richardson, 1979). As far as commercially produced materials for pupils is concerned, one of the earliest attempts was *Orientations*, a French course book published in the UK for fourth- and fifth-year students (Aplin, Miller & Starkey, 1985). Whilst the authors were certainly constrained by teacher expectations and the new examination syllabuses for fifth-year students, they none the less had wider educational aims beyond merely instrumental ones. These aims include placing human rights values at the centre of the foreign language curriculum alongside the instrumental and skills-based tendency.

The authors of *Orientations* selected authentic French texts which would promote a world view, which would challenge racist and sexist stereotypes and which would show concern for the environment. The unit on fashion, for instance, contains an interview and a map illustrating the links between French fashion and India where the garments are actually made. The section on 'La nature' includes a description of a Greenpeace protest on nuclear testing in Nevada. The unit on food contains illustrated material on the links between colonisation in Senegal and present-day food shortages. The accompanying exploitation of this material asks students to prepare a television debate on world hunger. Another exercise involves students in a role-play on how they might react to a racist incident on the Paris Metro. The photo illustrating a text on the women of Tchad shows three women cradling Kalashnikoffs.

The examples just cited are not merely tokenistic. The authors had taken the conscious decision that France should be shown to be a country whose people, like those in Britain, are concerned with issues of freedom, of justice, of social and economic change both nationally and internationally. French is presented as a language used by a variety of people in a number of countries to express their concerns, their hopes and their struggles, their enthusiasms. Students are given the opportunity to inform themselves and to discuss issues that go far beyond tourism. *Orientations* thus builds on the topic and situational approach that has been developed over a number of years. It proposes, however, a wide range of contexts and of actors, not restricting its scope to Europe. The broadening of the context is not a substitute for careful presentation and rehearsal of language patterns;

rather it aims to provide, through its intrinsic interest, the motivation which gives learners a desire to understand and to express themselves.

Other courses for the teaching of French in the UK now contain material from a wide range of perspectives (e.g. Stanojlovic & Whiter, 1988; Miller & Roselman, 1988). Such materials are part of a change in the educational climate. Understandably, instrumental values will always be important in school, where success or failure can be determinant for life chances. Teachers, however, are also concerned with broader educational aims. In the hands of teachers with a broad world view, the combination of a student-centred methodology, communicative activities and authentic materials enables foreign language teaching to regain its rightful place as the major vehicle for intercultural education.

References

APLIN, R., MILLER, A. and STARKEY, H. 1985, *Orientations*. London: Hodder & Stoughton.
BAUMGRATZ, G. 1985, Transnational and cross-cultural communication as negotiation of meaning. In D. SIXT (ed.) *Comprehension as Negotiation of Meaning*. Amsterdam: Goethe-Institut.
BRUMFIT, C. 1984, *Communicative Methodology in Language Teaching: the Roles of Accuracy and Fluency*. Cambridge: Cambridge University Press.
BYRAM, M. 1984 Cultural studies in language teaching. *Modern Languages* 65, 4, 204–12.
CLARK, J.L. 1987, *Curriculum Renewal in School Foreign Language Learning*. Oxford: Oxford University Press.
DES, 1987, *Modern Foreign Languages to 16*. Curriculum Matters 8. (An HMI series.) London: HMSO.
1988, *Modern Languages in the School Curriculum: A Statement of Policy*. London: HMSO.
FISHER, S. and HICKS, D. 1985, *World Studies 8–13: A Teacher's Handbook*. Edinburgh: Oliver & Boyd.
GIRARD, D. 1987, *Choix et distribution des contenus dans les programmes de langues*. Strasbourg: Council of Europe.
HICKS, D. and TOWNLEY, C. (eds.) 1982, *Teaching World Studies*. Harlow: Longman.
KLIPPEL, F. 1984, *Keep Talking. Communicative Fluency Activities for Langauge Teaching*. Cambridge: Cambridge University Press.
KRASHEN, S.D. 1981, *Second Language Acquisition and Second Language Learning*. Oxford: Pergamon.
MILLER, A. and ROSELMAN, E. 1988, *Arc en Ciel*. London: Mary Glasgow.
PIKE, G. and SELBY, D. 1988, *Global Teacher, Global Learner*. London: Hodder & Stoughton.
RICHARDSON, R. 1976/1979, *Learning for Change in World Society*. London: One World Trust.

RISAGER, K. and ANDERSEN, H. 1978, The relationship between socio-cultural and linguistic content in foreign language teaching. In MEY, J. and BASBOLL, H. (eds.) *Papers from the Fourth Scandinavian Conference of Linguistics*, Copenhagen.
SHAFER, S.M. 1987, Human rights education in schools. In N.B. TARROW (ed.) *Human Rights and Education*. Oxford: Pergamon.
STANOJLOVIC, J. and WHITER, H. 1988, *Zigzag*. London: Heinemann.
UR, P. 1982, *Discussions That Work*. Cambridge: Cambridge University Press.
VAN EK, J. 1975, *The Threshold Level*. Strasbourg: Council of Europe.

L'ALIMENTATION

LA COLONISATION: UN PEU D'HISTOIRE

Lisez la bande dessinée et essayez d'en extraire l'information suivante:
- les céréales traditionnnellement cultivées par l'Africain;
- les produits dont l'industrie française a besoin;
- à qui l'Africain vend les cultures de rapport (c'est-à-dire les produits qu'on cultive pour vendre et non pas pour consommer soi-même);
- comment l'Africain dépense l'argent qu'il obtient en vendant les cultures de rapport;
- pourquoi l'Africain quitte ses terres.

Des développements plus récents
Lisez la bande dessinée à la page 92.

1
Faites correspondre ces débuts de phrases aux suites qui sont données ci-dessous:
a Les paysans sénégalais cultivaient le mil et le sorgho...
b Les Français avaient besoin de cacahuètes...
c Les Français ont décidé d'utiliser du sol sablonneux du Sénégal...
d Le Sénégal est obligé d'acheter du blé à d'autres pays...
e Les pays riches préfèrent aujourd'hui utiliser le soja...
f Les paysans vont à la ville...
   i   pour fabriquer de l'huile;
   ii pour chercher du travail;
   iii pour se nourrir;
   iv pour cultiver l'arachide;
   v pour se nourrir;
   vi pour fabriquer de l'huile.

WORLD STUDIES AND FOREIGN LANGUAGE TEACHING

Francophones

2
Maintenant lisez ces phrases qui sont dans le désordre. Mettez-les dans le bon ordre afin d'en faire un paragraphe qui explique comment les Sénégalais ont été affamés.
a Les Sénégalais ne peuvent plus vendre leur arachide.
b Les pays riches n'ont plus besoin d'arachide.
c Les Français avaient besoin d'arachide pour faire de l'huile.
d Le Sénégal consacre la moitié de ses terres arables à la production d'arachide destinée à l'exportation.
e Les Sénégalais sont obligés d'acheter du blé à d'autres pays pour se nourrir.
f Ils ne peuvent plus acheter de blé.
g La cultivation du mil et du sorgno est négligée.
h Ils ont obligé les Sénégalais à cultiver l'arachide.

3
Jeu de rôle. L'un(e) des partenaires va jouer le rôle d'un(e) représentant(e) du Sénégal, qui va expliquer les revendications de son pays. L'autre va jouer le rôle d'un(e) représentant(e) de la France, qui va défendre la politique de son pays.

4
Imaginez que vous êtes fermier au Sénégal. Vous allez recevoir la visite de l'ambassadeur français dans votre village. Profitez de l'occasion pour lui envoyer une lettre de la part de tous les cultivateurs d'arachide du village. Vous devez non seulement lui exprimer vos revendications. Il faudra aussi lui faire comprendre votre colère.

fonctionner *to work*
le système fiscal
   the taxation system
à présent *now*
impôts *taxes*
faites pousser *grow*
cultures de rapport *cash crops*
cacahuètes *peanuts*
ailleurs *elsewhere*
a besoin *needs*
consommer *to consume*
dépenser *to spend*
quitter *to leave*
terres *land*
débuts *beginnings*
suites *endings*
les paysans *peasants*
sénégalais *Senegalese*
sablonneux *sandy*
le soja *soya*
fabriquer *to manufacture*
l'huile *oil*
se nourrir *to feed oneself*
dans le désordre
   in the wrong order
affamés *starved*
consacrer *to devote*
la moitié *half*
destinée à *intended for*
blé *wheat*
négligée *neglected*
les revendications
   grievances/demands

91

Orientations

Greenpeace n° 15 été 83

Essais nucléaires

LA TRAVERSÉE DU DESERT

Pour l'arrêt des essais

Le 16 avril dernier, quatre membres de Greenpeace – Harold Zindler d'Allemagne fédérale, Ron Taylor du Royaume-Uni, Jon Hinck et Brian Fitzgerald des Etats-Unis – ont franchi les limites du site du Nevada, pour protester contre les essais américains et britanniques qui y ont lieu. Cette action se situe dans le cadre d'une campagne internationale visant les pays qui poursuivent des essais nucléaires – Etats-Unis, Royaume-Uni, Union soviétique, France et Chine. Objectif de la campagne: la conclusion d'un traité d'Interdiction totale des essais nucléaires.

En 1981, le voilier, *Greenpeace III* a manifesté à Mururoa; en 1982, nous avons envoyé le *Sirius* à Leningrad pour protester contre les essais soviétiques; toujours en 1982, a eu lieu aux Etats-Unis une tournée en montgolfière des Etats situés sous le vent du Nevada, pour attirer l'attention du public sur cette guerre souterraine que les puissances nucléaires mènent sans pour autant la déclarer.

Les quatre hommes ont pénétré à pied dans le site, désert d'une superficie de 350 000 hectares, au moment où le Congrès américain débattait d'une résolution pour un «gel nucléaire» («Nuclear Freeze») bilatéral et contrôlable entre les Etats-Unis et l'URSS. L'un des points principaux était la suspension des essais nucléaires: Monsieur Reagan est en effet le premier président américain de l'ère nucléaire à abandonner comme objectif prioritaire la conclusion d'un traité international interdisant les essais. Le 5 mai, après 53 heures de débat houleux, la résolution a été adoptée par 278 voix contre 149.

Pour quelques millions de dollars

La saison d'expérimentation américaine avait commencé le 14 avril 1983 avec l'explosion d'une bombe de moins de 20 kilotonnes, surnommée *Turquoise*. D'autres devaient suivre, et les quatre marcheurs se trouvaient sur le site.

Une fois alertées, les autorités se sont mises à rechercher les intrus à l'aide d'hélicoptères. Mais en vain. Nous reprochant de faire ainsi dépenser l'argent des contribuables, M. Millar, du département de l'Energie, ne s'est évidemment pas inquiété des 595 millions de dollars qui seront dépensés cette année pour les seules opérations du Nevada et qui sont prélevés des impôts des citoyens américains.

Au bout de cinq jours, à court d'eau, les «occupants» se sont dirigés vers la ville de Mercury à l'intérieur du site, pour dialoguer avec les travailleurs. Le jeudi 21 avril, alors qu'ils abordaient Yucca Flats, la zone d'essais proprement dite, nos amis ont été interceptés par douze membres du service de sécurité, puis arrêtés. Le lendemain, ils ont été inculpés de violation de propriété privée. Le 4 mai, le juge a rendu son verdict.

À priori, le personnel du site aurait pu se montrer hostile à notre démarche. Pourtant, nous avons reçu des coups de fil de travailleurs nous apportant leur soutien. Et l'un d'eux de préciser: «*Je ne suis pas convaincu que les gouvernements aient la volonté politique d'arrêter la course aux armements*».

Louise Trussell

Une minute après un essai nucléaire souterrain dans le désert de Nevada

essais *tests*
franchi *breached*
dans le cadre *in the context*
un traité d'Interdiction total
 des essais nucléaires
 *a complete nuclear test
 ban treaty*
en montgolfière *in a hot air
 balloon*
souterraine *underground*
une superficie *an area*
houleux *stormy*
surnommé *nicknamed*
les intrus *the intruders*
des contribuables *taxpayers*
évidemment *obviously*
prélevés des impôts
 taken from the taxes
A priori *we might have
 expected that*
des coups de fil *telephone
 calls*

WORLD STUDIES AND FOREIGN LANGUAGE TEACHING   225

La Nature

ANALYSE DU TEXTE

Ce texte comporte certains faits et certains jugements de l'auteur qui ont été rassemblés dans un ordre spécifique pour essayer de persuader le lecteur d'un certain point de vue.

Voici 6 catégories d'information qu'on trouve dans ce texte. À vous de trouver les détails exacts.

1 Précisions sur l'action des quatre hommes
 - la durée de l'action (nombre de jours);
 - les dates du début et de la fin;
 - l'endroit où l'action a eu lieu;
 - l'objectif de l'action;
 - en quoi consistait l'action, précisément?
 - la fin de l'action.

2 Exemples d'actions précédentes
 - noms des trois pays contre lesquels on protestait;
 - moyens de transport utilisés.

3 Le contexte politique de cette action
 - ce qui se passait au Congrès américain;
 - résultat de cet événement;
 - la réaction probable du Président des Etats-Unis à ce résultat.

4 Précisions sur la série d'essais nucléaires
 - les deux nations concernées;
 - la première expérience de 1983;
 - le coût de la série d'essais.

5 Les réactions des autorités
 - comment ils ont recherché les 4 hommes;
 - le commentaire de M. Millar;
 - les circonstances de l'arrestation.

6 Les réactions des travailleurs
 - la façon dont ils ont montré leur avis.

Le verdict du juge

Vous trouverez le verdict à la page 197. Avant de le regarder, réfléchissez. À votre avis que était la peine imposée?
a Tous les quatre étaient libérés comme non-coupables.
b 200 dollars d'amende chacun.
c 5000 dollars d'amende chacun.
d 6 mois de prison.
e 2 ans de prison.
f La peine de mort.
A votre avis qu'est-ce qu'ils meritaient?

Travail écrit

Choisissez le sujet qui vous plaît le plus
a Imaginez que vous êtes un des quatre membres de Greenpeace. Vous écrivez une lettre à vos parents expliquant ce qui s'est passé.
b Vous êtes journaliste pour un journal qui est favorable aux essais nucléaires. Rédigez un reportage où vous traitez les membres de Greenpeace comme des criminels irresponsables.
c Travaillez avec un partenaire. Rédigez chacun 5 questions concernant l'article. Essayez de trouver une réponse aux questions de votre voisin. (Par exemple: Pourquoi les britanniques font-ils des essais nucléaires aux Etats-Unis?)

De gauche à droite: Brian Fitzgerald (U.S.); Jon Hinck (U.S.); Harold Zindler (Allemagne); et Ron Taylor (G.B.)

Yucca Flats, Centre d'essais nucléaires souterrains: ces cratères sont le résultat des essais.

Orientations

L'INDUSTRIE DU PRÊT-À-PORTER

Lisez cette interview avec Solange, qui vient d'ouvrir un magasin prêt-à-porter à Nantes.

Ann Vous dites que vous êtes là depuis très peu de temps...

Solange Ah oui, ça fait deux mois que je suis ouverte alors je ne me suis pas encore fait ma clientèle – ça vient petit à petit.

Ann Et qu'est-ce qui vous a donné l'idée de...

Solange De faire un magasin prêt-à-porter? Ben, parce que j'ai bien aimé le quartier, et puis le style rétro que je fais, j'ai trouvé que ça se marierait bien avec le style de la rue, les restaurants qui sont avoisinants, et le style de vêtements que je veux faire un petit peu bohème. Et par goût personnel aussi, j'ai voulu faire un magasin prêt-à-porter, quoi. Mais ce que je voulais éviter à tout prix c'est justement le style grande surface et je voulais faire quelque chose d'un peu personnalisé, pour faire ma clientèle.

Ann Et vous les trouvez où, vos vêtements?

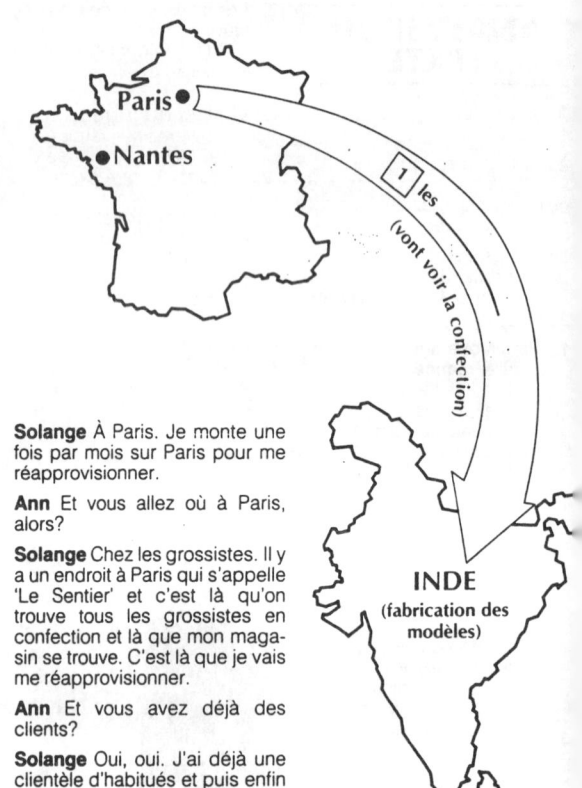

Solange À Paris. Je monte une fois par mois sur Paris pour me réapprovisionner.

Ann Et vous allez où à Paris, alors?

Solange Chez les grossistes. Il y a un endroit à Paris qui s'appelle 'Le Sentier' et c'est là qu'on trouve tous les grossistes en confection et là que mon magasin se trouve. C'est là que je vais me réapprovisionner.

Ann Et vous avez déjà des clients?

Solange Oui, oui. J'ai déjà une clientèle d'habitués et puis enfin il y a le bouche-à-oreille, enfin c'est ma meilleure publicité aussi: les gens qui viennent et qui ont donc leur modèle sur eux et qui m'envoient d'autres clients parce que ça a plu. C'est comme ça que je travaille.

Ann Est-ce que ce sont des jeunes?

Solange Jeunes et moins jeunes. Il y a un petit peu les deux. J'ai des mamans qui viennent avec leurs filles.

Ann Ah bon?

Solange Oui oui oui – qui achètent en premier lieu pour leurs filles et puis qui voyant mes modèles, parce que j'ai d'autres modèles, voyez-vous, qui sont un peu plus stylés, et qui viennent m'acheter également.

Ann Et ce sont des vêtements qui sont fabriqués en France?

Solange Non. Ils sont importés. Ils sont fabriqués en Inde, mais vous voulez la styliste est su Paris. La création est à Pari mais la fabrication est en Inde Tout ça parce que ça coût moins cher. C'est l'unique raison Mais la styliste est sur Paris. Le modèles sont créés à Paris.

Ann Et vous avez l'occasion d voyager?

Solange Non, non. Disons qu pour ma profession je vais u iquement sur Paris. Je dis pa

1 les (vont voir la confection) Paris • Nantes INDE (fabrication des modèles)

10

WORLD STUDIES AND FOREIGN LANGUAGE TEACHING

Modes

```
  3  les _____
(Solange et d'autres
détaillants viennent se
reapprovisionner ici)
```

```
la maison de couture
  2  la _____
(création des modèles,
choix de la matière,
choix des coloris)
```

● PARIS

```
  4  le _____
(présente sa collection à
Solange et à d'autres
detaillants)
```

le magasin prêt à
porter de Solange
(vente des modèles
au détail)

● NANTES

```
  5  les _____
(viennent acheter les
modèles)
```

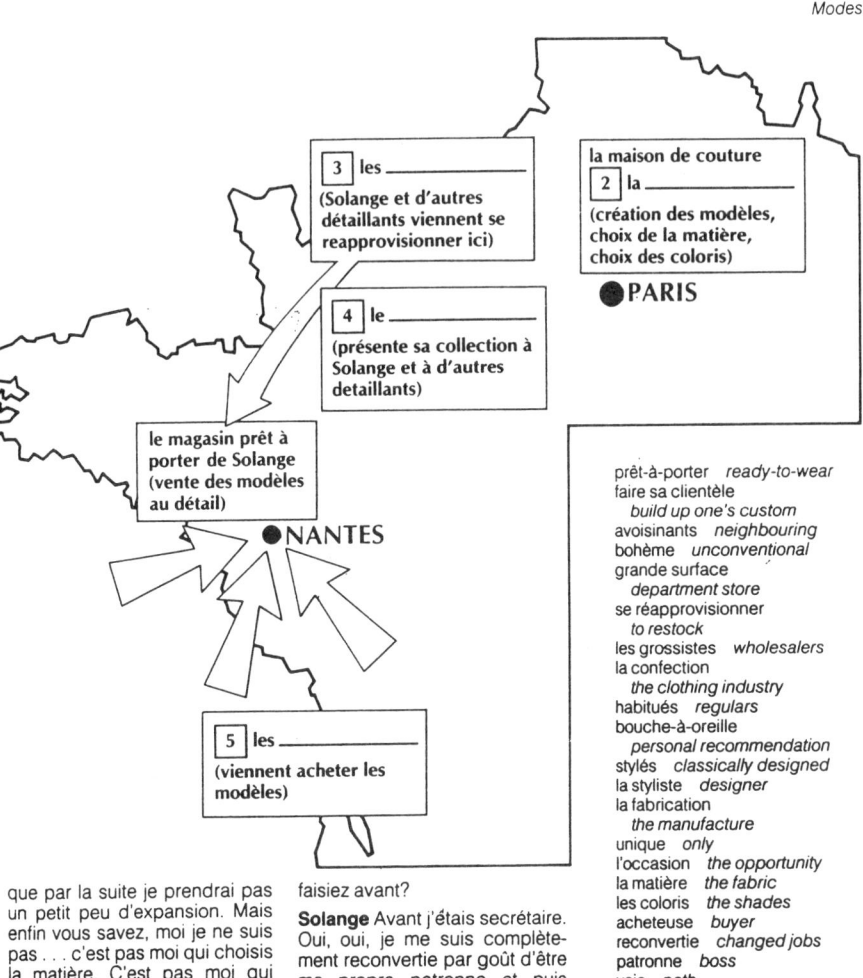

prêt-à-porter   *ready-to-wear*
faire sa clientèle
   build up one's custom
avoisinants   *neighbouring*
bohème   *unconventional*
grande surface
   department store
se réapprovisionner
   to restock
les grossistes   *wholesalers*
la confection
   the clothing industry
habitués   *regulars*
bouche-à-oreille
   personal recommendation
stylés   *classically designed*
la styliste   *designer*
la fabrication
   the manufacture
unique   *only*
l'occasion   *the opportunity*
la matière   *the fabric*
les coloris   *the shades*
acheteuse   *buyer*
reconvertie   *changed jobs*
patronne   *boss*
voie   *path*
détaillants   *retailers*
couture   *fashion*
étapes   *stages*

que par la suite je prendrai pas un petit peu d'expansion. Mais enfin vous savez, moi je ne suis pas . . . c'est pas moi qui choisis la matière. C'est pas moi qui choisis les coloris.

Ann Ah bon.

Solange Non, non, non. Moi je choisis simplement le modèle qui me plaît. Et c'est le représentant qui me présente sa collection. Et puis sur Paris il y a des filles qui s'appellent des acheteuses, qui sont attachées à une maison, et qui vont à l'étranger pour voir la confection par elles-mêmes.

Ann Et qu'est-ce que vous faisiez avant?

Solange Avant j'étais secrétaire. Oui, oui, je me suis complètement reconvertie par goût d'être ma propre patronne et puis parce que mes parents étaient dans le milieu du commerce et j'ai voulu suivre leur voie aussi. C'est un choix.

1
Regardez les schémas qui montrent les rapports qui existent entre toutes les personnes citées par Solange qui jouent un rôle dans l'industrie de la mode. Comment est-ce qu'on appelle ces personnes? Essayez de remplir les blancs.

2
Faites une redaction qui s'intitule *L'Industrie du Prêt-à-Porter*, ou vous raconterez les differentes étapes qui relient la commerçante et les clientes, en passant par la confection en Inde et toutes les personnes qui travaillent dans cette industrie.

11

15 Relating Experience, Culture and Language: A German – French Video Project for Language Teaching

GISELA BAUMGRATZ-GANGL

Introduction

The West German Goethe-Institut, Munich, has in recent years organised a series of workshops on 'regional textbooks' for German as a Foreign Language. One of the conferences was concerned with the theory of intercultural communication, but also with practical approaches to intercultural education in the context of learning and using a foreign language (Gerighausen & Seel, 1987.) This chapter is based on a contribution to that workshop and introduces a teaching unit which has been developed for French as a Foreign Language in Germany. *'Vivre l'école'* is one of the topics investigated by the German–French research project *Frankreichkunde im Französischunterricht*. It has been published in the series *Landeskundliche Unterrichtskonzepte für Französisch* (Alix *et al.*, 1988). This unit – like the others in this series – is an attempt to combine methods of foreign language teaching with theoretical concepts of perception and with practical considerations regarding transnational and transcultural communication.

The unit consists of a video film of 30 minutes length about a day in the life of a 15-year-old French girl; the film was shot by German pupils of the same age in the Collège of Chelles near Paris. It contains also a tape of pupils' interviews and four teaching sequences with detailed proposals for planning lessons concerning the topic of 'school'. These approaches were developed for school teaching, but can be transferred to adult education if the different learning styles and interests of adults are considered. Since the published unit contains all the details, this chapter will be confined to some of the theoretical and educational principles involved in this project combining personal experience, language acquisition, and access to a foreign culture.

The Representation of Culture in Teaching Transnational Communication

If language teaching material is not considered purely as an instrument of word acquisition or of introduction to grammatical aspects, the question of how to represent and treat culture arises. The choice of topic and its relation to action and situation present the central problem, because in any transnational encounter cultural knowledge and behaviour are closely interrelated (Baumgratz, 1985).

In teaching French at school, the opportunities of exchange visits, educational class trips, and tourist travel can be used. Since an exchange usually takes place at the end of the third year of French in Germany, we decided to prepare the pupils for cultural knowledge, language competence, and social abilities which they should have at their disposal. The encounter with ordinary school life and everyday family life should be a profitable experience for the host families, the exchange school, and the pupils themselves.

In beginners' language courses, without greater language competence to fall back upon, visual material offers an adequate way of presenting 'authentic' reality. Since films integrate image, motion, action and speech, they seem to be an ideal starting point. But the theory and history of film show that one had to move away from naive notions of the camera depicting reality 'as it is'. People had to realise that films are constructed just as texts, and merely offer readings of reality. Film reception shows how complex the representation of reality is in practice, and also how varied the responses can be with regard to different cultural perceptions, e.g. in the ways the films relate to cultural assumptions, experience and associations (Kluge, 1983).

Therefore, what at first sight looks like the ideal medium for cultural studies in language teaching contains, on closer inspection, the central problem of intercultural communication, i.e. the culturally conditioned perception and interpretation of material produced in the context of another society for another audience. In our search for an adequate film conveying a concrete and comprehensible image of life in a French Collège, we came across the French movie *Très insuffisant*. When watching this film we agreed quickly that it would not serve our purpose because it focuses on the deficiencies of the French school system and emphasises particularly serious shortcomings by caricature and exaggeration. Showing such a film to German pupils would presuppose that kind of complex knowledge of conflicts within the French educational system which needs to be acquired first of all. Only then would German pupils be able to reconstruct and understand some of the criticism of the institution from their knowledge of social conditions. We therefore decided to shoot our own film which would correspond better to our objectives and our age group.

In producing the film we were influenced by the following considerations. On the basis of the binding principles of pupil-centred teaching and reality-related contents, the film was to convey an image of the French school reality adapted to the experience of 14 to 15-year old German pupils. We therefore chose the following conditions for the film production. A French schoolgirl of that age attending the Collège of Chelles in the Paris area served as a figure of identification. This specific school was chosen because the person in charge of the video team had spent some time as an assistant teacher there and knew some of the French colleagues. He was also very familiar with the conditions of the school, which he considered an average rather than a model school.

In order to guarantee pupil participation from the start, the film was shot by 15-year-old pupils of a German comprehensive school who had previously made a film about their own school life. After attending lessons in France for some days, the group made a first outline of scenes. Certain structural similarities between their school at home and the Collège, such as having lunch at noon in the canteen, made orientation within the French school easier. The film crew had been instructed to convey one day in the life of a pupil from getting up to going to bed. Special emphasis was suggested for the time structure in order to show the relationship between leisure and work. The main points of the film's message were to be comprehensible even without any knowledge of French.

The pupils were asked to pay particular attention to differences and similarities between their own and the French school and to take them into account when planning the scenes. Also, the most important persons of the French school system should be shown while performing their duties. The German film crew was asked not to put too much emphasis on school facilities because a comparison of equipment was not intended. German lessons should definitely be filmed to show that French learners of German face similar problems as German pupils, learning French.

The film therefore contains the following characteristics. The pictures are authentic, i.e. the scenes were not prearranged but present normal lessons. All the school scenes are filmed from the perspective of pupils; their experience and expectation determine the film's view of French school reality. Background noise was preserved for authenticity's sake even at the expense of impairing the sound quality. However, with today's sound equipment a better acoustic quality may be achieved. This became evident during another project on class trips involving a video documentary of a typical quarter of Paris.

Relating Film and Class Discussion in Preparing for a Pupil Exchange

Starting out from the experience of filming their own school, the team of pupils were asked to present their view of French school life in such a way that as many structural characteristics of the Collège as possible actually become visible in their film. Thus the film's topic is not identical with a teaching unit preparing for an exchange. However, the film's aspects of school reality are taken up in the teaching unit and prepare the pupils indirectly for the experience of an exchange. For beginners' courses only certain aspects of the film were selected, those which are important for an exchange, but are also adequate for the pupils' restricted linguistic, cognitive, and emotional abilities. This way the film's potential was, of course, not fully exploited.

Evaluations of the teaching material have shown that the pupils perceive much of what the film conveys by way of 'atmosphere'. Brain-storming sessions after the first viewing indicated that pupils of this age group react strongly to aspects of school climate as expressed in the teaching method observed, the pupil – teacher relations, and the relationship among the pupils. They show similar concern with affective relations within the family. These responses provide a starting point for the teacher to try to mediate between native and foreign social conventions, between different institutional rules and the observable behaviour of groups and individuals living under cultural conditions specific to the respective society.

Video film and sound tapes can, of course, be exploited to different degrees depending on the interest and age group of the learners. What we are aiming at is a balance between the objectives and the capabilities of the learners, their activities and language competence, and contents and form of the teaching material.

Approaching School Life in a Foreign Culture

Teaching French prepares pupils for the actual situation of an exchange, and living in another country requires intercultural communication, that is, coping with varieties of foreign language articulation and description. In selecting or producing teaching material certain sequences of learning should be observed which relate to receptive, productive, and behavioural language competence. Curricula for 11+ courses assume that textbooks have laid the ground for studying and discussing complex authentic material. However, bad marks and lack of interest indicate that pupils are often not prepared for this kind of work. Frequently, their interest in the foreign language and culture will not be matched by their actual language achievement.

At this point we need to discuss our concept of 'authenticity'.

- 'Authentic' refers primarily to any spoken or written material produced within the foreign country and with a native audience in mind.
- The term 'authenticity' may also take on a political and social meaning, claiming some sort of objective truth and immediate realism for an author or a speaker. This is a reflection of ideological processes between social groups that must be taken into account in any evaluation of meaning (Schmitz, 1978: 280). Films, too, acquire authenticity only as social constructs and expressions of cultural norms.

Foreign language teaching is concerned with both of these dimensions of authenticity. School subjects like Social Studies face similar problems without the additional barrier of language; the work of foreign language teachers is even more difficult in this respect. But foreign language classes have an advantage, too. If pupils encounter the foreign reality on an adequate level of experience, a productive balance between distance and proximity may be reached: pupils are beginning to differentiate and may even show renewed interest in their own school situation. In order to approach this ideal in advanced classes, even beginners' courses need material that prepares them for authentic texts, but takes into consideration the learners' linguistic, intellectual, emotional and moral development.

One more dimension of 'authenticity' must be mentioned, namely the problems resulting from the 'outsider's view'. Any German observer and author produces his or her impressions of a section of French reality. The native cultural experience is bound to shape the perception of the new reality by relating and evaluating both fields of experience, first of all through recognition. In fact, the outsider as observer will approach a foreign reality with less anxiety if familiar traits are recognised. On the other hand, new environments that seem all too familiar may fail to arouse that kind of curiosity about surprising and not easily integrated observations. In all this, the 'outsider's view' must be analytical rather than naive because even on the level of perception familiar concepts and unfamiliar impressions need to be consciously related. On the visual level, too, this implies some degree of reaffirming and being aware of one's own subjectivity (Luria, 1981). This close interrelation between visual and conceptual perception, empirically demonstrated by Soviet and other psychologists, implies that any depiction of a foreign reality or experience is the product of coming to terms with one's own cultural and social experience (Baumgratz, 1985). Given that the backgrounds are similar for the author of an authentic text and the reader of this text, the analysis and mediation of the foreign cultural reality is facilitated.

Starting from this assumption, we felt that it was not sufficient for textbook authors to try and claim to produce pupil-centred material, but that it would be essential to include pupils and their peers themselves in the actual process of producing 'authentic' material. The film and the interviews were produced this way and form the basis of our teaching concept. It is intended as a model to be practised even under less fortunate conditions with respect to finance and equipment. We do not, however, claim that video is the only possible medium in this respect. In fact, pupil exchanges and class correspondence may provide various ways of producing material, for example, slides, letters, cassettes, photos. All of these authentic materials have the advantage of arising from situations of authentic intercultural communication and of encouraging just these.

Authenticity and Reality in Language Teaching

For our purposes we need to clarify in what form reality is depicted in a given document and which problems pupils encounter in decoding what refers to a foreign reality. Because in the formation of concepts visual sense, abstraction and generalisation are closely connected, the general problems of perception are located in this context too: the form of presentation determines the degree of abstraction from the actually visible. Any visual medium, such as photos, films, pictures or drawings, contains more elements of perceived reality than language texts which require greater imagination and greater faculties of abstraction and generalisation.

Essential elements of reality – in our case of school institutions – are visible in the picture, and at the same time the pictures introduce that degree of concreteness, which is necessary for the recognition of such elements in comparable situations. This assumption provides us with criteria of selection, combining, and sequencing in our work of producing teaching material for foreign language courses aiming at the acquisition both of cultural concepts and of language. For the purpose of language acquisition, the first step is to identify what the pictures convey. This identification is based on native language concepts even if these are not articulated or consciously applied. First language concepts play a central role in any perception because they provide the acquired instruments for perceiving reality. If this process is to be influenced by the teacher whenever false identifications occur or unidentifiable objects or actions are omitted, the learners' attention must be focused – by way of additional cultural information – on those passages which contain structural elements representative of, in this case, the specific French school reality. Photos can take over this function, supplemented by foreign language words and sentences to be associated. This exercise proves difficult whenever first language identifications do not fit. However, inferencing may help to relate persons and their actions to roles and functions within the institutional setting.

If the pupils are to leave this stage of intercultural 'guessing', explicit comparisons need to be encouraged. In perceiving new reality all of us tend to reduce the initial impression of foreignness by suppressing the deviating elements and emphasising those that confirm our expectation. This 'natural' cognitive strategy may be counteracted by intentionally alienating and questioning the familiar reality. This can be done by asking questions from the vantage point of the foreign reality, thus encouraging reconfirmation and critical awareness in the learners' minds. Such comparisons may lead to separate semantic elements which make up a larger concept requiring functional rather than lexical equivalence.

This can be observed in culturally specific settings like schools when we look at persons and their functions. These will be unlikely to correspond in different national school systems and therefore lexical equivalents will often be neither available nor useful. In order to detect functional equivalence, an analysis is necessary to identify the various functions fulfilled by one person. Recognising and identifying such functions within the foreign context may in turn lead to questioning one's own cultural and social reality. This requires, however, that specific elements of one's own environment can be isolated and expressed in terms of the native cultural system, but referring to transcultural social phenomena. A functional analysis of this kind can make pupils aware of relations of hierarchy and domination within any such institution.

Such functional comparison and the identification of similar structural elements should not, however, remain at the level of abstract systems. On returning to the level of social reality, questions about the actual behaviour of specific persons playing certain roles will arise. A variety of cases will help to outline possibilities and restrictions of an individual's behaviour, leading on to the general question of how people interpret and reconcile their roles and functions personally. Anticipation will only be possible at this level allowing pupils to recognise social roles in a specific case and to evaluate an individual's actual behaviour in a given function.

Defining any situation therefore requires recognising the structure and its elements and identifying the subjective interpretation and actual realisation of this structure. The internal cultural process of constituting meaning needs to be made transparent in teaching and accessible to cultural outsiders as potential participants in this meaning process, too. If teaching is successful in this respect, even 'natives' may start to reconsider their accepted concepts, attitudes, norms and behaviour. Ideally both sides in this intercultural communication might reach joint interpretations and, perhaps, better solutions if deficiencies of structures and behaviours in their respective cultural settings could be recognised and mutually conceded.

In language teaching the systems-and-structure approach needs to be supplemented by observations of groups and individuals and their attitudes towards social systems, e.g. teaching role, teacher–pupil relations, parents and children, and so on. Before any human communication can be fully appreciated, language is required that is capable of expressing and understanding subjective attitudes and personal interpretations. Simulating such communicative situations should be practised in the foreign language classroom because the language implications need to be felt and mastered. The willingness to deal with such situations increases with the amount of self-confidence gained from practice and experience. Teaching foreign language and cultural concepts should be geared to such situations extending beyond the classroom. Reality in foreign language teaching implies that the pupils come to acknowledge the pragmatic and cultural value of what they learn.

References

ALIX, C. *et al.* 1988 *Vivre l'école. Unterrichtskonzepte mit Schülermaterialien.* Paderborn: Schöningh.

BAUMGRATZ, G. 1985, Transnational and cross-cultural communication as negotiation of meaning. In Goethe-Institut (ed.) *Comprehension as Negotiation of Meaning*, pp.112–39. Munich: Goethe-Institut.

GERIGHAUSEN, J. and SEEL, P.C. (eds.) 1987, *Aspekte einer interkulturellen Didaktik*. Munich: Goethe-Institut.

KLUGE, A. 1983 *Bestandsaufnahme: Utopie Film*. Frankfurt: Zweitausendeins.

LURIA, A.R. 1981 *The Working Brain*. Harmondsworth: Penguin.

SCHMITZ, U. 1978, *Gesellschaftliche Bedeutung und sprachliches Lernen*. Weinheim: Beltz.

Part V
Towards an Intercultural Teacher Education

If cultural studies has been attributed little importance in the language classroom, the neglect in teacher education has been even more striking. And yet the significance of teacher education as a long-term influence is self-evident. The curricula which shape future teachers' experience in higher education are crucial in establishing their professional identity. Our review of the social history of language teaching in an earlier section showed how theorists have looked to the disciplines of the social sciences as a base for cultural studies. The same orientation is to be found in this section where three authors discuss how teachers can become more aware of the social and cultural dimensions of their subject.

Kane takes his starting point in the curricula for students in higher education in Germany. He argues for an ethnographic/symbolic approach to the study and analysis of culture by students and provides a taxonomy of objectives which could give precise direction and guidance to the revision of curricula. Zarate describes an experiment with teachers on in-service courses which draws on similar notions and begins to give teachers the ethnographic skills and viewpoint which will change their understanding of their purpose and professional identity. That that identity is largely shaped by training in literary criticism is acknowledged as the basis of another experiment described by Kuna. Far from denying its relevance, Kuna's account shows how a competence in reading literary texts can be broadened into an understanding of the nature of all kinds of social meanings and symbols.

There is clearly much to be done in teacher education and the traditions of many decades cannot be overturned in the short term. These three chapters nonetheless point the way towards the integration of cultural studies into teacher education, and as a consequence into the experience of foreign language teaching offered by each teacher to generations of learners in the course of a professional career.

16 The Acquisition of Cultural Competence: An Ethnographic Framework for Cultural Studies Curricula

LAURENCE KANE

The aim of this chapter is to discuss the present status of civilisation studies at university level and to suggest perspectives for its curricular development. The first difficulty arises when we start to look for a standard label to apply to the area of civilisation studies and do not find one. This failure suggests a subject area in search of its own identity, or in the process of change, or both. This is a welcome opportunity to discuss the situation of civilisation studies (or cultural studies as we would probably like to call them) in the universities of several different countries; my discussion will involve ascertaining whether the teaching of civilisation/cultural studies has become more important in the training of second language teachers, describing where the new emphases lie and the kind of welcome which new objectives have received from curriculum planners, colleagues and students as well as identifying the objectives which can be realised in the future. To help discussion, I would like to outline my own view of the situation in Germany, a view which will be a very partial and local one, partly because of the fragmentation caused by the German federal system.

From *Landeskunde* to Cultural Studies in West Germany

The position of cultural studies in the curriculum of advanced English learners at West German universities, in spite of several recent attempts to secure its role and upgrade its status, is still problematical. For the Federal State of Germany which I work in, Nordrhein-Westfalen, this can be illustrated by the resistance which the Ministry responsible for university curricula encountered when it decided to introduce civilisation studies (*Landeskunde*) in a modest way into the English curriculum for trainee teachers. To some extent the negative reaction from the teachers of literature and linguistics was predictable since *Landeskunde* has frequently been something of a pot-pourri of apparently unrelated elements containing, for instance, courses on the education system, the churches, the political parties, pop and folk music and art. This state of affairs presented the critics of the upgrading of *Landeskunde* with a fairly easy target. It could be claimed that the amorphous nature of *Landeskunde* disqualified it as a serious scholarly discipline. Furthermore, from a more practical point of view it could be argued that there is no significant *Landeskunde* tradition in university foreign language departments with the result that only a limited number of university lecturers capable of teaching the subject were available. The lack of library and other research resources meant that opportunities for original research would be very limited indeed. These arguments are not new, but they do not lack substance and have had to be taken seriously (Buttjes & Kane, 1978).

The response by the supporters of civilisation/cultural studies has been a dual one. On the one hand they have concentrated their attention on one aspect of civilisation studies, such as history or geography, and by specialising in an academically approved area have tried to invest the teaching of civilisation with the scholarly prestige which is allegedly missing. However well-intentioned this approach may be, it fails to satisfy some of the needs which courses in civilisation studies should arguably provide for. For instance, history as a substitute for *Landeskunde* fails to appeal because one feels that our students will need to devote much of their available time to acquiring knowledge about contemporary society, and because this type of specialisation will not provide sufficient opportunities either to practise the language or to acquire knowledge about contemporary usage.

The alternative to such strategies of specialisation has been cultural studies which I would like to define, perhaps slightly idiosyncratically, as follows. Cultural studies are concerned with the way belief systems are realised in a social context; contemporary society and the interplay between the small-scale interaction of individuals, social groups and communities and the larger social background are central to their concerns. Thus, cultural studies focus on a subset of the topics dealt with by the older *Landeskunde* while emphasising the interplay between the micro- and macro-levels of society. The replacement of the term 'civilisation'/ *Landeskunde* with the term 'cultural studies' is therefore not merely a terminological manoeuvre but an attempt to meet some of these objections to traditional *Landeskunde* by defining a subject area which is compact enough to be amenable to scholarly analysis, which is also teachable in the tertiary foreign language context in the sense that students can find intellectual access and yet not be overwhelmed by the sheer scale of the material, and which has developed its research methods which can serve as an example of how to tackle a social science topic in a methodical way.

The redefinition of *Landeskunde* as cultural studies implies that the older view of it as being completely restricted to providing ancillary services for linguistics and literature is inadequate, and that it has to be considered as much a subject in its own right as literature and linguistics. However, just as linguistics and literature provide foreign language students with opportunities of improving their language skills, it is clear that cultural studies should offer a similar or better level of opportunities for language learning. In fact, after examining the implications of the definition of cultural studies above it becomes evident that the mix of texts provided by cultural studies does indeed provide excellent language learning opportunities in a wide variety of contexts. Any restructuring of the old *Landeskunde* curriculum will need to concern itself with the provision of systematic opportunities for language acquisition.

Sociological Approaches to Culture Research

In the brief sketch of the curricular implications of cultural studies which now follows I would like to avoid a lengthy analysis of different definitions of culture and focus instead on approaches which emphasise the role of belief systems, the role of everyday life and the interplay between everyday life and macro-level social forces. As representative of those sociologists who emphasise the symbolic function of culture I have chosen the American Swidler. In a recent article she points out that the older totalising and encyclopaedic views of culture as the entire way of life of a people, including technology and material artefacts or everything one would need to know to become a functioning member of society, have been replaced by definitions which view culture as 'symbolic forms through which people experience and express meaning' (Swidler, 1986: 274). Culture as Swidler would define it consists in 'beliefs, ritual practices and art forms'. It is a drawback that this definition apparently excludes material artefacts or technological products, even though these can be the object of fetishistic and/or ritualistic cultural use. Nevertheless from the curricular point of view the focus on the symbolic meaning of cultural behaviour can be a useful guide to the selection of material. It provides a rationale for developing self-contained units in the curriculum since Swidler sees culture as a 'tool-kit' of symbols, stories, rituals and world-views out of which are constructed 'strategies of action', that is persistent ways of ordering action through time.

Another approach, which is closely associated with the Centre for Contemporary Cultural Studies in Birmingham, emphasises the embedding of a culture's symbolising practices within a framework of economically determined constraints (Baron, 1985). According to this view, it remains essential to understand the interplay of class systems and established institutions with the symbolic 'tool-kit' in order to fully appreciate how cultural processes function. Applying these ideas to a particular topic, for instance, to working-class culture in Great Britain, involves mapping out the cultural resources available to members of the working class in the forms of values, and lifestyles and relating these to the institutional and other macro-level constraints.

A third approach could be called the ethnographic approach. This approach emphasises the density, the 'thickness', as the American ethnographer Geertz calls it, of everyday social interaction. This approach implies a close attention to everyday interaction within a given social setting which is reminiscent of the Chicago school of in-depth research into the seedier corners of American society. Research into British working-class culture, particularly that associated with the Centre for Contemporary Cultural Studies has frequently contained elements of all these approaches. For instance, Willis in *Learning to Labour* (1980) combines an ethnographic investigation into tough working-class kids with an explanation of how the culture they create functions symbolically in the wider context of capitalism. Later work includes oral history, biographies and autobiographies as resources for the topic under discussion as, for instance, Blackwell and Seabrook do in *A World Still to Win* (Blackwell & Seabrook, 1985).

Since the 'thick' ethnographic/symbolic approach has been incorporated into cultural studies curricula in Germany and elsewhere, it seems worth trying to ascertain the kind of contribution this approach can make to curriculum studies (Sauer, 1987). To help do this three central questions which bear on the question of cultural studies curricula are discussed in the following section: the level of abstraction at which social problems should be set, the problem of authenticity and the problem of bias in cultural studies.

Ethnographic Research Parameters and Cultural Studies Curricula

Level of abstraction

Traditional approaches to civilisation/cultural studies have seldom given systematic consideration to the question of whether a social question should be approached at a micro-level through oral histories, accounts of personal experience and so on or at an institutional level. Frequently, they have tended to plump for either one approach or the other. Institutional or generalising approaches tend to fail to suggest the density and the contradictoriness of actual experience, while the more detailed accounts leave behind a feeling of randomness or arbitrariness. The ethnographic/symbolic approach outlined above gives a rationale for providing richly detailed accounts of everyday life. The detail is necessary to be able to understand the functioning of the cultural process in a clearly defined area of everyday life since culture is realised *through* the tangible experiences of everyday life: as Blackwell and Seabrook put it in discussing Hoggart's contribution to the analysis of working-class culture:

> One of the great strengths of *The Uses of Literacy* is that Hoggart's own reliance on personal testimony and observation itself expresses a characteristic working-class mode of discourse which embodies a distrust of the general and the abstract, and an affirmation of the tangible. This preference for the concrete and the particular is a kind of cultural counterpart of people's knowledge of, and control over, the familiar resistances of the materials with which they worked. (Blackwell and Seabrook, 1985: 25)

As we have seen Geertz takes a similar line; for him ethnography is 'thick description':

> What the ethnographer is in fact faced with ... is a multiplicity of complex conceptual structures, many of them superimposed upon or knotted into one another, which are at once strange, irregular and inexplicit, and which he must contrive somehow first to grasp and then to render ... Doing ethnography is like trying to read ... a manuscript – foreign, faded, full of ellipses, incoherencies, suspicious emendations, and tendentious commentaries, but written not in the conventionalized graphs of sound but in the transient examples of shaped behaviour. (Geertz 1973: 9–10)

This means that

> behavior must be attended to, and with some exactness, because it is through the flow of behaviour — or more precisely, social action — that cultural forms find articulation. Whatever, or wherever, symbol systems 'in their own terms', may be, we gain empirical access to them by inspecting events, not by arranging abstracted entities into unified patterns. (p.17)

Geertz's own description of his method is 'microscopic'.

This seems like a good description of what we are trying to do in our cultural studies courses. We clearly should not be attempting to train our students to become ethnographers. We do, however, wish our students to acquire some detailed knowledge of the target cultural patterns and to become aware of the complexity and contradictions of cultural discourse and the way in which ideologies are realised in everyday life. The 'microscopic' point of view should lead to students being able to acquire a repertoire of cultural patterns appropriate to interactional situations which have been targeted by them, or at least to obtain insight into how such a repertoire might be acquired. In addition the 'microscopic' point of view is appropriate for language students since the study of ethnographic material will increase their socially based language repertoire and their sociolinguistic awareness. Supplementing the 'microscopic' point of view with the symbolic approach will induce awareness of social embedding of micro-patterns and of relationships between the economic base and ideological practices.

The dual ethnographic/symbolic approach advocated here provides a rationale for both everyday culture and 'institutions', but it does have the drawback of seeming to overburden the curriculum, and this in spite of the relatively low priority and the limited time available to cultural studies within the university. The consequence must be to concentrate courses, apart from a small number of introductory lectures on small sectors of social life which offer the opportunity to combine the ethnographic and the symbolic approach. Courses might focus on studies of working-class culture, the culture of young people, the culture of leisure, the culture of racial minorities, and the social agents which are concerned with the transmission of ideology, for example the school system, the family and the mass media.

Authenticity and bias

A cultural studies programme along these lines should also have a beneficial impact on the problem of authenticity. Inauthentic materials are those which project an inaccurate picture of a society, though not necessarily through ill-will or bias. One of the major causes of inauthenticity is the lack of access to up-to-date materials. A glance at standard textbooks shows how difficult it apparently is to achieve this. Financial problems and the complexity of the publishing process certainly play a part here, but the wish to preserve certain cultural images (heterostereotypes) of the foreign country on the part of education ministries, publishers and teachers is also important. In the case of anglophile Germans these heterostereotypes have often stressed the eccentricity and oddness of British culture, but also certain class-based beliefs and practices (the gentleman, public schools, the 'establishment'). Frequently these features were held up uncritically for admiration, and sometimes for derision. However, the blame does not always lie with the foreigners, and so it is not just the heterostereotypes which may be misleading; a culture's own self-image may also be inconsistent with reality. There may also be interactions between the culture's own autostereotype and the heterostereotypes of foreign cultures. A further source of inauthenticity is the expectation that the behaviour of one class will be representative for all classes. This *'pars pro toto'* attitude affects both autostereotypes and heterostereotypes.

The ethnographic/symbolic approach does at least potentially offer some help here through its insistence on the importance of detail and by keeping textbook authors and students in touch with the result of ongoing research. There might, however, be some danger of replacing one stereotype by another if the range of topics becomes too limited. That could happen if we concentrated, for example, on working-class culture to the exclusion of everything else. The danger can be countered by choosing the limited range of topics we can realistically teach so as to suggest the variability of culture.

The kind of cultural studies advocated here should also be effective in countering charges of bias from both the right and the left against cultural studies. Describing a culture in detail makes it difficult to falsify the image of a country as a utopia (e.g. 'Merry Old England', America as the country of unlimited opportunity, etc.) or as an anti-utopia. A detailed presentation will show up the inadequacy of oversimplified stereotypes.

A Taxonomy of Cultural Studies Objectives

One way of summing up the argument and concentrating discussion is the following scheme which organises the objectives of cultural studies into a taxonomy with subgoals in three areas: the theoretical basis of cultural studies, the institutional and social framing of everyday life, and everyday life itself as a field of social action.

With respect to the theoretical basis of cultural studies the following subgoals can be identified:

- students should be able to recognise the social determination of behaviour
- students should be able to recognise that everyday behaviour has symbolic meaning
- students should have some knowledge of basic sociological models.

In the area of the institutional and social framework we might want to identify the following subgoals:

- students should be in a position to recognise differences and similarities between their own and the target society
- students should be in a position to identify some of the characteristic features of the target society – in the case of someone who is studying Britain as the target culture this would mean being able to identify key features of the British social system such as the persistence of the class system, the structure of British political life and other features
- students should also be in a position to understand some of the factors which determine the process of change in the target society – in the case of the student of England this would involve understanding changes in the economic structure, demographic changes due to the influx of immigrants in the post-war era and other changes. The illusion of a 'timeless' social system should be avoided at all costs
- students should also know something of the social agencies and institutions which are responsible for the transmission of social norms. This would include knowledge of the mass media and the education system, but also of family life.

In the area of everyday life we might want to identify the following subgoals involving recognition that:

- there are culture-specific patterns of face-to-face interaction which members of the target society conform to. This is obviously a fruitful field for comparisons with the students' first culture. Among points of comparison could be clothing, eating habits, gestures, proxemics etc.
- patterns of everyday interaction are themselves socially conditioned and reflect the larger social matrix
- patterns of everyday behaviour may differ by region or by class
- the significance of the relationships between individual biographies and everyday patterns of behaviour

- patterns of everyday behaviour are complex and require first-hand and intensive study.

Such objectives can only be realised in a miniaturised way in the type of projects which have been suggested above. Similar or more complete lists of objectives can, I hope, provide guidance for the construction of cultural studies curricula and also a guide to the mix of materials which are required, ranging from standard sociological descriptions to biographies, autobiographies and oral histories (Kane, 1986).

It is sometimes implied or explicitly argued that cultural studies in the language learning context should exclude social and institutional factors and concentrate on the micro-level of everyday interaction. Even in secondary education I believe that such a reductive approach, because of its lack of explanatory power, will fail to stir interest and, worse still, will lead to a concept of the target culture in which differences are viewed as peculiarities or eccentricities, and will be a source of cultural and linguistic misunderstanding. A minimalist stance on cultural studies would not do justice either to our students or the culture.

References

BARON, S. 1985, The study of culture. Cultural studies and British sociology compared. *Acta Sociologica* 28, 71–85
BLACKWELL, T. and SEABROOK, J. 1985 *A World Still to Win. The Reconstruction of the Post-War Working Class.* London: Faber & Faber.
BUTTJES, D. and KANE, L. 1978, Theorie und Zielsetzung der Landeskunde im Fremdsprachenstudium. *Anglistik und Englischunterricht* 4, 51–61.
GEERTZ, C. 1973, *The Interpretation of Cultures.* New York: Basic Books.
KANE, L. 1986, Work and community in Britain. In D. BUTTJES (ed.) *Panorama. English Cultures Around the World*, pp.1–17. Dortmund: Lensing.
SAUER, H. (ed.) 1987, *Amerikanische Alltagskultur und Englischunterricht.* Heidelberg: Winter.
SWIDLER, A. 1986, Culture in action. *American Sociological Review*, 50, 273–86.
WILLIS, P. 1980, *Learning to Labour. How Working Class Kids Get Working Class Jobs.* Farnborough: Gower.

17 The Observation Diary: An Ethnographic Approach to Teacher Education

GENEVIÈVE ZARATE

What can the sociologist, the ethnologist and the language teacher have in common, even though they are assigned by society the same task: to describe social facts with a high degree of scientific precision?

As an instrument of sociological and ethnological enquiry, the diary can, when used in the training of (future) teachers of French as a foreign language, lead them to pose a number of first order questions. What distinguishes an empirical view from one which is rigorously structured? How can lived experience be transformed into the object of writing? How can one separate out from dense reality the object observed? And it can then invite students to deal with such issues in a concrete way.

The Observation Diary: Definition of an Instrument of Training

In an experiment in teacher training in French as a foreign language (FFL) over a period of two years, the initial requirements on students were relatively simple.

Firstly, they were to choose a place accessible to direct observation. This requirement automatically excludes large-scale entities (town, age group, social group) and suggests that the object to be observed should be determined as a function of spatial limitations. In Table 17.1 the limiting cases can be observed. Is a team of supervisors of a leisure centre systematically identifiable with the reception area of the centre? Is the Parisian Metro accessible to direct observation by one single person?

Secondly, students were to choose a place which they frequented on a regular basis. At what point can one say that one frequents a place regularly? What degree of regularity creates a relationship of familiarity with a locality? In the students' choice the constraints of frequency had little influence; it is none the less noteworthy that weekly or fortnightly observations were more frequent than daily observation. The most significant constraint was to establish the observation project over a period of time (see Table 17.1), this being a condition presented as fundamental to the writing stage.

TABLE 17.1

Localities observed	No. of observations	Length
primary school	11	8 Apr – 29 May
university residence	28	26 Apr – 23 May
clothes shop	11	5 May – 24 May
café (Paris 16e)	15	27 Apr – 25 May
Pierrelaye station	12	30 Apr – 25 May
doctor's surgery		not dated
library	8	6 May – 27 May
tea room/pâtisserie	22	7 Apr – 21 May
baker's/pâtisserie	13	7 Apr – 24 May
staffroom in school	12	27 Apr – 26 May
towerblock lift	9	27 Apr – 23 May
school exit	10	28 Apr – 26 May
university restaurant	13	29 Apr – 22 May
corridor of *au pair* agency	11	8 Apr – 21 May
municipal swimming baths	8	20 Apr – 3 May
public park	10	14 Apr – 23 May
'civilisation' class	12	7 Apr – 18 May
baker's shop	14	26 Apr – 18 May
grocer's shop	12	6 May – 23 May
school (lycée)	11	27 Mar – 14 May
staffroom of school for handicapped	7	28 Apr – 22 May
flower shop	15	7 Feb – 7 May
entrance to apartment block	21	1 Dec – 27 Apr
team of monitors at leisure centre	11	14 Jan – 8 Apr
Courbevoie market	11	24 Dec – 7 Apr
men's section, department store	11	22 Nov – 27 Dec
Pompidou library	7	28 Dec – 5 Apr
school corridor	9	12 Jan – 8 Apr

Table 17.1 continued

Localities observed	No. of observations	Length
art class	4	9 Feb – 6 Apr
an apartment	16	7 Dec – 24 Apr
laundromat	9	23 Dec – 1 Mar
company telephone switchboard	7	19 Dec – 23 Apr
train compartment (Gare du Nord)	14	6 Dec – 28 Feb
private lessons in a school	7	25 Nov – 7 Apr
Paris Metro		monograph
tearoom in a mosque	15	6 Feb – 14 May
cheese shop	8	20 Mar – 10 May
supermarket	19	16 Jan – 11 Mar
crèche	27	14 Dec – 23 May
recording studio	9	7 Mar – 9 May

Thirdly, the students were required to choose a place where it was possible to observe a plurality of representations. Localities where there is constant movement (large stores, hallways, escalators, for example) can from this point of view prove particularly difficult to master in that the flow of regular users is intense, and of irregular and arbitrary composition. Repeated contact with the same interlocutors may be impossible. Conversely, the places where access is regulated (school yard, school staffroom) or where the regular users are to a high degree socially homogeneous (employees of the same status, for example) can make the collection of contrasting representations more problematic. In this case there is often a tendency for the content of the diary to be reduced to the narration of the psycho-affective relationships described below.

The question now arises as to what in the development of this diary is pertinent to the procedures of the anthropological process and what is relevant to the processes of training.

Although Mauss remarked in his *Manual of Ethnography* (1967: 7 and 9) that his lectures were intended to 'teach how to observe and classify social phenomena' and that 'the first method of work will consist of keeping a travel diary where will be noted each evening the work accomplished during the day' he none the less credited this first stage of the relationship with the field with only limited scientific credibility. The diary provides only fragmented and disparate information which will attain scientific value only when organised in the form of a monograph. Favret-Saada (1981) takes a quite different view. When publishing the whole of her research diary on witchcraft in Normandy, she writes:

> Usually the only part of ethnographic work which is known is the end product, the scientific monograph. But how, in the field, does a researcher set about determining his object of study, how does he choose 'good' informants, or distinguish what is worth noting in an encounter with a 'native'? How do numerous, often purely chance encounters with individual human beings, moved by diverse emotions, become transmuted into the analysis of a social system? What happened from day to day between the researcher and the 'natives' for the former to give a particular interpretation of the latter? (1981: 1589)

In this case the scientific credibility is due less to the social recognition which the ethnologist enjoys than to his ability to objectify the conditions arising in the here and now, which determined the structure of his observation. This type of diary not only allows a glimpse behind the scenes of observation (the false starts, the productive moments, the moments of progress, the failures) but above all it gives the events behind the scenes a scientific significance.

It is the latter view that we have adopted in the context of training, because it forms a break with the dominant models of pedagogic description of French as a foreign language. By making explicit the conditions of production of the description of a cultural fact, by making apparent the nature of the relationship between the observer and his object, this descriptive model offers an alternative to the naive vision of social facts which is dominated by the idea of truth, of panoramic description and by the textbook author's absolute authority ('France in Your Pocket', 'Everything about ...' or 'Keys to ...'). By choosing to define the object not as a function of the product of school study or of an abstract entity (transport, young people ...) but rather as a function of its accessibility to direct observation, we believe that this procedure has a greater chance of inducing reflection on the genesis of a description, on the development of knowledge and on the relativity of social representations.

It remains to be said that this diary was part of a university assessment procedure, and – not the least paradoxical element of the experiment – the teacher found herself confronted by the difficulty of assessing the diary of a locality which she had not observed herself, even less actually frequented.

The Gap between Empirical Observation and Structured Observation

In asking the apprentice ethnologist to be exhaustive and to 'neglect no detail' Mauss (1967: 10) expresses a descriptive principle whose application implies, but sometimes also demands, a sociological sensitivity.

Observational accuracy: conditions and obstacles

In the 87 diaries available, the requirement of accuracy is taken account of to differing extents. The minimal degree of accuracy is as follows:

- the date, the time of beginning the observation, accompanied less systematically by the finishing time;
- a plan of the location carried out on the spot (sometimes redrawn with a ruler afterwards) and/or a plan drawn from memory.

The first observation consists of a preamble (if the preamble is made explicit as such, it is because the diary has been copied out a second time). In the preamble there may be:

- an often minutely detailed description of the locality and its decor Georges Perec, Alain Robbe-Grillet and the '*Nouveau Roman*' (Perec or Robbe-Grillet are often present as descriptive models);
- the reconstruction of the total experiences of the locality (known history, conditions of the first entry into the locality, etc.);
- description of the identity of the social actors;
- the explicit status of the observer in this locality.

The accuracy requirement is, in general, very evident at this stage of the work, perhaps because the first act of writing is an invitation to account for all the data known to the observer but unknown to the potential reader of the diary (i.e. the teacher). This attempt to include all the available data is sometimes accompanied by a wish to anticipate future interactions or by a desire for a structured narrative ('As we shall see later'). In the latter case, however, the diary has been re-written in a fair copy. In fact, in the course of observation this desire for accuracy tends to dissolve. The observer has increasing difficulty in sorting out, in the information he or she has acquired, that which has already been given (a constantly increasing amount) from that which the reader does not yet know. As a consequence gaps appear in the information as an effect of the observer's microscopic view of the object. For example, an observation situated at one of the extension telephones of a company omitted to mention what that company manufacture. Another diary kept in a library leaves unclear the status of the observer – was she a reader, or a librarian, or ...?

The fact that the diary is written over a period of time exposes the observer to the phenomenon of repetition. In this case a loose observation might be defined as one which is more concerned with the systematic repetition of a previous situation – in which 'nothing happens' – than with the minute daily variations. Naive writing also tends to assert rather than describe and thus evades the construction of meaning; for example, when the interactions of a public shopping area are described as follows: 'There is a way of speaking particular to private conversations'; or when people are sitting at table in a school dining room: 'I sense there is bad feeling between people at the two ends of the table.' One of the difficulties of description is to pin down that which is inexpressible.

We considered that a certain degree of professionalism is attained when the accuracy of the observation is not narrowly correlated with the length of the observation. Thus a purchasing interaction between a newsagent and his customer, although very brief, is perceived as being shot through with great social density:

> Everything happens very quickly. The newsagent hands him the daily paper without the title having been mentioned. (This is where the notion of regularity appears.) The social interaction, or more simply, the complicity arises from the fact that (a) the person is recognised and does not need to ask for what he wants to buy and (b) the desire for speed but at the same time for intimateness (for personalisation) is legitimate.

Thus an exchange which is minutely noted changes the meaning of an interaction which a naive observer might have interpreted as *impersonal* because it was wordless.

Writing up the observation notes

Although there are some localities where observation and the writing of the diary can be concomitant (for example, in a library or café) there are others where this is not possible. In these cases writing has to be postponed, creating problems of memorisation. When these difficulties are integrated into the narrative the observer produces simultaneously the object of the observation and the data which allow the relativisation of the object produced. For example: 'I wrote all this a few days later from notes made when I returned to my office'; or 'Although I note everything in abbreviated form, it is still possible that my own language interferes with the discourse I observe and that I forget important parts of it; what is more I do not transcribe the silences and the phatic expressions.' The differentiated transcription of whole sections of conversation is thus one of the most difficult aspects of this work. Even the professionals themselves can stumble over this, as Favret-Saada remarks: 'Last night I stopped short, unable to remember the rest. The interview had lasted two and a half hours' (1981: 1593). The classical rules of the academic game, which consist of hiding the gaps in one's knowledge, are inverted and, in the final assessment, the diary which contains the analysis of the limits of the observation is marked high. This involves a rule of writing which it was necessary to make explicit from the very beginning of the work.

The students were asked not to reveal their observation project in the milieu observed. This is without doubt a debatable methodological choice, but one which does have a justification. Making the observation public can separate the observer from the milieu, change him or her into a voyeur and also change the locality into a stage and the participants into actors. This would create a degree of theatricality which it would be difficult to overcome in what is, after all, only an initiation into observation. Sometimes this discrete observation relationship is badly handled and is made public because the act of writing is unmasked ('I didn't want to tell him that I make a note of my remarks and so I told him I was doing some French homework'). It may also threaten the sense of security of the observed group; for example in the presence of political militants in the entrance to a university: 'The Arab students noticed me ...' or 'On one occasion, without my realising, a shopkeeper came up to me to see what I was writing, and he said nothing.' Because the exercise has a direct relationship to reality, the social sanction is immediate, as we see, when the academic exercise overrides respect for social constraints. With respect to academic assessment, these lapses are not penalised provided that they are integrated into the field notes and transformed into objects for analysis.

When the relationship between observer and milieu observed was objectified, we considered that the diary demonstrated scientific qualities. To be able to relate *a posteriori* the effects of surprise is to demonstrate an ability to reconstitute the origins of knowledge by recall, which is acquired at the moment of writing:

> Imagine my surprise to find that a long queue was waiting in silence, standing, as on the previous day. Couldn't they at least sit down?

Similarly, to re-establish in the diary the different perceptions of the observer which are current in the milieu observed demonstrates the ability to put into operation the process of objectivisation:

> My relationship with the customers is fairly satisfactory. I am seen sometimes as the mother of a small boy, sometimes as a young woman, less often as a Polish woman, and as a student only by those who actually know.

Or:

> My status is rather special, known to the baker as a consequence of her previous conversations with my father who has been a regular customer for nine years. So I am (a) the daughter of my father, which explains such exchanges as 'Well your father must be pleased to see you'; (b) a Helen of Troy who is exiled in an 'exotic' country – hence exchanges such as 'I don't suppose you have the same kind of bread over there?'; and (c) the wife of an Australian ... hence exchanges such as 'Don't you feel lonely a little ... it must be hard in the evenings?' (!)

Sociological sensitivity

It is sometimes difficult for students who have not been trained in this way to understand the sociological interest of a given situation. Take, for example, two conversations between an inhabitant of a block of flats and the postman, one of which takes place in the entrance to the flats, the other in a neighbouring street. The conversations can be interpreted in terms of repetition. The information contained in talk about the communal decoration of a Christmas tree or the arrival of a new member in an existing group is not always seen for what it is: an exceptional event which might re-focus the observations made up to that point. If the sociological implications are not properly perceived, they are shifted to the level of affective relationships, as the 'I' of the observer totally submerges the object of observation: 'I don't like her very much because she is hypocritical and is constantly telling lies all day long, to show her superiority'. This is then very close to the personal diary but a long way from the initial stages of training, i.e. the objectivisation of observation. These lapses are not always total. A psychologising remark – 'I find the person in charge – Cacharel – very sound' – can be 'corrected' by re-establishing the narration of the relations between protagonist and observer, by making explicit the positive signs of the relationship: 'She had been very kind to me, being prepared to help me find a bedsitter and a job'.

In contrast, we considered that the observation demonstrated real sociological relevance when, being sensitive to the process of daily creativity, it showed how users can alter the usual function of a locality. For example: 'This [railway] waiting room is far from being anonymous, I will even be able to compare it to a café or a newsagent's shop'; Or: 'The train ... takes on the character of private spaces where everyone controls his bit of space in his own way; one can read, sing, sleep, dance, play cards.' In this case, the diary attempts to 'uncover the surreptitious forms taken by the disparate, tactical and impromptu creativity of groups or individuals' and takes account of 'those processes and tricks of the consumer which, in the extreme case, form the basis of an anti-discipline' whose hidden presence has been emphasised by de Certeau (1980: 14).

Decoding the implicit

The development of a new way of seeing, which breaks down the image of a familiar locality and transforms it into an object of surprise, is one of the intended benefits of this exercise. In the final stage, the diarist can uncover the implicit rules which structure the observed locality. In order to facilitate the relatively difficult organisational task involved, we suggested that localities whose explicit functions are the same but whose implicit use may be different should be placed in parallel. As they are a relatively homogeneous social group, the students often choose localities whose functions are the same, as is evident from Table 17.1: for example, libraries, entrance hall, cafés, baker's shops. None the less, the localities are sufficiently diverse for the social networks to be different and for the comparison of two diaries to bring out noticeable variations in localities whose function seems identical. This provides the opportunity to note simple effects of 'the illusion of nominal constancy' which Bourdieu (1987) warns against. For example, the comparison of two libraries shows on the one hand the rules of mutual help between neighbouring readers to reserve the place of a reader who is absent for a moment, despite the presence of other people. In the second case, the constraints are more determined by the personalities of the librarians:

> The few existing rules are generally respected (there is no smoking, people finish their coffee before entering, they don't eat in the library). There is a tendency to go a little further either when Mrs T is absent, and the duty librarian is known, or at the end of the week, or even more so just before the holidays.

It is not always easy to know the status of an informant. It is on the basis of knowledge acquired 'from the inside', shared with the employees of a store or the salespeople of a department, that one can manage to distinguish between the window-dresser who is not one of the staff and the designer who is. It is not always easy to distinguish among the members of staff of a shop as to who is the boss and who the employee. Being on the look-out for clues of this kind is an introduction to the pleasure of resolving an enigma. Two foreign 'cleaners' who speak rather broken French and who are in charge of the running of a laundrette, turn out to be the owners:

> Since they don't know how to deal with technical questions (of a machine which has broken down) they refer people to a telephone number pinned to the wall and this means that almost no-one is aware of the fact that the laundrette belongs to them, and everyone thinks they are cleaners.

How can the teacher assess the observation of a locality which he/she does not know at first hand? If one accepts that the purpose of the diary is to transform empirical knowledge of a locality into a rigorously structured object, then the assessment can be carried out according to the following criteria:

- does the observer identify and assess the sociological relevance of the situations he/she narrates?
- does the description give an account of the specificity of the observed locality and of the daily practices of its users?
- are the meanings produced by the particular experience of the observer made explicit?

The View from Abroad

In so far as the work was carried out jointly by French and foreign students it might be expected that there would be two kinds of writing from the two groups: a view drowned in familiarity for the former and a naive view full of surprises for the latter. In fact, if there are traces of a view from abroad, it is neither ingenuous nor abrasive in the manner of Persans de Montesquieu's *Lettres Persannes*. Remember that the very conditions of the work – a locality which one uses oneself, training spread over a whole university year – do not favour the viewpoint of the new arrival. An observer does clearly confirm his characteristic of being a foreigner when he evaluates the differences in behaviour from the practices current in his own country. For example, hygiene (an ice cream licked in turn by a dog and its owner), politeness ('I've given up a lot of my sociability in order to conform with the practices of this country, without really getting to know what it's like'), decency (appearing in pyjamas in the entrance hall of a block of flats) are all noted negatively. But the signs of indignation remain relatively discreet ('At one point he had even put his feet on the table to feel more at ease. He really thought he was at home'), made more palatable no doubt in the name of the required process of objectivisation, as perceived by the writer.

The view from abroad is also apparent in the concern to point out the differences observed between the culture of origin and the host culture. This type of remark tends to systematise the divergence, either by stating the difference in the form of laws of a national character ('I have never seen a Portuguese or a Spaniard wear a cap in this café; educated Frenchmen don't either' or 'it's rare in France for people to know their neighbour's name') or by identifying the divergences in the functioning of an institution (the function of a fireman or of a headteacher, for example). It is as if the view from abroad retained only those properties of the chosen locality which have a certain degree of generality. The diary then tends to descend into the description of what creates the specificity of the observed locality.

When the characteristic of being a foreigner is less marked, the view from abroad becomes evident in other signs. It is apparent in the choice of the observed localities: the interstices between the home country and the host country (telephone kiosks, university halls of residence, local radio broadcasting for a given community, etc.); or places of exile where national solidarity is daily reinforced (tearoom which at certain times of the day serves as the Iranian club; an *au pair* agency which recruits in a specific geographical region: 'We sometimes feel as though we are a miniature Nordic consulate'). The dynamics of the signs of recognition at the heart of a community are transcribed in their ambiguity:

> As he left he slipped in, among the usual forms of politeness, a 'thankyou' in Arabic which seemed to me to be an invitation to start a conversation in that language in order to get to know each other. But I didn't take advantage of the opportunity.

Or:

> I recognised the language he was speaking: Ewe, a language of Togo. That's how I recognised him to be a compatriot. He on the other hand doesn't know me as such.

The process of decoding an implicit meaning is more the object of hypothesis than of certainty:

[Talking about a child of school age brought to the 'centre.] I deduce from that that it is a place which is intended for children who have problems.

Finally, the differences do not reflect exclusively a demarcation along national lines. One diary, talking about the students of a university residence, establishes in the conclusion the following different groups: 'the Greeks versus the others; the people living on the same floor versus the others; the residents who speak French versus the others; the residents with the same social status versus the others'. Notice none the less that the refocusing of a view which is socially constructed remains the exception:

> It was the first time that I had become aware of my own requirements – as far as the surface of life is concerned, the hygiene of the fittings etc. – and as a consequence of my social position: educated bourgeois (all the family is in teaching) from the established middle class in a rich European country.

If this definition of social identity is due to the required activity of objectivisation, it has to be emphasised that this operation is all the more likely to take place when the mother culture exists in a positive symbolic relationship with the observed foreign culture.

In Conclusion

The immediate gains of this kind of training may not appear obvious to those who favour 'the concrete' and 'the field'. Indeed these diaries are not 'new' material for us in class. That is, no doubt, a limitation of the work. The intention is, however, quite different. Whereas the training of teachers of culture is usually conceived of in terms of identifying sources of information, of creating exercises and writing tasks, our concern is to propose, as antecedent, a critical reflection on an objective view of the culture to be taught. In this case the teacher will 'naturally' take up the position of spectator or impartial judge. Our concern, further, is to challenge the position of the teacher in the social space which he or she directs in class.

References

BOURDIEU, P. 1987, *Choses dites*. Paris: Editions de Minuit.
BOURDIEU, P. CHAMBOREDON, J.C. and PASSERON, J.C. 1968, *Le Métier de Sociologue*. Paris: Mouton/Bordas.

DE CERTEAU, M. 1980, L'invention du quotidien. *Arts de Faire*, 10 October.
FAVRET-SAADA, J. 1981, *Corps pour corps*. Paris: Gallimard.
FREMONT, A. 1979, Journal de guerre d'un géographe en Algèrie. *Herodote*. (January/March), 5–35.
LECERF, Y. 1985, Ethnologie à Paris VII: indexicalité, journaux, récits, quasi-journaux. *Pratiques de Formation* 9, 59–77.
LEIRIS, M. 1974, *L'Afrique fantome*. Paris: Gallimard.
LEVI-STRAUSS, C. 1983, *Le Regard éloigné*. Paris: Plon.
MAUSS, M. 1967, *Manuel d'éthnographie*. Paris: Payot.

18 From Integrative Studies to Context Theory: A Project in In-service Education

FRANZ KUNA

Culture as Social System or Context of Meanings

After decades of linguistic and anthropological research and in the light of recent developments in sociology and culture theory, Oscar Wilde's statement that people when they talk about the weather mean something else appears to be truer than ever. While no-one, as yet, denies 'the fact-stating functions of ordinary language and the cause-seeking inclinations of the human mind', there is general agreement on the view that 'the man-as-scientist approach to language and thought can be stretched only so far' (Schweder & LeVine, 1984: 12). Whilst it is true that many people in the contemporary world, as scientists, statisticians, or logicians of all types, are involved in some of the more reductive functions of language, 'ordinary language and thought aims to do more than merely report and represent the causal structure of reality, and relatively few utterances or practices serve a pure and exclusive assertive function' (Shweder & LeVine, 1984: 12). Contemporary anthropologists have even gone further than this: 'Language is all', they seem to be saying. If to Geertz culture is 'an historically transmitted pattern of meanings embodied in symbols, a system of inherited conceptions expressed in symbolic form by means of which men communicate, perpetuate, and develop their knowledge about and attitude towards life' (1973: 89) then the various components of culture − such things as beliefs, customs, taboos, techniques, rituals, ceremonies, institutions, codes, etc. − are not merely what they seem to be, but are, above all, units of meaning; they are signs, which work like the signs of language.

Culture thus defined is not merely a complex social system, an integrated pattern of human knowledge, belief and behaviour, but above all a 'pattern of meanings', that is to say a language system by which values, ideals and beliefs are communicated, and transmitted to succeeding generations.

The highly pluralistic view of the function of human language as contained in contemporary culture theory is backed up by contemporary social psychology. What we have been witnessing for some time now is a kind of post-Piagetian and post-Skinnerian interest in language acquisition. Language acquisition is at the same time cultural acquisition, and vice-versa.

> What psychologists have discovered is that logic is not all there is to thinking and that abstract traits are not all there is to affective and interpersonal functioning. With that discovery, what something 'means', how to talk about meaning, and how to study it have become central issues. (Shweder & LeVine, 1984: 4)

Moreover, psychologists of a more psychoanalytical bent have emphasised the fact that children build up their 'maps of reality' only gradually, and without critical analysis, which means that the words of our language remain very largely imprecise and undefined. Words and whole utterances therefore have many meanings, with some of these meanings even acting as kinds of synonyms for inner states of being. At this point we are again reminded of Wilde's statement, when he implies that with their references to the weather, people are more likely to refer to their well-being or the opposite rather than to meteorological facts.

The imprecision of words and meanings is of course, of primary interest to writers and literary critics. And it is not surprising that for some time now literary theorists and structural semioticians have been working with a view of language which tends to be closely tied up with views of culture, communication, social intercourse, and even of problems like the constitution and representation of self. Moreover, there is a tendency to postulate types of meaning which are said to be external to language rather than internal. According to this view 'funniness', for example, would be in the audience rather than in the clown, or in a receptive reader rather than in a funny text. If the question of whether meanings are internal or external actually seems a futile one to discuss further it is nevertheless symptomatic of current views of language that certainly the structuralists amongst semioticians and radical reception theorists are particularly prone to emphasising the importance of 'context' over the importance of the 'mere' text. Meaning is not in the language, they seem to be saying, but something that needs to be constantly negotiated on the basis of the 'gaps' contained in all language, particularly in literary texts and sophisticated speech acts. Understanding meanings is thus a process of discovery, a permanent act of 'contextualisation' in response to the referential function of language.

There can be no doubt that the belief in the polysemic nature of language, and of cultural facts taken as signs, lies at the heart of cultural sciences today. With all their differences, reception theorists amongst literary scholars, '*Didaktiker*' amongst educational scientists (particularly in Europe) and anthropologists and cultural theorists associated with names like Clifford Geertz, Paul Kay or Jürgen Habermas would have no difficulty in agreeing that 'texts' (in the widest sense of the word) are not occasions for a quest for once-and-for-all explanations but rather for an open-ended negotiation of meaning. If their demand is a just one then the implications for the teaching of language and literature are far-reaching. It seems that as language teachers and literary critics we are not called upon to teach language as if it had a fixed (internal) structure of meaning, or literature as if it were a specific body of knowledge, but as if language and literature were cultural facts amongst other cultural facts and therefore in need of comparative treatment and structural analysis. The idea would not be to teach pupils how to search for identifiable types of meaning but to create a sense of the plural function of all language systems and of the interpretive possibilities in the face of concrete instances. The idea would be, as it were, to restore corrupt and worn-out meanings – the result of everyday, mechanistic or 'technological' usage – to the life they have been distilled from: 'to the turmoil of emotional experience', as Thomas Blackburn put it somewhat dramatically (1960: 19). Today we might say that readers and interpreters of language should consider it their primary duty to restore ideas and abstractions to the contexts they grew from. And 'context' means what is both inside and outside the minds of readers.

Teaching Literature in Context: The INSET Project

In the following I should like to describe a small-scale experiment in the teaching of literary criticism which attempted to realise some of the intentions implied in the above, and which was designed for use within a new type of INSET-project set up by members of the University of Klagenfurt, Austria. This will give me an opportunity to report briefly on a, in many ways, unique project, and to spell out some of the theoretical assumptions which underlie both the teaching experiment and the project for which it was designed.

The so-called PFL-project[1] was designed to provide a new type of in-service training for higher secondary school teachers from all over Austria. The idea was not to *instruct* the teachers independently of their actual needs in the everyday classroom situation, but to create a framework within which teachers were able to organise their own professional development. The following were some of the principles which governed the planning of the programme:

1. Work started from the academic and pedagogical problems individual teachers had actually encountered in their own classroom, and not from the structure of scientific knowledge of any of the disciplines involved, or from any personal interests members of the course team might have had.
2. Members of the course team were not supposed to act as 'experts' or as prophets in the wilderness, but rather as 'counsellors' who were able to make flexible use of whatever initiatives members of the course were willing to take, or of the wealth of material they had prepared and brought with them in order to cater for 'emergencies'. Their problem was to react quickly to situations, problems and questions they very often could not anticipate, define or raise in advance.
3. The course team was put together on a strictly interdisciplinary basis. Of the ten people originally involved, four came from the Department of English Language and Literature (representing both the discipline of English Studies and the Teaching of English/*Fachdidaktik*), four from the Department of Education (representing a range of educational subjects) and two were teachers who were associated with the University in a number of ways. Whilst at first the difficulties in co-operating seemed insurmountable, a kind of workable *modus vivendi* was ultimately achieved through a combination of long planning sessions, team seminars devoted to the discussion of problems of interaction and project design, and sheer luck and good-will.
4. Most of the work was to be done, over two years, at three one-week residential seminars, in regional working groups, and at the participants' schools. The duties of the course team were strictly limited to providing an organisational framework for the work of the participants, to counselling, and, finally, to the production of input in the form of self-instructional material.

That the project has survived in this form, and is now institutionalised as a two-year university course, is rightly considered a miracle by those who were involved from the beginning, either as participants or members of the project team, in planning and completing the first PFL-programme. The conflicts and tensions between members of the project team, between individual participants, and, above all, between participants and the course team frequently reached breaking-point. The temptation to desert the role of the 'counsellor' and to revert to traditional forms of communicating 'knowledge' was enormous. Moreover, it was not always easy to persuade the participating teachers that it was exclusively up to them to provide the bulk of the material for any work that was going to be of any use to them at all. However, by strictly adhering to the principles outlined above, enough organisational know-how and interactive skills were gradually acquired by those involved to make the project a continuing success.

In 1965 Wimsatt postulated three tasks the literary critic had to face when analysing and interpreting poems: *explanation, description* and *explication*. The first activity referred to the apparent need to explain the 'explicit' (dictionary) meaning of the poem; the second had to do with the problem of describing the formal properties of the poem conceived as *Gestalt*, and the third with giving an account of what Wimsatt called 'implicit meaning'. When Wimsatt refers to 'the strongly directive and selective power of such meaning – the power of the *pattern*, of the main formally controlling purpose in the well-written poem (in terms of Gestalt psychology, the principle of "closure")' (1965: 226), then we know what he thinks of verbal structures and their meaning. Poems are entities, which can be described like the shape of cathedrals, and the shape together with the explicit meaning determines the implicit – *the* meaning of the poem. This ontological view of poetry and language has led to a situation in which everybody from Susan Sontag ('Against Interpretation') to structuralists and reception theorists have been busy redressing the balance. In the late 1980s we had good reasons for believing that poems are not entities but rather what speech act theorists call 'locutionary acts'. We do not react to poems as if they were instances of 'la langue'; on the whole most of us today react to them as if they were instances of 'la parole'. Moreover, we no longer believe that all the meaning we apparently find in language actually is in the language, but rather feel that it derives from contexts in which it is produced. And we have learnt how to distinguish between sentence-meaning and utterance-meaning. We also know that there is another component of the speech act – called by J.L. Austin 'the rhetic act' – 'which includes the assignment of reference and may be described more generally as contextualization' (Lyons, 1981: 182).

But there is a practical problem of considerable dimension. It is well-known that the generation of Wimsatt was far more successful in discovering a *praxis* for their theoretical and ideological concern than we seem to be. Today, after more than 20 years of hectic efforts in such areas as semiology and reception theory, theory still dominates practice. There are many more truly exciting books and articles on theory than there are on practical analysis. Most of us today will honestly believe in the wisdom of content-analysis and context theories, but at the same time find it extremely difficult – as Todorov has frequently pointed out – to talk about content, to contextualise, and quite generally to make use of what we might call the 'democratic' properties of language. Why should this be so? And what can we do to bring our practice into line with theory?

Analysing a Poem: An Experiment in Context Theory

The following experiment, which was used in the project described above, is designed to help both teachers and pupils to gain insights into the problem, and to discover for themselves a way of reading literary texts without closing all doors, and without succumbing to the temptation of secretly looking for, and selecting, the kind of explanations that make any further comments superfluous. I shall first describe the experiment, and then spell out some of the implied theoretical assumptions.

A discussion of Ted Hughes' poem 'Lineage'

The critical aims were twofold:

1. Understanding the poem in its contexts (the problem of contextualising language)
2. Learning to become sensitive to the intersubjectivity of subjective judgements.

The educational aims were defined as:

1. Learning to interact and exchange opinions in small groups;
2. Developing a sense of the 'significance' (personal meaning) of literary texts.

Method of Teaching

The form of interaction was that of task- and pupil-orientated discussion, which took place in a small group framework. The role of the teacher was limited to 'procedural tasks' and 'counselling'; taking responsibility for the definition and communication of purpose, task and agenda and for providing inputs without in any way influencing or determining the discussion. The teacher would provide an introduction which comprised brief comments only on author and poem, which may take a form such as the following:

'As we can see at a glance the form of the poem follows some sort of genealogical pattern; there is an effect of litany, of liturgical performance. Why? What kind of "lineage" is the poem referring to? In another sense the poem appears to be a sequence of words partly relating to anatomy, partly to areas of human feeling and activity, partly to religion. Why are all the words written in capital letters? Are we presented here with a string of familiar but possibly complex symbols or metaphors? If so, what kind of experiences, references and contexts will help us to understand the sequence? This is in fact the question I should like you to concentrate on, on the question of meaning, on what the poem means to you. I find this poem intriguing but have not tried to come to any conclusions about it. So all I can do is to provide you, from time to time, with other texts, which I have found of interest in relation to Ted Hughes' text.'

Input provided by teachers typically comprised contextual material, which may be found of relevance by the group for an understanding of the text. Material which the 'teacher' either provided at appropriate intervals or had ready for discussion included excerpts from the Gospels according to St John ('In the beginning was the Word') and St Matthew (containaing the typical Biblical lineages), old and more recent statements on the Virgin Mary (e.g. from John Harthan, *Books of Hours and Their Owners*, or from pop songs and beat lyrics of the 1950s and 1960s), on the ideological, religious and physical implications of pop (e.g. from Nik Cohn, *Modern Pop. From the Beginning*), on variations on the creation myth (e.g. from Goethe's *Faust*) or formulations of Egyptian myths and the function of 'crow' as an Egyptian symbol of death, and above all on the pros and cons of the alternative culture movements of the 1960s (plenty of suitable passages can be found in such books as *Beatitude Anthology*, C.A. Reich's *The Greening of America*, Norman Mailer's *The American Dream*, Herbert Marcuse's *One Dimensional Man*, but also in reports on the disintegration of alternative culture movements through the emergence of such social phenomena as the Manson Movement and suicidal sects).

'Lineage' was published in 1970 in Ted Hughes' collection *Crow*. It is not difficult to see that the poem is a pessimistic and conservative reaction to 'the swinging sixties' and their messianic desire for a new society. In the 1960s a powerful need was felt to break up what by many was considered to be an oppressive fossilised structure, the 'Granite' or 'Moloch' (A.

Ginsberg) of contemporary society. Through its progression of typical contemporary images ('Violet', 'Guitar', 'Sweat') the poem 'Lineage' evokes a by now familiar story: the attempt to reverse the original creation sequence in the various, frequently hysterical quests for deliverance and for a new mankind. This time it is not God who stands at the beginning of everything, but the new Adam who will 'beget' the new woman (not Eve but Mary!) and then, after the image of the new man, God. Was the attempt successful? Hughes' answer is obviously 'no'. And events towards the end of the 1960s – the disintegration of the 'flower'-movements, the chaos, brutalities and even murders inside the remaining sects, and the cultural pessimism resulting from all this – seem to prove him right.

Nevertheless, Hughes' answer, as implied in the poem 'Lineage', reflects only one point of view. There were many other points of view, particularly at the time when the poem was written, and there have been many different answers, attitudes and contributions since to what clearly has acquired the dimensions of a cultural debate. It is for this reason that Hughes' poem should not be read on its own. Though the poem's speaker appears to adopt a rather self-assured, even knowing and prophetic pose, the poem's imagery is ambiguous, because it is imbued with the meanings the images had, or still have, in different contexts and utterances. The Russian Formalists, Bakhtin above all, were particularly sensitive to the fact that the individual words of a text always also refer to matters beyond the text in which they occur. It is therefore 'illegitimate', as Bakhtin puts it, to limit the analysis of a text to the analysis of the text itself. Understanding a text does not merely mean the understanding of 'explicit' and 'implicit' meanings (in Wimsatt's sense) of single texts, but more importantly, the understanding of texts in their contexts, and the understanding of meanings resulting from the comparison of texts.

The Practice of Contextualisation: Some Observations and Conclusions

It is not difficult to see why an earlier generation of critics was not much interested in context. If one considers texts to be 'things in themselves', entities, closed autonomous structures, then the question was which features and properties gave such texts their identity. Texts were seen rather like evolving stars, artful verbal structures evolving from Babylonian chaos and background noise. They were considered to be 'unique' forms or unique 'vessels of meaning', and not incomplete structures interrelating with other incomplete structures. The art of interpretation was one of isolating meaning from its context, and of identifying it as something shaped by specific formal intentions. Today we are much more aware of 'the impossibility of defining the frontiers or limiting the context of "literature"' (Eliot, 1926: 3) and of a duty, as it were, to restore texts to the contexts from which they have emerged.

There is neither enough space here nor a particular need to describe in detail what happened on the various occasions at which the experiment was tried out. Generally speaking it can be said that those sessions at which the participants did not quite accept the challenge of initiating a 'dialogue' (Bakhtin) between the various texts, of bravely establishing and deciding on available contextual meaning, were a failure. A favourite temptation was to use the other texts not as texts or contexts in their own right but as 'background' material in order to 'explain' and 'elucidate' the basic text. It should not be surprising that attempts along these lines will sooner or later end in selective (not to say arbitrary) importation of meaning into the text from the outside (thereby internalising context), and in formal criticism. Only where the group did not deviate from its aim to read one text in the light of another text (without destroying their identity) was it possible to gain insight into the contextual nature of words and meaning and what appears to be a fundamental ambiguity and inbuilt dialectical open-endedness in all language acts.

In conclusion I should like to put together, in thesis-like fashion, some of the principles which are involved in reading and interpreting as acts of 'contextualisation'.[2]

- Context is everything that can meaningfully and actively be related to texts. It is not what you can put into 'introductions' or footnotes, i.e. mere 'background', an amorphous, *ad hoc* arrangement of so-called extra-literary facts. It is what can be felt and experienced as an integral aspect of the content and 'repertoire' of texts.
- Contextualisation is the attempt to identify relevant units of meaning in mere 'background' material and the experience of establishing active relationships between texts, and between texts and extra-textual areas of meaning.
- There is no difference between the act of contextualisation and the act of interpretation as far as the relationship between text and reader (as interpreter and 'contextualiser') is concerned. That is to say, in both cases the subject/object problem will be the same. In both cases the reader will be responsible for discovering and 'realising' (a term of reception theory) lines of interpretation. A 'sociologist' or 'historian' may be able to suggest what may be relevant context, but ultimately

- it is the reader of texts himself who has to make a decision on the basis of his experience of meaningful relationships.
- It is therefore obvious that acts of contextualisation are dependent on ideological dispositions, sociocultural competence and personal experience.
- The difficulty in the handling of context is not of a theoretical, but of a practical kind. It lies in the problem of how to prove to another reader the relevance of a postulated relationship between textual and extra-textual matters.
- Contexts are not constants. Like interpretations, they are 'unstable' and 'provisional'. They are not given units of meaning, but in each individual case have to be 'constituted' in the consciousness of the reader.
- The relationship between texts and contexts is a dialectical one; it is one of cause and effect. Texts are dependent on contexts, but they are not totally determined by them.
- It is impossible to determine objectively what W. Iser calls the '*Appellstruktur*' of literary texts, this is to say the number and variety of 'indicators' (L. Hjelmslev, R. Barthes) of connotations and contextual relationships in a text. The act of determining indicators (or 'connotators', as they were also called by Hjelmslev and Barthes) implies the same 'risks' as the act of interpretation and contextualisation. All depend on the competence, social-cultural experience and intellectual integrity of the reader.

The most important point about context was made, as early as 1940, again by M. Bakhtin, when he distinguished between context in the social sciences and context in the natural sciences. In the latter, context is simple: it is constituted by the objective, 'subject-less' system, or the theoretical environment, within which all scientific work is conducted. In the former, context is complex: it is what is ultimately happening in the minds of human beings. Context is 'personalistic', as Bakhtin puts it; it is 'an endless dialogue, in which the last word is never spoken'. It is the complex system of cross-references between texts, individuals, disciplines, decades, centuries. There is a reciprocal relationship between texts and their contexts, even if we are not always aware of it. If this were not so the reading of texts would be a peculiarly futile and meaningless affair. It would be like talking to oneself. But whilst it is not possible, by definition, to separate texts from contexts, it is possible to intensify (and of course to suppress) the interaction between the two by conscious effort. There is a difference between reading, say *Middlemarch* against the vague background of prejudiced and ill-remembered knowledge about the Victorian age or against the rather more precise contexts of the major intellectual debates of the 1860s. Only when we make a conscious effort at contextualisation will we be able to achieve a meaningful process of interaction between texts and their readers. As it happens, a conscious effort of this kind has been attempted, not by a critic, but by a writer. Whatever else John Fowles' book *The French Lieutenant's Woman* may be — most people would agree that it is one of the best novels written since the war — it is also a perfect model for the contextualisation of meanings, whether they belong to the past or to the present.

Notes

1. Full reports on the project (PFL is an abbreviation of *'Pädogogik und Fachdidaktik für Lehrer'*) can be found in Herbert Altrichter, 'The Austrian INSET-Project "PFL". Establishing a framework for self-directed learning', *British Journal of In-Service Education* 12 (1986) 3, pp.170–7; P. Posch, 'University support for independent learning – a new development in INSET', in Research Institute for Higher Education (ed.) *The Changing Functions of Higher Education*, Hiroshima University, 1985, pp.42–51.
2. Full and useful comments on the *'Methode der Kontextualisierung'* can be found in Kuno Schuhmann, 'Literaturgeschichte und Literatur in der Geschichte. Zur Kontextualisierung literarischer Texte', in his *Praxisbezüge der Anglistik*, Hoffman Verlag, Grossen-Linden, 1980, pp.7–56.

References

BLACKBURN, T. 1960, *An Anthology of English Poetry 1945–60*. London: Putnam.
ELIOT, T.S. 1926, The idea of a literary review.*The New Criterion* 4. 4.
GEERTZ, C. 1973 *The Interpretation of Cultures*. New York: Basic Books.
LYONS, J. 1981 *Language, Meaning and Context*. London: Fontana.
SHWEDER, R.A. and LEVINE, R.A. 1984, *Culture Theory. Essays on Mind, Self and Emotion*. Cambridge: Cambridge University Press.
WIMSATT, W.K. 1965, *Hateful Contraries. Studies in Literature and Criticism*. Lexington: University of Kentucky Press.

Part VI
Towards an Integrated View of Language Learning

The social and political significance of foreign language teaching has been an underlying theme throughout this book. It was raised in the earliest sections and reappeared in the illustrations from empirical research, the discussions of teaching materials and textbook analysis and the accounts of teacher education. At a point in time when travel, the media and international relations are bringing peoples and cultures more frequently in contact with each other, proximity paradoxically makes us aware of potential distance and difference. At the time of writing, the publication of one novel – Salman Rushdie: *The Satanic Verses* – has created a major international crisis of relations and again demonstrated how important and how difficult intercultural understanding within as well as across national frontiers will always be.

The contribution of foreign language teaching to the improvement of the situation has to be recognised, but those within the language teaching profession must also realise the limitations. In this final section authors address these issues by discussing the potential of an intercultural pedagogy (Borrelli), the attainable levels of intercultural competence in school (Kordes) and the need to establish a wider concept of which languages can and should be taught to whom (Broadbent and Oriolo).

Although the structure of this volume has taken us from accounts of culture studies in the past, descriptions of new intitiatives in the present and onto the wider perspectives for the future, there can be no conclusions or rounding off. The authors of this final section make that quite clear. There is still much to do, many new ideas to develop in theory and practice, many people to be drawn into a recognition of a richer, more socially responsible kind of language teaching through which intercultural understanding and communication can really take place.

19 Intercultural Pedagogy: Foundations and Principles

MICHELE BORRELLI

Intercultural Pedagogy Within a General Theory of Education

Intercultural and general pedagogy developed in the various schools of thought in the Federal Republic of Germany (FRG) as well as in other countries try to respond to educational problems side by side rather than by pooling their efforts and resources. This tendency is especially evident in the FRG. More than in other countries intercultural education, or 'foreigner pedagogy', is firmly established at most institutions of higher education. In addition to the traditional courses concerned with general and historical pedagogy, intercultural studies are offered. There is further evidence as titles of master theses, doctoral dissertations and research about intercultural education have greatly increased in the FRG during recent years.

This development raises the question as to how this coexistence came about and what legitimate reason keeps it alive. If, upon closer examination of this theoretical development, it turns out to be the case that the division between general and intercultural pedagogy is not artificially based, then we would have to check to see what is questionable, insufficient or perhaps even 'false' about the paradigms of traditional and general pedagogy. This cannot be done here, since neither general nor intercultural pedagogy can be regarded as a uniform set of theories. Nevertheless it is necessary to think about the theoretical foundations of pedagogy, whether or not it feels an obligation towards traditional categories of education or towards intercultural paradigms.

Meanwhile I will turn towards a different aspect: namely the scientific and theoretical understanding of intercultural pedagogy. Intercultural pedagogy is not to be understood as a set of statements, designed simply to supplement the traditional educational opportunities, to enrich the field of education with a new variant, discipline or perspective – for example, that of the integration of migrant children into the school systems and societies of the receiving countries. Furthermore the addressee of intercultural education is not only the foreign pupil, teenager, adult or any specific group but rather the educatee as such. Thus intercultural pedagogy does not differ from other concepts of systematic pedagogy with respect to its object. The object of our pedagogic efforts remains the same: the educatee. The question still on the floor is, do the preconceptions and settings concerning the object remain the same? This question will be raised here briefly in order to emphasise the theoretical and pedagogical understanding of intercultural education.

Constituting intercultural education as a discipline

If we are to establish intercultural pedagogy as a social science, which pedagogical, critical and theoretical paradigms will be indispensable? One close look at the history of pedagogy should suffice to prove that the science of pedagogy cannot be conceived of as purely logical or methodological without giving up the political, economic, historical framework within which it is operating.

The science of pedagogy cannot be seen outside, but rather inside experiences and processes within society. This goes for the object of science as well as for the research and the function of science, hence for intercultural pedagogy that takes its scientific character seriously. Just as the science of society means criticism, a constituent element of education is critical questioning. Just as with science in general, intercultural pedagogy as a science cannot remain indifferent or passive towards its object, society. Intercultural pedagogy claiming to be scientific is like critical science being obligated to criticism. It does not earn its legitimacy as an educational theorem as a substrate, derivative or subsystem of society, but rather because it is conceptualised as an ideologically critical category of society.

Intercultural education as an ideologically critical category of society distances itself *per se* from so-called neutral and unbiased concepts of science. The substantial implication of intercultural pedagogy as an ideologically critical category of society is the transformation of that very society. Our understanding of society is by no means abstract. It is based on a set of categories that can scarcely be explained even with the traditional paradigms of natural science. It is the idea of a better, more humane society and future. Correlating with it, our understanding of education means the regaining of lost humanity by negating racism and the power of human beings over human beings. This understanding of science and education distances itself from paradigms of objectivity of a naive empiricism. No empiricism could confirm or sufficiently refute this design of a better society and future. The limitations of a positivist methodolgy manifest themselves blatantly as well as the questionable nature of a pedagogy that places its task and function at the service of an unbiased methodology. Intercultural education within the framework of societal theory cannot be understood as free of ideology. As a result, we have normatively decided to let it emerge as an ideologically critical category of society. Intercultural pedagogy as a critical category means intervention into societal practice rather than affirmation.

Intercultural pedagogy as a science that understands itself outside this intervention looking for a possible autonomous and unbiased space, a pedagogical province or island, remains outside practical life and thus socially irrelevant, even if the mystification of the 'objective' (Adorno) caused by it would make it highly ideological. In this case, this would mean a factual ideology, confirming the status quo. Intercultural pedagogy as the science of eduction devoid of its critical potential with respect to society, does not practise objectivity, but consequently rather ideology, an ideology of domination and power. If intercultural pedagogy as the science of education distances itself from the normative categories of societal transformation, it will at the same time be unable to perceive and intervene into that complex reality which is constantly being set into motion by economic imperialism. It would limit its task to the educatee. Thus it would place its object, namely the educatee, outside the whole society and its contradictions. It would put him beyond that concrete totality, society itself, with its conflicts that need to be solved and the institutions that have to be questioned and perhaps abolished.

Intercultural education as a critical theory of society

If we are to understand intercultural pedagogy as the science of education as well as the critical theory of societal transformation, it will not simply be a theoretical construct independent of concrete practice. Quite the contrary: educational theory and societal reality are not opposed, but are related to each other directly. Their correlate is identical: the humanisation of society. The overpowering force is societal reality seen from the perspective of the suggested criticism of ideology: educational theory as criticism. This correlate assures that intercultural education, as well as practice in the sense of a revolutionary force, will not be blind, estranged, entangled by pseudo-facts and thus a reproduction of mere affirmation. Consequently, intercultural pedagogy as a science is not abstract, but rather is evoked by the context of social reality. It is not particular or limited to children of minority groups. Intercultural pedagogy is obliged to the societal totality, explicitly to the negation of national boundaries, which estrange and taint societal reality and its processes, in which case it might and would probably have to define itself as a resistance movement.

From a pedagogical viewpoint this category of negation hints at a process that would have to be initiated from within society as a service to the future. This process would have to be planned in co-operation with the educatee. Humanisation and liberation could be two reciprocal categories which, as a part of this social movement, work as normative preliminary decisions for the design and search for an improved society. Thus intercultural pedagogy as a science cannot be abstracted from ongoing societal processes. On the contrary, it participates in the transformation of society as a critical and normative regulative.

Emancipation and Practice as Paradigms of Intercultural Pedagogy

Which paradigms could be appropriate for an intercultural pedagogy presenting itself as a science? The paradigms of enlightenment and practice would have to be stressed. The enlightening character of intercultural education as a criticism of ideology would lie in the questioning of political, social and economic realities and the legitimacy of power as well as in consciousness-raising for structures that stabilise power. The degree to which social reality is affirmed would decrease in relation to the liberating character inherent in the process of emancipating people – migrants as well as the majority in the receiving countries – from a status as political minors to the subject of the historic process. This is our pedagogical task and should be the aim of our effort.

Thus, intercultural pedagogy as the science of education cannot give up its general and enlightening, that is, its universal character without giving itself away. This universal character, being a fundamental constituent of intercultural pedagogy as the science of education, is not directly opposed to the societal reality. On the contrary, the necessary correlate of our understanding of education is that dimension of the science of pedagogy depending on its practical application. The critical instance of intercultural pedagogy is not only the basis for the practice of enlightenment, nor is it only a critical interpretation of social reality with the perspective of democratising and humanising it, but it is also an existential condition for the constitution of intercultural pedagogy as the science of education. This needs further explanation, especially with regard to the legitimacy of our scientific principles.

The legitimacy of intercultural education

Thinking about the legitimacy of the scientific principles of intercultural pedagogy, we avoid empirical explanations. Our scientific principles are legitimised on the basis of *a priori* definitions and foundations. The scientific legitimacy has already been marked by methodological preliminary decisions. The legitimacy evades general validity, without losing its right to claim universal validity. Regarding itself as criticism of ideology, intercultural pedagogy will not need an empirical explanation in order to legitimise itself as a pedagogical system.

Pedagogical legitimacy will evidently have to be understood as enlightenment within the correlation between social reality and criticism of ideology, if that legitimacy is not abstract, indifferent and neutral to the theoretical and social context from which it arises. Social practice would never reach beyond its own affirmation without the critical stage that turns into a critical movement. The criticism of ideology seen outside social practice would result in sophistry and its own mystification. Therefore, intercultural pedagogy as a pedagogical system claiming to be scientific can be conceptualised under the following two conditions: (1) it cannot work without scientific foundations based upon justified principles; (2) the critical stage is necessary – the enlightening and enlightened practice as a reference and as a methodological preliminary decision for its construction.

The pedagogical and scientific question is where the legitimacy of the cultural and intercultural finds its theoretical foundations in scientific terms. To this purpose, reflecting upon the connection between culture and power proves to be of pedagogical relevance. The underlying hypothesis of this connection is as follows: culture and power are not antinomic. Culture and power are dialectically connected and therefore inseparable like the two sides of a coin. To be more precise: culture relates to the institutionalised societal norms. Where culture is turned into the institutionalised form of societal legitimacy, it becomes the institutionalised power. Culture and power condense in a dominant culture, finally in the culture of those in power. The dominant, predominant culture becomes its own social scale. It takes on the shape of a law. Its transformation into power even ensures that it is consolidated as a cultural hegemony. This entails pedagogical demands, meaning that it is relevant to pedagogy as a system as well as to the practice of pedagogy.

Related to the practice of pedagogy, our task can be defined as follows: what needs to be questioned within our conscience, within our individual and societal being, is the subjective and the objective condition of being constrained within institutionalised power involving individuals, groups and peoples. Subjective restraint becomes evident in the restricted capability of perception in the individual case. This is where we find the reduced and biased perception of the individual resulting from cultural hegemony, from socialisation into institutionalised power and from the cultural colonisation of an individual's thinking. Objective constraint encompasses the global societal constraint. It is transferable to all countries, knows no boundaries, involves man as a species and threatens to become an ontological constraint. With respect to societies and societal practice this objective restraint becomes visible in ritualised everyday life, in the adaptation of human thinking and acting in response to the perception of fixed roles, norms and values prescribed by the institutionalised power. The human being, socialised and 'differently' socialised, the human being who thinks 'in a different way', the different mentality which allegedly or actually separates us from other people who have experienced a different socialisation in other countries, give evidence of the bias and of the constraints of institutionalised power. Every human being is the expression and at the same time a carrier of a specific type of socialisation. He is entangled in the autonomy of his socialisation. He is so truly convinced of the validity and obviousness of his thoughts and deeds that he does not realise his own bias. He is equally unaware of the objective societal constraints so that he cannot perceive the limitations, the historicity of societal reality, the relativity and thus dubiousness of institutionalised power. He is so little conscious of his own conscience that he does not have to question it any more. His thinking has become so self-evident to him that he has been unable to see his own cultural ghetto.

Intercultural education as criticism of ideology

With regard to pedagogy as a system it has to be stressed that intercultural pedagogy as an ideologically critical category includes into its reflection this double constraint which is inherent in the individual and in the society as a whole. Intercultural pedagogy as the theory, practice and science of education is confronted with this double form of constraint in any society, and indeed came into existence out of the necessity to help overcome this constraint. The overcoming of constraints affects man as an individual and man as a species. Its legitimacy lies in its attempt to help man to liberate himself from the chains of power that alienate and estrange his thought and action.

With regard to its scientific principles, intercultural pedagogy will neither be able to choose its approach towards its legitimacy nor will it be obliged to follow a certain methodology, a foreigner-specific pedagogical structure and organisation of learning. If, however, intercultural pedagogy wants to fulfil its own claim, that is, to make the constraints of the individual and the society more transparent, questionable and solvable, it will have to accomplish far more than the conventional and traditional pedagogy, because it is difficult to recognise the individual as well as the societal constraints and even more so to question them with the traditional curricula. On the contrary, the traditional curricula are partly responsible for this stage of awareness. Years or decades might be necessary to question and revise only those historical distortions and mistakes that have been and still are being pressed into the hearts and minds of schoolchildren. Nationally oriented curricula are and will remain racist-oriented curricula. Therefore intercultural education has to develop new, anti-racist curricula. This demand is inherent to intercultural pedagogy, if it does not want to be the transmitter of societal affirmation such as nationalism and racism.

As soon as intercultural pedagogy is seen as enlightening practice, its contrast to affirmation becomes decisive and radical. From a pedagogical viewpoint the institutionalised shape of power, the cultural hegemony in which social reality as a whole as well as the educatee as an individual are involved, has to be made questionable and breachable. We have to help the conscience reach its own critical development. Finally, we have to awaken society from its lethargy and turn it towards critical action.

With regard to its empirical principles intercultural pedagogy has to define itself within the enlightened practice and within societal organisation and movement. The ideological terrain of racism, cultural racism and cultural colonialism must be drained. The substantive task of the practice of interculturality is to break racism. The more political and economic enlightenment becomes relevant for the society, beyond a merely empirical educatee, in such a way that it is turned into societal practice, intercultural pedagogy will turn from a set of statements to practice, theory of practice or living theory.

Thus, practice is all the more 'true', the more it manages to adopt theory. In analogy: theory will be all the more 'true', the more it manages to absorb practice. As a result, theory and practice are not arbitrary. If this understanding of intercultural pedagogy as theory and practice is valid, the question is: Does it empirically suffice to take only the educatee into account in order to constitute pedagogy as a system? According to our preliminary decisions for the establishment of intercultural pedagogy as a science, we can summarise: intercultural pedagogy can never be conceptualised outside, but rather must be conceptualised *inside* society. Intercultural pedagogy is not an affirmative expression of social reality, but its critical ferment.

The reference of a pedagogical system encompasses the individual educatee as well as the societal context in its totality, of which the educatee is a part. Finally we will have to help the educatee to understand the societal framework in its entirety, in order not to deprive him from becoming a conscious participant in the whole. But it will also be of fundamental importance for intercultural education to make the dominance of institutionalised cultural hegemony questionable for indigenous as for 'foreign' schoolchildren. We will be concerned with recognising and abolishing this culture of power. Finally, we will have to break the constraints of the educatee – already pointed out several times – together with the societal constraint in institutionalised dominance and turn it into enlightened and human practice.

Education and humanistic values

It has become more than evident that the pedagogical task of intercultural education shuns the national categories of affirmation, the racist implications of nationally oriented education and societal practice. Intercultural education implies the human being and dedicates itself to human rights as does any system that uses the name of pedagogy. Education strives for humanity in two different ways, one being an individual act of liberation towards oneself, the other as a collective act of liberation towards the societal whole, towards the human as species. Both tasks in their dialectic are necessary for education. Intercultural pedagogy as the science of education, and its didactics, will adopt both tasks into the educational process of reflection and draw the necessary conclusions, at first the formation of a pedagogical justification, secondly the didactic construction of education with respect to the societal practice as suggested above.

One more thing needs to be explained in order to avoid misunderstanding connected with the concept of culture. The task of intercultural education as intending to prevent cultural affirmation in the interest of the educatee and the society as a whole, cannot be the mediation of an additive culturalism, i.e. multiculturalism. Intercultural education cannot work as an intermediary of the respective national cultures. Education neither needs mediation nor can it be mediated. Cultures cannot be taught as facts, either, since they are not static but dynamic.

Those who now believe that it is the responsibility of intercultural education to acknowledge various cultures have certainly made a pedagogically more correct statement than those who set their own culture as an aim and credo of education. Both, however, miss the point of education and consequently of an educational model which defines itself as intercultural. Let us stress one more point: from a pedagogical perspective the 'inter'-cultural does not mean a symbiotic unity of different cultures. We lack the necessary elements that could create such an intercultural symbiosis. We have to reject the intercultural symbiosis as well as the mediation of an additive culturalism, because both concepts are unable to counteract the affirmative nature of an institutionalised culture. Intercultural symbiosis expands affirmation by adding further affirmations. Like multiculturalism it is incapable of making societal affirmation questionable and easy to handle for schoolchildren. Both concepts, multiculturalism and intercultural symbiosis, have thus proven to be useless for the construction and legitimacy of intercultural pedagogy. Therefore we need a notion of culture that knows how to question culture itself. Pedagogy will want to and have to tie itself to this explicative, questioning notion of culture.

Culture as an Educational Concept

But from what notion of culture could intercultural pedagogy start? We will attempt to define culture from a pedagogical viewpoint: three criteria constitute the character of culture. In the first place, it cannot be confined to national boundaries; secondly, it is shaped by an historical experience of society, i.e. it is not a product of elites; thirdly, it is a thinking experience, i.e. conscious being. The notion that culture cannot be confined to boundaries points out the universal content of the concept. The statement that culture is an historical experience of society refers to the societal practice that constitutes culture. Our second criterion, furthermore, hints at the dynamic character of the state of affairs and points to the possibility and necessity of surmounting historic-societal experience. Since this experience also can be understood in the sense of a surmounting of conscience, the third criterion of culture is valid: culture has furthermore to be understood and defined as a thinking experience.

The pedagogically relevant implication upon which a concept of culture as I have elucidated relies, is as follows: culture must also be equated with a thinking experience. Thinking is a constitutive part of the human being. The legitimacy of this philosophical and anthropological implication is established by the fact that culture can always and only find its content and inner sense in connection with the human experience, *cultus atque humanitas*. Understood in this way, culture is more than the abundance of the human material production. Culture is dynamic and we have to deal more and more with its procedural character. Thus, we can speak of culture and make substantial statements about it, as long as we reflect its historical, its procedural and its dynamic character. We can speak of culture and hit on pedagogy, if we are willing to question and, if necessary, abolish the self-assessment and obviousness of culture.

From a pedagogical viewpoint: intercultural education is either a synonym (a) for the plurality of thinking experiences that need to be initiated and obtained by means of educating processes, (b) for the complexity of societal experiences to be reflected, or (c) for the plurality of cultural formations and their legitimacy to be questioned – or it simply means the handing down of the historically established (i.e. power and dominance) status quo, affirmation.

Culture as continuing criticism of culture

The counterproposition of cultural affirmation would be as follows: if culture is not a constant movement and the attempt to become conscious of itself and thus historically conscious; if the constitutive and essential element of culture is not its own criticism, then it will remain on an ahistoric level as a simple reflection of the established power structures.

Naturally, this implies pedagogical consequences. If, from a pedagogical viewpoint, we do not start with a dynamic concept of culture and regard the suspension of culture by means of cultural criticism as the task of education and culture, then we are forced to teach without questioning its own particular and institutionalised culture to each ethnic group. A static and ahistoric notion of culture would lead to the consequence that the efforts for an intercultural pedagogy would have to be replaced by the juxtaposition of institutions of learning for the respective cultures. To be more concrete, this means that we would have to have in Germany, for example, Turkish, Greek, Yugoslavian, Italian, Spanish, Portuguese and even Tunisian schools in which transmitters of the respective cultures would transplant cultural assets into the hearts and minds of the culture receivers. In other words, we would deal with *intra*cultural rather than *inter*cultural education. That would be the negation of what is meant here by intercultural education.

However, in order to minimalise the cultural affirmation of education as pointed out, we need a critical, self-reflecting intercultural approach. How could the general and crucial pedagogical task of this intercultural approach be defined? It is the main task of intercultural education to liberate itself from the generalised form of ontological constraint (this is true for all schoolchildren in all countries), from the constraint of the societal being in established historicity (i.e. the established power and dominance in which reality and conscience are involved), to liberate itself in the sense of becoming aware of this thinking and of societal deeds caught up in historicity. Our pedagogical hope could be specified as follows: may this liberation enable people to make individual and co-operative decisions within the historic process of thinking and doing.

Culture and intercultural education

What follows from this definition of culture? Intercultural as well as education in general cannot serve this liberation of being and conscience by means of 'cultural harmonies' or 'cultural affirmation'. On the contrary, intercultural education should make use of the dissonance of the being and of the contradictions of the conscience in the hope of making the subjective and objective constraints questionable, transparent and surmountable.

Therefore, if we are to ask ourselves, what should be integrated and enculturated it will become clear that our education problem is reduced to an integration of subcultural peculiarities and of special ways. On the other hand it is evident that more common than divisive features mark the intercultural situation. Intercultural pedagogy will have to deal with the content of these problems, as can be concluded from the preceding and following thoughts.

Intercultural education starts from the empirical human as does the theory of intercultural pedagogy from the concept of the human being. As is well known, the concept of the human can be unfolded, in the tradition of Plato and Aristotle, without forcing anyone by means of commensurate argumentation to agree with this philosophical and anthropological hypothesis. The human is defined as '*zoön logon echōn*', i.e. a living being endowed with reason, and as '*zoön politikon*', i.e. a living being depending on socialisation. Within the context of the above-mentioned fundamental axioms this would mean that the human is defined by thinking and that only thought makes him human. From a pedagogical point of view this means that every human being has the right to think with his own head and should not be hindered but rather encouraged.

What follows from this for intercultural education? Intercultural education has to start from the provisional conscience of each educatee:

- By integrating the educatee into the process of reflecting upon human experience and perception, intercultural education will underline the preliminary character of thought.
- By including the educatee in the reflection of his and strange ('foreign') constraints of thought and by questioning his and strange preliminary, philosophising conscience, the first task of intercultural education will have to be self-criticism.
- It will try to call the following into our conscience: the historicity of the being and the conscience within economic, political, ideological, institutional, normative constraints as well as constraints caused by behaviour and individual thinking and feeling.
- Finally, it will attempt to confront the educatee with his and strange categories of thought, of judgement and prejudice and those presuppositions which are fundamental for these judgements and prejudices, to make him aware of them and enable him to rethink them.

20 Intercultural Learning at School: Limits and Possibilities

HAGEN KORDES

The Acquisition of Intercultural Competence: An Investigation

For a long time the question of intercultural learning has been tackled in a way typical for schools: in the form of topics in regional studies (*Landeskunde*), guiding pupils in such a way that they could develop their understanding of the other culture; or in the form of rationales for learning targets, bringing about the gradual collapse of prejudices and the development of international understanding. The pupils were an empty space within this didactic programme. They were the 'vacuum' which we, the educationalists, crammed with topics and targets, and they remained the vacuum, because the processes of learning had to remain to a large extent hidden.

I have studied these processes of intercultural learning for many years – as far as they have developed within the medium of school learning – and gave particular attention to these processes during a three-year investigation involving 112 learners of French in Germany (Kordes, 1991). I followed their progress from their entry into the sixth form (*Oberstufe*) until their final examinations, and sometimes beyond this to their entry into an occupation or to university. The four didactic frameworks to be presented in the following as possible modes of intercultural learning at school, are based on these studies.

Since this outline presents an abstraction from this experience, the three most important results need to be stated in advance. First, within the general development of foreign language communication competence, the development of intercultural competence is far behind the other dimensions of foreign language education. It has to be stated that there is no simultaneity of development: the development of intercultural competence keeps pace neither with language (and action-) competence, nor with reflective and professional competences. More precisely: more than a third of all the young students remained in a monocultural stage; only with great difficulty did the majority advance to an intermediate intercultural level, which, among other things, comprises the willingness and capability to see their own cultural norms in relative terms; an insignificant minority of just six pupils reached a 'transcultural stage', in which the character of one's own culture is recognised by being exposed to a foreign culture. Further details of this model of stages will be given below.

Second, foreign-language learning at school is accompanied by numerous critical experiences which affect pupils' identity problems; such experiences of cultural and intercultural identity only arise late and sporadically. With regard to the question as to why they were learning French in addition to their school curriculum, we made the following discovery with the help of interviews, informal feedback and by registering critical events. In the 11th grade (first year of *Oberstufe*) the outstanding crisis-like feelings which many of the pupils had produced feelings of reduced self-esteem and inadequacy concerning the system of rules of the target language (problems of deficiency: 'I don't get the grammar!') and the feeling of incompetence concerning communication in the target language (problems of insufficiency: 'I'm not able to talk as sensibly as I can in German and even in English!'). In isolated cases this was accompanied by a critical attitude towards the French classes. This attitude expressed itself in an increasingly intense fear of not being adequately trained in the target language as far as general background and vocational training aspects were concerned. This latter criticism became more clearly recognisable and more frequent in the following year.

However, the feelings of inferiority manifest in the preceding year further dominated the attitude of many pupils regarding French classes. At the same time critical and more radical remarks concerning school and school career arose expressing the suspicion that the curriculum withheld essential aspects of foreign language education from the pupils. This criticism further increased during the third year (13th grade) continuing until the final exams, where the feeling of inferiority observable in the first year diminished considerably. A critical tendency, which, in the previous year, could only be seen in the attitudes of two pupils, spread among the majority of pupils. This tendency to alienate themselves from the school-based French classes, whose norms now appeared out of touch with life because of intercultural experiences, were made by pupils in France and elsewhere (problems of alienation: 'I want to learn French, so that I can talk with

French friends. Instead we are reading boring texts and are crammed full with out-dated vocabulary of Molière, Sartre, etc. That gets us nowhere as far as our love for France in concerned ...'). That is, only at the end of their foreign language school career did some of the pupils achieve a critical insight into the intercultural dimension, so that they were able to see that school could only offer them an artificial foreign language education, but withheld the essential aspects: a vivid encounter with foreigners.

Third, intercultural learning in foreign language instruction is mainly defined as a cognitive strategy of knowledge and as a *Landeskunde* model. *Landeskunde* is essentially equated with the usual lessons on text analysis: the content of these lessons consists of historical topics, of topical interests, and of literary or political texts which usually focus on bicultural tension. It is the task of the teacher, and consequently of the pupils, to carry out an elaborate text analysis. The procedure in *Landeskunde*, which is added to the conventional text analysis, is usually one of (historical, cultural) contextualisation. Within certain limits, cultural norms of behaviour are treated in relative terms. Possible ways of intercultural learning, which have to do with competence and identity as well as direct communication with native speakers and other francophone foreigners, are officially omitted in this kind of instruction. Where such people appear in lessons, they primarily 'serve' the continuation of the principal thrust of the subject matter, and the improvement of pronunciation and expression. To a large extent the teachers remain the only model for the pupils as far as their interlingual and intercultural competence are concerned (Kordes, 1991).

Intercultural Learning: The Final Task in School Foreign Language Learning

Pupils acquire meaningful foreign-language and intercultural learning if they link the medium of foreign language instruction with developmental tasks (Kordes, 1982). In this case, they link development with foreign language instruction in a dialectic sense: they generate themselves tasks of their own development, but, at the same time they are exposed to generalised developmental tasks. This dialectic becomes understandable if we visualise the fundamental contradiction which dominates foreign language education in general. Initially pupils feel an 'absolute love' (Kordes, 1991) for the foreign language. They are fascinated by the possibility of speaking a foreign language, of getting to know foreign people with their stimulating and exciting behaviour, perhaps of living 'the way they live' and engaging in the 'adventure' of an actual change of personality. However, these longings for omnipotence are soon given up in the course of school-based language learning: learning vocabulary, grammar, phrases, analysing texts ... These things fragment foreign language education and lead pupils into strictly determined patterns.

In order to achieve a realistic concept of fundamental foreign language education on a theoretical level, the reconstruction of educational interrelations is necessary. First of all this has to be done in the way pupils experience it, not in the way the curriculum intends it. If we interpret the crisis-like experiences of the students in the right way, we can extract the different levels of their learning from the complexity of foreign language education. With the help of the three years of investigation, ideas concerning the succession of tasks of development, which had intitially been rough and intuitive, could be stated more and more precisely on a conceptual level, and verified on an empirical level. On condition that pupils are confronted not only with the reality of ordinary foreign language education, but with the practice of international co-operation (whether in commercial correspondence or literature and *Landeskunde*) and from the point of view that their development leads from foreign language learner to foreign language speaker (i.e. a person who, as a foreigner, exposes himself to foreign situations) the following succession of tasks of development became evident (cf. Kordes, 1991):

- developmental task 1, in the transitional phase: coping with disrupted interlingual interaction;
- developmental task 2, in the structural phase: coping with disrupted international co-operation;
- developmental task 3, in the final phase: coping with disrupted intercultural communication.

Developmental task 1: Coping with disrupted interlingual interaction

Up to the beginning of the *Oberstufe* most of the pupils preserved their longing for total communication. Latently, they maintained a naive interest in the country and its people, in the culture of the foreign language: foreign language learning is a good thing, it was fun as long as it was effected with ease in earlier years. However, in higher grades, and with the transition into a higher level course it became increasingly difficult. The more complex the situations, requirements and tasks, the greater the tendency of the pupils to separate the latent demands into the first, feasible and evident stage. In this way pupils meet the intitial obstacle in their foreign language education:

foreign language as a system of rules and actions. Most pupils never tire of stressing the fact that French is 'belle mais difficile'. They cannot help but concentrate at first on this feature of foreign language education, no matter how much they are longing for the more exciting aspects of content.

Here they find themselves confronted for the first time with the dangers and possibilities reflected in learning a foreign language. They see the dangers in the abstraction of the language of transactions, and even in the interaction of the content of international co-operation (in conversations, commercial correspondence and texts). They have to fight the fear of not being able to get their language into a system and they run the risk of feeling fundamentally deficient. Moreover, they have a fear of not being able to express themselves or of expressing themselves in a childish way. They are also afraid of appearing artificial or primitive and hence have a feeling of insecurity. In this phase, the learning horizon is almost inevitably reduced to the acquisition and stabilisation of language rules and conscious action (see Figure 20.1).

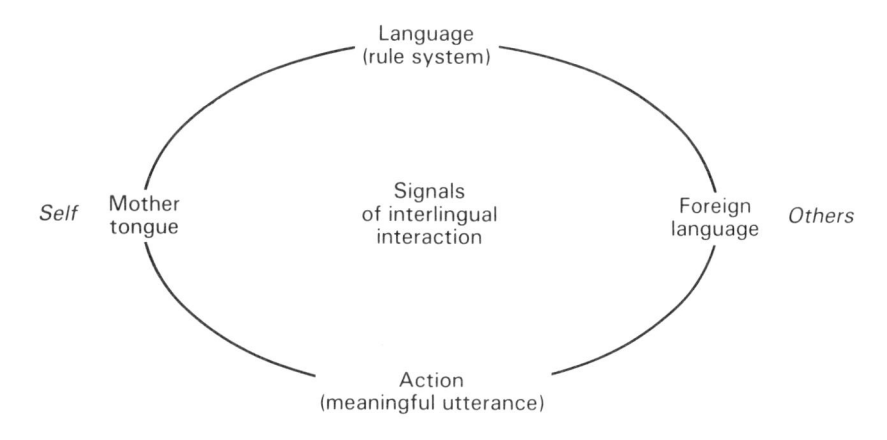

FIGURE 20.1 *Interlingual interaction – developmental task 1*

Pupils turn their main attention – partly consciously and partly unconsciously – to the interferences between mother tongue and foreign language. Their learning is oriented to the balance and co-ordination of both of them, in particular to the reduction of those mother-tongue interferences in the foreign language which lead to mistakes, redundancies or misunderstandings. It is their goal to transfer their own insights and intentions fairly well into the other language. It is still irrelevant who is the addressee and how well he may understand. Their language expression is concentrated on *signals* of interaction, which are more or less transferred point by point and which are gradually available for them as accumulated linguistic means. The spectrum of their learning activities ranges from attempting correct translation into French to finding adequate French expressions. The feeling of these young people for the French language, within this first stage of development, is regulative and strategic. They have a tendency to be as curious about words and rules as others are curious about how a diesel engine functions.

Developmental task 2: Coping with disrupted international co-operation

As soon as pupils feel that they are standing on firm ground — that their expressions are based on a more or less adequate grammatical system — and that to some extent they are able to express themselves satisfactorily, their attention can turn towards their interlocutor and to the co-operative and communicative contents of international interactions. Their attention in this case always moves between the poles of an orientation to the practical aspects of foreign language acquisition (for journeys, jobs, career and studies) and an orientation to the problems of international co-operation. Consequently, they find themselves confronted with dangers and opportunities. Dangers ensue from the fragmentation which many of them now perceive as an aspect of foreign language education at school. This makes them vacillate between dropping out and resignation. On the other hand, opportunities arise from the first impressions and experience of how foreign language interaction may become productive ('I made the French laugh', 'I bargained the prices of the hotel down', etc.) and reflexive ('Now I can understand why there is no peace movement', 'Camus made me take notice of something, now I think a lot more about the meaning of life ...')

Their main attention is now focused on the relationship between themselves and the contents, as well as the patterns, of international co-operation: economic, businesslike transaction, on the one hand, and literary, aesthetic communication on the other. The linguistic signals, which were the centre of interest in the first stage of development, now stop being a mere goal and begin to become a means for the realisation of this relation between oneself and the contents of international co-operation. Consequently, the pupils' learning effort is oriented to this balance and co-ordination of linguistic means and pragmatic purposes of international exchange of opinions and interpretations of information and products, of arguments and proofs — and, therefore, simultaneously to the co-ordination of learned standard expressions and personal remarks. These

INTERCULTURAL LEARNING AT SCHOOL

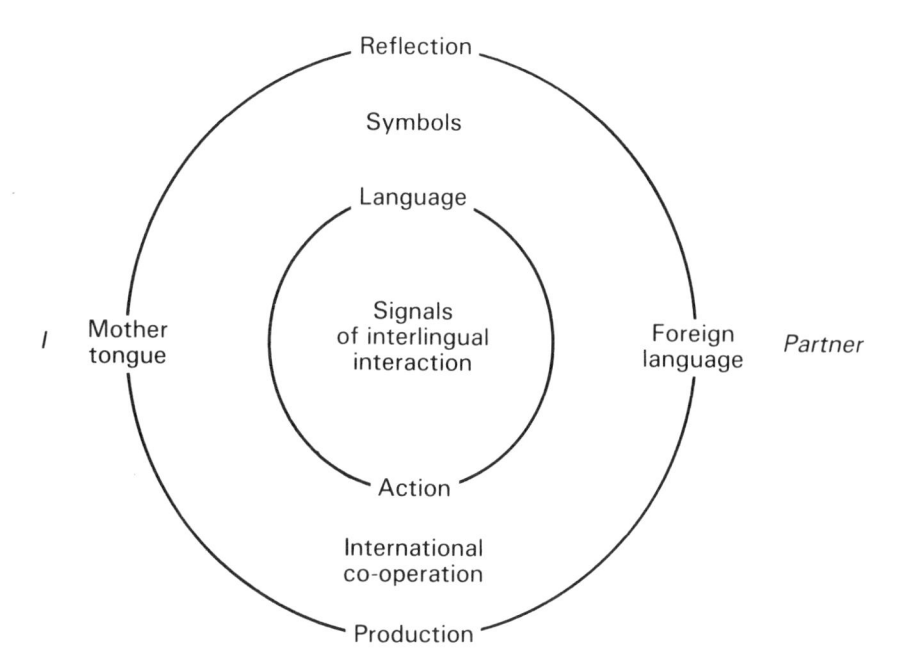

FIGURE 20.2 *International co-operation – developmental task 2*

remarks are at this point less focused on the signals of interlingual interaction but are more *symbols* of international co-operation. As for the acquisition of symbols, foreign language acquisition now reaches an 'educated standard', as it were. An increasingly large store of reproduced and reflected symbols now underpins and influences the linguistic means (see Figure 20.2).

Although attention is still focused on linguistic correctness and adequacy of expressions, it concentrates increasingly on meaning, on well-formed expressions of content, on linguistic aspects as well as on substance and relevance. The language of the foreigner is no longer a mere obstacle, it is now available for the reflection and reproduction of the symbolic content of international exchange.

Developmental task 3: Coping with disrupted intercultural communication

Together with increasing competence, still within the medium of school, some pupils develop an awareness of the fact that without encounter with and experience of the foreign culture, knowledge of the language and culture remains superficial. Only when intercultural experience becomes significant can the voluntary extension of the personality which is characteristic of advanced foreign language education begin to develop. The acquisition of the foreign language can only attain the quality of a new sense of identity through the encounter with the foreign culture and the foreign people. The experience of foreignness, possibly in the form of an alienation or culture shock, challenges the individual and social identity. For those learners who are living in another country as individual foreigners or members of a foreign minority, it is especially imperative for their self-esteem that they be able to expose their own identity to the foreignness. Foreign language instruction has to enable them to do this. Consequently, the task of intercultural learning presents the last significant stage within the complex encounters of pupils with foreign elements in language, within the situation and within human beings.

The dangers and opportunities linked with this task of development are just as far-reaching as they are uncertain. Dangers can already arise superficially in moments of home-sickness and rootlessness but they originate just as much in rejection and imitation of foreign habits. These dangers increase with the fear of losing one's own integrity, way of thinking or even personality. Dangers may also express themselves in the form of feedback, be it that pupils despise conversation within French classes, that they hold their own cultural identity in contempt or that they even let an unconscious racism show through the guise of the cosmopolitan. In contrast to this, opportunities result directly from the chance to cope with these dangers: to rediscover one's own cultural identity, the ability to get along with the apparent French 'chaos', etc. The scope of learning activities is thus widened: the self and the foreign element stretch more or less completely to the learning horizon. Living and learning largely coincide. The centre of interest of learning activities is now focused on *symptoms*, that is to say on the latent cultural meaning structures which are more or less hidden behind interlingual disturbances and international conflicts or behind the everyday actions and habits of foreigners. The more the language learner is confronted with the practice of interlingual interaction and has developed the appropriate aspects of competence and identity, the more the remaining latent dimension of intercultural communication will come to the fore (see Figure 20.3).

In brief, interlingual and international relations remain a considerable potential for unsolved sociocultural interferences resulting from the fundamental patterns of behaviour and judgement of people of different cultural spheres. Language interaction as well as political and economic co-

INTERCULTURAL LEARNING AT SCHOOL 295

```
                    Cultural
                    identification

                    Symptoms

                    Reflection

                    Language

Self   Mother       Signals           Foreign    Foreigner
       tongue       of interlingual   language
                    interactions

                    Action

                    International
                    co-operation

                    Production

                    Cultural
                    relativisation
```

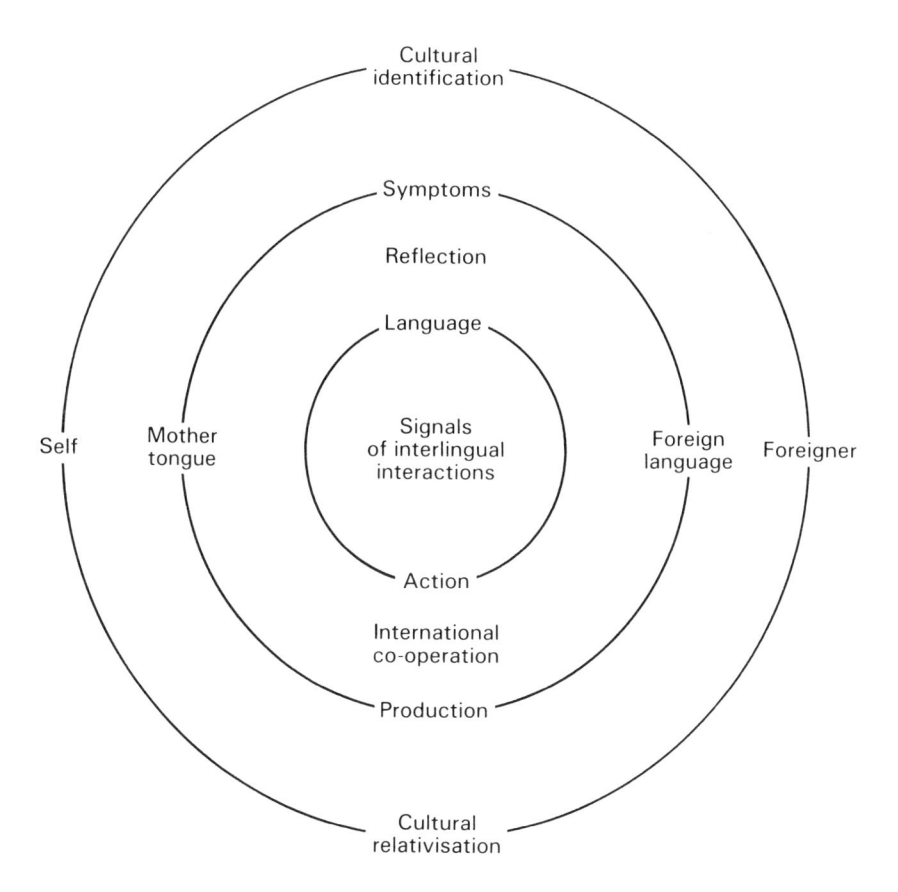

FIGURE 20.3 *Intercultural communication – developmental task 3*

operation represent the surface of a deeper structure which can accurately be described as intercultural communication between the self and the foreign element. Since interlocutors come from different cultures they have each internalised their own everyday rules, which others, consciously or unconsciously, may break. In this situation the learner is always at a disadvantage if he exposes himself to a foreign situation. The foreigner, as a local inhabitant, always has an advantage since his rules automatically claim validity, even if the foreigner tries to adjust himself to the needs of the other. Potentially he will not be able to avoid breaking a number of cultural rules since he does not know them or cannot 'tolerate' certain effects of these rules (e.g. female German pupils who are annoyed by the chauvinistic behaviour of French men). Thus the third task of development is the one in which the learner of a foreign language has to consolidate his capacities of interlingual interaction (e.g. in a culturally sensitive choice of words or in an expression of communicative acts which is appropriate to the situation) and of intercultural co-operation (e.g. in the clarification of prejudices and limits of tolerance originating in his own culture).

In the ideal case, which pupils will hardly ever achieve, the foreign language learner takes over the role of mediator. As a mediator he is able to decipher those sociocultural interferences which decisively restrict interlingual interaction and international co-operation. The foreign language learner knows about the latent cultural embedding of misunderstandings and inconsistencies. If one were to carry the idealisation of the interculturally competent person to an extreme, the following constellation of capacities would result:

1. He realises that interlocutors from two different cultures do not know the complexity of roles and positions (and partial ambiguity) of their foreign counterpart and that they therefore tend to a behaviour which is not appropriate in that situation (e.g. German pupils' and teachers' lack of understanding concerning the apparently authoritarian role-specific behaviour of French teachers, and at the same time the 'chaotic' manner of discussion among the French).
2. He recalls that interlocutors cannot dissociate themselves from their role-specific and position-specific behaviour to such an extent that their behaviour appears to be comprehensible and understandable to the other (e.g. the consternation of German pupils or teachers who do not feel that they are appreciated sufficiently in their role as guests or in their position as a teacher or as representatives of a partner country).
3. He realises that interlocutors with different cultural backgrounds are frequently not able or not willing to tolerate, or even learn to tolerate, inconsistencies or ambivalences within the norms of the foreigner (e.g. the difficulties of many German pupils with respect to the ambivalence of apparent sex-specific behaviour).

This idealisation has heuristic value since, as we have mentioned before, intercultural learning may not develop within the medium of foreign language education at school. Certainly this apparently negative result has much to do with the fact that French is learnt as a second or third language, where high level courses in the *Oberstufe* are attended almost exclusively by young women. Cognitive text-learning 'from top down' as well as implications of sex-specific socialisation certainly play a decisive part in the enormous delaying of the cultural dimension. On the other hand this result cannot be taken for granted in a time of increasing internationalisation of the world, in which young women especially are participating to an increasing extent.

However, it may be that this internationalisation is taking place only on a superficial level in the form of an Americanisation with the help of 'Dallas', Micky Mouse, Coca Cola and McDonalds. If we associate this constant stream from the media with an increasing tendency of the current young generation to stay at home, young people appear to us to be almost offending culture. They are reduced to ekeing out, in front of the gogglebox, a miserable existence with the above-mentioned Dallas, or other Disneylands. These young people are hardly exposed to the 'danger' of an alienation shock. For example, although this latent internationalisation has led many Germans to think chaos is marvellous because there is 'always something going on', most of them are not even up to the chaos of a chaotically organised school excursion to France. On the contrary, they emphasise antipathies and aggression even more openly than their parents. The goal not to be branded as 'alien' or 'German' in another country may be the goal of some immigrant children but it is not the goal of pupils in general. If we value the opportunities of intercultural learning at school we have to start at the point pupils have reached in their process of learning to live, coinciding with the spirit of the times.

From *Landeskunde* to Intercultural Learning

The fact that the intercultural dimension gains significance only for a minority of pupils at a late stage introduces an underlying issue which should at least be mentioned here. First of all, pupils need a knowledge of the foreign language to feel secure. First within language classes and at a later point in the encounter with foreigners they try to 'dominate' the language, to get the menacing aspect of foreigners under control (bad marks mean loss of self-esteem; insecurity leads to aggression). This attitude, which is particularly widespread among German pupils, contrasts in general with the fact that most French pupils just 'master' the foreign language, but they do not dominate it. The wish to dominate would require a penetration of the foreign world as well as an exposure of oneself to this world. However, most French pupils oppose such didactic intentions insistently and successfully. German pupils, on the other hand, do not tend to show such open resistance. Nevertheless, resistance can also be found, although only in the implicit forms of protection and in latent structures of oppression – in their endeavour to dominate the situation of foreignness (maybe even the foreigner). They try to dominate it with the help of an extensive knowledge of the language.

The *Landeskunde* model

This syndrome finds a certain equivalence in the dominant model of *Landeskunde* epitomised in the curricula. The goals are predominantly directed at the reduction of prejudice and at the development of international understanding. Because of her role, as well as because of her position in German culture, the teacher tries hard to overcome her own prejudices and to convert the pupils' prejudices into considered judgements. However, this didactic interaction results in a model of *Landeskunde* which does not only prevent the utterance of prejudice, but which also prevents the expressions of stages of development, since prejudices are normally an expression of presuppositions and surprise in which biographically and culturally significant habits and modes of action find expression. In many different foreign language school careers we found the same experience: teachers as well as pupils start learning as soon as they dare to utter prejudices that should not even exist, referring for example to the 'chaos' of the French, the 'pasha-like' behaviour of the men, the 'affected' behaviour of the women, their cynicism, racism and so on. It seems as if it were necessary to rediscover such prejudices although the developing process of learning is frequently first of all directed against oneself ('to describe oneself *vis-à-vis* the others', 'provincial Germans', 'German petit-bourgeois conformism'), whereas foreigners are idealised.

Significant cultural experiences and learning at school

With the rash elimination of prejudices, foreign language education deprives itself of its only possibility of finding access to learners' − and teachers' − significant biographical experiences. Normally those significant intercultural experiences take place outside school, during journeys and holidays. If, however, they arise from the milieu of the school itself (e.g. during a students' exchange or a study trip) they are glossed over didactically (Müller, 1981). Usually school does not offer the space for experiences which permit such events to gain importance or which set off the needs for identification, whether these needs are the longing for freedom and love, or inner drives of fascination aroused because of the greater liveliness of the foreigner; whether it is the yearning for separation from familiar and cultural dependencies or the misery of being unhappy − not loved in one's own country; or whether it is the urge to secure one's own personal and cultural identity. Probably these meaningful experiences are excessive as learning targets at school: it is neither possible nor sensible that school or even foreign language education should make further demands on young people; nor is it possible that pupils make a foreign culture an integral part of their learning culture.

This relative intercultural ignorance is by no means an individual deficit of lazy or narrow-minded pupils. Instead, it mirrors their biographical situation. To express this in exaggerated terms, their situation is one of semi-culturism: an insufficient shaping of their own (German) cultural identity (a fact which has to be explained historically) coincides with a poor handling of foreign cultural identification and prejudices. Certainly this is not only the fault of *Landeskunde* at school, although this is definitely not the form of teaching which will promote significant intercultural learning.

Intercultural learning instead of *Landeskunde*

Landeskunde contains a series of implicit premises and requirements which altogether produce a real block of intercultural learning. We have already critically examined the first assumption – that prejudices have to be eliminated and instead thoughts of German–French friendship or international friendship developed. Significant intercultural learning starts only at the point where teachers expose themselves to the prejudices, aversions and aggressions as well as to the longings and fascinations which are more or less based on the experiences and sufferings of pupils. The assumption that the main concern was to convey to pupils an understanding of international problems which are alien to their immediate field of experiences (Kordes, 1986), holds them back from a real confrontation with people of another language, culture and concept of the world.

The topics of intercultural learning cannot be inferred from *Landeskunde*, history, politics or 'current events'. They originate rather in intercultural situations in which pupils as foreigners have to cope with a foreign situation or culture. Judgements and prejudices, sympathies and antipathies, linguistic hindrances or awareness as well as the experiences hidden behind them represent the first real material of foreign language education in the form of intercultural learning.

The assumption that topics and texts elicited from pupils have in the final analysis to be designed for a learning target or a determined structure of analyses leads pupils to use their experiences and prejudices as mere illustrations of basic terms and problems. Pupils keep their own interests and stages of development out of foreign language classes. In terms of intercultural learning, however, the situations and emotions introduced by pupils do not serve as illustrations of concepts in *Landeskunde* but serve the joint perception of their own everyday learner culture, and as such they are at their disposal for the practical and reflexive development of their learner culture and interculture.

The assumption that language classes as well as pupils' understanding of culture would benefit if a determined topic is agreed upon in advance in the end only denies pupils the freedom to pursue their own goals. Moreover, it discriminates against deviations and rejections as 'disturbances' which cause damage to the class and therefore have to be eliminated. However, precisely these disturbances can be sources for the discovery that interpersonal problems at home as well as at school (e.g. problems of hegemony between teacher culture and learner culture or discrepancies of orientation between girls and boys) at the same time always have intercultural connotations and equivalents. The most important aspect is that these are the only intercultural problems in which pupils can directly interfere (Kordes, 1986).

The assumption that difficulties with linguistic expressions and comprehension are merely a linguistic problem which can be solved in a linguistic way prevents foreign language education from perceiving and dealing with fears and frustrations which are tied to culture but which are taken to be personal fears. Intercultural learning on the other hand takes rejections and defence reactions, which on the surface find expression in language inhibitions and fears, seriously and perceives them as specific problems not only of interpersonal but also of intercultural communications. Consequently, even the basic assumption of conventional learning at school is seen in relative terms. It is the assumption that teachers are ahead of pupils regarding their readiness to negotiate and their freedom from prejudice and that they have to convey these attitudes to the pupils. It may be possible to estimate how far teachers are ahead of pupils as far as their knowledge is concerned, but regarding their capacity and readiness for intercultural learning only those who insist on antiquated linear ideas of the development of intercultural competence and identity will assume they are at a more advanced stage.

The Development of Intercultural Learning: Introducing a Model

A mobilisation of intercultural learning can only be started by the acceptance of intercultural situations (within and outside school) and their

INTERCULTURAL LEARNING AT SCHOOL 301

treatment. The way pupils and teachers deal with them and take the chance to extend them again and again in the course of a school career gives us an indication of an implicit line of intercultural learning development. We describe this learning development – analogous to the development of interlingual learning (Jakabovits, 1970) – as a transitional stage('interculture') between the culture of the learner and another culture. The native culture forms the monopolised starting point, which for the individual is decisive, whereas the foreign culture forms the opposing pole (see Figure 20.4).

```
Native culture                                                    Target culture
┌──────────┐────────────────────────────────────────────────────►┌──────────┐
└──────────┘      │                  │                  │        └──────────┘
                  ▼                  ▼                  ▼
           ┌──────────┐─ ─ ─►┌──────────┐─ ─ ─►┌──────────┐
           └──────────┘      └──────────┘      └──────────┘
           Learner culture 1  Learner culture 2  Learner culture 3
           (interculture)     (interculture)     (interculture)
```

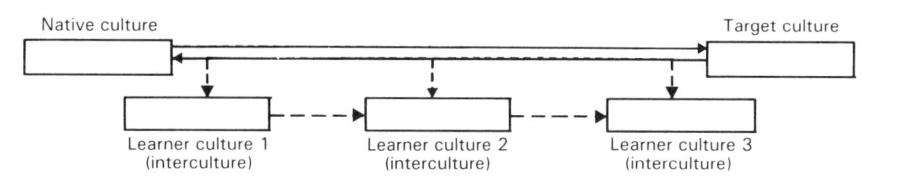

FIGURE 20.4 *The development of intercultural learning*

In closer characterisation of the different stages of the development of intercultural competence (Kordes, 1982: 85–6), we start from the premise that the 'threshold' of this learning process is one of 'intercultural understanding': the learner is capable of recognising aspects of intercultural or international conflicts in the situations with which he is confronted. He is able to differentiate between the different kinds of reaction and differences of institutions between his own culture and the foreign culture. He is also able to see the kinds of reaction and the norms of his own culture in relative terms. The boundaries of this 'threshold' go beyond the learner's own learning culture, beyond the point where he stands timidly between the cultures without a perspective on his own identity; hence the idealised 'final stage' of the development of intercultural competence which expresses itself in transcultural procedures. With the help of these procedures the learner develops his own criteria according to which he can judge a situation or a goal taking both cultures into consideration – sometimes even judging a situation from a point of view beyond both cultures and trying to find a meaning for himself. The more he apparently removes himself from his own culture and turns towards target cultures, the more he is going to regain and perceive his own culturally shaped identity, mirrored by the foreign culture.

This characterisation should be sufficient to avoid misunderstandings. By no means does the model of development suggest a linear progression towards becoming 'transcultural', or cosmopolitan. Just as culture is not learnable in the final analysis, the development of intercultural competence cannot simply be 'built up'. The model of development simply depicts qualities on an abstract and heuristic level whose processes in reality run forwards and backwards, and in all directions.

Catalysts and products of intercultural learning

Although a foreign culture is even less learnable than a foreign language, nevertheless intercultural learning is possible. There are, however, fewer opportunities to control intercultural learning than is the case with foreign language acquisition. On the other hand catalysts which encourage the development of intercultural learning and possible procedures can be stated.

The didactic change which we are suggesting here is significant. Instruction is not the primary influence. Culture shock or, more precisely, catalytic cultural experiences and situations precede the process of teaching and learning and the didactic which encompasses this process. It is not education which makes people receptive to intercultural learning; on the contrary, it is a shock which produces intercultural learning and the corresponding educational study. Then again the process of learning is carried out with the help of other processes which may have to be enriched and supported pedagogically and didactically. Nevertheless these processes have a 'generative' character, that is to say, they cannot be 'taught' from outside with the help of learning targets and courses. Instead they require constant new impulses and experiences in order to mobilise them for intercultural re-orientation and reconstruction.

Intercultural learning, just as any kind of significant learning, does not simply arise from everyday experience. Catalysts are necessary. The catalyst of intercultural learning is a new cultural experience, a culture – or alienation – shock which sets young people in such a critical situation that they feel 'confused' and 'crazy'. They have to feel this way since the new experience is ambiguous: it does not only irritate because there is something surprising about the foreign exterior, but further there is something 'inside' the self which is confused.

This culturally caused shock leads to intercultural learning only if the learner is no longer capable of coping with the experience of foreign culture with the help of the familiar and well-known range of action of his own culture. Moreover, the tendency to 'rationalisation' and the rejection of experience fail. At that point a new orientation – that is, learning in a signficant way – becomes necessary. Old types of experience have to be unconsciously examined and reorganised according to the new problems of action. These intellectual proceedings which examine and reorganise familiar patterns of behaviour are procedures, that is to say intellectual tools, with the help of which the learner can cope with critical experiences. If this 'symbolic work' leads to the production of new forms and structures, the procedures prove to be acceptable; if this development takes place, i.e. if new structures are developed by coping with critical experiences, the procedures prove to be successful. The development itself is then carried out as a serious of procedures, during which the learners work on an increasing reflexive abstraction of the concrete experience of foreignness. We emphasise this 'becoming reflexive', since within the medium of school chances of 'becoming productive' are poor. At least six such procedures, which are to a large extent responsible for the development of processes of intercultural learning – through the three stages with their corresponding monocultural, intercultural and transcultural procedures – can be demonstrated.

In principle all these procedures deal with the secondary form of human 'egocentric attitude', that is ethnocentric attitude. The development of intercultural learning consists in the transition from one form of ethnocentric attitude to another. This occurs dialectically. The intellectual structures which release the learner from a more 'primitive', monocultural stage, then hold him prisoner in the next stage of 'intercultural' ethnocentric attitude. Considered from the point of view of development theory, ethnocentric attitudes do not merely present a negative by-product of developed acculturation and enculturation processes. At this stage of development the learner has new experiences and reflections at his disposal with the help of which he revises and reorganises his behaviour at the preceding stage. Monocultural procedures basically rely on assimilation strategies ('the others are actually just the same as we are and they intend to be like that; they simply haven't reached our stage of development'). Intercultural procedures rely on contrasting strategies ('the others are different; they can and have to be different'). Transcultural operations rely on identification strategies which on the one hand are made automatic through intercultural experience, but which on the other come to terms with native cultural limitations and influences.

In view of the ambiguity of critical cultural experiences, intercultural learning (in the sense of finding new orientations) has to proceed on two levels: on the one hand it has to be directed 'outwards' towards the understanding of the latent culture of others, the 'foreigners'; on the other hand it has to be directed 'inwards', so as to cope with one's own feelings and identifications. Consequently each stage contains two procedures, which signify both sides of the same handling of experiences: the aspect of intercultural competence with development directed outwards and the aspect directed inwards. Both sides together characterise the task of each stage of development (see Figure 20.5).

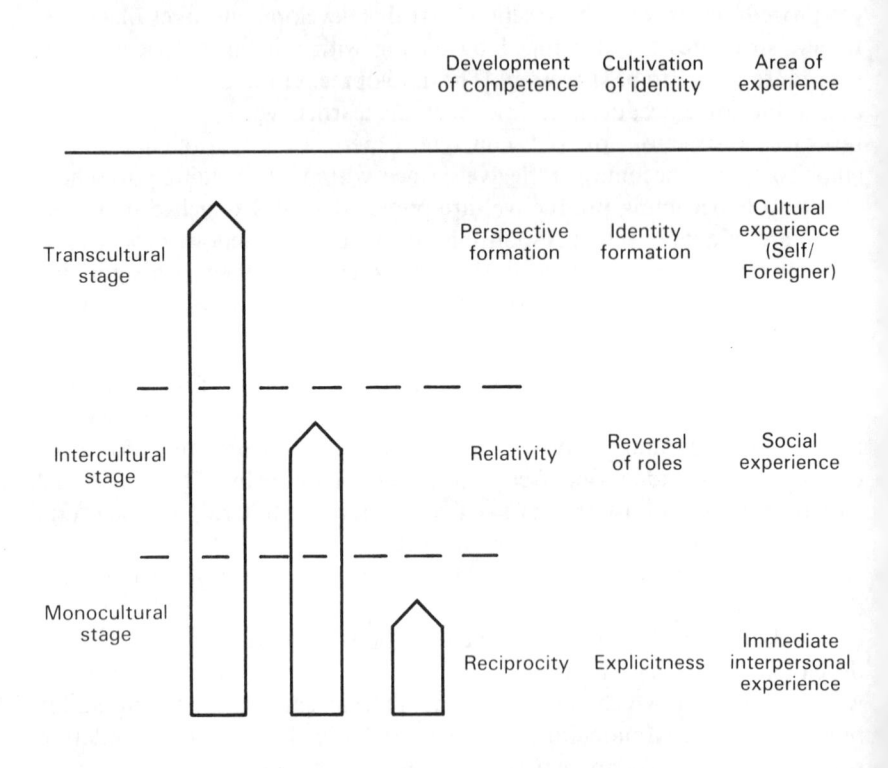

	Development of competence	Cultivation of identity	Area of experience
Transcultural stage	Perspective formation	Identity formation	Cultural experience (Self/ Foreigner)
Intercultural stage	Relativity	Reversal of roles	Social experience
Monocultural stage	Reciprocity	Explicitness	Immediate interpersonal experience

FIGURE 20.5 *Stages of intercultural learning*

The development towards the 'transcultural' stage does not imply the fiction of the sublime figure of light who is floating over the depressions of the real, culturally shaped world. What we are describing here are dialectic developments of structures which exist because of a task of development: identification with the foreign culture, closely related with a feeling of uneasiness within the native culture — sometimes too an uneasiness about culture, about civilisation, in general, for example in the conclusion that civilisation again and again produces anti-civilisation, namely destruction, misery, unemployment and so on. The love and warmth, freedom and solidarity, for which we are all longing has never been real, neither in our culture, nor in primitive cultures, nor in the idealised foreign culture; however, the longing is still legitimate. And no matter how difficult and hopeless it may appear, the capacity of developing perspectives and identity is, finally, the most important condition to ensure that big or small Auschwitzes are not repeated, ever again.

References

JAKABOVITS, L.A. 1970, *Foreign Language Learning. A Psycholinguistic Analysis of the Issues.* Cambridge, Mass.
KORDES, H. 1982, *Vorwärtrückwärts oder das unheimlich totale Lernen.* Münster: Mimeo.
——1986, *Aus Fehlern Lernen.* Münster: Mimeo.
——1991, *Wie Schülerinnen lernen, sich mit Angehörigen fremder Sprache und Kultur zu verständigen.* Wetzlar: Büchse der Pandora.

21 Language Education Across Europe: Towards an Intercultural Perspective

JOHN BROADBENT and LEONARDO ORIOLO

'Community Languages in the Secondary Curriculum?'

'How can you possibly succeed, in London, in educating children of Italian origin into the norms of an English-speaking society, whilst at the same time preserving the language and culture of their heritage?

This question was raised privately by an Italian official at the Colloquium held towards the end of 1987 to report on the work of the European Commission's Pilot Project on 'Community Languages in the Secondary Curriculum'. Posed in this way, the question seems to invite the answer 'You can't do it. It's impossible'. And yet the promotion of the language and culture of origin has been one of the main forms of positive action recommended by officials responsible for the education of children of migrant workers across the member states of the European Community. There is difficulty in answering the question, not because bilingual and intercultural strategies are intrinsically difficult to implement, but because the concepts of language, culture and society which underpin the educational policies formulated at governmental level are in most cases blatantly oversimplified. Often they erroneously presuppose a neatly homogenous and static society, extending conveniently to the borders of each individual nation-state. There is in consequence a tendency towards narrow ethnocentricity in the selection of the forms of culture to be transmitted via each national school system.

The Pilot Project on 'Community Languages in the Secondary Curriculum' had, as its name implies, focused much more centrally on questions of language policy in secondary education than it had upon

LANGUAGE EDUCATION ACROSS EUROPE

cultural transmission. The use of the term 'community' in connection with 'language' does carry with it important associations with collectively defined forms of culture: 'community language' was adopted largely to differentiate the pedagogic approaches developed for a foreign language as opposed to those which need to be taken when a language is used by a local community and when it is part of the affective experience of at least some of the pupils in a particular school. 'Community language' was not used to refer exclusively to the select few official languages of the European Community, but to *all* of the languages which are used in the member states; including those languages brought by migrant workers and refugees.

There are a number of contextually determined differences in the approaches which should be made for community language teaching as opposed to those traditionally adopted for foreign language teaching. Although the participating colleagues involved in the teaching of Italian, Panjabi and Urdu as community languages in the secondary timetable had at some time or other all confronted issues involving conflicts of culturally derived values, unfortunately no specific forum was organised in the EC Pilot Project mentioned above in order to arrive at any collectively refined stances. Indeed, the direction taken by the Project tended to see language as an instrument to be broadened and developed in the classroom by certain kinds of teacher intervention, including the exposure to new experiences, rather than as a vehicle for maintaining pre-existent forms of culture.

A number of statements were circulated in the EC Pilot Project through confidential working papers to which amendment was invited from all participants. The fact that the following statements were unchallenged suggests that they reflect a concensus right across the Project, to the effect that:

> the curriculum of the secondary school should provide space for the study of a number of optional languages in addition to the main medium of instruction;
>
> all the forms of language brought from home into the school are to be regarded as valid tools for learning in their own right;
>
> steps should be taken to encourage every pupil to value the forms of language used in the home, and to develop them towards the educated standards obtaining in the country of heritage;
>
> that language is an inseparable part of culture as well as being a vehicle for its transmission, so that an intercultural approach inevitably requires insights into different languages;
>
> that all forms of discrimination are to be counteracted, and

that each individual student should have rights to determine the balance of language and culture which he or she chooses to adopt.

These pious principles become difficult to realise when there is such a clear hierarchy in the languages offered in British schools, as indeed there is in schools throughout the world; when certain varieties of language, such as Creoles and languages without a written tradition, are characterised as unsuitable for educational purposes; and when speakers of Panjabi and Urdu, Arabic and Chinese, even Turkish and Italian, are subject to racist abuse wherever their collective power and relative numbers are insufficient to counteract the anti-social behaviour directed towards them.

Needless to say, to offer an optional two hours of tuition per week in a pupil's own language within a curriculum delivered during at least 20 pupil-teacher contact hours, as happened in the larger fraction of those few schools which worked with the EC Pilot Project, is hardly an equitable basis upon which a balanced biculturalism or bilingualism can be built. The language teacher can do little more than correct some of the most glaringly ethnocentric forms of misrepresentation purveyed in different areas of the curriculum. This is not to suggest that the work which has been attempted should now be revoked, as indeed may be beginning to happen as a result of the publication by the Department of Education and Science of a National Curriculum document (DES, 1987), which ascribes a place to 'modern foreign languages' in its core, but makes no explicit reference to the locally used languages which have been identified in several distinct areas of the United Kingdom. Contrary to the position implied by this silence, there is an urgent requirement to strengthen the position of languages which are additional to the traditionally accepted medium or media of instruction in each of the European states.

Choosing the Most Relevant Languages

In the extremely diverse context of local educational autonomy currently obtaining in the United Kingdom, there are examples of schools which arrange for every child to receive some tuition in the language(s) spoken at home, but such schools are very much the exception. In others, various members of staff, most often those concerned with the teaching of English, or of English as a Second Language, have made attempts to find places in the curriculum to refer to and build upon the language knowledge which students already possess. Their initiatives include after-school and lunchtime language clubs; school assemblies involving the use of different languages; multilingual collections of research books and works of literature in the library; the display of signs and pupils' work in all of the languages present; language awareness programmes; language taster courses; various social and cultural activities including the celebration of relevant festivals, and often involving parents; links with local supplementary schools, sometimes for the purpose of enabling pupils to be entered as candidates for language examinations through an approved centre; the organisation of visits, sometimes exchange visits to countries or other areas of Britain in which the languages spoken by at least some pupils in the school are a main means of communication; the encouragement of pen-pal correspondence, and so on.

Sooner or later, decisions must be taken to extend the range of languages offered in the timetables of most schools in England beyond the mere provision of French, beyond the tiny pockets in which German, Italian, Russian and Spanish exist as second options, into a full-blown multilingual policy, capitalising on the language resources available in so many inner city schools. The argument is often advanced that there are too many languages to cater for adequately, but this cannot be allowed to become an excuse for a failure to offer particular languages when they are spoken by significant sections of a school population and are widely used in the area surrounding a particular school.

Once a decision has been taken to promote within the school day the most commonly used language or languages, those forms of language must be seen to be used as educational tools in their own right, and not just as subjects to be studied. This means that significant parts of the conceptual and informational content of the school curriculum must eventually be delivered through more than a single language.

A Feasibility Study

Early in 1982, discussions began towards the design of a Pilot Project to be funded by the European Commission which would look at practice in the provision for locally used languages within the timetable of state schools in England. This EC Pilot Project came to involve some 30 teachers of three main locally used languages, working with four employing authorities – the City of Birmingham, the Inner London Education Authority, the Italian Embassy and Nottinghamshire – in its study of the teaching of Italian, Panjabi and Urdu in mainstream secondary schools. A number of other authorities assisted the Project with expertise and examples of practice. Through the network established by the Italian Embassy for the deployment of their teachers, the Project was also able to develop constructive relationships with Bedfordshire, Warwickshire, and, in South Wales, West Glamorgan.

The four aims decided upon by the EC Pilot Project's Management Committee, consisting of representatives of the four employing authorities plus the DES and Her Majesty's Inspectorate, proved to be extremely ambitious. The Project aimed to facilitate:

- exploration of opportunities and constraints for the inclusion of community languages in the normal curricular arrangements of secondary schools;
- exchange of ideas on methodology (including dialogue with teachers of foreign languages);
- exchange of materials for diverse situations and contexts, given different age/ability, group sizes, allocation of times and learning objectives.

Opportunities and Constraints

In seeking to draw a consensus view from the participating teachers of community languages, the Project assembled evidence concerning a wide range of provision in British schools as well as analysing in some detail the practice obtaining in the authorities mentioned above. Tentative findings include the following points:

1. The numbers of children opting to study a community language are increasing, as are public examination entries in most community languages.
2. Continuity in terms of bilingual development for children who speak a community language at home and who have received some tuition in that language during their years of primary schooling requires that the earliest possible start be made in the secondary phase. Previous research undertaken for the European Commission has established the case for promoting both languages of bilingual children during the early years and primary phase of schooling.
3. Of the timetable frameworks observed in the Pilot Schools, the arrangements which best suited the promotion of community languages offered access to at least two languages in addition to English within a curricular core extending from the age of 11 to the age of 16.
4. There is still a crippling shortage of adequately trained personnel able and willing to build on the existing linguistic expertise in the population of school age.

The presence of at least one community language specialist on the established staff of a school clearly enhances the integration of provision within the normal life of the school. Currently schools in England often use the resources of a peripatetic teacher available from a central pool, and such teachers will inevitably experience difficulty in securing recognition for their practice and ideas. It seems, for example, that community language teachers can be more successful if they also teach other highly desired subjects in the curriculum. Ideally they should be native speakers of the languages they are promoting, although there is also a case for deploying side by side with native speakers, some teachers who have grown up bilingual and others who have acquired the language in later life.

With regard to the existing teaching of languages other than English in England, it would seem that the Department of Education and Science in Britain at one time held the view that pupils learn more successfully from teachers who have shared similar problems in studying the target languages. A consultative paper on *Foreign Languages in the School Curriculum* claimed:

> It is widely held that foreign languages are best taught by teachers who are native speakers in English or Welsh rather than by foreign teachers employed, as exchange teachers or otherwise, to teach their native language. (DES, 1983).

The French Ministry of Education seems to have held a similar view with regard to the teaching of Portuguese in French schools: it argues that pupils of Portuguese origin should receive their tuition from teachers of similar origin, whilst pupils of French origin should be taught by teachers again of their own nationality and mother tongue. The shortcomings of such simple administrative formulae lie largely in the fact that human society is not so simple: family backgrounds, cultural experience and relative levels of linguistic competence all vary widely within any category which is posited solely on the grounds of nationality or even of mother tongue. There are of course a multitude of different contexts arising out of the political oppression of certain languages, such as Kurdish in Turkish speaking communities and Panjabi amongst Urdu users. There is also the question of dialectal variation, which is very much a part of the educational scene in many countries from which migration is still occurring, including Italy. There, for the first time in history, junior school curricula are being designed to take account of different local dialects and historical traditions. It follows from their work that it may not be absolutely necessary that teachers should share a knowledge of the same dialect as their pupils, or that they have the same cultural (or subcultural) background. It is more important that the teacher should have a consistently positive approach to the linguistic and cultural factors which may affect the pupils' performance. Admitting that native speakers of a particular language are also likely to be the most effective users of that language, the main priority would seem to lie in the development of an adequate educational philosophy and pedagogy to allow them to pass on their skills.

A combination of teachers, involving both native speakers and colleagues who have learned a relevant community language in later life, would seem to offer the most satisfactory recipe for evolving effective teaching strategies and for weakening prejudice and racism when it is expressed towards a particular linguistic group. This, at any rate, was the resoundingly successful experience of one of the EC Pilot Project Schools in Bedfordshire. In Berlin, the campaign for collaborative teaching for bilingual students argues for a structure which involves a Turkish teacher working alongside a German teacher, each nationality acting as a representative of a distinct variety of culture. Although current research findings strongly support bilingual team teaching of this kind, inequality of status and citizenship can undermine successful working relationships. Even the most committed proponents of team teaching seem not to have recognised that a clear division of roles in the classroom, with one teacher typically representing Turkishness and another Germanness, is unlikely to reflect the cultural complexities which arise within a dynamic multilingual community or to result in anti-racist intercultural understandings on the part of a mixed school population. In the most supportive of the secondary schools which worked with the EC Pilot Project, at least one teacher of the targeted community language had been taken on to the staffing establishment. Their efforts to offer this language in the curriculum are no longer dependent upon, but are supplemented by, the teachers drafted in through the good offices of various national embassies, or in the case of Commonwealth languages through the financial support of the Home Office.

Language Loyalty Amongst the Learners

The denial of their linguistic and cultural heritage by pupils under pressure from often hostile circumstances in state schools in Britain is a very real problem which mother tongue teachers continually have to face. In general, adolescents need to be able to feel equal or superior to others, to be accepted by their peer group, and also to define themselves within forms of culture from which adults are necessarily excluded. This need seems to be accentuated amongst those adolescents who experience their heritage as an obstacle in their relations with pupils of their own age.

It is not possible to generalise about the responses of all bilingual children to their home language when it is offered in school or outside of it. In England, many pupils attending out-of-school mother tongue classes are obliged to do so by their parents. Even if for some the classes provide an opportunity to go out and to meet their peers in a generally sympathetic context, compulsion inevitably creates conflicts and hardly contributes to motivation. Similarly in mainstream school provision it can happen that pupils find themselves placed in language provision against their will. The extent of their possible resistance to learning their language in school will largely depend on the social and economic status of the parents, on the standing of the country of heritage in the eyes of the surrounding society, on the attitudes to linguistic and cultural difference purveyed by the school and so on. In England, some bilingual pupils exhibit a tendency to ascribe to their non-English family background many of the social and psychological problems which are typical for their age and level of personal development; they may be ashamed of their background, and, by extension, ashamed of the language and culture of their parents. This makes them, in their own perception at least, different from their peers – a minority – and in consequence likely victims of derision or social exclusion. Moreover, whenever the mother tongue is a dialect, it is likely that it will be considered inferior to the standard variety by the parents themselves. This inevitably has its effect upon the children so that they may come to use the mother tongue only when obliged to do so and with evident unwillingness when they are confronted by other pupils in the same age group.

This kind of reaction may change radically, if the hostility comes clearly from outside of the pupil him or herself. Under such circumstances, a pupil may adopt a nationalistic stance, defending their loyalty to their country and to their origins. This opposite response often, once compulsory schooling is over, turns into a need to research into one's real heritage and identity, at which stage the advantages of bilingualism become clearer.

Some students in secondary schools in England clearly have worked out their reasons and purposes for studying their home language, or rather, at secondary level, the language which would be recognised as the norm amongst educated people in the country of their heritage. One Italian student in Bedford expressed her position in the following way:

> I can already speak my dialect with my relatives here and in Italy. In school I want to learn to use Italian flexibily, so that when I go to Italy I can take part in all of the things Italian people do, watching television, and so on.

There is little scientific evidence as yet which would allow us to posit characteristic personal responses to biculturalism as manifested in different contexts. Nevertheless, the above insights revealed through careful interviewing of pupils over the period of the EC Pilot Project in the UK do have important implications for the teaching objectives, the methods, the course content, the materials, and the ideal relations with the pupils' families to be promoted as part of the teaching of a community language.

Methodology

There is little experience which has been investigated and collated in ways that allow general conclusions to be applied in different contexts. The didactic hypotheses which arise from particular forms of practice and research need to be tested in a variety of places. Some general rules of good experiential pedagogy were shown by the EC Pilot Project in the UK to have a direct relevance to the teaching of community languages – the importance of initiating activities in the classroom which create the greatest involvement amongst the pupils, for example.

Participants in the Project reached a consensus that the syllabus content and methodology of community language teaching is best derived in the first place from the needs of children who share in the relevant cultural heritage, without excluding the needs of students with no family connection with the language in question. Social reasons rather than pedagogical ones have predominated in the debate in England to suggest that where particular languages are made available within the state school curriculum, they should be made available to all.

The resultant wide range of attainment existing in community language classrooms includes that of pupils who have no family connection with the language studied. The range has been analysed in such a way as to facilitate the development of relevant parallel syllabuses and schemes of work depending on the immediate purposes and needs of the learners, whether these are of a transactional nature, or more reflective and creative, or again more specialised in vocational terms. The formulation of relevant methods and syllabuses for community languages is likely to have a useful spin-off for the effective teaching of foreign languages as well, especially in classrooms where it is necessary to cater for a wide range of attainment.

Unifying learning centres and the activities which flow from them needs to start out from a centre of interest which is directly linked to the concrete situation and experience as shared by the particular group of pupils being catered for. Similarly, the forms of communication which are encouraged should start out from the existing language resources possessed collectively by the pupils and from their collective needs and purposes for learning. These would seem to be minimum requirements in order to stimulate and motivate pupils under the circumstances sketched above. In other words, it is important particularly in the early stages to avoid stressing differences between individual pupils, since this is likely to have negative consequences amongst adolescents working in a group situation. This is, of course, not to suggest that there should not be a general emphasis placed on the value of the language used at home, or on the positive interests expressed by individual pupils for music, fashion, sport, news items and so on. Such concrete examples should be used to underline the importance of a knowledge of various languages and of the value of bilingualism in the life of the school and also in the world of work. For greater credibility amongst the students, these positive attitudes need to be constructed and reinforced by teachers of other subjects, a factor which greatly strengthens the argument for team teaching and interdisciplinary approaches.

Ethnocentric Bias in the Curriculum

Bilingual colleagues participating in the EC Pilot Project were anxious, in the schools to which they were assigned, to work alongside teachers of a wide variety of different subjects, in order to reinforce the concepts otherwise transmitted solely by the medium of English. This helped to strengthen the grasp of bilingual students over the more formal educational uses of their home langauges. There were successful examples of partnership teaching of Science, Home Economics, History, Social Studies, Drama, Art, Needlework and so on. In almost every discipline, some corrections needed to be made to redress the ethnocentric bias present in existing approaches. Two of the most glaring examples of this related to History and to Social Studies. In History it proved illuminating for participating students to become aware of the ways in which the same period of history could be viewed from different perspectives – as, for example, the 1857 historical episode known variously as the 'Sepoy Mutiny' or as the First War of Indian Independence. Similarly, with Social Studies the presentation of the concept of the nuclear family as the most successful social structure in modern society conflicted very obviously with the sophistication of the Panjabi and Urdu vocabulary used to describe the roles and relationships in the extended families in which many pupils were nurtured. It is worth quoting at some length the following passage from a standard British school textbook by Jack Nobbs (1981) for the stereotype which it offers of nuclear family structure, and the negative implications for members of extended ones:

> The nuclear family was not always the most popular type in Britain. When there was a scarcity of houses, transport, and job opportunities away from home, it was customary for father, mother, children and grandparents to live together under one roof. This large family unit is called an extended family. In Saxon times the family was extended to include grandparents with their children, sons' wives, daughters' husbands, grandchildren, cousins, aunts, uncles, nephews, nieces. They all lived in the long hut. It must have been quite a gathering. There are still villages where all the people are related, although in civilised societies relations usually divide up into close knit groups with separate homes ...
>
> In working-class urban areas such a Bethnal Green in the East End of London, the extended family often continues to be more important than the nuclear family; this is bound up with the wife maintaining a close relationship with her mother after marriage.

Colleagues working with the Pilot Project made wide-ranging efforts to enrich the cultural experience offered to students. Song and drama have both proved to be effective ways of passing on an awareness of the various stages in Italian history, including the waves of migration, which are quite difficult to present to insecure adolescents who may be unwilling to recognise the privations experienced by their direct ancestors.

Syllabus Design

Given the extremely heterogeneous composition of community language classes, it has often proved difficult to reconcile the competing sets of objectives advanced for particular languages, and consequently to design sufficiently balanced syllabuses. A confusing range of conflicting rationales has been adduced in different British secondary schools to justify the provision of languages other than English. At one end of the spectrum is the set of objectives drawn up principally to justify the teaching of foreign languages, mainly relating to language learning as a valid mental discipline in its own right which perhaps also offers access to alternative forms of culture. At the other end lies the set of objectives used for strengthening the case for maintaining and supporting the language and culture of minority groups from the earliest years onwards, so as to ease the transition from home to school, or so as to reaffirm the cognitive development and self-image of students who may have received important parts of their socialisation and education through the medium of a language different from the medium of instruction obtaining in the national school system. Experience in various parts of the European Community suggests that the two kinds of learning context, the two sets of objectives, the two kinds of teaching methodology present apparently insuperable difficulties, whether policy veers towards integration or towards segregation.

There do seem to be advantages in using languages other than English for grappling with the conceptual content of a multicultural curriculum and an adequate linguistic preparation is necessary to underpin this in almost all areas of cultural development – visual arts, architecture and interior decoration, food and cuisine, fashion, dance, popular and classical music, design and technology, drama, and literature.

Language knowledge provides an ever-expanding gateway into the kinds of cultural experience which are made available in the schools and other institutions of a multicultural society. At the same time, care must be taken not to trivialise or stereotype through the information provided about the cultural practices of identifiable groups. One way of monitoring for this is to filter out the information which the present members of a particular group would prefer not to share with out-group peers. A debate along these lines was provoked by the desire of the Panjabi teachers in the Project to offer typical foods and to present an evening of Panjabi folk dances as part of the End-of-Project Colloquium; when approached to offer a similar output, the teachers of Italian rejected the idea of putting their culture on show, for fear of reinforcing stereotypes of singing and spaghetti-eating. Where a focus on celebrations and festivals has proved to be a valuable part of the language teaching syllabus, such festivals have often been an integral part of the relationships between the school and its surrounding community. By and large, the Project teachers rejected the view that language teaching should concern itself with religious beliefs and practices, although clearly there is a fine distinction between religious observance and social occasions based on a religious calendar.

Discussions about the elements of Italian culture which should be promoted revealed that pupils, including those who are deeply loyal to their Italianness, have different standards and different levels of maturity with regard to the aspects which they wish to see reinforced. At one level, it is fast cars and modern Italian fashion and design which pupils would prefer to see put at a premium; the willingness to delve into Italian art, and into the history of Italian migration seems to evolve at a later stage of maturity and self-confidence. In any multicultural school there is a danger of transmitting damaging Eurocentric value judgements about the superiority of one particular national culture or product over another. The dilemmas are perhaps easier to resolve in the upper secondary or tertiary phase, when students can be expected to have the necessary maturity to create their own cultural syntheses, drawing on the whole range of experience available in the local community.

Materials Production

The ongoing intention of the EC Pilot Project was to bring the teachers closer to an understanding of the needs, aspirations and capabilities of their pupils, and to encourage collaborative work in the design of teaching materials. Analysis of the kinds of competence identified amongst learners of community languages within the Project suggested different levels of teaching target to be located somewhere between specialised skills for fluent users of the community language (such as story-telling, translation, public speaking, and so on), and a transactional foundation for students who may have no knowledge of the language, and no family connections with it. Teaching materials designed by groups of teachers in the Project consequently attempted to address the different levels of existing competence by devising tasks at different levels of difficulty around a repeating series of themes, such that overall cohesion can be maintained in a classroom containing a wide range of individual attainment.

It is self-evident that teaching materials cannot be culturally neutral, although in the EC Pilot Project there was a preference for approaching the inevitable dilemmas from the utilitarian standpoint of the professional language teacher. One such formulation asked what cultural images should be presented in the books used, for example, for developing early literacy in Urdu, given that the learners we are servicing have to an increasing extent been born and brought up in Britain. This particular issue had surfaced at a very early meeting held to open a dialogue between teachers of foreign languages in British schools as opposed to teachers of languages which have been revealed to be widely used in the UK itself by pupils and their parents. Teachers of Italian, Panjabi and Urdu working with the EC Pilot Project were describing their materials to teachers of French and German. One Urdu teacher in particular explored the inadequacy of teaching materials imported from Pakistan and India, since many of the cultural references were beyond the experience of British-born pupils. Pictures of houses, streets and policemen had proved to be as unfamiliar as the descriptions of weather conditions. This particular teacher had accordingly set about providing simple Urdu texts to accompany pictures of English houses, streets and policemen whose appearance would be more familiar. The foreign language teachers present demurred, arguing that Urdu teaching materials should represent the characteristic flavour of life amongst Urdu-speaking people in Pakistan and India. Just as materials for teaching French showed French policemen, so too materials for teaching Urdu in Britain should show Pakistani police. The compromise reached in discussion suggested portraying the existing norms for both societies. It was from this compromise suggestion that the germ of contrastive intercultural strategy could evolve.

Examples of teaching materials need to be produced to professional standards before circulation to other colleagues. There is a healthy tendency for community language teachers to wish to create their own materials with particular groups of students in mind. However, in order to maintain high standards of production and to reduce the wastage of effort involved, there is a strong case for building up a national team with proven ability in the design of materials for each community language. The preparation of teaching materials for community languages in secondary schools is unfortunately seen principally as the preparation of worksheets, and the value of using a variety of media is often neglected.

Recent developments in educational technology mean that teaching materials for a number of community languages can be stored on computer, and printed out, or amended to suit the needs of particular groups of students. Although curriculum development support units in different local education authorities, and the EC Pilot Project itself, have assisted in the printing and distribution of individually produced materials, this assistance has not as yet proved to offer a viable return in either pedagogical or financial terms. It would seem that practically all of the resources which have so far been made available both inside and outside the Project are insufficiently accessible for any users other than their immediate designers. Project teachers have in any case had very little time to realise their ideas in terms of professionally produced resources. The successful development of teaching resources cannot be based merely on good will or on a spare time commitment, which means that in future supply teachers must be found to replace teachers engaged in development work. Above all, finance needs to be made available for comparative work across national boundaries.

The syllabus which is proposed by the Italian government for use with pupils of Italian origin in England is in fact the same syllabus as is recommended for use in Italy itself. It relates to a curriculum framework constructed around blocks of informational content, rather than one underpinned by the 'areas of experience' approach commonly obtaining in British schools. This is not to attempt to suggest that one way of defining the curriculum is necessarily better than the other, but rather to highlight the conflict of expectations. For the Italian government, those expectations are based on an unwritten assumption that the education of Italian pupils should be the same as they would have received in Italy. The desire is to ensure that they can function fully as Italian citizens should they return to Italy. The assumption of the British authorities, on the other hand, is often that pupils must put behind them the cultural differences between thmselves and the rest of the school population if they wish to compete on equal terms. There is simply not time for the Italian Embassy teacher, whether working in after-school classes or in mainstream schools, to cover the amount of ground expected by the Italian syllabus. Nor does it seem possible to many teachers in the English school system that the whole of the normal English curriculum can be delivered to students for whom English is their second language. The possibility, then, of forming adults who are capable of moving between countries and languages, and of operating with equal ease in each, seems an impossible ideal. Basing its arguments on relatively impressionistic insights gained during the three years of the Pilot Project's work, this chapter wishes to argue that it is the very processes of cultural transmission occurring in schools in Europe, and the narrow nationalistic ideologies which are reinforced by the institutional structures of schooling, which make the endeavour seem so idealistic.

Assessment of Performance

Nationally evolved systems of education continue to handicap rather than facilitate the free movement of people across Europe, let alone the globe. Education ministers have so far failed in all attempts to harmonise the different systems operating within the European Community, although they do agree that each state should recognise qualifications awarded by the others. The definition of equivalent levels of performance in school-leaving examinations, and common rules of access to higher education could serve as a valuable basis for mutual recognition of qualifications and study periods wherever these may be completed.

The range of examinations in languages across Europe should be sufficiently broad to differentiate across the range of attainment occasioned by a spread of candidates from beginners to fluent mother tongue speakers: the higher examinations should give recognition to the superior levels of linguistic expertise which can be acquired by candidates who are part of a community which uses the target language in its daily life, whilst the lower grades should nevertheless represent a useful achievement and an ability to achieve genuine standards of communicative competence in real-life situations. There would seem so be value in formulating statements of performance in language use which can allow for international comparison.

The criteria underlying the new General Certificate of Secondary Education in England, Northern Ireland and Wales would seem to offer some of the flexibility needed for the different levels of language competence identified. Parallel initiatives which offer unit/credits for successfully completed modules and which stress the value of course work in evaluating performance increase the likelihood of progress in this area. The Secondary Examinations Council is involved in encouraging further developments with regard to languages like Chinese, Greek and Urdu which are spoken by significant numbers of pupils in the state system.

The new examinations are, in addition, likely to have a useful backwash effect in ensuring that teachers prepare students for communicative uses of language, but given the overriding criterion of 'successful communication with a sympathetic native speaker', examiners are going to need to be more sensitive about questions of linguistic variation and 'grammatical accuracy'.

Bilingual Approaches and Intercultural Education

Accuracy in terms of the successful use of educated varieties of Italian, Panjabi and Urdu was one of the major preoccupations of the team of community language teachers working with the EC Pilot Project in the UK. To date this preoccupation seems largely to have arisen because of the requirements of public examinations. A number of colleagues started out from a deficit theory in analysing learners' errors in their use of Italian and English, or Panjabi, Urdu and English. Contrastive analyses were drawn upon to facilitate the discovery by the students themselves of how the standard varieties seemed to function. The discovery of general syntactical rules seemed to yield richer results in terms of improvements in written accuracy than did formal explanations and extensive correction of errors. By analysing the different sources of the languages they were attempting to use, bilingual pupils could become more conscious of appropriacy and convention. At the same time they increased their control over the forms of language they were acquiring. Similar processes might yield similarly positive results in terms of cultural studies, working on 'interculture' instead of 'interlanguage'. Perhaps if students are provided with a methodology for discovering the recent history of the cultural practices which have in part determined their current behaviour, they will be better placed to decide on the balance of culture which they decide to adapt and develop into the future.

As is so often the case, the nagging doubts which lay behind the formulation of the Italian official's question have not really surfaced in the public debates, or in national and international remedies. In the 1987 Colloquium itself there would in any case hardly have been time even to hint at the more fundamental underlying issues within an agenda already crammed with discussions on curriculum planning, language pedagogy and materials. The Project had tended to concentrate on the maintenance and extension of the pupils' existing language resources towards utilitarian goals of their own choosing, such as talking to relatives or other forms of social interaction, writing letters, answering the telephone, helping out in supplementary schools, reading newspapers or novels and so on. In other words the direction agreed collectively by participants in the Project inevitably has left open a number of questions to be investigated further. This chapter could do little more than offer some of the incidental insights that grew out of a language-centred focus in action research, a focus which recognised the dynamically changing nature of language and culture in our society.

(This chapter incorporates the views of other colleagues in the EC Pilot Project.)

References

BROADBENT, J. 1987, *The Inclusion of Community Languages in the Normal Curricular Arrangements of Local Education Authority Maintained Schools in England and Wales* (The 1984–1987 Report of the EC Pilot Project 'Community Languages in the Secondary Curriculum'). London: University of London Institute of Education.

DES 1983, *Foreign Languages in the School Curriculum* (consultative paper). London: DES/Welsh Office.

1987, *The National Curriculum 5–16: A Consultation Document*. London: DES.

NOBBS, J. 1981, *Modern Society: Social Studies for CSE* (2nd edn). London: George Allen and Unwin.

ROBINSON, J. 1988, *Community Languages in the Secondary Curriculum*. Report of the End-of-Project Colloquium, held at the University of Warwick, 28th–30th September 1987. London: University of London Institute of Education.

List of Contributors

Patricia Allatt*
Department of Social Administration, Teesside Polytechnic, Middlesbrough, England.

Gisela Baumgratz-Gangl
Centre d'Information et de Recherche sur l'Allemagne Contemporaine, 9, rue de Teheran, F-75008 Paris, France.

Michele Borrelli
Bergische Universität, Institut für interkulturelle Pädogogik, Postfach 10 01 27, D-5600 Wuppertal 1, Federal Republic of Germany.

John Broadbent
University of London, Institute of Education, Centre for Multicultural Education, Bedford Way, London WC1 OAL, England.

Dieter Buttjes*
Universität Dortmund, Institut für Anglistik und Amerikanistik, Postfach 50 05 00, D-4600 Dortmund 50, Federal Republic of Germany.

Michael Byram*
University of Durham, School of Education, Durham DH1 1TA, England.

Astrid Ertelt-Vieth
Justus-Liebig-Universität, Institut für Slawistik, Karl-Gloeckner-Str. 21, D-6300 Giessen, Federal Republic of Germany.

Veronica Esarte-Sarries*
University of Durham, School of Education, Durham DH1 1TA, England.

Laurence Kane*
Universität Dortmund, Institut für Anglistik und Amerikanistik, Postfach 50 05 00, D-4600 Dortmund 50, Federal Republic of Germany.

Gottfried Keller*
Gustav-Heinemann-Schule, Schul-und Sportzentrum, D-3520
Hofgeismar, Federal Republic of Germany.

Dieter Kerl
Friedrich-Schiller-Universität, Sektion Sprachwissenschaften, Otto-
Engau-Str. 7, DDR-6900 Jena, German Democratic Republic.

Hagen Kordes
Westfälische Wilhelms-Universität, Institut für pädogogische Lernfeld
und Berufsfeldforschung, Georgskommende 33, D-4400 Münster,
Federal Republic of Germany.

Angelika Kubanek
Katholische Universität Eichstätt, Sprach-und Literaturwissenschaftliche
Fakultät, Ostenstr. 26, D-8078 Eichstätt, Federal Republic of Germany.

Franz M. Kuna*
Universität für Bildungwissenschaften, Institut für Anglistik und
Amerikanistik, Universitätsstr. 65, A-9010 Klagenfurt, Austria

François Mariet
Univèrsité de Paris-Dauphine, Place du Maréchel de Lattre de Tassigny,
F-75775 Paris Cedex 16, France.

Meinert A. Meyer*
Westfälische Wilhelms-Universität, Institut für pädogogische Lernfeld
und Berufsfeldforschung, Georgskommende 33, D-4400 Münster,
Federal Republic of Germany.

Leonardo Oriolo
University of London, Institute of Education, Centre for Multicultural
Education, Bedford Way, London WC1 OAL, England.

Karen Risager*
Roskilde Universitetscenter, Postbox 260, DK-4000 Roskilde, Denmark.

Hugh Starkey*
Westminster College, North Hinksey, Oxford OX2 9AT, England.

Susan Taylor*
University of Durham, School of Education, Durham DH1 1TA, England.

Genevieve Zarate
Bureau pour l'Enseignement de la Langue et de la Civilisation,
Françaises à l'Etranger, 9, rue Lhomond, F-75005 Paris, France.

* Participants at the Durham Symposium, 1986.

Index

Note: Page references in italics indicate tables and figures.

Acculturation 6, 303
Accuracy 22, 23, 27, 156-7, 217, 321
 – observational 252-3
Acquisition,
 – culture 3-4, 5, 18-19, 262
 – language 3-4, 9, 22, 78, 216-17, 234, 241, 262, 294
Action, in learning 137-8
Action! Graded French 79-81
Age,
 – and attitudes to cultures 107
 – and textbook content 183-4, 190
Alienation 234, 294, 302
American Studies 34, 37, 55, 56-7, 60
Andersen, H. & Risager, K. 43
Area studies 56-7, 63-72
 – consolidation 70-2
 – differentiation and complexity 69-70
 – in East Germany 66-8
 – evolution 64-5
 – status 64, 65-6, 69
Attitudes,
 – to language learning 104, 117-18, 315
 – to other cultures 78, 79-80, 132, 175, 197
 – qualitative analysis 107-10
 – statistical analysis 106-7
 – in textbooks 188
 – *see also* generalisation, cultural; prejudice; stereotypes
Auslandsstudien 55

Austin, J.L. 265
Austria, teacher training 263-8
Authenticity 21, 79, 179-80, 201-2, 214-15, 220, 231, 232-5
 – and teacher training 244-5
Author of textbook 188, 192, 206
Awareness,
 – cultural 9, 19-20, *20*, 23-6, 27, 28-9, 195, 197-8, 205
 – language 19-20, *20*, 22-3, 28-9, 244, 309

Bachelard, Gaston 86, 91
Background studies 17, 49, 74-83
 – and communicative approach 77-9
 – and graded objectives 76-7
 – and teacher training 75, 80, 81-2
 – and textbooks 79-81
Bakhtin, M. 268, 269, 270
Baldwin, James 88
Barley, N. 24
Barthes, R. 270
Baumgratz, G. 137-8, 155, 218
Baumgratz-Gangl, G. 180, 228-35
Behaviourism 58, 216, 218
Bias,
 – in curriculum 315-16
 – in textbooks 194, 245
Bilingualism, and language awareness 22-3
Blackburn, Thomas 263
Blackwell, T. & Seabrook, J. 242, 243
Bokmal 34

Borrelli, Michelle 273, 275-86
Bourdieu, P. 86, 92, 256
Bower, R. 7
Braudel, F. 86
Britain,
— language teaching 31-2, 55, 73-83, 103-18, 209-10, 211-17, 306-22
— perceptions of Germany *121*, 122-3, 125-8, *126*, *127-8*, *129*, 140-1
Broadbent, John & Oriolo, Leonardo 273, 306-22
Brøgger, F.C. 43
Brown, H.D. 6
Brumfit, C. 217, 218
Buckby, M. 79-80
Buisson, Fernand 86
Buttjes, Dieter 3-14, 31, 47-61, 203
Byram, M. 17-30, 31-2, 73-83, 213-14, 320
Byram, M. & Schilder, H. 49
Byram, M. *et al.* 101, 103-18

Centre for Cultural Studies, Birmingham 242
Change, in knowledge 105
Civilisation studies 239-40, *see also* cultural studies
Clark, J.L. 212, 213
Class,
— and culture 242, 244-5
— and textbook content 183, 184, 188-9, 190, 212, 213
Co-operation, international 143, 175, 290, 292-3, *293*, 296
Comenius 52
Communication,
— intercultural 7, 8, 12, 59
 disrupted 293-7, *295*
 research 101-2, 103-18, 120-37, 136-57, 159-75
 secondary pupils 138-41, *139*, 144-57, 232
 teaching 229-31
— as negotiation of meaning 13, 137-8, 143, 148
Communicative approach 21-2, 23, 40, 42, 53, 58, 60, 76, 78-9, 212, 216-18

Community language 306-22
Comparison, cross-cultural 19-20, 24, 161-75, 194, 205, 228-35
Competence,
— communicative 18, 40, 54, 58, 77-9, 287, 321
— cultural 19, 23, 26, 132, 270
— grammatical 79
— intercultural 9, 12, 19, 24-5, 42, 136-57, 198, 273
 acquisition 287-97
 definition 136-8
 development 154-7, 287-8, 289-97, 300-5, *304*
 levels 138, 141-57, 288
 see also performance, intercultural
— linguistic 21, 22, 78, 140, 157, 198, 229, 288
— social 103-4
— teacher 156
Conflict, cultural, *see* difference, intercultural
Conte, Rafael 94
Context,
— and *Landeskunde* 289
— social 4, 7, 164-8, 181, 219-20, 240
— theory 262-3, 265-71
Contrastive analysis 13
Cook-Gumperz, J. 4
Correspondence, foreign language 157, 233
Council of Europe 209, 211-12, 218
Cultural studies,
— content 40-1, 161
— justification 9, 40, 157, 160
— objectives 245-7
— politicisation 59-60
— and social history,
    Britain 73-83, 211
    East Germany 66-72
    France 84-99
    Scandinavia 33-44
    West Germany 47-61, 174-5
— *see also* area studies; background studies; *Landeskunde*
Culturalism, additive 282-3
Culture,
— and critique of culture 284-5

- definition 241-2, 261, 279
- as educational concept 283-6
- 'hidden' 159-75
- and intercultural education 285-6
- in language learning 17-30
- and national identity 55
- perceptions 159-60, 161, 229-35, 280
- representation 229-31
- *see also* acquisition, culture

Culture shock 206, 294, 302

Curriculum,
- Britain 74-6, 209-10, 211, 217, 308
- higher education 237, 239-47
- W. Germany 156-7, 239-47, 281, 298

Datta, A. 200
De Certeau, M. 256
Deficit theory 321
Denmark,
- cultural relations 36-7, 55
- economic relations 35-6
- history 34-5
- language teaching 31, 33, 37-40, 41-2, 44, 213

Descartes, René 84, 86
Deutschkunde 55-6
development, language, ethnographic approach 3-4, 7-8, 12, 19, 110-17

Dewey, John 138
Dialect,
- and language learning 22, 311, 312
- and standardisation 5

Difference, intercultural 142-54, 165-7, 171-5, 194, 201, 230, 257-9

Disciplines,
- evolution 63-72
- and intercultural education 11, 276-8

Distance, cultural 172, 194, 195, 205

Diversity, *see* difference

Durham Project,
- aims and methods 104-5
- data analysis 105-17

Ebuna, Obi 205
Economics, and interculturalism 95-7
Education,
- bilingual 6, 308, 309, 321-2
- comprehensive 32, 73-6, 105-18
- development 179, 193, 195, 198-201, 206
- ecological 199, 204, 219
- general, and foreign language teaching 39, 40, 41
- intercultural,
  catalysts 302-5
  as criticism of ideology 277, 278, 280-2
  and culture 283-6
  development 299-305
  and general education 276-8
  legitimacy 279-80, 281
  paradigms 278-83
- intracultural 284-5
- and knowledge as written 4
- primary 37, 39, 41, 44, 106, 117, 311
- secondary 22
  England 306-22
  English in 58
  French in 38-9, 105-18
  German in 39
  W. Germany 138-41, 144-54, 155-7
- *see also* teacher training

Elbeshausen, H. & Wagner, J. 42
Eliot, T.S. 202, 269
Empathy, need for 9, 60, 138, 143, 217
England, *see* Britain, language teaching
English,
- and cultural studies 54
- in Germany 37-8, 49, 200-1
- as L2 33, 42-3, 44, 50, 58, 60, 144, 189, 193-206
- as *lingua franca* 6-7
Enlightenment, and intercultural education 278-9, 281
Ertelt-Vieth, Astrid 101-2, 159-75
Ethnocentricity 49, 51, 55, 56, 92, 98, 204, 210, 303, 306-7

– research findings 105-6, 107-8, 142, 315-16
Ethnography,
– and cultural awareness 24-5, 87, 237
– and language development 3-4, 7-8, 12, 19, 110-17
– and teacher training 242-7, 248-59
Etiemble, F. 88
Europe,
– cultures 26
– intercultural language learning 13, 26, 31-2, 33-44, 47-61, 63-72, 73-83, 84-99
– language education 306-22
European Commission Project on Community Languages 305-8, 309-22
– and assessment of performance 320-1
– and ethnocentric bias 315-16
– feasibility study 309-110
– and intercultural education 321-2
– and language loyalty 312-14
– methodology 314-15
– and syllabus design 316-18
– and teaching materials 318-20
European Studies 75
Evaluation, social 166-7, 171-3
Examinations,
– in community languages 310, 320-1
– influence 75-6, 78-81, 104, 212, 217, 219
Exchange, student 26, 101, 120-37, 193, 229, 231, 309
Experience,
– cultural 19-21, *20*, 26-8, 28-9, 106, 110, 117-18, 231, 294
and pupil exchanges 120-37, 232-3, 298-9
– teachers' 111-12, 115, 117, 237
– of Third World 196-7, 201

Favret-Saada, J. 250-1, 254
Ferry, Jules 87, 94
Finkenstaedt, T. 59
Fisher, S. & Hicks, D. 210, 211

Fiske, J. 7-8
Fluency 22, 23, 27, 217
Folklorisation 90-1, 99
Form, and content 52, 53-4, 58, 231, 292
Formalism, Russian 268
Fowles, John 271
Fragmentation, linguistic 185-6, 290, 292
France, language teaching 32, 84-99
French, as L2 33, 38-9, 41, 50, 59-60, 74-5, 76-81, 104-18, 219-20, 229-35, 248-59

Geertz, C. 8, 43, 242, 243-4, 261, 263
Gender, and attitudes to cultures 106-7, 117-18
General Certificate of Secondary Education (England) 81, 104, 217, 321
Generalisation, cultural 129-31, *130*, 132, 165, 195, 210, 233
Geography, and cultural studies 240
German, as L2 33, 38-9, 230
Germany, East 31, 59, 66-72
Germany, West 11, 31, 47-61, 82, 136-57
– and intercultural education 275, 287-305
– as multicultural 196-7
– perceptions of Britain 122, *122*, 123-5, *124-5*, *129*, *130*, 140-1, 200-1, 203, 245
– perceptions of France 228-35
– perceptions of Russia 161-75
– and teacher training 239-47
– Third World in textbooks 193-206
Girard, D. 211
Goody, Jack 90, 92
Graded Objectives in Modern Languages movement 77, 78-9, 212

Habermas, Jürgen 262-3
Hall, E.T. 159
Halliday, M.A.K. 7
Hart, D. *et al.* 78
Hegel, G.W.F. 92

Historicity, and culture 9
History,
 — and bias 315-16
 — and cultural studies 240
 — European 86, 88-9, 93-4
Hjelmslev, L. 270
Hoggart, R. 243
Holt, S. 71
Hughes, Ted 266-8
Hurman, A. 25-6
Hymes, D. 78

Identity,
 — cultural 3, 8, 60, 89, 141, 189, 288, 294, 299, 301
 — intercultural 89, 288, 294
 — national 5-6, 12, 19, 27, 55, 90, 191
 — personal 8, 137, 143, 149, 154, 157, 298-9
 — social 259, 294
Ideology, and intercultural education 277, 278, 279, 280-2
Immersion techniques 27, 78, 218
Immigrants,
 — acquisition of L2 6
 — portrayed in textbooks 183
 — West Germany 196-7, 276
India, in W. German textbooks 203
Indicators 270
Individualisation, and textbook content 184, 190
Inference 234
Information, intercultural 97
INSET project 263-5, 266-8
Insight into culture 78, 79, 104-6
Inspectorate, England 17, 82, 103-4, 213, 214
Interaction,
 — classroom 4-5
 — interlingual 290-2, *291*, 296
Interculturalisation 12-13, 84-99
 — and educational theory 275-8
 — and European history 86, 93-4
 — and European traditions 85-90
 — and language teaching 94-9
 — and social sciences 90-3
Interculture 301, 322
Interference, language 290

Internationalisation 37, 64, 84-5, 195, 297
Interpretation, and contextualisation 269-70
Iser, W. 269, 270
Italian, in British schools 307-8, 309, 313, 317-18, 320, 321

John-Steiner, V. 8

Kane, Laurence 237, 239-47
Kay, Paul 262-3
Keller, Gottfried 101, 120-37, 139-40
Kerl, Dieter 31-2, 63-72
Klippel, F. 219
Knowledge,
 — cultural 23, 43, 55, 77-9, 120, 229-30, 244
 — and language 3, 7, 289, 317
 — and literacy 4
Kohlberg, L. 143-4
Kordes, Hagen 142, 273, 287-305
Krashen, S.D. 216-17
Kubanek, Angelika 179, 193-206
Kulturkunde 49, 50, 55-7, 59, 61
Kuna, Franz 237, 261-71

Laboratory, language 58, 74
Lacuna system 159, 167, 168-74, *169*, *170*, 175
Landeskunde 17, 49-50, 58, 82, 240-1, 287, 289
 — critique 137, 299-300
 — in Scandinavia 31, 41, 43
Language, functions 6-7, 261-3
Language, first,
 — and learning L2 18-19, 23, 26, 234, 291
 — in secondary education 307-22
Language learning 21-2
 — and cultural studies 241
 — and culture 6, 17-21, 28-30, 288-9
    educational motives 8, 52, 55, 57, 59, 82-3, 211
    pragmatic motives 8, 52, 59, 94, 95-7, 155
 — final school stage 289-97
 — theory 179

see also awareness, cultural;
awareness, language;
communicative approach;
experience, cultural; language
teaching
Language reform   8-9, 12, 50, 51-5, 57, 61
Language teaching   5, 21, 25
– aims   17, 29, 58, 77, 103-5, 111, 118, 198, 211-14, 220, 298, 316-17
– changing content   212-14
– and comprehensivisation   73-83
– content   212-14
– effects,
  on perceptions   101, 103-18
  qualitative analysis   110-17
– intercultural   6-7, 8-9, *10*, 61, 94-8, 159-60
  and research   11-14
  West Germany   49-56
– modernisation   57-9, 60
– and personal identity   8
– social history   31-2, 33-44, 47-61, 63-72, 73-83, 84-99, 237
  Britain   31-2, 73-83
  East Germany   63-72
  France   32, 84-99
  Scandinavia   31, 33-44
  West Germany   47-61
– theory   11, 12, 48, 53, 58, 60, 200, 203
– and World Studies   211-12
see also communicative approach
Learning, and developmental tasks   154-7
Linguistics, and culture   7, 241
Literacy,
– in community languages   318
– and transition from oracy   4-5
Literary criticism   237, 263-71
Literature,
– and context   263-71
– and cultural studies   11, 60, 87-8
– and foreign language teaching   57, 59, 156, 201, 241
Loyalty,
– language   312-14
– national   13, 317

Lyons, J.   265

Mapping, cognitive   191, 262
Mariet, François   32, 84-99
Marxism, and area studies   63, 66, 71
Massey, Donald   194
Materials, teaching   12, 14, 40, 42, 43-4, 57, 60
– Britain   74-5, 318-20
see also authenticity; textbooks; video
Mauss, M.   250, 252
Meaning,
– and culture   7-8, 79, 163-8, 171-3, *173*, *174*, 237, 261-2, 294
– and literary criticism   265, 268-70
– negotiation   9, 13, 137-8, 143, 148, 157, 201, 262-3
– symbolic   159, 166-7, 171-2, *171*, 246
Media,
– and interculturalism   91, 93, 108
– and Third World   193, 201
Methods, teaching,
– active   211, 215, 216
– audiolingual   18, 74-5, 77, 216, 217-18
– changes   216-17
– direct   156
– enquiry-based   215
– intercultural   273, 275-86, 287
– pupil-centred   118, 210, 211, 220, 230-1, 233, 266-7
– systems-and-structure approach   235
– task-oriented   266-7
– team teaching   312, 315
– and world studies   180
see also communicative approach
Meyer, Meinert   101-2, 136-57
Mind engagement   216-17
Mobility, geographic   88, 94-5
Modern Studies   55
Modernism and textbooks   191
Motivation for language learning   9, 52, 74, 217-18, 220, 313, 315

INDEX

Multiculturalism and interculturalism 283

Nation-states,
— and cultural studies 50, 53
— and national language 5-6, 306
Nationalism 88-9, 92, 93, 96, 281
Nietzsche, F. 91, 92
Nobbs, Jack 315-16
Norway,
— cultural relations 36-7, 44
— economic relations 35-6
— history 34-5
— language teaching 31, 33, 37-40, 42-3, 44

Oberndörfer, Dieter 196-7
Observation diary 248-51, *249-50*
— and differing viewpoints 257-9
— empirical/structured 252-7
— and locality 256-7, 258
— and sociological sensitivity 255-6
— writing 253-5
Ochs, E. & Schieffelin, B.B. 3-4
Oracy, and transition to literacy 4-5
Orientations 219-20, *224-7*

Page, B. & Hewitt, D. 77
Panjabi, in British schools 307-8, 309, 317, 318, 321
Panofsky, Erwin 86
Performance, intercultural 160
— assessment 320-1
— case studies 144-54
— levels 141-4
Pfaffenberger, W. 205
Phillipson, R. & Skutnabb-Kangas, T. 42
Philology, and area studies 70
Philosophy, and interculturalism 86
Photographs, in textbooks 181, 183, 185, 190, 234
Pickett, D. 49
Pike, G. & Selby, D. 210
Politeness, and cultural difference 166-7, 171-2, 257-8
Politikdidaktik 198-9
Postmodernism and textbooks 191
Power, and culture 279-80, 281-2

Practice, and intercultural education 281-2
Prejudice 103, 164-5, 175, 287, 298-9, 312, see also generalisation; stereotypes
Problem-solving in language learning 216-17
Process, in World Studies 215
Protectionism 96-7
Psychology of language 22

Quasthoff, U. 163

Racism,
— and curricula 89, 281, 282, 312
— in textbooks 204, 211, 219
Reading, cultural variation 12
Realia, foreign 52, 53-4, 55, 168
Realism,
— in textbooks 9, 179, 182, 185, 190, 191, 201-2
— in visual material 229-31, 232-5
Reception theory 262-3, 265, 269
Regionalism 88
Reification of language 4
Relativism, cultural 80, 189-90, 212
Relevance 76-7, 78, 175
Repertoire, language 244
Research, intercultural 11-14, 101-2, 104-18, 136-57, 138-2, 175, 240-1
— sociological approaches 241-2
Richardson, Robin 210, 215
Rights, human 87, 96, 209, 211, 218, 219, 282
Risager, K. 31, 33-44, 179, 181-92
Risager, K. & Andersen, H. 213
Russia, perceptions of W. Germany 161-75
Russian, as L2 161

Scandinavia, textbooks 183-92
Schemata, modification 18, 23-7
Schieffelin, B.B. & Ochs, E. 4, 7
School, in foreign culture 230-1, 232-3, 234-5
Section biculturelle 27-9
Séférian, M.A. 41-2
Semantics, European 98
Sevaldsen, J. 41

Sexism, in textbooks 115-16, 184, 211, 219
Shweder, R.A. & LeVine, R.A. 261, 262
Smith, L.E. 7
Social sciences,
 – and area studies 67, 71
 – and background studies 75
 – and interculturalisation 90-3, 101, 232
 – in teacher training 81
 – W. Germany 57, 59-60
Social studies,
 – and bias 315-16
 – and culture 9
Socialisation,
 – and cultural acquisition 3, 5, 22, 92-3, 175, 200, 280
 – and L2 learning 19, 103-4, 105
 – and language acquisition 3-4, 7, 18
Society, and intercultural education 276, 277-8, 279-80
Sociology,
 – and culture research 241-2
 – and teacher training 56
Sontag, Susan 265
Sorokin, Ju.A. 171
Sorokin, Ju.A. & Markovina, I.Ju. 167, 168
Speech act 21, 265
Spicer, A. & Riddy, D.C. 82
Standardisation, language 5-6
Starkey, Hugh 179-80, 209-20
Stereotypes 25, 101, 109, 120-37, *124-5*, 142, 146, 197, 213, 315-16
 – autostereotype 121, 123, 126-8, *127-8*, *129*, 140-1, 168, 171-2, 245
 – heterostereotype 90-1, 121-8, *121-2*, *124-5*, *126*, *127-8*, *129*, *130*, 140-1, 148-50, 168-72, 245
 – in textbooks 188, 206
Stern, H.H. 11, 48, 49
Strategy, learning 234
Structuralism 58, 60, 262, 265
Student, role 180
Style, teaching 112-15, 118, 216, 217-18

Subjectivity in textbooks 189, 190, 191
'Survival courses' 27, 77, 78-9
Svensson, S.E. 43
Sweden,
 – cultural relations 36-7, 44
 – economic relations 36
 – history 34-5
 – language teaching 31, 33, 37-40, 43-4
Swidler, A. 241-2
Syllabus, design 316-18, 320
Symbolism, cultural 8, 173-4, 241-2, 243-5, 261
Symbols, social 237

Teacher,
 – and aims of language teaching 29-30, 111-18
 – and community languages 311-12
 – competence 156
 – role 29-30, 289, 298
Teacher training 12, 14, 54, 56-7, 237
 – and background studies 75, 80, 81-2
 – in cultural studies 239-47, 248-59, 263-71
 – in-service 248-59, 263-71
Text,
 – and culture 7, 9, 60, 262-71
 – language as 4
Textbooks,
 – characters in 183-6, 189
 – and communicative approach 79-81
 – and contemporary issues 186-7
 – content analysis 182-7
 – cultural content 9, 14, 17-18, 56, 58, 110, 112-18, 179-80, 181-92
 – evaluation 179, 188-92, 194-201, 205-6
 – functions 181-2, 185-6, 191
 – intercultural issues 187-8, 190
 – and modernism/postmodernism 191
 – Third World in 201-6
 – World Studies 214-15, 219-20

see also authenticity
Third World, in W. German textbooks   193-206
Tolerance, promotion   9, 78, 79, 98, 104-6, 111, 143, 198, 203
'Tourism' approach to language teaching   19, 58, 76-81, 116, 184, 197, 214-15, 217
Treml, A. & Seitz, K.   198-9
Triviality in textbooks   186, 188-9

United States,
 −influence   31, 34, 58
 −mediating language and culture   11, 82
Universalism, and interculturalism   85, 86-8, 89, 92, 143-4, 278, 283
Urdu, in British schools   307-8, 309, 318-19, 321

Values,
 −cultural   18, 63-72, 261-2, 307
 −in education   282-3
 −political   59-60
 −transcultural   13, 211
Van Ek, J.   212
Video   180, 228-35
Visits, school, effects   101, 110, 118, 120-37

Wesenkunde   56, 67
Willis, P.   242
Wimsatt, W.K.   265, 268
Wittgenstein, L. von   136-7
Work, portrayal in textbooks   115-16, 185, 189, 214
World studies   179-80, 198-206, 209-20
 −and foreign language teaching   213, 217-18
 −'process' in   215
World Studies Project   209-10, 211
Wuthnow, R. *et al.*   8

Zarate, Geneviève   237, 248-59